A FORGOTTEN EMPIRE
(VIJAYANAGAR)

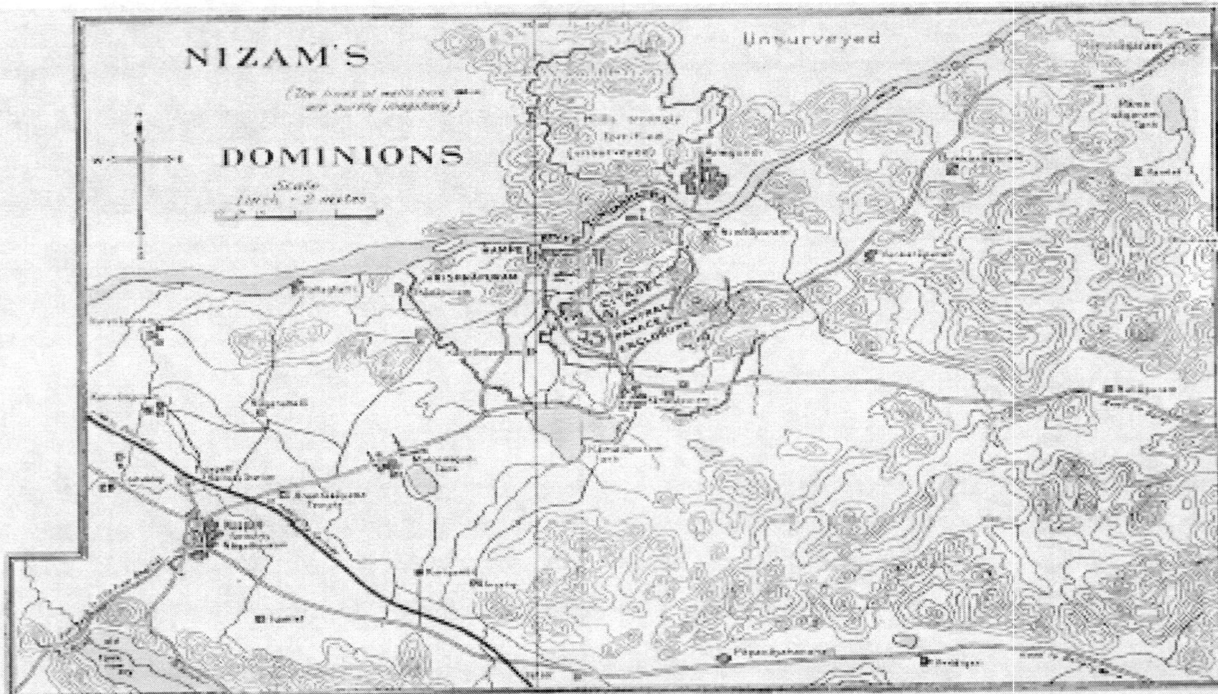

MAP OF VIJAYANAGAR WITH ENVIRONS.

A FORGOTTEN EMPIRE

(VIJAYANAGAR)

A CONTRIBUTION TO THE
HISTORY OF INDIA

ILLUSTRATED

ROBERT SEWELL

GYAN

Published by

Gyan Publishing House
5, Ansari Road
Daryaganj, New Delhi-110002
Phone: 011-47034999, 9811692060
E-mail: books@gyanbooks.com

Distribution Network
gyanbooks.com
India, USA, Canada, UK, Australia, France

ISBN : 978-81-212-3397-2 (PB)
First Published, London, 1900

2nd Impression 2020

Printed at: Gyan Press, Delhi.

A Forgotten Empire
Author: Robert Sewell

A Forgotten Empire

(Vijayanagar)

A Contribution to the History of India

BY

ROBERT SEWELL

M.R.A.S., F.R.G.S., LATE OF H.M. INDIAN CIVIL SERVICE

AUTHOR OF "THE AMARÂVATI TOPE, AND EXCAVATIONS ON ITS SITE IN 1877," "SKETCH OF THE DYNASTIES OF SOUTHERN INDIA," "ECLIPSES OF THE MOON IN INDIA," ETC.; JOINT AUTHOR OF "THE HINDU CALENDAR"

LONDON

SWAN SONNENSCHEIN & CO., LTD.

1900

CORRECTIONS

On page 319 (text and note 1) I have boldly identified the "Symamdary" of the chronicler Nuniz with Rajahmundry, fancying that the initial syllable might have been accidentally dropped by the sixteenth-century copyist. I find that I did him an injustice. Paragraph 69 of the Annual Report on Epigraphy in the Madras Presidency for the year ending with June 1900 shows that the place referred to by Nuniz must be Simhâchalam, in the Vizagapatam District, the old name of which was *Simhâdri*. We should therefore pronounce "Symamdary" as if the first *a* were long and the second short.

It will be noticed that Nuniz places this town a hundred leagues from Kondapalle; and this is not far from the truth, the distance to Rajahmundry being only a hundred miles.

Our text tells us that Krishna Deva Râya while at Simhâchalam "gave alms to the temples," &c., and the extant inscriptions confirm this statement. Two of these, in the Vishnu Temple, dated in A.D. 1515–16, mention the King's conquest of Udayagiri, Kondavîd, Kondapalle, and Rajahmundry, and state that the two Queens of Vijayanagar presented jewels to the temple. Another records grants by Krishna Deva of villages which had belonged to the King of Orissa. An inscription at Chidambaram in the south relates that a tower of a temple at that place was erected by King Krishna Deva after his return from Simhâdri, where he had planted a pillar of victory.

The King of "Orya," or Orissa, at this time was Pratâpa Rudra Gajapati.

What became of the insulting inscription alleged by Nuniz to have been engraved on a temple at Simhâchalam? Is there any trace of it to be found? or any local legend relating to it? Perhaps some resident of the district will be sufficiently interested to make inquiries.

Page 131, line 3 from foot.

After "Rajahmundry" *add* "and Simhâchalam, near Vizagapatam where he halted, &c."

Page 158, line 23.

For "A.D. 1530" *substitute* "1529."

Page 165.

A careful study has been made during the current year of a number of inscriptions at Conjeeveram, and two of these have yielded the date of the coronation of King Achyuta, viz. Thursday, October 21, A.D. 1529—"the fifth *tithi* of the second half of the solar month Vrischika in the Virôdhin year, which corresponded to the Saka year 1452."

This does not, of course, give us the date of Krishna Deva's death. Another inscription of three years earlier, *i.e.* in Saka 1449, seems to show that Achyuta was then ruling as co-regent with his predecessor.—(*Paragraph 70 of the Report on Epigraphy, Madras, for the year ending June* 30, 1900.)

R. SEWELL.

November 1900.

PREFACE

THE two Portuguese chronicles, a translation of which into English is now for the first time offered to the public, are contained in a vellum-bound folio volume in the Bibliothèque Nationale in Paris, amongst the manuscripts of which institution it bears the designation "*Port. No.* 65." The volume in question consists of copies of four original documents; the first two, written by Fernão Nuniz and Domingo Paes, being those translated below, the last two (at the end of the MS.) letters written from China about the year 1520 A.D. These will probably be published in translation by Mr. Donald Ferguson in the pages of the *Indian Antiquary*.

The first pair of original papers was sent with a covering letter by some one at Goa to some one in Europe. The names are not given, but there is every reason for believing that the recipient was the historian Barros in Lisbon.

Both these papers are in the same handwriting, which fact—since they were written by separate Portuguese merchants or travellers at Vijayanagar in different years, one, I believe, shortly subsequent to 1520 A.D., the latter not later than about 1536 or 1537—conclusively proves them to be copies of the originals, and not the originals themselves.[1] I have inserted[2] a facsimile of two pages of the text, so that no doubt may remain on this point. The first portion consists of the conclusion of the text of Fernão Nuniz; the second of the covering letter

[1] The letters from China were copied by a different hand.

[2] Below, facing p. 235.

written by the person who sent the originals to Europe; the third of the beginning of the text of Domingo Paes.

Paes being the earlier in date (about 1520) I have given his account of personal experiences first, and afterwards the historical summary composed by Nuniz about the year 1536 or 1537.

I have stated that the person to whom the documents were sent from Goa was probably the celebrated historian Barros. He is alluded to in the covering letter in the words: "It seemed necessary to do what your Honour desired of me," "I send both the summaries . . . because your Honour can gather what is useful to you from both;" and at the end of the long note on "Togao Mamede," king of Delhi, quoted in my introduction, "I kiss your Honour's hand."

Since the first *Decada* of Barros was published in 1552,[1] this argument is not unreasonable; while a comparison between the accounts given by Nuniz and Barros of the siege and battle of Raichûr sufficiently proves that one was taken from the other. But we have fortunately more direct evidence, for the discovery of which we have to thank Mr. Ferguson. I have mentioned above that at the end of the MS. volume are copies of two letters concerning China. These were written subsequent to the year 1520 by Vasco Calvo and Chris-

[1] Barros was apparently never himself in India, but held an official position in the India Office in Lisbon. His work was completed in four *Decadas*. Couto repeats the fourth *Decada* of Barros, and continues the history in eight more *Decadas*. The first three *Decadas* of Barros were published in A.D. 1552, 1553, and 1563, bringing the history down to 1527, under the title of *Dos feitos que os Portugueses fizeram no descubrimento e conquista dos mares e terras do Oriente*. His fourth *Decada*, published by Couto, dealt with the period A.D. 1527 to 1539, and contained an account of the events that occurred during the governorships of Lopo Vaz de Sampaio and Nuno da Cunha. Couto's own eight *Decadas* covered the subsequent period down to 1600. The combined work is generally called the *Da Asia*. Couto completed his publication in 1614. The fourth *Decada* was published in 1602, the fifth in 1612, the sixth in 1614, the seventh in 1616, the year of his death. Couto spent almost all his life in India, for which country he embarked in 1556.

tovão Vieyra. Mr. Ferguson has pointed out to me that, in the third *Decada* (liv. vi. cap. ii.); after quoting some passages almost verbatim from this chronicle of Nuniz regarding Vijayanagar; Barros writes: "According to two letters which our people had two or three years afterwards from these two men, Vasco Calvo, brother of Diogo Calvo, and Christovão Vieyra, who were prisoners in Canton, etc. . . ." He also mentions these letters in two subsequent passages, and quotes from them. This renders it certain that Barros saw those letters; and since they are copied into the same volume which contains the chronicles of Nuniz and Paes, we may be sure that Barros had the whole before him. It is of little importance to settle the question whether the chronicles of Nuniz and Paes were sent direct to Barros —whether, that is, Barros himself is the addressee of the covering letter—or to some other official (the "our people" of the passage from Barros last quoted); but that Barros saw them seems certain, and it is therefore most probable that the Paris MS. was a volume of copies prepared for him from the originals.

* * *

These documents possess peculiar and unique value; that of Paes because it gives us a vivid and graphic account of his personal experiences at the great Hindu capital at the period of its highest grandeur and magnificence—"things which I saw and came to know" he tells us—and that of Nuniz because it contains the traditional history of the country gathered first-hand on the spot, and a narrative of local and current events of the highest importance. known to him either because he himself was present or because he received the information from those who were so. The summaries of the well-known historians already alluded to, though founded, as I believe, partly on these very chronicles, have taken all the life out of them by eliminating the personal factor, the presence of which in the originals gives them their greatest charm. Senhor Lopes, who has published these documents in the original Portuguese in a recent work,[1] writes in his introduction: "Nothing that we know of in any language can compare with them, whether for their historical importance or for the description given of the country, and especially of the capital, its products, customs, and the like. The Italian travellers who visited and wrote about this country—Nicolo di Conti, Varthema, and Federici—are much less minute in the matter of the geography and customs of the land, and not one of them has left us a chronicle." They are indeed invaluable, and throw an extraordinary light on the condition of Vijayanagar as well as on several doubtful points of history.

Thus, for instance, we have in Nuniz for the first time a definite account of the events that led to the fall of the First Dynasty and the establishment of the second by the usurpation of Narasimha. Previous to the publication of these chronicles by Senhor Lopes we had nothing to guide us in this matter, save a few vague and unsatisfactory lines in the chronicle of the historian Firishtah.[2] Now all is made clear, and though as yet the truth cannot be definitely determined, at least we have an explicit and exceedingly interesting story. Paes too, as well as Nuniz, conclusively proves to us that Krishna Deva Râya was really the greatest

[1] *Chronica dos Reis de Bisnaga*, by David Lopes, S.S.G.L. Lisbon, 1897: at the National Press. The extract given is taken from his Introduction, p. lxxxvi.

[2] Firishtah was a Persian of good family, and was born about 1570 A.D. Early in his life he was taken by his father to India, and resided all his life at the Court of the Nizâm Shâhs of Ahmadnagar, rejoicing in royal patronage. He appears to have begun to compile his historical works at an early age, since his account of the Bijapûr kings was finished in 1596. He appears to have died not long after the year 1611, which is the latest date referred to in any of his writings.

of all the kings of Vijayanagar, and not the mere puppet that Firishtah appears to consider him (Firishtah does not mention him by name); for Paes saw him on several occasions and speaks of him in warm and glowing terms, while Nuniz, whose narrative was evidently first-hand, never so much as hints that his armies were led to victory by any other general but the king himself. Nuniz also gives us a graphic description from personal knowledge of the character of Krishna's degenerate successor Achyuta, whose feebleness, selfishness, cowardice, and cruelty paved the way for the final destruction of the great empire.

By the side of these two chronicles the writings of the great European historians seem cold and lifeless.

* * *

I have mentioned the publication of Senhor Lopes. It is to that distinguished Arabic scholar that we owe the knowledge of the existence of these precious documents. He it was who brought them to light in the first instance, and to him personally I owe the fact of my being able to translate and publish them. His introduction to the *Dos Reis de Bisnaga* is full of valuable matter. India owes him a debt of gratitude for his services; and for myself I desire to record here my sincere thanks for the disinterested and generous help he has so constantly accorded to me during the last two years.

My thanks are also due to Mr. Donald Ferguson for his careful revision of the whole of my translations.

As to the illustrations, I am indebted, for permission to reproduce the photographs, to Colonel W. W. Hooper, to the Government of Madras, to the officer commanding the Duke of Cornwall's Light Infantry for views taken by one of the officers of the regiment with the regimental camera; and to Messrs. Nicholas & Co., Madras, for the views of the old palaces at Kondapalle and Chandragiri. I have specially to thank Mr. F. Dunsterville for most kindly sending to England for me the negatives of the three photographs taken by him. I desire further to express my appreciation of a particular kindness done to me by Colonel R. C. Temple, C.I.E., in the matter of this publication. And lastly to acknowledge gratefully the liberality of H.E. the Governor of Madras and the Members of his Council, who by subsidising this work have rendered its publication possible.

* * *

I trust that my remarks regarding the causes of the downfall of Portuguese trade in the sixteenth century will not be misunderstood. It is not in any spirit of criticism or comparison that I have written those passages. History, however, is history; and it is a fact that while the main cause of the small success which attended the efforts of the Portuguese to establish a great and lasting commerce with India was no doubt the loss of trade after the destruction of Vijayanagar, there must be added to this by the impartial recorder the dislike of the inhabitants to the violence and despotism of the Viceroys and to the uncompromising intolerance of the Jesuit Fathers, as well as the horror engendered in their minds by the severities of the terrible Inquisition at Goa.

* * *

A word as to my spelling of names. I have adopted a medium course in many cases between the crudities of former generations and the scientific requirements of the age in which we live; the result of which will probably be my condemnation by both parties. But to the highly educated I would point out that this work is intended for general reading, and that I have therefore thought it best to avoid the use of a special font of type containing the proper diacritical points; while to the rest I venture to present the plea that the time has passed when Vijayanagar needs to be spelt "Beejanuggur," or Kondavîdu "Condbeer."

Thus I have been bold enough to drop the final and essential "a" of the name of the great city, and spell the word "Vijayanagar," as it is usually pronounced by the English. The name is composed of two words, *vijaya*, "victory," and *nagara*, "city," all the "a's" to be pronounced short, like the "u" in "sun," or the "a" in "organ."

"Narasimha" ought, no doubt, to be spelt "Nrisimha," but that in such case the "ri" ought to have a dot under the "r" as the syllable is really a vowel, and I have preferred the common spelling of modern days. (Here again all three "a's" are short.)

As with the final "a" in "Vijayanagara," so with the final "u" in such names as "Kondavîdu"—it has been dropped in order to avoid an appearance of pedantry; and I have preferred the more common "Rajahmundry" to the more correct "Râjamahendri," "Trichinopoly" to "Tiruchhinâpalle," and so on.

This system may not be very scientific, but I trust it will prove not unacceptable.

* * *

The name of the capital is spelt in many different ways by the chroniclers and travellers. The usual Portuguese spelling was "Bisnaga;" but we have also the forms "Bicheneger" (*Nikitin*), "Bidjanagar" (*Abdur Razzâk*), "Bizenegalia" (*Conti*), "Bisnagar," "Beejanuggur," &c.

CONTENTS

HISTORY

CHAPTER I

CHAPTER V

Deva Râya I. (A.D. 1406 to 1419)

CHAPTER VI

Deva Râya II. (A.D. 1419 to 1444 or (?) 1449)

CHAPTER VII

The City of Vijayanagar in the Reign of Deva Râya II. (A.D. 1420 (?), 1443)

CHAPTER VIII

Close of the First Dynasty (A.D. 1449 to 1490)

CHAPTER IX

The First Kings of the Second Dynasty (A.D. 1490 to 1509)

CHAPTER X

The Reign of Krishna Deva Râya (A.D. 1509 to 1530)

CHAPTER XI

The Siege and Battle of Raichûr, and Close of Krishna's Reign (A.D. 1520 to 1530)

CHAPTER XII

The Buildings, Works, and Inscriptions of Krishna Deva

CHAPTER XIII

The Reign of Achyuta Râya

CHAPTER XIV

The Beginning of the End

CHAPTER XV

Destruction of Vijayanagar (A.D. 1565)

CHAPTER XVI

The Third Dynasty

CHAPTER XVII

The Story of Barradas (1614)

THE CHRONICLES

NARRATIVE OF DOMINGO PAES

(About 1520)

CHRONICLE OF FERNÃO NUNIZ

(ABOUT A.D. 1535)

CHAPTER I

CHAPTER II

CHAPTER III

CHAPTER IV

CHAPTER V

CHAPTER VI

CHAPTER VII

CHAPTER VIII

CHAPTER IX

CHAPTER X

CHAPTER XI

CHAPTER XII

CHAPTER XIII

CHAPTER XIV

CHAPTER XV

CHAPTER XVI

CHAPTER XVII

CHAPTER XVIII

CHAPTER XIX

CHAPTER XX

CHAPTER XXI

CHAPTER XXII

CHAPTER XXIII

APPENDICES

LIST OF ILLUSTRATIONS

MAPS

A TYPICAL BIT OF VIJAYANAGAR SCENERY

WITH TEMPLE ON SUMMIT OF HILL

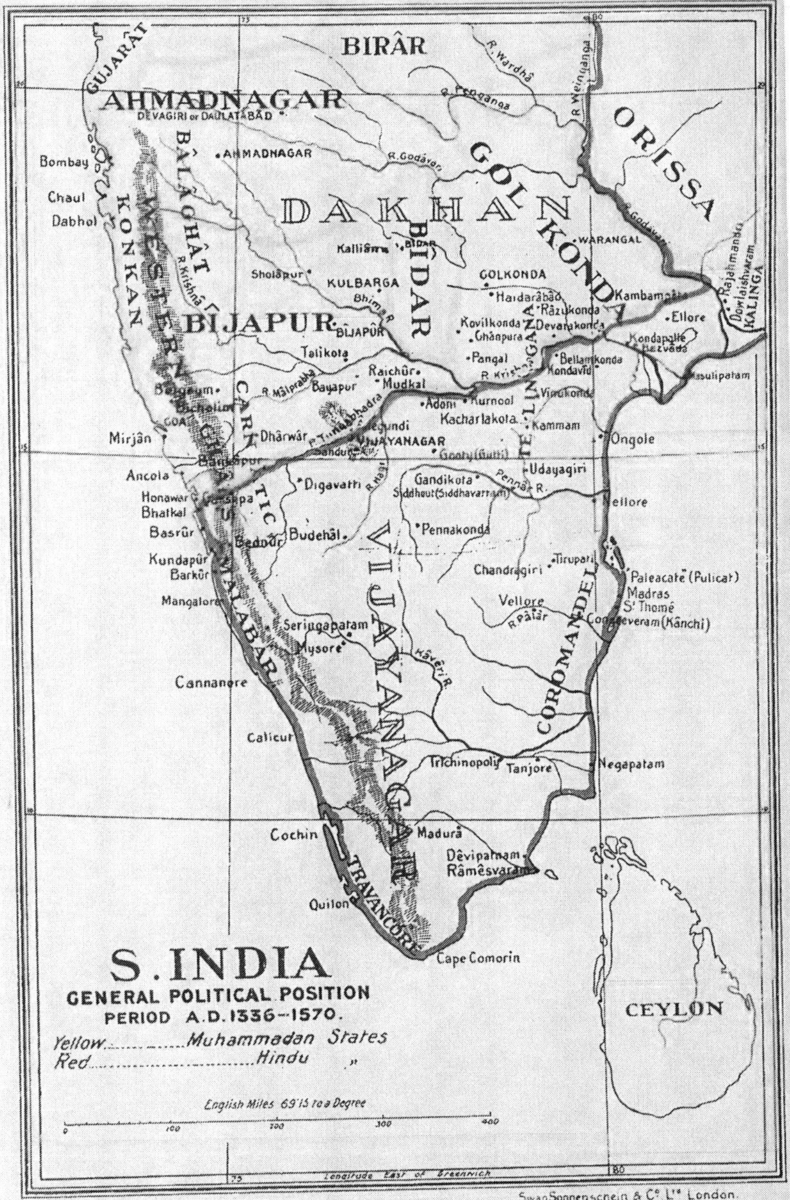

R. Sewell, del.

Swan Sonnenschein & Co. Ltd. London.

A FORGOTTEN EMPIRE

VIJAYANAGAR

CHAPTER I

INTRODUCTION

Introductory remarks—Sources of information—Sketch of history of Southern India down to A.D. 1336—A Hindu bulwark against Muhammadan conquest—The opening date, as given by Nuniz, wrong—"Togao Mamede" or Muhammad Taghlaq of Delhi—His career and character.

IN the year 1336 A.D., during the reign of Edward III. of England, there occurred in India an event which almost instantaneously changed the political condition of the entire south. With that date the volume of ancient history in that tract closes and the modern begins. It is the epoch of transition from the Old to the New.

This event was the foundation of the city and kingdom of Vijayanagar. Prior to A.D. 1336 all Southern India had lain under the domination of the ancient Hindu kingdoms,—kingdoms so old that their origin has never been traced, but which are mentioned in Buddhist edicts rock-cut sixteen centuries earlier; the Pândiyans at Madura, the Cholas at Tanjore, and others. When Vijayanagar sprung into existence the past was done with for ever, and the monarchs of the new state became lords or overlords of the territories lying between the Dakhan and Ceylon.

There was no miracle in this. It was the natural

result of the persistent efforts made by the Muhammadans to conquer all India. When these dreaded invaders reached the Krishnâ River the Hindus to their south, stricken with terror, combined, and gathered in haste to the new standard which alone seemed to offer some hope of protection. The decayed old states crumbled away into nothingness, and the fighting kings of Vijayanagar became the saviours of the south for two and a half centuries.

And yet in the present day the very existence of this kingdom is hardly remembered in India; while its once magnificent capital, planted on the extreme northern border of its dominions and bearing the proud title of the "City of Victory," has entirely disappeared save for a few scattered ruins of buildings that were once temples or palaces, and for the long lines of massive walls that constituted its defences. Even the name has died out of men's minds and memories, and the remains that mark its site are known only as the ruins lying near the little village of Hampe.

Its rulers, however, in their day swayed the destinies of an empire far larger than Austria, and the city is declared by a succession of European visitors in the fifteenth and sixteenth centuries to have been marvellous for size and prosperity—a city with which for richness and magnificence no known western capital could compare. Its importance is shown by the fact that almost all the struggles of the Portuguese on the western coast were carried on for the purpose of securing its maritime trade; and that when the empire fell in 1565, the prosperity of Portuguese Goa fell with it never to rise again.

Our very scanty knowledge of the events that succeeded one another in the large area dominated by the kings of Vijayanagar has been hitherto derived partly from the scattered remarks of European travellers and the desultory references in their writings to the politics of the inhabitants of India; partly from the summaries compiled by careful mediæval historians such as Barros, Couto, and Correa, who, though to a certain degree interested in the general condition of the country, yet confined themselves mostly to recording the deeds of the European colonisers for the enlightenment of their European readers; partly from the chronicles of a few Muhammadan writers of the period, who often wrote in fear of the displeasure of their own lords; and partly from Hindu inscriptions recording grants of lands to temples and religious institutions, which documents, when viewed as state papers, seldom yield us more than a few names and dates. The two chronicles, however, translated and printed at the end of this volume, will be seen to throw a flood of light upon the condition of the city of Vijayanagar early in the sixteenth century, and upon the history of its successive dynasties; and for the rest I have attempted, as an introduction to these chronicles, to collect all available materials from the different authorities alluded to and to weld them into a consecutive whole, so as to form a foundation upon which may hereafter be constructed a regular history of the Vijayanagar empire. The result will perhaps seem disjointed, crude, and uninteresting; but let it be remembered that it is only a first attempt. I have little doubt that before very long the whole history of Southern India will be compiled by some writer gifted with the power of "making the dry bones live;" but meanwhile the bones themselves must be collected and pieced together, and my duty has been to try and construct at least the main portions of the skeleton.

Before proceeding to details we must shortly glance at the political condition of India in the first half of the fourteenth century, remembering that up to that time the Peninsula had been held by a number of distinct Hindu kingdoms, those of the Pândiyans at Madura and of the Cholas at Tanjore being the most important.

The year 1001 A.D. saw the first inroad into India of the Muhammadans from over the north-west border, under their great leader Mahmûd of Ghazni. He invaded first the plains of the Panjâb, then Multân, and afterwards other places. Year after year he pressed forward and again retired. In 1021 he was at Kalinga; in 1023 in Kâthiâwâr; but in no case did he make good his foothold on the country. His expeditions were raids and nothing more. Other invasions, however, followed in quick succession, and after the lapse of two centuries the Muhammadans were firmly and permanently established at Delhi. War followed war, and from that period Northern India knew no rest. At the end of the thirteenth century the Muhammadans began to press southwards into the Dakhan. In 1293 Alâ-ud-dîn Khilji, nephew of the king of Delhi, captured Devagiri. Four years later Gujarât was attacked. In 1303 the reduction of Warangal was attempted. In 1306 there was a fresh expedition to Devagiri. In 1309 Malik Kâfur, the celebrated general, with an immense force swept into the Dakhan and captured Warangal. The old capital of the Hoysala Ballâlas at Dvârasamudra was taken in 1310, and Malik Kâfur went to the Malabar coast where he erected a mosque, and afterwards returned to his master with enormous booty.[1] Fresh fighting took place in 1312. Six years later Mubârak of Delhi marched to Devagiri and inhumanly flayed alive its unfortunate prince, Haripâla Deva, setting up his head at the gate of his own city. In 1323 Warangal fell.

Thus the period at which our history opens, about

[1] According to tradition the wealth carried off was something fabulous. See Appendix B.

the year 1330, found the whole of Northern India down to the Vindhya mountains firmly under Moslem rule, while the followers of that faith had overrun the Dakhan and were threatening the south with the same fate. South of the Krishnâ the whole country was still under Hindu domination, but the supremacy of the old dynasties was shaken to its base by the rapidly advancing terror from the north. With the accession in 1325 of Muhammad Taghlaq of Delhi things became worse still. Marvellous stories of his extraordinary proceedings circulated amongst the inhabitants of the Peninsula, and there seemed to be no bound to his intolerance, ambition, and ferocity.

Everything, therefore, seemed to be leading up to but one inevitable end—the ruin and devastation of the Hindu provinces, the annihilation of their old royal houses, the destruction of their religion, their temples, their cities. All that the dwellers in the south held most dear seemed tottering to its fall.

Suddenly, about the year 1344 A.D., there was a check to this wave of foreign invasion—a stop—a halt—then a solid wall of opposition; and for 250 years Southern India was saved.

The check was caused by a combination of small Hindu states—two of them already defeated, Warangal and Dvârasamudra—defeated, and therefore in all probability not over-confident; the third, the tiny principality of Ânegundi. The solid wall consisted of Ânegundi grown into the great empire of the Vijayanagar. To the kings of this house all the nations of the south submitted.

If a straight line be drawn on the map of India from Bombay to Madras, about half-way across will be found the River Tungabhadrâ, which, itself a combination of two streams running northwards from Maisûr, flows in a wide circuit north and east to join the Krishnâ not far from Kurnool. In the middle of its course the Tungabhadrâ cuts through a wild rocky country lying about forty miles north-west of Bellary, and north of the railway line which runs from that place to Dhârwâr. At this point, on the north bank of the river, there existed about the year 1330 a fortified town called Ânegundi, the "Nagundym" of our chronicles, which was the residence of a family of chiefs owning a small state in the neighbourhood. They had, in former years, taken advantage of the lofty hills of granite which cover that tract to construct a strong citadel having its base on the stream. Fordable at no point within many miles the river was full of running water at all seasons of the year, and in flood times formed in its confined bed a turbulent rushing torrent with dangerous falls in several places. Of the Ânegundi chiefs we know little, but they were probably feudatories of the Hoysala Ballâlas. Firishtah declares that they had existed as a ruling family for seven hundred years prior to the year 1350 A.D.[1]

The chronicle of Nuniz gives a definite account of how the sovereigns of Vijayanagar first began to acquire the power which afterwards became so extensive. This account may or may not be accurate in all details, but it at least tallies fairly with the epigraphical and other records of the time. According to him, Muhammad Taghlaq of Delhi, having reduced Gujarât, marched

[1] It is highly probable that amongst the hills and crags about the upper fortress of Ânegundi there may be found remains of a date long prior to the fourteenth century; and it is much to be regretted that up to now no scientific examination of that tract, which lies in the present territories of Haidarâbâd, has been carried out. Want of leisure always prevented my undertaking any exploration north of the river; but from the heights of Vijayanagar on the south side I often looked wistfully at the long lines of fortification visible on the hills opposite. It is to be hoped that ere long the Government of Madras may place us in possession of a complete map of Vijayanagar and its environs, showing the whole area enclosed by the outermost line of fortifications, and including the outworks and suburbs. Hospett and Ânegundi were both part of the great city in its palmy days, and Kampli appears to have been a sort of oupost.

southwards through the Dakhan Bâlâghât, or high lands above the western ghâts, and a little previous to the year 1336[1] seized the town and fortress of Ânegundi. Its chief was slain, with all the members of his family. After a futile attempt to govern this territory by means of a deputy, Muhammad raised to the dignity of chief of the state its late minister, a man whom Nuniz calls "Deorao," for "Deva Râya," or Harihara Deva I. The new chief founded the city of Vijayanagar on the south bank of the river opposite Ânegundi and made his residence there, with the aid of the great religious teacher Mâdhava, wisely holding that to place the river between him and the ever-marauding Moslems was to establish himself and his people in a condition of greater security than before. He was succeeded by "one called Bucarao" (Bukka), who reigned thirty-seven years, and the next king was the latter's son, "Pureoyre Deo" (Harihara Deva II.).

We know from other sources that part at least of this story is correct. Harihara I. and Bukka were the first two kings and were brothers, while the third king, Harihara II., was certainly the son of Bukka.

The success of the early kings was phenomenal. Ibn Batuta, who was in India from 1333 to 1342, states that even in his day a Muhammadan chief on the western coast was subject to Harihara I., whom he calls "Haraîb" or "Harîb," from "Hariyappa" another form of the king's name; while a hundred years later Abdur Razzâk, envoy from Persia, tells us that the king of Vijayanagar was then lord of all Southern India, from sea to sea and from the Dakhan to Cape Comorin—"from the frontier of Serendib (Ceylon) to the extremities of the country of Kalbergah . . . His troops amount in number to eleven lak," *i.e.* 1,100,000. Even

[1] Nuniz erroneously gives the date as 1230. The error will be commented on hereafter.

so early as 1378 A.D., according to Firishtah,[1] the Râya of Vijayanagar was "in power, wealth, and extent of country" greatly the superior of the Bâhmanî king of the Dakhan.

The old southern states appear (we have little history to guide us) to have in general submitted peaceably to the rule of the new monarchy. They were perhaps glad to submit if only the dreaded foreigners could be kept out of the country. And thus by leaps and bounds the petty state grew to be a kingdom, and the kingdom expanded till it became an empire. Civil war and rebellion amongst the Muhammadans helped Harihara and Bukka in their enterprise. Sick of the tyranny and excesses of Muhammad Taghlaq, the Dakhan revolted in 1347, and the independent kingdom of the Bâhmanîs was for a time firmly established.

The chronicle of Nuniz opens with the following sentence:—

> "In the year twelve hundred and thirty these parts of India were ruled by a greater monarch than had ever reigned. This was the king of Dili,[2] who by force of arms and soldiers made war on Cambaya for many years, taking and destroying in that period the land of Guzarate which belongs to Cambaya,[3] and in the end he became its lord."

After this the king of Delhi advanced against Vijayanagar by way of the Bâlâghât.

This date is a century too early, as already pointed out. The sovereign referred to is stated in the following note (entered by Nuniz at the end of Chapter xx., which closes the historical portion of his narrative) to have been called "Togao Mamede."

> "This king of Delhi they say was a Moor, who was called

[1] Scott, i. 45, 46.

[2] Delhi.

[3] The Portuguese historians often mistook "Cambay" for the name of the country, and "Gujarât" for one of its dependencies.

Togao Mamede. He is held among the Hindus as a saint. They relate that once while he was offering prayer to God, there came to him four arms with four hands; and that every time he prayed roses fell to him from out of heaven. He was a great conqueror, he held a large part of this earth under his dominion, he subdued . . . (*blank in original*) kings, and slew them, and flayed them, and brought their skins with him; so that besides his own name, he received the nickname . . . which means 'lord of . . . skins of kings;' he was chief of many people.

"There is a story telling how he fell into a passion on account of (*being given?*) eighteen letters (*of the alphabet to his name?*), when according to his own reckoning he was entitled to twenty-four.[1] There are tales of him which do indeed seem most marvellous of the things that he did; as, for instance, how he made ready an army because one day in the morning, while standing dressing at a window which was closed, a ray of the sun came into his eyes, and he cried out that he would not rest until he had killed or vanquished whomsoever had dared to enter his apartments while he was dressing. All his nobles could not dissuade him from his purpose, even though they told him it was the sun that had done it, a thing without which they could not live, that it was a celestial thing and was located in the sky, and that he could never do any harm to it. With all this he made his forces ready, saying, that he must go in search of his enemy, and as he was going along with large forces raised in the country through which he began his march so much dust arose that it obscured the sun. When he lost sight of it he made fresh inquiries as to what the thing was, and the captains told him that there was now no reason for him to wait, and that he might return home since he had put to flight him whom he had come to seek. Content with this, the king returned by the road that he had taken in his search for the sun, saying that since his enemy had fled he was satisfied.

"Other extravagances are told of him which make him out a great lord, as, for instance, that being in the Charamaodel country he was told that certain leagues distant in the sea there was a very great island, and its land was gold, and the stones of its houses and those which were produced in the ground were rubies and diamonds: in which island there was a pagoda, whither came the angels from heaven to play music and

[1] *Sic.* The meaning is doubtful.

dance. Being covetous of being the lord of this land, he determined to go there, but not in ships because he had not enough for so many people, so he began to cart a great quantity of stones and earth and to throw it into the sea in order to fill it up, so that he might reach the island; and putting this in hand with great labour he did so much that he crossed over to the island of Ceyllao, which is twelve or fifteen leagues off.[1] This causeway that he made was, it is said, in course of time eaten away by the sea, and its remains now cause the shoals of Chillao. Melliquiniby,[2] his captain-general, seeing how much labour was being spent in a thing so impossible, made ready two ships in a port of Charamaodell which he loaded with much gold and precious stones, and forged some despatches as of an embassy sent in the name of the king of the island, in which he professed his obedience and sent presents; and after this the king did not proceed any further with his causeway.

"In memory of this work he made a very large pagoda, which is still there; it is a great place of pilgrimage.

"There are two thousand of these and similar stories with which I hope at some time to trouble your honour; and with other better ones, if God gives me life. I kiss your honour's hand."[3]

To conclusively establish the fact that this account can only refer to Muhammad Taghlaq of Delhi, who reigned from 1325 to 1351, it is necessary that we should look into the known character of that monarch and the events of his reign.

Nuniz states that his "Togao Mamede" conquered Gujarât, was at war with Bengal, and had trouble with the Turkomans on the borders of Sheik Ismâîl, *i.e.* Persia.[4] To take these in reverse order. Early in

[1] There is evidently a confusion here between tales of the doings of Muhammad Taghlaq and much older legends of Râma's Bridge and his army of monkeys.

[2] Mallik Nâib. (See the chronicle below, pp. 296, 297.)

[3] "Your honour" was probably the historian Barros (see preface).

[4] Sheik Ismâîl's power in Persia dates from early in the sixteenth century. Duarte Barbosa, who was in India in 1514 and wrote in 1516, mentions him as contemporary. He had subjugated Eastern Persia by that time and founded the Shiah religion. Barbosa writes: "He is a Moor and a young man," and states that he was not of royal lineage (Hakluyt edit. p. 38). Nuniz was thus guilty of an anachronism, but he describes Persia as he knew it.

the reign of Muhammad Taghlaq vast hordes of Moghuls invaded the Panjâb and advanced almost unopposed to Delhi, where the king bought them off by payment of immense sums of money. Next as to Bengal. Prior to his reign that province had been subdued, had given trouble, and had again been reduced. In his reign it was crushed under the iron hand of a viceroy from Delhi, Ghiyâs-ud-dîn Bahâdur "Bura," who before long attempted to render himself independent. He styled himself Bahâdur Shâh, and issued his own coinage. In 1327 (A.H. 728) the legends on his coins acknowledge the overlordship of Delhi, but two years later they describe him as independent king of Bengal.[1] In 1333 Muhammad issued his own coinage for Bengal and proceeded against the rebel. He defeated him, captured him, flayed him alive, and causing his skin to be stuffed with straw ordered it to be paraded through the provinces of the empire as a warning to ambitious governors. With reference to Gujarât Nuniz has been led into a slight error. Muhammad Taghlaq certainly did go there, but only in 1347. What he did do was to conquer the Dakhan. Firishtah mentions among his conquests Dvârasamudra, Malabar, Ânegundi (under the name "Kampila," for a reason that will presently be explained), Warangal, &c., and these places "were as effectually incorporated with his empire as the villages in the vicinity of Delhi."[2] He also held Gujarât firmly. If, therefore, we venture to correct Nuniz in this respect, and say that "Togao Mamede" made war on the "Dakhan" instead of on "Gujarât," and then advanced against Ânegundi (wrongly called "Vijayanagar," which place was not as yet founded), we shall probably be not far from the truth. The history of "Togao Mamede" so far is the history of Muhammad Taghlaq.

1 "Chronicle of the Pathan Kings of Delhi," by Edward Thomas, p. 200.

2 Firishtah (Briggs, i. 413).

Then as to the extraordinary stories told of him. True or not, they apply to that sovereign. Muhammad is described by contemporary writers as having been one of the wonders of the age. He was very liberal, especially to those learned in the arts. He established hospitals for the sick and alm-houses for widows and orphans. He was the most eloquent and accomplished prince of his time. He was skilled in many sciences, such as physic, logic, astronomy, and mathematics. He studied the philosophies and metaphysics of Greece, and was very strict in religious observances.

"But," continues Firishtah, from whom the above summary is taken, "with all these admirable qualities he was wholly devoid of mercy or consideration for his people. The punishments he inflicted were not only rigid and cruel, but frequently unjust. So little did he hesitate to spill the blood of God's creatures that when anything occurred which excited him to proceed to that horrid extremity, one might have supposed his object was to exterminate the human species altogether. No single week passed without his having put to death one or more of the learned and holy men who surrounded him, or some of the secretaries who attended him."

The slightest opposition to his will drove him into almost insane fury, and in these fits he allowed his natural ferocity full play. His whole life was spent in visionary schemes pursued by means equally irrational. He began by distributing enormous sums of money amongst his nobles, spending, so it is said, in one day as much as £500,000. He bought off the invading Moghuls by immense payments instead of repelling them by force of arms. Shortly after this he raised a huge army for the conquest of Persia, his cavalry, according to Firishtah, numbering 370,000 men. But nothing came of it except that the troops, not receiving their pay, dispersed and pillaged the country. Then he decided to try and conquer China and sent 100,000 men into the Himalayas, where almost all of them miserably perished; and when the survivors returned in despair the king put them all to death. He tried to introduce a depreciated currency into his territories as a means to wealth, issuing copper tokens for gold, which resulted in entire loss of credit and a standstill of trade. This failing to fill the treasury he next destroyed agriculture by intolerable exactions; the husbandmen abandoned their fields and took to robbery as a trade, and whole tracts became depopulated, the survivors living in the utmost starvation and misery and being despoiled of all that they possessed. Muhammad exterminated whole tribes as if they had been vermin. Incensed at the refusal of the inhabitants of a certain harassed tract to pay the inordinate demands of his subordinates, he ordered out his army as if for a hunt, surrounded an extensive tract of country, closed the circle towards the centre, and slaughtered every living soul found therein. This amusement was repeated more than once, and on a subsequent occasion he ordered a general massacre of all the inhabitants of the old Hindu city of Kanauj.[1] These horrors led of course to famine, and the miseries of the Hindus exceeded all power of description. On his return from Devagiri on one occasion he caused a tooth which he had lost to be interred in a magnificent stone mausoleum, which is still in existence at Bhîr.

But perhaps the best known of his inhuman eccentricities was his treatment of the inhabitants of the great city of Delhi. Muhammad determined to transfer his capital thence to Devagiri, whose name he changed to Doulatâbâd. The two places are six hundred miles apart. The king gave a general order to every inhabitant of Delhi to proceed forthwith to Devagiri, and prior to the issue of this order he had

[1] Elphinstone, "History of India," ii. 62.

the entire road lined with full-grown trees, transplanted for the purpose. The unfortunate people were compelled to obey, and thousands—including women, children, and aged persons—died by the way. Ibn Batuta, who was an eye-witness of the scenes of horror to which this gave rise, has left us the following description :—

"The Sultan ordered all the inhabitants to quit the place (Delhi), and upon some delay being evinced he made a proclamation stating that what person soever, being an inhabitant of that city, should be found in any of its houses or streets should receive condign punishment. Upon this they all went out; but his servants finding a blind man in one of the houses and a bedridden one in the other, the Emperor commanded the bedridden man to be projected from a balista, and the blind one to be dragged by his feet to Daulatâbâd, which is at the distance of ten days, and he was so dragged; but his limbs dropping off by the way, only one of his legs was brought to the place intended, and was then thrown into it; for the order had been that they should go to this place. When I entered Delhi it was almost a desert."[1]

It is characteristic of Muhammad's whimsical despotism that shortly afterwards he ordered the inhabitants of different districts to go and repeople Delhi, which they attempted to do, but with little success. Batuta relates that during the interval of desolation the king mounted on the roof of his palace, and seeing the city empty and without fire or smoke said, "Now my heart is satisfied and my feelings are appeased."

Ibn Batuta was a member of this king's court, and had every opportunity of forming a just conclusion. He sums up his qualities thus :—

"Muhammad more than all men loves to bestow gifts and to shed blood. At his gate one sees always some fakir who has become rich, or some living being who is put to death. His traits of generosity and valour, and his examples of cruelty and violence towards criminals, have obtained celebrity among the people. But apart from this he is the most humble of men and

[1] Lee's translation, p. 144.

the one who displays the most equity; the ceremonies of religion are observed at his court; he is very severe in all that concerns prayer and the punishment that follows omission of it . . . his dominating quality is generosity. . . . It rarely happened that the corpse of some one who had been killed was not to be seen at the gate of his palace. I have often seen men killed and their bodies left there. One day I went to his palace and my horse shied. I looked before me and I saw a white heap on the ground, and when I asked what it was one of my companions said it was the trunk of a man cut into three pieces. . . . Every day hundreds of individuals were brought chained into his hall of audience, their hands tied to their necks and their feet bound together. Some were killed, and others were tortured or well beaten."[1]

A man of these seemingly opposite qualities, charity, generosity, and religious fervour linked to unbridled lust for blood and an apparently overmastering desire to take life, possesses a character so *bizarre*, so totally opposed to Hindu ideals, that he would almost of necessity be accounted as something superhuman, monstrous, a saint with the heart of a devil, or a fiend with the soul of a saint. Hence Muhammad in the course of years gathered round his memory, centuries after his death, all the quaint tales and curious legends which an Oriental imagination could devise; and whenever his name is mentioned by the old chroniclers it is always with some extraordinary story attached to it.

Nuniz, therefore, though accurate in the main, was a century too early in his opening sentence. His "Togao Mamede" can be none other than Muhammad Taghlaq.

Henceforward this will be assumed.[2]

[1] Sir H. Elliot's "History of India," iii. 215.

[2] If we add together the number of years of the reigns of kings of Vijayanagar given by Nuniz prior to that of Krishna Deva Râya ("Crisnarao"), we find that the total is 180 (Senhor Lopes, Introduction, p. lxx.). The date of the beginning of the reign of Krishna Deva Râya is known to be 1509–10 A.D.; whence we obtain 1329–30 A.D. as the foundation of the empire in the person of "Dehorao" according to the chronicle. This is not quite accurate, but it helps to prove that "1230" is a century too early.

CHAPTER II

ORIGIN OF THE EMPIRE (A.D. 1336)

Muhammad's capture of Kampli and Ânegundi—Death of his nephew Bahâ-ud-dîn—Malik Nâib made governor of Ânegundi—Disturbances —Harihara Deva Râya raised to be king of Ânegundi—Mâdhavâchârya Vidyâranya—The city of Vijayanagar founded—Legends as to the origin of the new kingdom.

THE city of Vijayanagar is, as already stated, generally supposed to have been founded in the year 1336, and that that date is not far from the truth may be gathered from two facts. Firstly, there is extant an inscription of the earliest real king, Harihara I. or Hariyappa, the "Haraîb" of Ibn Batuta,[1] dated in A.D. 1340. Secondly, the account given by that writer of a raid southwards by Muhammad Taghlaq tallies at almost all points with the story given at the beginning of the Chronicle of Nuniz, and this raid took place in 1334.[2]

For if a comparison is made between the narrative of Batuta and the traditional account given by Nuniz as to the events that preceded and led to the foundation of Vijayanagar, little doubt will remain in the mind that both relate to the same event. According to Ibn Batuta,[3] Sultan Muhammad marched southwards against

[1] Batuta was a native of Tangiers, his name being Sheik Abû' Abdullah Muhammad. He arrived at the Indus on the 1st Muharram A.H. 734 (September 12, 1333 A.D.), and he seems to have resided in India till 1342.

[2] The narrative is given in the French translation of Ibn Batuta's travels, by Defrémery and Sanguinetti (vol. iii. pp. 318–320). See also Sir Henry Elliot's "History of India" (vol. iii. pp. 615–616).

[3] Firishtah's account is somewhat different, and he gives the date A.H. 739, or July 20, 1338, to July 9, 1339. But I consider the narrative of Ibn Batuta to be far the most reliable, since he wrote from personal experience, while Firishtah compiled his story two and a half centuries later.

his rebel nephew, Bahâ-ud-dîn Gushtasp, who had fled to the protection of the "Rai of Kambîla," or "Kampila" as Firishtah calls the place, in his stronghold amongst the mountains. The title "Rai" unmistakably points to the Kanarese country, where the form "Râya" is used for "Râjah;" while in "Kambîla" or "Kampila" we recognise the old town of Kampli, a fortified place about eight miles east of Ânegundi, which was the citadel of the predecessors of the kings of Vijayanagar. Though not itself actually "amongst the mountains," Kampli is backed by the mass of rocky hills in the centre of which the great city was afterwards situated. It is highly natural to suppose that the "Rai," when attacked by the Sultan, would have quitted Kampli and taken refuge in the fortified heights of Ânegundi, where he could defend himself with far greater chance of success than at the former place; and this would account for the difference in the names given by the two chroniclers. Ibn Batuta goes on to say that the Râya sent his guest safely away to a neighbouring chief, probably the Hoysala Ballâla, king of Dvârasamudra in Maisûr, then residing at Tânûr. He caused a huge fire to be lit on which his wives and the wives of his nobles, ministers, and principal men immolated themselves, and this done he sallied forth with his followers to meet the invaders, and was slain. The town was taken, "and eleven sons of the Rai were made prisoners and carried to the Sultan, who made them all Mussalmans." After the fall of the place the Sultan "treated the king's sons with great honour, as much for their illustrious birth as for his admiration of the conduct of their father;" and Batuta adds that he himself became intimately acquainted with one of these—"we were companions and friends."

There are only two substantial points of difference between this story and the traditional Hindu account given by Nuniz. One of these concerns the reason for the Sultan's attack. According to the Hindus it was a war undertaken from pure greed of conquest; according to Muhammadan story it was a campaign against a rebel. The second is that while the Hindus declare that none of the blood royal escaped, Batuta distinctly mentions the survival of eleven sons, and proves his point incontestably. But this does not vitiate the general resemblance of the two accounts, while the synchronism of the dates renders it impossible to believe that they can refer to two separate events. We may suppose that since the eleven sons became followers of Islâm they were for ever blotted out of account to the orthodox Hindu.

After the capture of the fortress the Sultan, according to Ibn Batuta, pursued Bahâ-ud-dîn southwards and arrived near the city of the prince with whom he had taken refuge. The chief abandoned his guest to the tender mercies of the tyrant, by whom he was condemned to a death of fiendish barbarity.

> "The Sultan ordered the prisoner to be taken to the women his relations, and these insulted him and spat upon him. Then he ordered him to be skinned alive, and as his skin was torn off his flesh was cooked with rice. Some was sent to his children and his wife, and the remainder was put into a great dish and given to the elephants to eat, but they would not touch it. The Sultan ordered his skin to be stuffed with straw, to be placed along with the remains of Bahâdur Bura,[1] and to be exhibited through the country."

To continue briefly the story given by Nuniz. After the capture of Ânegundi in 1334 the Sultan left Malik Nâib (whom Nuniz calls "Enybiquymelly" in his second chapter, and "Mileque neby," "Meliquy niby," and "Melinebiquy" in the third) as his local governor, and retired northwards. The country rose against the

[1] This was Ghiyâs-ud-dîn Bahâdur Bura of Bengal, mentioned above.

usurpers, and after a time the Sultan restored the principality to the Hindus, but made a new departure by raising to be Râya the former chief minister Deva Râya, called "Deorao" or "Dehorao" by Nuniz. He reigned seven years. During his reign this chief was one day hunting amongst the mountains south of the river when a hare, instead of fleeing from his dogs, flew at them and bit them.[1] The king, astonished at this marvel, was returning homewards lost in meditation, when he met on the river-bank the sage Mâdhavâchârya, surnamed *Vidyâranya* or "Forest of Learning," — for so we learn from other sources to name the anchorite alluded to—who advised the chief to found a city on the spot. "And so the king did, and on that very day began work on his houses, and he enclosed the city round about; and that done, he left Nagumdym, and soon filled the new city with people. And he gave it the name *Vydiajuna*, for so the hermit called himself who had bidden him construct it."[2]

Thus, in or about the year A.D. 1336, sprung into existence the great city which afterwards became so magnificent and of such wide-spread fame.

The chronicle continues by saying that the king constructed in the city of Vijayanagar a magnificent temple in honour of the sage. This temple I take to be the great temple near the river, still in use and known as the temple of Hampi or Hampe, having a small village clustering about it. On the rocks above it, close to a group of more modern Jain temples, is to be seen a small shrine built entirely, roof as well as walls, of stone. Everything about this little relic proves

[1] This tale is told of the rise of almost every kingdom, principality, or large zamindâri in Southern India, the usual variant being the discovery of a hidden treasure.

[2] I think that there can be little doubt that this derivation, though often given, is erroneous, and that the name was "City of Victory," not "City of Learning,"—*Vijaya*, not *Vidya*. *Vydiajuna* evidently represents *Vidyârjuna*.

it to be of greater antiquity than any other structure in the whole circuit of the hills, but its exact age is doubtful. It looks like a building of the seventh century A.D. Mr. Rea, superintendent of the Madras Archæological Survey, in an article published in the *Madras Christian College Magazine* for December 1886, points out that the fact of mortar having been used in its construction throws a doubt upon its being as old as its type of architecture would otherwise make it appear. It is quite possible, however, that the shrine may have been used by a succession of recluses, the last of whom was the great teacher Mâdhava. If we stand on that rock and imagine all the great ruins of the city visible from thence, the palaces and temples, the statues and towers and walls, to be swept out of existence, we have around us nothing but Nature in one of her wildest moods—lofty hills near and far, formed almost entirely of huge tumbled boulders of granite, but with trees and grass on all the low ground. It was a lonely spot, separated by the river from the more inhabited country on the farther side, where dwelt the chiefs of Ânegundi, and was just such as would have been chosen for their abode by the ascetics of former days, who loved to dwell in solitude and isolation amid scenes of grandeur and beauty.

We shall, however, in all probability never know whether this hermit, whose actual existence at the time is attested by every tradition regarding the origin of Vijayanagar, was really the great Mâdhava or another less celebrated sage, on whom by a confusion of ideas his name has been foisted. Some say that Mâdhavâchârya lived entirely at Sringêri.

There are a number of other traditions relating to the birth of the city and empire of Vijayanagar.

One has it that two brothers named Bukka and Harihara, who had been in the service of the king of

Warangal at the time of the destruction of that kingdom by the Muhammadans in 1323, escaped with a small body of horse to the hill country about Ânegundi, being accompanied in their flight by the Brahman Mâdhava or Mâdhavâchârya Vidyâranya, and by some means not stated became lords of that tract, afterwards founding the city of Vijayanagar.[1]

Another states that the two brothers were officers in the service of the Muhammadan governor of Warangal subsequent to its first capture in 1309. They were despatched against the Hoysala Ballâla sovereign in the expedition under the command of Malik Kâfur in 1310, which resulted in the capture of the Hindu capital, Dvârasamudra; but the portion of the force to which the brothers belonged suffered a defeat, and they fled to the mountainous tract near Ânegundi. Here they met the holy Mâdhava, who was living the life of a recluse, and by his aid they established the kingdom and capital city.

A variant of this relates that the two brothers for some reason fled direct from Warangal to Ânegundi. This account redounds more to their honour as Hindus. Though compelled first to accept service under their conquerors, their patriotism triumphed in the end, and they abandoned the flesh-pots of Egypt to throw in their luck with their co-religionists.

A fourth story avers that the hermit Mâdhava himself founded the city after the discovery of a hidden

[1] Buchanan ("Mysore," &c., iii. 110), while on a visit to Beidûr in Mysore in 1801, was shown by one Râmappa Varmika a Sanskrit book in his possession called the *Vidyârâyana Sikka*, which relates that the founders of Vijayanagar were Hukka and Bukka, guards of the treasury of Pratâpa Rudra of Warangal. These young men came to the Guru, or spiritual teacher, Vidyâranya, who was head of the monastery of Sringêri, and the latter founded for them the city of Vijayanagar. This was in 1336, and Hukka was made first king. But this story entirely leaves out of account the most important point. How could two brothers, flying from a captured capital and a conquered kingdom, suddenly establish in a new country a great city and a sovereignty?

treasure, ruled over it himself, and left it after his death to a Kuruba family who established the first regular dynasty.

A fifth, mentioned by Couto,[1] who fixes the date as 1220, states that while Mâdhava was living his ascetic life amongst the mountains he was supported by meals brought to him by a poor shepherd called Bukka, "and one day the Brahman said to him, 'Thou shalt be king and emperor of all Industan.' The other shepherds learned this, and began to treat this shepherd with veneration and made him their head; and he acquired the name of 'king,' and began to conquer his neighbours, who were five in number, viz., Canara, Taligas, Canguivarao, Negapatao, and he of the Badagas, and he at last became lord of all and called himself Boca Rao." He was attacked by the king of Delhi, but the latter was defeated and retired, whereupon Bukka established a city "and called it Visaja Nagar, which we corruptly call Bisnaga; and we call all the kingdom by that name, but the natives amongst themselves always call it the 'kingdom of Canara.'" Couto's narrative seems to be a mixture of several stories. His wrong date points to his having partly depended upon the original chronicle of Nuniz, or the summary of it published by Barros; while the rest of the tale savours more of Hindu romance than of historical accuracy. He retains, however, the tradition of an attack by the king of Delhi and the latter's subsequent retirement.

Another authority suggests that Bukka and Harihara may have been feudatories of the Hoysala Ballâlas.

Nikitin, the Russian traveller, who was in India in 1474, seems to favour the view that they belonged to the old royal house of the Kâdambas of Banavâsi, since

[1] *Decada* VI. l. v. c. 4.

he speaks of "the Hindoo Sultan Kadam," who resided at "Bichenegher."[1]

Here we have a whole bundle of tales and traditions to account for the origin of the great kingdom, and can take our choice. There are many others also. Perhaps the most reasonable account would be one culled from the general drift of the Hindu legends combined with the certainties of historical fact; and from this point of view we may for the present suppose that two brothers, Hindus of the Kuruba caste, who were men of strong religious feeling, serving in the treasury of the king of Warangal, fled from that place on its sack and destruction in 1323 and took service under the petty Râjah of Ânegundi. Both they and their chiefs were filled with horror and disgust at the conduct of the marauding Moslems, and pledged themselves to the cause of their country and their religion. The brothers rose to be minister and treasurer respectively at Ânegundi. In 1334 the chief gave shelter to Bahâ-ud-dîn, nephew of Muhammad of Delhi, and was attacked by the Sultan. Ânegundi fell, as narrated by Batuta, and the Sultan retired, leaving Mallik as his deputy to rule the state. Mallik found the people too strong for him, and eventually the Sultan restored the country to the Hindus, raising to be râjah and minister respectively the two brothers who had formerly been minister and treasurer. These were Harihara I. ("Hukka") and Bukka I.

[1] "India in the Fifteenth Century," Hakluyt edit., p. 29.

THE FIRST VIJAYANAGAR DYNASTY

[The following shows the pedigree of this dynasty as given in the *Epigraphia Indica* (iii. p. 36). Inscriptions not yet satisfactorily examined will probably add to the information given.]

- SAMGAMA.
  - HARIHARA I. (or Hariyappa).
  - KAMPA.
    - SAMGAMA
  - BUKKA I., *m. Gaurî* (or *Gaurâmbikâ*).
    - HARIHARA II., *m. Malâmbikâ.*
      - BUKKA II.
      - DÊVA RÂYA I., *m. Hêmâmbikâ.*
        - VÎRA VIJAYA, *m. Nârâyanâmbikâ.*
          - DEVA RÂYA II.
            - MALLIKÂRJUNA.
              - RÂJASÊKHARA.
              - VIRÛPÂKSHA II.
            - VIRÛPÂKSHA I.
          - PRATÂPA DEVA RÂYA.
  - MÂRAPA.
  - MUDDAPA.

CHAPTER III

THE FIRST KINGS (A.D. 1336 TO 1379)

Rapid acquisition of territory—Reign of Harihara I.—Check to Muhammadan aggression—Reign of Bukka I.—Kampa and Sangama?—The Bâhmanî kingdom established, 1347—Death of Nâgadeva of Warangal—Vijayanagar's first great war—Massacres by Muhammad Bâhmanî—Battle at Adoni, 1366—Flight of Bukka—Mujâhid's war, 1375—He visits the Malabar coast—Siege of Vijayanagar—Extension of territory—Death of Mujâhid, 1378.

THE city of Vijayanagar, thus founded about the year 1335, speedily grew in importance and became the refuge of the outcasts, refugees, and fighting men of the Hindus, beaten and driven out of their old strongholds by the advancing Muhammadans.

The first rulers of Vijayanagar, however, did not dare to call themselves kings, nor did even the Brahmans do so who composed the text of their early inscriptions. It is for this reason that I have spoken of Harihara I. and Bukka I. as "Chiefs." The inscription referred to of Harihara in 1340 calls him "Hariyappa *Vodeya,*" the former name being less honourable than "Harihara," and the latter definitely entitling him to rank only as a chieftain. Moreover, the Sanskrit title given him is *Mahâmaṇḍalèśvara,* which may be translated "great lord"—not king. And the same is the case with his successor, Bukka, in two inscriptions,[1] one of which is dated in 1353. Already in 1340 Harihara is said to have been possessed of very large territories, and he was the acknowledged overlord of villages as far north as the Kalâdgi district, north of the Mâlprabha, a country that had been over-

[1] *Journal Bombay Br. R.A.S.*, xii. 338, 340.

run by Muhammad Taghlaq. That this was not a mere empty boast is shown by the fact that a fort was built in that year at Bâdâmi by permission of Harihara.

And thus we see the first chief of Vijayanagar quietly, and perhaps peacefully, acquiring great influence and extensive possessions. These so rapidly increased that Bukka's successor, Harihara II., styles himself *Râjâdhirâja*, "king of kings," or emperor.

But to revert to the first king Harihara, or, as Nuniz calls him, "Dehorao," for *Deva Râya.* He reigned, according to our chronicle, seven years, "and did nothing therein but pacify the kingdom, which he left in complete tranquillity." His death, if this be so, would have taken place about the year 1343. Nuniz relates that he founded a temple in honour of the Brahman hermit, his protector. This was the great temple at Hampe close to the river, which is still in full preservation and is the only one among the massive shrines erected at the capital in which worship is still carried on; the others were remorselessly wrecked and destroyed by the Muhammadans in 1565. As already stated, the traveller Ibn Batuta refers to this king under the name of "Haraîb" or "Harîb" in or about the year 1342. If the traditions collated by Nuniz, according to which Harihara I. lived at peace during the seven years of his reign, be true, his death must have occurred before 1344, because in that year, as we learn from other sources, Krishna, son of Pratâpa Rudra of Warangal, took refuge at Vijayanagar, and, in concert with its king and with the surviving Ballâla princes of Dvârasamudra, drove back the Muhammadans, rescued for a time part of the Southern Dakhan country, and prepared the way for the overthrow of the sovereignty of Delhi south of the Vindhyas. I take it, therefore, that Harihara died in or about the year A.D. 1343.

As to his having reigned quietly, I know of only one statement to the contrary. An inscription of Samgama II. recording a grant in 1356, and referred to below, states that Harihara I. "defeated the Sultan;" but perhaps this only alludes to the fact that Muhammad Taghlaq had to abandon his hold on the country.

The next king was Harihara's brother, Bukka I. ("Bucarao"), and according to Nuniz he reigned thirty-seven years, conquering in that time all the kingdoms of the south, even including Orissa (Orya). Without laying too much stress on conquests by force of arms, it seems certain that most if not all Southern India submitted to his rule, probably only too anxious to secure a continuance of Hindu domination in preference to the despotism of the hated followers of Islâm.[1] According to the chronicle, therefore, the death of Bukka I., as we must call him, took place about the year A.D. 1380. As to inscriptions of his reign, Dr. Hultzsch[2] mentions that they cover the period from about 1354 to 1371, while the first inscription of his successor, Harihara II., is dated in 1379.[3] If, then, we assume that Bukka I. reigned till 1379, we find the chronicle so far accurate that Bukka I. did in fact reign thirty-six years, though not thirty-seven—A.D. 1343 to 1379.

But meanwhile we have another story from an inscription on copper-plates which is to be seen preserved in the Collector's office at Nellore. It has been

[1] There is an undated inscription, published in Dr. Hultzsch's "South Indian Inscriptions" (vol. i. p. 167), on a rock not far from the summit of the lofty hill on which stands the virgin fortress of Gutti or Gooty in the Anantapur District, according to which that stronghold belonged to King Bukka. The place is seventy-eight miles east of Vijayanagar.

[2] *Epig. Ind.*, iii. 36.

[3] An inscription of 1368-69 (Saka 1290, year Kîlaka) mentions Mâdhavâchârya Vidyâranya, apparently as still living. *Ind. Ant.*, iv. 206.

[4] See my "Antiquities of Madras," ii. 8, No. 58; Hultzsch's *Epig. Indica*, iii. 21.

carefully edited by Mr. H. Krishna Sâstri. According to this it would appear that Bukka I., who undoubtedly was a man of war, usurped the throne. It asserts that the father of Harihara I., who was named Samgama, had five sons. The eldest was Harihara himself, the second Kampa, and the third Bukka. We want to know who succeeded Harihara. There is extant an inscription of Bukka dated in 1354, and there is this Nellore inscription dated in 1356. The latter comes from a far-off country near the eastern coast, and it relates that Kampa succeeded Harihara, and that Samgama II., son of Kampa, succeeded his father, and granted a village in the Nellore district to the Brahmans on a date which corresponds to May 3, A.D. 1356. It implies that Samgama had succeeded his father Kampa exactly a year previous to the grant. Thus it claims that Kampa was king from 1343 to 1355. We know nothing more of this, and there is only one other document at present known to exist which was executed in the reign either of Kampa or of Samgama. This is alluded to by Mr. Krishna Sâstri, who refers us to the colophon of the *Mâdhavîyâ Dhâtuvritti*, according to which its author, Sâyanâchârya, uterine brother of the great Mâdhavâchârya, was minister to king Samgama, son of Kampa. The only possible inference is that the succession to Harihara was disputed, and that somehow Bukka got the upper hand and at least as early as 1354 declared himself king, afterwards claiming to have immediately succeeded Harihara. It will be seen farther on that in almost every case the kingdom was racked with dissension on the demise of the sovereign, and that year after year the members of the reigning family were subjected to violence and murder in order that one or other of them might establish himself as head of the State.

On the assumption, therefore, that the reign of

Bukka I. lasted from 1343 to 1379, we turn to Firishtah to learn what were this king's relations with the followers of Islâm, now supreme on the north of the Krishnâ.

Just after his accession, as it would appear, occurred the successful campaign alluded to above, in which a combination of Hindus from different States drove back the invaders. Here is Firishtah's account of what took place.[1] He is speaking of the year A.H. 744, which lasted from May 26, A.D. 1343, to May 15, 1344, and he says that Krishna Naik, son of Rudra Deva of Warangal, went privately to Ballâla Deva and urged him to join a combination of Hindus with the view of driving out the Muhammadans from the Dakhan. The Ballâla prince consented, and Krishna Naik promised, when the preparations were complete, to raise all the Hindus of Telingana and place himself at their head.

Ballâla Deva then built the city of Vijayanagar,[2] raised an army, and the war began. Warangal, then in the hands of the Muhammadans, was reduced, and its governor, Imâd-ul-Mulkh, retreated to Daulatâbâd or Devagiri. The two chiefs then induced other Rajahs of the Malabar and Kanara countries to join them, and the joint forces seized the whole of the Dakhan and expelled the Muhammadans there, "so that within a few months Muhammad Taghlak had no possessions in that quarter except Daulatâbâd."

So far the Muhammadan historian. It is necessary to observe that this success of the Hindus was only temporary, for their enemies still swarmed in the Dakhan, and immediately after this contest the Hindus appear to have retired south of the Krishnâ, leaving

[1] Briggs, i. 427.

[2] This is in itself absurd, and carries with it its own refutation. It would be manifestly impossible for the city to be "built" in so short a time, and, moreover, it would have been sheer waste of time for the Prince to have employed himself in such a way. The sentence was probably introduced merely to account for that city having been built *about* this period.

the distracted country a prey to temporary anarchy. This, however, was of short duration, for though the domination of the Sultan of Delhi in that tract was completely destroyed, yet three years later, viz., on Friday the 24th Rabî-al-âkhir A.H. 748, according to Firishtah, a date which corresponds to Friday, August 3, A.D. 1347, Alâ-ud-dîn Bâhmanî was crowned sovereign of the Dakhan at Kulbarga, establishing a new dynasty which lasted for about 140 years.

A few years after this there was a successful invasion of the Carnatic country by Alâ-ud-Dîn; but though the army returned with some booty Firishtah does not claim for him a decisive victory. He does, however, claim that the new Sultan extended his territory as far south as the river Tungabhadra, "the vicinity of the fortress of Adoni." Alâ-ud-dîn died at the age of sixty-seven on Sunday, February 2, A.D. 1358,[1] and was succeeded by Muhammad Shâh. The Râya of Vijayanagar had presented Alâ-ud-dîn with a ruby of inestimable price, and this, set in a bird of paradise composed of precious stones, the Sultan placed in the canopy over his throne; but some say that this was done by Muhammad, and that the ruby was placed above his umbrella of State.

Early in the reign of Muhammad it was discovered that the gold and silver coins of the Bâhmanî Sultans were being melted down in large quantities by the Hindus of Vijayanagar and Warangal, and numbers of the merchants were put to death. At the same time Bukka I., supported by his friend at Warangal, de-

[1] Firishtah says on 1st Rabî-ul-awwal A.H. 759; A.H. 761 (A.D. 1359–60) according to the *Burhân-i-Maâsir*. But the author of the latter work says that Alâ-ud-dîn reigned thirteen years ten months and twenty-seven days, which would make the date of his death the 22nd of Rabî-ul-awwal A.H. 762, or January 31, A.D. 1361. He does not, therefore, appear to be very accurate. Firishtah gives in words the length of his reign as "eleven years two months and seven days."

manded the restoration of certain territories,[1] and as the Sultan was not ready for war, he "during a year and a half kept the ambassadors of the Raies at his court, and sent his own to Beejanugger to amuse his enemies." Finally he resolved on war, and made extravagant counter-demands on the Hindus. Bukka joined forces with Warangal, and Muhammad waged war on the latter state, plundering the country up to the capital, and retiring only on receipt of a large indemnity. Firishtah does not relate that any further campaign was at that time initiated, and we are therefore free to suppose that the Muhammadans were unable to press their advantage. Warangal was not long left in peace, and it may be well to glance at its subsequent history before returning to the events of the reign of Bukka at Vijayanagar.

After an interval, enraged at an insult offered or supposed to have been offered by the Rajah of Warangal, Muhammad made a rapid advance to the former's city of "Vellunputtun," as it is spelt by Firishtah, or "Filampatan," according to the author of the *Burhân-i-Maâsir*. He seized it, slaughtered the inhabitants without mercy, and captured the unfortunate prince Vinayaka Deva.[2] The Sultan "commanded a pile of wood to be lighted before the citadel, and putting Nagdeo in an engine (catapult), had him shot from the walls into the flames, in which he was consumed." After a few days' rest the Sultan retired, but was followed and harassed by large bodies of Hindus and completely routed. Only 1500 men returned to Kulbarga, and the Sultan himself received a severe wound in his arm.

[1] Certain inscriptions published by Mr. Rice state that the general who commanded Bukka's armies about this time was Nadegonta Mallinâtha, son of Nadegonta Sâyyana. These bear date A.D. 1355–56 and 1356–57.

[2] Called "Nagdeo" in Scott's translation (i. 19).

This was followed by a joint embassy from Bukka of Vijayanagar and the prince of Warangal to the Sultan of Delhi, in which they offered to act in conjunction with him should an army be sent southwards by that monarch in order to regain his lost power in the Dakhan; "but Feroze Shah, being too much employed with domestic commotions to assist them, did not attend to their representations." Thus encouraged, Muhammad assembled fresh forces and despatched them in two divisions against Warangal and Golkonda. The expedition was successful and the Râjah submitted, the Sultan receiving Golkonda, an immense treasure, and a magnificent throne as the price of peace. The throne was set with precious stones of great value, and being still further enriched by subsequent sovereigns was at one time valued at four millions sterling.[1] Warangal finally fell in A.D. 1424, and was annexed to the Bâhmanî kingdom, thus bringing the Muhammadans down to the River Krishnâ all along its length except in the neighbourhood of the east coast.

Now for the principal events of Bukka's reign and the affairs of Vijayanagar. The story deepens in interest from about the year 1365, and for two centuries we can follow the fortunes of the Hindu kingdom without much difficulty.

Early in A.D. 1366[2] the Sultan opened his first regular campaign against Vijayanagar. Originating in an after-dinner jest, it ended only after such slaughter that Firishtah computes the victims on the Hindu side alone as numbering no less than half a million. The story is told us by an eye-witness, one

[1] Briggs, ii. 307.

[2] There is a confusion of dates here in Firishtah; but he definitely fixes the month and year when Muhammad set out, and we may accept it for the present. The *Burhân-i-Maâsir* implies that the war against Vijayanagar took place prior to the campaign against Warangal. Firishtah places it certainly after the "Vellunputtun" affair.

Mullah Dâûd of Bîdar, who was seal-bearer to Sultan Muhammad.[1]

"One evening, when the spring of the garden of mirth had infused the cheek of Mahummud Shaw with the rosy tinge of delight, a band of musicians sung two verses of Ameer Khoossroo in praise of kings, festivity, and music. The Sultan was delighted beyond measure, and commanded Mallek Syef ad Dien Ghoree to give the three hundred performers a draft for a gratuity on the treasury of the roy of Beejanuggur. The minister, though he judged the order the effect of wine, in compliance with the humour of the Sultan wrote it, but did not despatch it. However, Mahummud Shaw penetrated his thoughts. The next day he inquired if the draft had been sent to the roy, and being answered, not, exclaimed, 'Think you a word without meaning could escape my lips? I did not give the order in intoxication, but serious design.' Mallek Syef ad Dien upon this, affixed the royal seal to the draft, and despatched it by express messenger to the roy of Beejanuggur. The roy, haughty and proud of his independence, placed the presenter of the draft on an ass's back, and, parading him through all the quarters of Beejanuggur, sent him back with every mark of contempt and derision. He also gave immediate orders for assembling his troops, and prepared to attack the dominions of the house of Bhamenee. With this intent he marched with thirty thousand horse, three thousand elephants, and one hundred thousand foot to the vicinity of the fortress of Oodnee;[2] from whence he sent detachments to destroy and lay waste the country of the faithful."

The Râya, in spite of the season being that of the rains, pressed forward to Mudkal, an important city in the Raichûr Doâb, or the large triangle of country lying west of the junction of the Krishnâ and Tungabhadrâ rivers, a territory which was ever a debatable ground between the Hindus and Mussulmans, and the scene of constant warfare for the next 200 years. Mudkal was

[1] Firishtah (Scott, i. 23).

[2] Adoni as now called; Âdhvani as properly spelt. This is a fine hill-fortress with extensive lines of walls, a few miles south of the River Tungabhadrâ and on the line of railway between Madras and Bombay.

captured, and all the inhabitants, men, women, and children, put to the sword. One man only escaped and carried the news to Kulbarga.

"Mahummud Shaw, on hearing it, was seized with a transport of grief and rage, in which he commanded the unfortunate messenger to be instantly put to death; exclaiming that he could never bear in his presence a wretch who could survive the sight of the slaughter of so many brave companions."

The same day—*i.e.* on a day in A.H. 767, in the month of Jamâd-ul-awwal, which lasted from January 14 to February 13, A.D. 1366—the Sultan marched southwards taking a solemn oath—

"that till he should have put to death one hundred thousand infidels, as an expiation for the massacre of the faithful, he would never sheathe the sword of holy war nor refrain from slaughter. When he reached the banks of the Kistna, he swore by the power who had created and exalted him to dominion, that eating or sleep should be unlawful for him till he had crossed that river in face of the enemy, by the blessing of heaven routed their army, and gladdened the souls of the martyrs of Mudkul with the blood of their murderers. He then appointed his son Mujahid Shaw to succeed him, and Mallek Syef ad Dien regent of his kingdom. He resigned all his elephants, except twenty, to the prince, gave him his advice, and sent him back to Kulbarga. He then crossed the river with nine thousand chosen horse without delay. The roy of Beejanuggur, notwithstanding his vast army, was so alarmed[1] that he sent off all his treasure, valuable baggage, and elephants towards his capital, intending to engage the next morning, or retreat, as he should find it adviseable. The night being stormy and heavy rain falling, the elephants and other beasts of burden stuck frequently in the mud,[2] and were not able to advance

[1] We must never forget that the narrative of Firishtah is necessarily tinged with bias in favour of the Musalmans, and that it was not compiled till the end of the sixteenth or beginning of the seventeenth century A.D. The "infidels" are, of course, the Hindus, the "faithful" the followers of Muhammad the Prophet.

[2] The country in question is a plain composed of a deep alluvial deposit, generally overlying gravel, and known as "black cotton soil." After heavy rain it is practically impassable for traffic for some days.

above four miles from the camp. Mahummud Shaw heard of the enemy's movement during the night, and immediately marched towards them, leaving his encampment standing. Towards the dawn he arrived at the roy's camp, and the alarm being given, so great was the confusion, that the infidels fled with the utmost precipitation towards the fortress of Oodnee, leaving everything behind them. Mahummud Shaw entered the camp of their market and baggage, putting all to death without any distinction; and it is said that the slaughter amounted to seventy thousand men, women, and children."

Muhammad passed the hot weather and the season of the early rains that year near Mudkal, and after being reinforced marched against Adoni—"in the plains of which, on the banks of the Tummedra (Tungabhadrâ), the roy of Beejanuggur had taken up his station in his own territories, having given the command of Oodnee to his sister's son. Here he had collected a great army, and brought elephants and all the splendid insignia of empire from Beejanuggur."[1]

The Sultan had with him a train of artillery[2] and in a short time crossed the Tungabhadrâ, "and entered the domains of Beejanuggur, which were now for the first time invaded by a Muhammadan sovereign in person." This remark of Firishtah's is historically correct, for the Delhi Sultan's attack on Ânegundi took place on the north bank of that river.

Before continuing the story I must note that Firishtah calls the king of Vijayanagar "Kishen Roy," otherwise Krishna Râya; but there can be no doubt that his real name was Bukka. The historian collected his information more than two hundred years after these events, and often misnamed the Hindu kings of whom he writes.

[1] The expression of Firishtah last quoted is deserving of note, as it implies that, according to tradition in his time, the Râya of Vijayanagar had by the year 1366 A.D. become a great and important sovereign.

[2] Briggs (ii. 312, n.) considers it unlikely that the armies could have possessed artillery at so early a date.

Muhammad, then, crossed the Tungabhadrâ, and only about twenty-five miles intervened between him and the great fortress of Adoni, which is situated on a precipitous range of hills about that distance from the river. The Tungabhadrâ at this portion of its course may be considered as forming the arc, west to north, of a quarter circle having Adoni for its centre, the radius roughly measuring about twenty-five miles. The river is fordable at most seasons of the year, lying as it does in a shallow rocky bed with low banks. It is difficult to locate with any certainty the scenes of this campaign, but I gather generally that, finding the Muhammadans aiming at the reduction of Adoni, Bukka marched out with a very large force to intercept this move, and placed himself on the south bank of the Tungabhadrâ, in the neighbourhood of the threatened fortress. The Sultan crossed somewhere near the present town of Siruguppa, and the great battle that ensued took place in the open cotton-plains, perhaps near Kavutâl ("Kowtall" on the Ordnance Map).

Here is Firishtah's account:[1]—

"Roy Kishen Roy (*i.e.* Bukka), on receiving the intelligence (that Muhammad had crossed), called together all the first nobles of his court, and consulted on the best mode of opposing the mussulmauns. It was agreed that Hoje Mul,[2] a maternal relation to the roy and commander of his armies, should have the conduct of the war. Hoje Mul, vain to excess, on receiving his command, asked the roy if he should bring the prince of the mussulmauns alive a prisoner into his presence, or present him only his head upon a spear. Kishen Roy replied, that a living enemy, in any situation, was not agreeable, therefore he had better put him to death as soon as he should take him. Hoje Mul, having received his dismission, marched to oppose Mahummud Shaw with forty thousand

---

[1] Scott's edit., i. 27.

[2] Briggs gives the name as Bhoj-Mul. He *may* be the Mallayya or Mallinâtha mentioned above (p. 31, note).

horse and five hundred thousand foot. He commanded the Bramins to deliver every day to the troops discourses on the meritoriousness of slaughtering the mahummedans, in order to excite zeal for expelling them. He ordered them to describe the butchery of cows,[1] the insults to sacred images, and destroying of temples, practised by the true believers.

"Mahummud Shaw, when the enemy arrived within fifteen coss [2] of his camp, commanded his general, Khan Mahummud, to muster the troops, who were found to be fifteen thousand horse and fifty thousand foot. Ten thousand horse and thirty thousand foot, with all the artillery, he advanced under Khan Mahummud Khan.

"On the 14th of Zeekaud (A.H. 767, or Thursday, July 23, A.D. 1366), the armies of light and darkness met. From the dawn till four in the afternoon, like the waves of the ocean, they continued in warm conflict with each other, and great numbers were slain on both sides. Mooseh Khan and Eeseh Khan, who commanded the right and left wings of Khan Mahummud's line, drank the sherbet of martyrdom, and their troops broke; which misfortune had nearly given a blow to the army of Islaam. At this instant Mahummud Shaw appeared with three thousand fresh horse. This restored the spirits of Khan Mahummud as also of the disordered troops, who rallied and joined him. Mukkrib Khan, advancing with the artillery, was not wanting in execution, greatly disordering the enemy's horse and foot. He asked leave to charge and complete the rout. Khan Mahummud upon this, detached a number of the nobility to support him, and permitted him to advance; which he did with such rapidity that the infidels had not time to use fireworks (*i.e.* cannon), but came to short weapons such as swords and daggers. At this time an elephant, named Sheer Shikar,[3] belonging to Khan Mahummud, refused the guidance of his driver, and rushed into the center of the enemy's line, where he was stopped by the elephants of Hoje Mul Roy, and his driver was killed. Khan Mahummud with five hundred horse followed, and the elephant becoming unruly, turned upon the enemy, throwing their ranks into confusion. Hoje Mul Roy, after receiving a mortal wound, fled, and his followers no longer made resistance. The infidels,

---

[1] Sacred animals to the Hindus.

[2] About forty-two miles.

[3] The Tiger-Hunter.

seeing their center broke, fled on all sides. The scymetars of the faithful were not yet sheathed from slaughter when the royal umbrella appeared. The sultan gave orders to renew the massacre of the unbelievers. They were executed with such strictness that pregnant women, and even children at the breast, did not escape the sword.

"Mahummud Shaw halted a week on the field, and dispatched accounts of his victory to his own dominions. In performance of his vow of massacre he next marched towards the camp of Kishen Roy, who, thinking himself unable to oppose notwithstanding his numerous force, fled to the woods and mountains for shelter. The sultan followed him from place to place for three months, putting to death all who came in his way, without distinction. At length Kishen Roy took the road of Beejanuggur, his capital. The sultan, pursuing, soon arrived with his army near the city."

To make a long story short, the Sultan besieged Vijayanagar in vain for a month, and then retreated across the Tungabhadrâ, harassed at every step by masses of the Hindus from the city. He halted at last in an open plain, and the king also pitched his camp at no great distance. Muhammad's retreat had been deliberately carried out in order to draw on his enemy, and cause him by over-confidence to neglect proper precautions. The ruse was successful. The Muhammadans made a sudden and unexpected night-attack. Bukka (called, as before, "Kishen") was off his guard, having indulged in wine and the amusements provided by a band of dancing-women. The slaughter was terrible, and the Râya fled to Vijayanagar, ten thousand of his troops being slain;—"But this did not satisfy the rage of the sultan, who commanded the inhabitants of every place round Beejanuggur to be massacred without mercy."

Then Bukka tried to make peace, but the Sultan refused.

"At this time a favourite remarked to the sultan that he had only sworn to slaughter one hundred thousand Hindoos, and not totally to destroy their race. The sultan replied that though twice the number of his vow might have been slain, yet till the roy should submit, and satisfy the musicians, he would not pardon him or spare the lives of his subjects. To this the ambassadors, who had full powers, agreed, and the money was paid at the instant. Mahummud Shaw then said, 'Praise be to God that what I ordered has been performed. I would not let a light word be recorded of me in the pages of time!'"

The ambassadors then pleaded that no religion ordained that the innocent, and particularly helpless women and children, should suffer for the guilty :—

"If Kishen Roy had been faulty, the poor and wretched had not been partakers in his crimes. Mahummud Shaw replied that the decrees of providence had so ordered, and that he had no power to alter them."

The ambassadors finally urged that as the two nations were neighbours, it were surely best to avoid unnecessary cruelty, which would only embitter their relations with one another ; and this argument had effect.

"Mahummud Shaw was struck by their remarks, and took an oath that he would not in future put to death a single enemy after victory, and would bind his successors to observe the same lenity."

For some years, no doubt, the promise was fulfilled, but we read of wholesale massacres perpetrated by sovereigns of later date. As to Muhammad, Firishtah glories in the statement that he had slaughtered 500,000 Hindus, and so wasted the districts of the Carnatic that for several decades they did not recover their natural population.

Thus ended the war, and for some years there was peace between Vijayanagar and Kulbarga.

Muhammad Shâh died on 21st April A.D. 1375,[1] and was succeeded by his son Mujâhid, then nineteen years

[1] 19th Zîlkada A.H. 776 (Firishtah). The *Burhân-i Maâsir* says in A.H. 775.

old. Shortly after his accession Mujâhid wrote to Bukka Râya (still called "Kishen Roy" by Firishtah[1]), "that as some forts and districts between the Kistnah and Tummedra (Tungabhadrâ) rivers were held by them in participation, which occasioned constant disagreements, he must for the future limit his confines to the Tummedra, and give up all on the eastern side to him, with the fort of Beekapore and some other places." This "Beekapore" is the important fortress of Bankâpur, south of Dhârwâr. The Dakhâni sovereigns always looked on it with covetous eyes, as it lay on the direct route from Vijayanagar to the sea, and its possession would paralyse Hindu trade.

The Râya replied by a counter-demand that the Sultan should evacuate the whole of the Doâb, since Raichûr and Mudkal had always belonged to the Ânegundi family. Bukka declared the Krishnâ river to be the true boundary, and asked that the elephants taken by Sultan Muhammad should be restored.

The Sultan's answer was a declaration of war. He advanced in person, crossed both the rivers, and arrived before Adoni. On hearing that the Râya was encamped on the bank of the Tungabhadrâ, he left one force to besiege the fortress, sent another to advance towards Vijayanagar, and himself marched, probably in a north-westerly direction, towards the river, "by slow marches and with great caution." The Hindu prince at first prepared to receive his attack, but for some reason[2] lost

[1] The *Burhân-i Maâsir* calls the Râya "Kapazah." Major King says that even the vowel marks are given, and there can be no doubt about the name. I venture to hazard a conjecture that if the word had been written "Pakazah," transposing the first two consonants—a mistake occasionally made by writers dealing with, to them, outlandish names—the sound of the word would suggest *Bukka Shâh*. There is no name that I have met with amongst those borne by the kings of Vijayanagâr in the remotest degree resembling "Kapazah."

[2] Firishtah relates a story which is hardly sufficient to account for Bukka's faint-heartedness. He says that Mujâhid went one day while on the march

heart and retired to the forests on the hills of Sandûr, south of his capital.

Firishtah here pays a tribute to the interest felt by the inhabitants of this part of India in the new city, then only forty years old, but evidently growing in grandeur year by year.

> " Mujahid Shaw, having heard great praises of the beauty of the city, advanced to Beejanuggur ; but thinking it too strong to besiege at present, he moved in pursuit of the enemy in the field."

Now follows a passage on which it is difficult to place full reliance, but which only echoes common tradition. It runs to the effect that, on the advance of the Sultan, the Râya

> " fled through the woods and hills towards Seet Bunder Ramessar followed by the sultan, who cut passages for his cavalry through forests before inaccessible. In this manner the roy fled from place to place for six months, but never dared to appear without the woods. It was in vain that the favourites of the sultan represented the pursuit as fruitless and destructive to the troops. He would not desist. At last his good fortune prevailed. The health of Kishen Roy and his family became affected by the noxious air of the woods, and they were warned to quit them by the physicians. . . . Driven by necessity, he retired by secret paths to his capital of Beejanuggur. The sultan despatched an army after him, while he himself, with the ameer al amra Bahadur Khan and five thousand men, went to amuse himself with the sight of Seet Bunda Ramessar.
>
> " The sultan at this place repaired a mosque which had been built by the officers of Sultan Alla ad Dien Khiljee. He broke down many temples of the idolaters, and laid waste the country ; after which he hastened with all expedition to Beejanuggur."

It is a fact that a mosque is declared to have been

after a man-eating tiger of great ferocity, and shot it with a single arrow through the heart. "The idolaters, upon hearing of this exploit, were struck with dread." At the present day, at least, there are no tigers in the country between Adoni and Vijayanagar, though panthers are plentiful enough

erected by Malik Kâfur on the sea-coast in 1310, but apparently not at Râmesvaram, which lies in the extreme south of India, on the eastern coast opposite the island of Ceylon. Moreover, it is extremely improbable that a Muhammadan sovereign could, in the fourteenth century A.D., have penetrated so far south with such a handful of men. They would have been harassed at every step by myriads of Hindus, who, though doubtless trembling at the sight of a Muhammadan, would, we may be sure, never have permitted 5000 men to traverse in peace 1000 miles of forest and mountain; for Râmesvaram is fully 500 miles from Vijayanagar. Malik Kâfur's expedition is said to have taken place after the conquest by him of the Ballâla Râjah of Dvârasamudra in Maisûr, when he erected a mosque on the *sea-coast of Malabar*, and therefore nowhere near Râmesvaram. Colonel Briggs has observed this difficulty,[1] and thinks that the place alluded to must be Sadâsivaghur, on the western coast, south of Goa, adding, "The spot . . . is called Cape Ramas on our maps."[2] He believes, however, that the remains of an old mosque do exist at Râmesvaram, and its date should be settled. Leaving it to others better informed to throw light on this point, I return to Bukka Râya and his doings.

Firishtah says that there were two roads to Vijayanagar:

"one fit for the passage of armies, the other narrow and difficult. As the former was lined with ambushes, he chose the latter, through which he marched with a select body of troops, and appeared suddenly in the suburbs of the city."

If Mujâhid came up from the Malabar coast, the former of these two roads would perhaps be the usual route

[1] Firishtah, ii. 332 n.

[2] A French map of A.D. 1652, published by Mr. Danvers ("Portuguese in India," end of vol. i.), shows at this spot "C. de Rames," but the modern Ordnance map has no place of that name in the vicinity.

adopted by travellers, which leads through open undulating plains. Avoiding this route, the Sultan may have turned the Sandûr hills by a flank movement to his right, and approached either along the valley of Sandûr or along the valley which now carries the main road from Bellary to Vijayanagar, between the Sandûr hills and the hills that surround the latter city.

"Kishen Roy was astonished at his boldness, and sent myriads of his people to defend the streets. The sultan drove them before him and gained the bank of a piece of water which alone now divided him from the citadel, in which Kishen Roy resided. Near this was an eminence, upon which stood a temple covered with plates of gold and silver set with jewels, much venerated by the Hindoos, and called in the language of the country Puttuk. The sultan, esteeming the destruction of it as a religious obligation, ascended the hill, and having razed the temple, possessed himself of the precious metals and jewels."

The piece of water alluded to may have been the picturesque lake at Kâmalâpuram; but which was the temple that Mujâhid destroyed? It seems useless to speculate, considering that the historian only wrote from tradition after a lapse of two centuries. There are many temples on hills to choose from, and several pieces of water. But the strangest part of the story is that we are not told how the Sultan succeeded in penetrating the outer lines of works, and in reaching a spot which divided him only from the inner citadel or palace enclosure. It must, however, be remembered that though in A.D. 1443 Abdur Razzâk saw seven lines of walls, we are not certain how many there were in the days of Bukka Râya.

At this point Mujâhid was attacked and nearly lost his life.

"The idolaters, upon seeing their object of veneration destroyed, raised their shrieks and lamentations to the sky.

They obliged Kishen Roy to head them and advanced resolutely in astonishing numbers. Upon which the sultan formed his disposition. He laid aside his umbrella, and with one of his arms-bearers, an Afghaun named Mhamood, crossed a small rivulet to observe the numbers and motions of the infidels. A Hindoo, who knew the sultan from the horse he rode, resolved, by revenging the destruction of his gods and country, to gain immortal reputation for himself. He moved unperceived through the hollows and broken ground along the bank of the rivulet, had gained the plain, and was charging towards the sultan at full speed, when Mujahid Shaw, at a lucky instant, perceiving him, made a sign to Mhamood Afghaun, who without delay charged the Hindoo. Mhamood's horse rearing, he fell to the ground. His antagonist, having every advantage, was on the point of putting him to death, when sultan Mujahid Shaw advanced with the quickness of lightning. The Hindoo, changing his object, aimed a heavy stroke at the sultan, giving at the same instant a shout of triumph, which made the spectators believe his blow was effectual. Luckily, a helmet of iron saved the head of the sultan, who now inflicted such a wound on his enemy that he was divided from the shoulder to the navel and fell dead from his horse,[1] upon which the sultan remounted Mhamood and joined his army on the other side of the rivulet."

A battle ensued in which the Hindus were defeated; but while the invading force had hardly recovered from their fatigue, the Râya's brother[2] "arrived at the city from his government with a reinforcement of twenty thousand horse and a vast army of foot."[3] The fighting then became furious. In the middle of the battle the Sultan's uncle, Dâûd Khân,[4] fearful for the safety

[1] It should be noted that Firishtah has previously described Mujâhid, though he was then only about twenty years old, as a remarkably powerful man. He states that at the age of fourteen he had broken the neck of an opponent in a wrestling match.

[2] Probably Mârappa or Muddappa.

[3] It will be seen hereafter that the kingdom was divided into provinces, held by nobles on condition of maintaining large armies ready for service at any moment.

[4] Some authorities say that Dâûd was Mujâhid's cousin.

of his sovereign, quitted his post at "Dhunna Sodra"[1] and joined in the engagement with distinguished gallantry. The Muhammadans were again victorious; but the enemy, having taken advantage of Dâûd Khân's movement, had captured the abandoned position, and thus seriously threatened the Sultan's retreat. He therefore left the field, and by skilful manœuvring enabled the whole of his force to extricate themselves in safety from the hills. With between sixty and seventy thousand prisoners, mostly women, he retreated from Vijayanagar and sat down before Adoni; but after a siege lasting nine months the attempt was abandoned, and the Sultan retired to his own territories. Thus ended the campaign.

Firishtah gives a short account of the kingdom of Vijayanagar at this period (about 1378 A.D.), from which the following extracts are taken.

"The princes of the house of Bahmanee maintained themselves by superior valour only, for in power, wealth, and extent of country the roies of Beejanuggur were greatly their superiors;" and he implies that at this time, as certainly in after years, all Southern India had submitted to the sway of the Râya.

"The seaport of Goa,[2] the fortress of Malgaon,[3] . . . be-

[1] "Dhunna Sodra" is, I think, a lake or tank in the plain on the eastern edge of the Vijayanagar hills, close under a lofty hill called, in the Trigonometrical Survey Taluq map, "Dannsundram," for (probably) Dharma Samudram. On the summit of this hill is a great Trigonometrical Survey pillar. The hill is 500 feet high, and lies within the limits of the village of Kanvi Timmâpuram. Commanding, as it does, the route by which a force issuing from the capital would attempt, by rounding the hills, to cut off the only line of retreat open to the invaders towards the north-east, the importance of the post to the Muhammadan army could not be over-estimated.

[2] Senhor Lopes tells me that he recently found in the archives of the Torre do Tombo in Lisbon (*Corpo Chronologico*, Part iii. packet 11, No. 107) a copy of a copper-plate grant which was executed by the chief of Goa in A.D. 1391 in the name of "Vîrahariar," king of Vijayanagar, the suzerain. This was "Vîra" Harihara II. It was copied in A.D. 1532, and translated into Portuguese.

[3] Probably Belgaum.

longed to the roy of Beejanuggur, and many districts of Tulghaut[1] were in his possession. His country was well peopled, and his subjects submissive to his authority. The roies of Malabar, Ceylon, and other islands and other countries kept ambassadors at his court, and sent annually rich presents."[2]

We must revert for a moment to the Sultan's uncle and his behaviour before Vijayanagar. It will be remembered that, filled with the best intentions, he had quitted his post to defend his king.

"The sultan, on seeing the standard of Daood Khan, was enraged, but stifled his displeasure till the gale of victory had waved over the standards of the faithful. He then called Daood Khan before him, and gave him a harsh reprimand for quitting a station so important that, should the enemy gain possession, not a mussulmaun could make his escape from the city."

Dâûd treasured up his resentment at this treatment, and, being joined by other disaffected nobles, secretly plotted the assassination of the Sultan. The conspirators waited till Mujâhid was on his way from Adoni towards Kulbarga, and then one night, that of Friday, April 16, A.D. 1378,[3] while the Sultan was asleep in his tent, Dâûd, accompanied by three other men, rushed in and stabbed him. There was a struggle, and the unfortunate monarch was despatched by the blow of a sabre.[4] Dâûd at once proclaimed himself Sultan as

[1] The Tulu-ghât, or the Tulu country on the Malabar coast.

[2] Compare the passage in the Chronicle of Nuniz, p. 302 below, where, writing of a period a few years later, he says, "The king of Coullao (Quilon) and Ceylon, and Paleacate (Pulicat), and Pegu and Tanaçary (Tenasserim), and many other lands, pay tribute to him"—the Râya.

[3] 17th Zîl-hijja, A.H. 779.

[4] Meadows Taylor, in his "History of India," relates (p. 163) that on one occasion Mujâhid, during his attack on Vijayanagar, penetrated into the second line of works, where there was a celebrated image of the monkey-god, Hanumân. The Sultan dispersed the Brahmans who tried to protect it, and struck the image in the face, mutilating its features. "A dying Brahman lying at the foot of the image cursed the king. 'For this act,' he said, 'thou wilt die ere thou reachest thy kingdom.' A prophecy which was literally fulfilled. The image, hewn out of a large boulder of

nearest of kin—Mujâhid having no children—and being acknowledged, proceeded to Kulbarga, where he was proclaimed.

The assassination of his nephew availed Dâûd but little, as the country was at once divided into two opposing factions, and on May 21, A.D. 1378,[1] after a reign of only one month, the murderer was himself assassinated while at prayer in the great mosque of the capital. Meanwhile Bukka Râya overrun the Doâb, advanced as far as the river Krishnâ, and invested the fortress of Raichûr.

Dâûd was succeeded by Alâ-ud-dîn's youngest son Mahmûd I.,[2] Mujâhid's sister Ruh Parvar Agah having blinded Dâûd's son, then a boy of eight years, in order to prevent dissension. Mahmûd was apparently welcome to all parties, for even the Râya raised the siege of Raichûr and agreed to pay him the tribute exacted by Muhammad Shâh; so at least says Firishtah. And during the whole of his reign of nearly twenty years there was peace and tranquillity at home and abroad. He died on the 20th April A.D. 1397.[3]

The decease of Bukka I. of Vijayanagar must apparently, for reasons shown, be placed at about A.D. 1379.

granite, still remains, and shows the marks of the king's mutilation." I do not know to which image the historian alludes. There are several statues of Hanumân in the second line of works, two of them lying south of the temple of Mâlavanta Raghunâthasvâmi.

[1] 21st Muharram A.H. 780.

[2] The name is generally given as Mahmûd, and so Firishtah names him, but Dr. Codrington (*Numismatic Chronicle*, 3rd Series, vol. xviii. p. 261) points out that the name on all the coins of this Sultan is "Muhammad," and not "Mahmûd;" and this is confirmed by the *Burhân-i Maâsir* and two other authorities (Major King in *Ind. Ant.*, July 1899, p. 183, note 39). I think it best, however, to adhere to Firishtah's nomenclature to prevent confusion.

[3] 21st Rajab A.H. 799. The 26th according to the *Burhân-i Maâsir*.

CHAPTER IV

GROWTH OF THE EMPIRE (A.D. 1379 TO 1406)

Harihara II.—Fîrûz Shâh of Kulbarga—Fresh wars—Assassination of a prince in 1399 A.D.—Bukka II.

BUKKA I. was succeeded by Harihara II., his son by his wife Gaurî. Nuniz calls the new king "Pureoyre Deorao," and "Pureoyre" seems to be a rough Portuguese version of the name Harihara; *h* and *p* representing the same sound in the Kanarese and Telugu languages. According to the inscriptions,[1] Harihara II. reigned at least twenty years, and he was the first king who gave himself imperial titles under the style of *Mâhârâjâdhirâja*. He gave many grants to the temples, and consolidated the supremacy of his dynasty over all Southern India. Sâyana, brother of Mâdhavâchârya, appears to have been his chief minister, as he was to King Samgama II.[2] Mudda is mentioned in two inscriptions of A.D. 1379 and 1382 as the king's general. Another of his generals was called Iruga. He was son of Chaicha, minister of Bukka II. His name appears on a pillar in a Jain temple near Kâmalâpura at Vijayanagar in an inscription bearing date A.D. 1385; which proves that the king was tolerant in religious matters. There seems also to have been a general named Gunda living in his reign, but his date is uncertain.[3] According to another inscription,[4] King

[1] See Rice's "Mysore Inscriptions," p. 55 (A.D. 1379); *Journal Bombay Branch Royal Asiatic Society*, xii. 340 (A.D. 1399).

[2] See above, p. 28. Professor Aufrecht believes that Sâyana died A.D. 1387.

[3] "Mysore Inscriptions," p. 226.

[4] *Journal Bombay Branch Royal Asiatic Society*, ix. 227.

Harihara early in his reign expelled the Muhammadans from Goa; and the last inscription of his reign at present discovered[1] mentions that one Bâchanna Udaiyâr was then governor of that place.

The king's wife, or one of his principal wives, was Mallâdevî, or Mallâmbikâ. The extent of his domination is shown by the fact that inscriptions of his reign are found in Mysore, Dhârwâr, Conjeeveram, Chingleput, and Trichinopoly.[2] He was a worshipper of Siva under the form Virûpâksha, but appears to have been singularly tolerant of other religions. The latest actual date of the reign afforded by inscriptions is October 15, A.D. 1399.[3]

Ghiâs-ud-dîn, a boy of seventeen, eldest son of the late Sultan Mahmûd, had succeeded his father on the throne of Kulbarga; but on June 14, 1397,[4] he was treacherously blinded during an entertainment by an ambitious slave, after a reign of only one month and twenty days. His younger brother, Shams-ud-dîn, was then placed on the throne, but after a reign of five months was blinded and deposed by his cousin Fîrûz, second son of the late Sultan Dâûd. Fîrûz was by birth undoubtedly of the elder branch, and he became one of the most celebrated monarchs of his line, ascending the throne on November 15, A.D. 1397.[5] He must have then been well advanced in years, as Firishtah says he was "old" in A.D. 1419.

The date of the last inscription of Harihara II. as yet brought to light is, as before stated, October 15, A.D. 1399. There are two inscriptions extant of Bukka II., his eldest son, both dated in A.D. 1406,[6] and several of

[1] In this the king is called "*Mahâmandalesvara*, son of Vîra Bukka *Udaiyâr*, Lord of the four seas."

[2] *Epig. Ind.*, iii. pp. 115–116.

[3] *Op. cit.*, p. 119.

[4] 17th Ramazân A.H. 799 (Firishtah).

[5] 23rd Safar A.H. 800 (Firishtah).

[6] *Epigraphia Indica*, iii. 36, *n*. 3.

the latter's successor, the younger brother of Bukka II., whose name was Devarâya I., and whose reign lasted till at least A.D. 1412.

It will be remembered that the first king of Vijayanagar, Harihara I., was an old man (Nuniz says "very old"), and reigned seven years. His successor, Bukka, his brother, reigned thirty-seven years according to Nuniz, and perhaps, therefore, it would be best not to assume too great an age for Harihara I. However this may be, it would appear that when the peaceful monarch Harihara II., son of Bukka I., came to the throne, his father must have died at a very advanced age, and he himself must have been by no means young. He reigned at least twenty years, as before stated, and we are therefore justified in assuming that at the close of his reign (in A.D. 1399) he was quite an old man. With this in our minds, let us turn to Firishtah's narrative of the reign of Firûz Shâh Bâhmanî, beginning with his accession in November A.D. 1397.

He tells us that in the Hijra year 801 (13th September 1398 to 3rd September 1399), month not given—

> "Dewal Roy of Beejanuggur, with thirty thousand horse and a vast army of foot, invaded the royal territories between the rivers, with a design to reduce the forts of Mudkul and Roijore" (Raichûr).

And in a later passage we are told that the campaign was at an end a few months before the end of Hijra 801; *i.e.* a few months before the end of August A.D. 1399. The first movement of the Hindu army must therefore have taken place at the beginning of the cold season of A.D. 1398, probably not earlier than December in that year, when the great cotton plains across which the troops had to march were passable. It can hardly be supposed that King Harihara II., then quite old and always a lover of peace, would without motive have waged this sudden war and himself led his armies into the field, and it seems more likely that the invasion was a bold dash made by his son with the king's permission. The Muhammadan historians admit an unbroken peace of twenty years previous to this date.

It seems, therefore, that the chronicles of Nuniz, the writings of Firishtah, and the extant inscriptions all agree together, and that we must place the death of Harihara II. at the close of the year A.D. 1399. Little more can be said about the events of his reign.

The new king, his eldest son, Bukka II., must have been a man of middle age, as he had a son old enough to take the field with him before he himself came to the throne.

"This king ('Pureoyre')," says Nuniz, "had a son, who by his death inherited the kingdom, who was called Ajarao; and he reigned forty-three years, in which time he was always at war with the Moors."

I can give no explanation as to why Nuniz calls the successor of Harihara II. "Ajarao," nor as to his estimate of forty-three years for his reign. The names and lengths of reigns given to "Ajarao's" successors by our chronicler prove that by "Ajarao" he means two kings, Bukka II. and his successor, Deva Râya I.; and the period covered by their combined reigns was only fourteen years, not forty-three.

Nuniz states that the successor of Harihara II. greatly improved the city of Vijayanagar, raising fresh walls and towers, increasing its extent, and building further lines of fortification. But his great work was the construction of a huge dam in the Tungabhadrâ river, and the formation of an aqueduct fifteen miles long from the river into the city. If this be the same channel that to the present day supplies the fields which occupy so much of the site of the old city, it is a most extraordinary work. For several miles this channel is cut out of the solid rock at the base of the hills, and is one of the most remarkable irrigation works to be seen in India. No details are given of the wars he engaged in, except that, besides his campaigns against the Moors, he took "Goa, Chaul, and Dabull," and reduced the Choromandel side of the peninsula to loyalty and obedience to his rule.

We learn a great deal more about the doings of Bukka II. and Deva Râya I. from Firishtah than from Nuniz, and I make no apology for quoting copiously from the former author, whose writings throw much light on the period.

Bukka's first war began with the invasion already alluded to. It took place during his father Harihara's reign, apparently about the month of December A.D. 1398 (rather later than earlier). The wide cotton plains of that tract are only passable during prolonged dry weather, and the prince would certainly not have risked an advance while there was any likelihood of rain falling. Bukka's son accompanied his father, and the objective was the country of the Doâb, and particularly the fortresses of Mudkal and Raichûr, then in the hands of the Bâhmanî Sultan. Sultan Fîrûz moved to meet him, slaughtering on the way a Hindu chief or zamindar and seven or eight thousand of his followers, "who had always been very troublesome and refractory." The Râya had advanced to the northern frontier of the debatable land and was encamped on the river Krishnâ, then in full flood, having large bodies of troops posted to oppose the passage of the Muhammadans.

"Sultan Feroze Shaw,[1] on his arrival near the river, held a council of war with his chief officers, but received no advice that to him appeared satisfactory.

"While the sultan was debating in his own mind how to act, Cauzi Serauje, seeing his concern, offered, if the sultan

[1] Firishtah (Scott, p. 76).

would permit him, to cross the river with a few of his friends, whom he would select for that purpose, to assassinate Dewal Roy or his son, as he found most convenient. . . .

"The sultan approving the measure, some hundreds of hurdles covered with leather[1] were prepared expeditiously for the troops to cross, Cauzi Serauje, with seven of his friends disguised as holy mendicants, proceeded to the roy's camp, and repaired to the quarter where the dancing-girls resided.[2] Here the cauzi pretended to be enraptured with a courtesan, and was guilty of a thousand extravagances to support his character. In the evening the girl, having adorned herself in her richest ornaments, prepared to go out, on which the cauzi, like a jealous and distracted lover, falling at her feet, entreated her to stay, or let him attend her, and not rend his heart by her absence. The woman upon this informed him that she was ordered to attend an entertainment by the roy's son, and durst not disobey, nor could she take him with her, as only musicians and dancers would be admitted. The cauzi upon this replied that he played on the same instrument as herself, and had, besides, some curious accomplishments that would highly please the roy's son. The dancing-girl, thinking him in jest, out of contempt gave him her mundal,[3] and desired him to play, which he did in so masterly a manner that she was delighted, saying that his company would give her superiority over her fellows and do her honour with the roy's son. Accordingly he with his companions attended the girl to the tents of the young roy.

"As is the custom of Dekkan, many sets of loolies[4] and dancing-girls were ordered to perform at the same time, and having finished their parts, the roy's son called for the players and mummers. The dancing-girl now obtained leave for the cauzi and one of his companions to show their feats. Having assumed the dress of women, they entered ogling and smiling,

---

[1] Rather, I think, basket-boats. These are described in the text of Paes (below, p. 259 as being in use on these rivers in the sixteenth century, just as they are to-day. They are circular in shape, and are made of wicker-work of split bamboo covered all over outside with leather. Colonel Briggs, writing of these boats (Firishtah, ii. 371), in a footnote says, "A detachment of the British army crossed its heavy guns without even dismounting them over the Toongbudra in 1812 in these basket-boats."

[2] These women always accompanied the Râya's armies. Nuniz says that large numbers of them were at the Hindu camp at Raichûr in 1520.

[3] A stringed instrument.

[4] Youths trained to sing and dance in public.

and so well imitated the mummers in playing on the mundal, dancing, and mimicry, that the roy's son was charmed with their performances. At length they each drew a dagger, and, like the dancers of Dekkan, continued to flourish them for some time, making a thousand antic postures in advancing, retreating, and turning round. At last, suddenly rushing upon the roy's son, they plunged both the daggers into his breast, afterwards attacking his companions. Their remaining friends, who were watching without the tent, on hearing an alarm, ripped up the curtain, and entered to assist them. Many of the company, being much intoxicated, were easily put to death. The cauzi with his friends extinguished all the lights, and, making their escape through the rent, mingled with the crowd. The outcry soon became general round the tents. Great confusion ensued, and various reports and alarms took place. Some said that the sultan had crossed the river and surprised the camp, others that one of his chiefs, with twelve thousand men, had cut off both the roy and his son. The night was uncommonly dark, and the camp extended near ten miles, so that circumstances were variously reported, and the different chiefs, ignorant of the real cause of the alarm, contented themselves with waiting in their several quarters under arms. About four thousand of the sultan's troops, in this interim, crossed the river in boats and rafts which had been prepared for the purpose. The enemy's foot, stationed to oppose the passage, terrified by the alarm in camp and the approach of the sultan's forces, fled in confusion without waiting to be attacked. Before the morning Feroze Shaw had crossed the river with his whole army, and at dawn assaulted the enemy's camp with great fury. Dewul Roy, grieved by the death of his son and panic-struck at the bravery of the assailants, made but a faint resistance. Before sunrise, having taken up his son's corpse, he fled with his army. The sultan gained immense plunder in the camp, and pursued him to the vicinity of Beejanuggur. Several actions happened on the way, all of which were fortunate to the sultan, and the roads were heaped up with the bodies of the slaughtered Hindoos."

Bukka reached Vijayanagar in safety and took refuge behind its fortifications, while the Sultan sent his brother Ahmad (afterwards Sultan), whom he had honoured with the title of "Khânkhânân," to ravage the rich districts south of the city. Ahmad fulfilled his instructions and returned with numberless prisoners, and amongst them many Brahmans. The relatives of these in the city begged the aged Râya (Harihara II., still alive) to offer ransom, and after much negotiation the Sultan accepted "ten lakhs of oons"[1] and agreed to the execution of a treaty.

According to this treaty, which was entered into a few months before the close of the Hijra year 801, *i.e.* a few months before 3rd September A.D. 1399, the boundaries of the two kingdoms were to be the same as before the war, and each party agreed to refrain from molesting the subjects of the other. This does not look as though the Sultan had gained any very material advantage in the campaign, since the true boundary was always a subject of dispute. I obtain the date above given from Firishtah's sentence:—"In a few months after the conclusion of this campaign, and the beginning of the year 802, the sultan marched to punish Nersing," a chief who had raised disturbances on the borders of Berar.

The *Burhân-i Maâsir* passes over this war with great brevity. It states that the Sultan began it, and that at its close he accepted a large indemnity and promise of payment of annual tribute. The date given is identical.

Not long after this war, but certainly not before October 15, A.D. 1399, Harihara II. died, and was succeeded by Bukka, his son.

We have little to guide us as to the events of Bukka's reign, but Firishtah states that he ceased to pay tribute to Fîrûz Shâh, partly owing to instigation from Gujarât, Mâlwa, and Khandeish. In Hijra 808 (June 1405 to June 1406 A.D.) four years' tribute was owing, but the Sultan took no notice, and waited for a more convenient time.

[1] Assessed at "near £400,000" (Scott, Firishtah, p. 79, note).

Bukka was followed on the throne of Vijayanagar by his brother Deva Râya I., the date of whose coronation is fixed by an inscription at Hasan in Mysore as November 5, 1406.[1] The last inscription of Bukka Râya at present known bears a date corresponding to April 30th in that year—in Hindu reckoning, the 12th day of the first half of the month Vaiṣâkha, in the (expired) Saka year 1328, the name of the cyclic year being "Vyaya."[2]

[1] "Mysore Inscriptions," Rice, p. 279, No. 150. Professor Kielhorn in *Ind. Ant.*, xxiv. p. 204, No. 304, and note.

[2] "South Indian Inscriptions," i. 82 (Dr. Hultzsch).

CHAPTER V

DEVA RÂYA I. (A.D. 1406 TO 1419)

The amorous monarch, Deva Râya I.—The farmer's beautiful daughter—The king's escapade—The city threatened—A Hindu princess wedded to a Muhammadan prince—Fîrûz Shâh's anger—Pertâl's marriage—King Vijaya—Probable date of accession of Deva Râya II.

FIRISHTAH tells us of an event that must have taken place towards the end of the year A.D. 1406, in which the principal actor was the king of Vijayanagar. This king I believe to have been Bukka II.'s successor, his younger brother, Deva Râya I. The story relates to a mad adventure of the Râya which he undertook in order to secure for himself the person of a beautiful girl, the daughter of a farmer in Mudkal. His desire to possess her attained such a pitch, that he made an expedition into the debatable land north of the Tungabhadrâ for the sole purpose of capturing the girl and adding her to his harem. I have already shown reasons for supposing that Bukka II. was a middle-aged man at his accession, and it is not unreasonable to suppose that this hot-blooded monarch was his younger brother, who began to reign in November 1406 A.D. His escapade must be narrated in full as told by Firishtah, since it led to very important consequences.

"There resided in the town of Mudkul a farmer, who was blessed with a daughter of such exquisite beauty, that the Creator seemed to have united all his powers in making her perfect."

This attractive person was educated by an old Brahman, whose admiration of her led him to think that she would prove a desirable member of the Râya's household.

"He proceeded to Beejanuggur, and being introduced to the roy, spoke in such praise of the beauty and accomplishments of the young maid, that he was fired with the desire of possessing her, and entreated the bramin to procure her for him of her parents in marriage. This request was what the bramin earnestly wished, and he immediately agreed to satisfy him; upon which the roy despatched him with rich gifts and great promises of favours to the parents, and the title of ranee, or princess, for their beautiful daughter. The bramin lost no time in his journey, and, upon his arrival at the farmer's house, delivered to him and his wife the roy's orders, that they should repair to Beejanuggur with their daughter. The parents were overjoyed at such unexpected good fortune, and calling for the young maid, laid before her the rich gifts of the roy, congratulated her on being soon to be united to a great prince, and attempted to throw upon her neck a golden collar set with jewels, as a token of immediate espousals, and which, if done, could not have been broken off.

"The beautiful virgin, to their great astonishment, drawing her neck from compliance, refused to receive the collar, and observed, that whoever entered the haram of Beejanuggur, was afterwards not permitted to see even her nearest relations and friends; and though they might be happy to sell her for worldly riches, yet she was too fond of her parents to submit to eternal absence from them, even for all the splendour of the palace of Beejanuggur. This declaration was accompanied with affectionate tears, which melted her parents; who, rather than use force, dismissed the bramin with all his gifts, and he returned, chagrined and disappointed, to Beejanuggur. . . .

"When the bramin arrived at Beejanuggur, and related to the roy the failure of his scheme, the prince's love became outrageous, and he resolved to gratify it by force, though the object resided in the heart of Feroze Shaw's dominions.[1] For this purpose he quitted Beejanuggur with a great army, on pretence of going the tour of his countries; and upon his arrival on the banks of the River Tummedra, having selected

[1] We must remember that the narrator is a loyal Muhammadan. Mudkal was in the tract always in dispute between the two kingdoms.

five thousand of his best horse, and giving the reins of his conduct to love, commanded them, in spite of the remonstrances of his friends, to march night and day with all expedition to Mudkul,[1] and, surrounding the village where Pertal[2] lived, to bring her prisoner to him, with her whole family, without injury."

The unexpected, however, happened. The king neglected to send the Brahman to warn Pertâl's family, and on the arrival of news at Mudkal that a large force of the Râya's troops was approaching, the inhabitants fled, and amongst them the girl and her relatives. The troops therefore returned, but on the way looted the country. They were attacked by superior forces and 2000 of them were slain. This led to a war.

"In the beginning of the winter of the year 809 (*i.e.* the winter of A.D. 1406),[3] he (the Sultan) moved in great force, and arrived near Beejanuggur, in which Dewul Roy had shut himself up. An assault was made upon the city, and the Sultan got possession of some streets, which, however, he was obliged to quit, his army being repulsed by the Carnatickehs. Dewul Roy, encouraged by his success, now ventured to encamp his army under protection of the walls, and to molest the royal camp. As the mussulmauns could not make proper use of their cavalry in the rocky unevenness of ground round Beejanuggur, they were somewhat dispirited. During this, Sultan Feroze Shaw was wounded by an arrow in the hand, but he would not dismount; and drawing out the arrow, bound up the wound with a cloth.

"The enemy were at last driven off by the valour and activity of Ahmed Khan and Khankhanan, and the Sultan moved farther from the city to a convenient plain, where he halted till his wounded men were recovered."

He halted here for four months, holding the Râya a prisoner in his own capital, while bodies of troops harassed and wasted the country south of Vijayanagar,

[1] About forty miles north. [2] Briggs gives her name as "Nehal."

[3] Briggs says, "In the beginning of the year 809." This would be the month of June, and the months following would have been unfavourable for the march of armies. I prefer Scott's rendering.

and attacked the fortress of Bankâpûr. The "convenient plain" was probably in the open and rich valley near the town of Hospett, south of the city; for the Sultan could not have ravaged the country to the south unless he had been master of the whole of this valley for many miles. Bankâpûr was taken, and the detached forces returned bringing with them 60,000 Hindu prisoners; on which the Sultan left Khânkhânân to hold Vijayanagar, while he himself attempted to reduce the fortress of Adoni, "the strongest in possession of the enemy."

Deva Râya then began to treat for peace, and was compelled to submit to conditions to the last degree humiliating. He agreed to give the Sultan his daughter in marriage, to indemnify him with an immense treasure, and to cede for ever the fort of Bankâpûr.[1]

"Though the roies of Carnatic had never yet married their daughters but to persons of their own cast, and giving them to strangers was highly disgraceful, yet Dewul Roy, out of necessity, complied, and preparations for celebrating the nuptials were made by both parties. For forty days communication was open between the city and the sultan's camp. Both sides of the road were lined with shops and booths, in which the jugglers, drolls, dancers, and mimics of Carnatic displayed their feats and skill to amuse passengers. Khankhanan and Meer Fuzzul Oollah, with the customary presents of a bridegroom, went to Beejanuggur, from whence at the expiration of seven days they brought the bride, with a rich portion and offerings from the roy, to the sultan's camp. Dewul Roy having expressed a strong desire to see the sultan, Feroze Shaw with great gallantry agreed to visit him with his bride, as his father-in-law.

"A day being fixed, he with his bride proceeded to Beejanuggur, leaving the camp in charge of Khankhanan. On the way he was met by Dewul Roy in great pomp. From the

[1] Firishtah generally calls this place "Beekapore" (Scott, i. 47, 69, 85, 86, &c.), but on p. 301 he spells the name "Binkapore." Bankâpûr was one of the principal fortresses in the Carnatic. It is the "Bengapor" or "Vengapor" of our chronicles. (See below, p. 122.)

gate of the city to the palace, being a distance of six miles,[1] the road was spread with cloth of gold, velvet, satin, and other rich stuffs. The two princes rode on horseback together, between ranks of beautiful boys and girls, who waved plates of gold and silver flowers[2] over their heads as they advanced, and then threw them to be gathered by the populace. After this the inhabitants of the city made offerings, both men and women, according to their rank. After passing through a square directly in the centre of the city,[3] the relations of Dewul Roy, who had lined the streets in crowds, made their obeisance and offerings, and joined the cavalcade on foot, marching before the princes. Upon their arrival at the palace gate, the sultan and roy dismounted from their horses, and ascended a splendid palanquin, set with valuable jewels, in which they were carried together to the apartments prepared for the reception of the bride and bridegroom, when Dewul Roy took his leave, and retired to his own palace. The sultan, after being treated with royal magnificence for three days, took his leave of the roy, who pressed upon him richer presents than before given, and attended him four miles on his way, when he returned to the city.

"Sultan Feroze Shaw was enraged at his not going with him to his camp, and said to Meer Fuzzul Oollah that he would one day have his revenge for the affront offered him by such neglect. This declaration being told to Dewul Roy, he made some insolent remarks, so that, notwithstanding the connection of family, their hatred was not calmed."

Fîrûz returned after this to his capital and sent for the lovely Pertâl, and on her arrival, finding that her beauty surpassed all report, he gave her in marriage to his eldest son, Hasan Khân, when "the knot was tied amid great rejoicings and princely magnificence." The lady's husband is described by Firishtah as being "a weak and dissipated prince." He was heir to the throne, but was easily ousted by the valiant Ahmad "Khân-

[1] This again points to the Muhammadan camp having been in the neighbourhood of Hospett, south of Vijayanagar.

[2] "Plates of gold filled with incense and silver flowers. —Briggs (ii. 386).

[3] This square is the open space mentioned by both Nuniz and Paes. On the left of it, as the cortège advanced, was the palace.

khânân," and lived privately at Fîrûzâbâd, "entirely devoted to indolence and pleasure." The last we hear of him is that his usurping uncle, Ahmad Shah I., treated him kindly, "gave him the palace of Firozeabad for his residence, with an ample jaghire (estate), and permission to hunt or take his pleasure within eight miles round his palace, without restriction to time or form." Hasan "was more satisfied with this power of indulging his appetites than with the charge of empire. While his uncle lived he enjoyed his ease, and no difference ever happened between them; but he was afterwards blinded and kept confined to the palace of Firozeabad." This must have been after A.D. 1434.

Deva Râya I. lived till at least 1412 A.D., and was succeeded by his son Vîra-Vijaya, whom Nuniz calls "Visaya," and who, he says, reigned six years. The last extant inscription of Deva Râya I. is dated in A.D. 1412–13, the first of his successor Vijaya in 1413–14. Vijaya's last known inscription is one of 1416–17, and the first yet known of his successor, his eldest son, Deva Râya II., is dated Monday, June 26, 1424–25. Nuniz gives Deva Râya II. a reign of twenty-five years.

I am inclined to think that Deva Râya II. began to reign in 1419, for the following reason. The informants of Nuniz stated that during Vijaya's reign he "did nothing worth relating," and the chronicle records that during the reign which followed, namely that of Deva Râya II., there was "constant warfare." Now we have it from Firishtah that in 1417 Fîrûz, Sultan of Kulbarga, commenced a war of aggression against the Hindus of Telingana. He besieged the fortress of Pangul,[1] seventy miles north-east of Adoni, for a period of two years, but the attempt to reduce it ended in failure owing to a pestilence breaking out amongst both men and horses.

[1] Scott has it "Mankul" (i. 90), but Briggs (ii. 389) corrects this into "Pangul," which is undoubtedly correct.

"Many of the first nobility deserted the camp and fled with their followers to their jaghires. At this crisis Dewul Roy collected his army, and having obtained aid from the surrounding princes, even to the Raja of Telingana (Warangal), marched against the sultan with a vast host of horse and foot."

This then took place in 1419 A.D., and since this energetic action was not consonant with the character of Vijaya, the *fainéant* sovereign, "who did nothing worth recording" in all his career, we must suppose that it took place as soon as Deva Râya, his successor, was crowned; when the nobles surrounding him (he was, I believe, quite young when he began to reign),[1] filled with zeal and ambition, roused the Hindu troops and in the king's name plunged into war against their country's hereditary foe.

If this be correct, the reign of Deva Râya II., granting that it lasted as stated by Nuniz for twenty-five years, ended in A.D. 1444. Now the chronicle tells us a story of how this Deva Râya's son and successor, "Pina Rao,"[2] was attacked by his nephew with a poisoned dagger, and died from the effects of his wounds after a lapse of six months. Abdur Razzâk, more reliable because he was not only a contemporary but was at Vijayanagar at the time, relates the same anecdote of Deva Râya II. himself, making the would-be assassin the king's brother, and definitely fixing the date beyond a shadow of a doubt. The event occurred on some day between November 1442 and April 1443—the outside limits of Razzâk's visit to Calicut—during his stay at which place

1 His grandfather, Deva Râya I., was young enough at the beginning of his reign (A.D. 1406) to plunge into amorous intrigues and adventures, and he reigned only seven years at most. His son and successor, Vijaya, reigned only six years. Vijaya's son, Deva Râya II., therefore, was probably a mere boy when he came to the throne in A.D. 1419.

2 *Pina* = *Chinna* (Telugu) or *Chikka* (Kanarese), and means "little" or "young." (See the tale told by Barradas below, p. 222 ff., of the events of 1614 A.D.) The name is very common in Southern India, and was generally applied to the Crown Prince.

he says it happened. Abdur Razzâk does not mention the king's death, and this therefore had not supervened up to the time of the traveller leaving the capital in December 1443. On the assumption that we need not be too particular about Nuniz's "six months," we may conclude that the attack was made about the month of April 1443, and that Deva Râya II. died early in 1444 A.D. There is still, however, a difficulty, as will be noticed below, inscriptions giving us the name of a Deva Râya as late as 1449 A.D., but it is just possible that this was another king of the same name.

Putting together the facts given above, we find that the twenty-five years of the reign of Deva Râya II. lay between 1419 and 1444 A.D.

CHAPTER VI

DEVA RÂYA II. (A.D. 1419 TO 1444 OR (?) 1449)

A fresh war, 1419—Success of Vijayanagar—Death of Fîrûz—Sultan Ahmad attacks Deva Râya—The latter's adventure and narrow escape—Ahmad at the gates of the city—He nearly loses his life—Submission of Deva Râya—Fall of Warangal—Sultan Alâ-ud-dîn—Deva Râya's precautions—His attempted assassination, 1443—The story as told by Abdur Razzâk—Expedition against Kulbarga—Improvements at the capital—Probable date of the king's death—Was there a King Deva Râya III.?

THERE was war then with Kulbarga in 1419, Deva Râya II. being king of Vijayanagar. The Sultan had been unsuccessful in his attack on the Warangal fortress, Pangul, and the troops of Vijayanagar marched against him with horse, foot, and elephants. Fîrûz Shâh gave battle forthwith, though he judged his forces to be inferior. Firishtah does not mention where the fight took place.

"Meer Fuzzul Oollah, who commanded the troops of Islaam, charged the infidels with heroic vigour, and, routing their center, proceeded to attack their right wing. He was on the point of gathering the flowers of victory, when one of his own attendants, bribed for the purpose by Dewul Roy, gave him a mortal wound on the head, and he instantly quaffed the sherbet of martyrdom. This fatal event changed the fortune of the day; the sultan was defeated, and with the utmost difficulty, by the most surprising and gallant efforts, made his escape from the field. The Hindoos made a general massacre of the mussulmauns, and erected a platform with their heads on the field of battle. They followed the sultan into his own country, which they wasted with fire and sword, took many places, broke down many mosques and holy places, slaughtered the people without mercy; by their actions seeming to discharge the treasured malice and resentment of ages. Sultan Firoze Shaw, in the exigence of distress, requested aid of the sultan of Guzarat, who, having but just acceded to the throne, could afford none.

At last fortune took a turn favourable to his affairs, and the enemy, after repeated battles, were expelled from his dominions by the Sultan's brother, Khankhanan; but these misfortunes dwelt on the mind of Firoze Shaw, now old, and he fell into a lingering disorder and lowness of spirits."

The Sultan desired the throne for his son Hasan, husband of the beautiful Pertâl, but on Ahmad Khânkhânân taking up arms to support his intended usurpation and advancing, supported by most of the nobles, to the capital, Fîrûz gave way and nominated him Sultan in his stead.

Fîrûz died on September 24, A.D. 1422,[1] and Khânkhânân became Sultan of Kulbarga under the title of Ahmad Shâh I.

The first act of the new monarch, after "impressing the minds of his people with affection to his government"—probably, that is, after an interval of a few months—was to strengthen his army in order to take revenge for the invasions of the Râya; and having made all preparations he advanced to the attack. Deva Râya's generals collected their troops, sent for aid to Warangal, and marched to the Tungabhadrâ where they encamped. From this it appears that they had retired from the Doâb after their successful raid. The Sultan arrived on the north bank of the river opposite the Hindu camp, and *laagered*, if we may use the term now in fashion. Firishtah says that he "surrounded his camp with carriages (carts and waggons), after the usage of Room (Turkey in Europe), to prevent the enemy's foot from making night-attacks. Here he halted for forty days." We are now, therefore, probably in the dry season at the beginning of the year A.D. 1423, for if the river had been in flood there would have been no fear of the enemy's crossing it. In the early months of the Christian year that river is usually shallow in the

[1] 7th Shawwâl A.H. 825. Firishtah, (Scott) p. 95, gives the length of the reign, and his figures yield this result.

open country east of the Hindu capital and away from the hills that surround it, having only thin streams running in its rocky bed. Indeed, Firishtah himself tells us that the river was at that time fordable.

Then ensued a dramatic episode. The Muhammadan cavalry had crossed the river and devastated the country of the Râya, who remained inactive, and the Sultan determined on a direct frontal attack. The troops of Warangal deserted the Râya and withdrew.

"Early in the morning Lodi Khan, Aulum Khan, and Dillawer Khan, who had marched during the night and forded the river at a distance, reached the environs of the enemy's camp. It happened that the roy was sleeping, attended by only a few persons, in a garden, close to which was a thick plantation of sugar-cane.[1] A body of the mussulmauns entered the garden for plunder, and Dewul Roy, being alarmed, fled almost naked into the sugar-cane plantation. Here he was found by the soldiers, who thought him only a common person, and having loaded him with a bundle of canes, obliged him to run with it before them. Dewul Roy, rejoiced at his being undiscovered, held his peace, and took up the burden readily, hoping that he should be discharged as a poor person, or be able to make his escape.

"They had not gone far when the alarm of Sultan Ahmed Shaw's having crossed the river, and the loss of the roy, filled the camp, and the Hindoos began to disperse. The sultan entered the camp, and Dewul Roy's masters, hoping now for more valuable plunder than sugar-cane, hastened to join their own friends, leaving him to shift for himself. Dewul Roy ran with his own troops, and about noon came up with some of his nobles, by whom he was recognised and received with great joy. His safety being made known, his army rallied into some order; but, as he regarded the late accident as an ill omen, he laid aside all thoughts of engaging in the field, and fled to Beejanuggur.[2]

---

1 The spot was therefore probably close to one of the old irrigation channels, supplied by dams constructed across this river under the Râyas.

2 It is difficult to reconcile this story with the fact of the Râya's tender age at this date, for I think it is certain that he was then quite a boy. Is it possible that the Muhammadan chroniclers, from whom Firishtah obtained

"Ahmad Shaw not stopping to besiege the city, overran the open country, and wherever he came, put to death men, women, and children, without mercy, contrary to the compact made by his ancestor Mahummud Shaw with the roies of Beejanuggur. Laying aside all humanity, whenever the number of the slain amounted to twenty thousand, he halted three days, and made a festival in celebration of the bloody work. He broke down the idol temples, and destroyed the colleges of the Bramins. During these operations a body of five thousand Hindoos, enraged to desperation at the destruction of their country and the insults of their gods, united in taking an oath to sacrifice their lives in attempting to kill the sultan, as the grand author of all their sufferings. For this purpose they employed spies to observe his motions, that they might seize the first opportunity of action.

"It happened, that the sultan going to hunt, in the eagerness of chase separated from the body of his attendants, and advanced near twelve miles from his camp.[1] The devoted infidels, informed of the circumstance, immediately hastened to intercept him, and arrived in sight when even his personal attendants, about two hundred Moguls, were at some distance from him. The sultan alarmed, galloped on in hopes of gaining a small mud enclosure which stood on the plain as a fold for cattle, but was so hotly pursued, that some broken ground falling in his way, he was not able to cross it before his pursuers came up. Luckily some archers at this instant arrived to his aid, so that the enemy were delayed sufficiently to give the sultan time to reach the enclosure with his friends. The infidels attempted to enter, and a sharp conflict took place; all the faithful repeating the creed of testimony, and swearing to die, rather than submit. . . . Their little troop being mostly

---

the narrative, mistook for the king an adult member of the family who commanded the army? Such mistakes were certainly made in later years. The chroniclers seem to have taken little pains to ascertain the actual names of the Hindu kings. It must, however, be noted that a little later on Firishtah speaks of Deva Râya's son.

[1] There is no clue as to where this event took place, except that it was not very close to Vijayanagar. The Sultan must have been near some hills with a plain below, because he met with open ground difficult for a horse to cross, in his eagerness to reach a mud enclosure in a plain. The description is applicable to numberless places in the vicinity, and it is useless to speculate. As he was on horseback, it is possible that he was riding down antelope.

killed and wounded, the assailants advanced close to the wall, which they began to throw down with pickaxes and hatchets, so that the sultan was reduced to the extremity of distress. At this critical juncture arrived Abd-al-Kadir, first armour-bearer to the sultan, and a body of troops, with whom, fearful of some accident having happened to occasion his absence, he had left the camp in search of his master. The infidels had completed a wide breach, and were preparing to enter, when they found their rear suddenly attacked. The sultan with his remaining friends joined Abd-al-Kadir in attacking the enemy, who after a long struggle were driven off the field, with a loss of a thousand men, and about five hundred of the mussulmauns attained martyrdom. Thus the sultan, by the almost inspired caution of Abd-al-Kadir, acceded, as it were, a second time, from the depths of danger to the enjoyment of empire.[1] It deserves place among the records of time, as a remarkable event, that two sovereigns at the head of armies, should fall into such danger for want of numbers, and both escape uninjured. . . .

"After this event Ahmed Shaw, having laid waste the whole country, marched to Beejanuggur, which he kept so closely blocked up, that the inhabitants were reduced to the greatest distress; when Dewul Roy, to spare his people, sent ambassadors to the sultan entreating peace, to which he consented, on condition that he would send the tribute of as many years as he had neglected to pay,[2] laden on his best elephants, and conducted by his son, with his drums, trumpets, and all the other insignia of state, to his camp. Dewul Roy, unable to refuse compliance, agreed to the demands, and sent his son with thirty favourite elephants, loaded with treasure and valuable effects. The sultan sent some noblemen to meet him, and after being led in ceremony through the market and great

---

[1] Before Ahmad's accession, his brother, the late Sultan Fîrûz, had designed, in order to secure the throne for his own son Hasan, that Ahmad, should be blinded. Ahmad was warned of this and left Kulbarga in time to secure his safety.

[2] This is the Muhammadan version. Nothing is said regarding this tribute by Firishtah in describing the terms of the peace of 1399 A.D. It is possible, however, that tribute was really paid. It had apparently been exacted by Muhammad Shaw Bâhmanî, and agreed to by Bukka Râya I. who confirmed the arrangement on the accession of Dâûd Shâh's brother Muhammad. (See above, p. 47.)

streets of the camp, he was brought to the presence.[1] The sultan, after embracing, permitted him to sit at the foot of his throne, and putting on his shoulders a magnificent robe, and girding him with a sabre set with jewels, gave him twenty beautiful horses of various countries, a male elephant, dogs for the chase, and three hawks, which the Carnatickehs were till then strangers to the use of. He then marched from the environs of Beejanuggur, and on his arrival on the bank of the Kistnah dismissed the roy's son and returned to Koolburga."

To form some idea of the date of this cessation of hostilities we must see what follows in Firishtah's narrative. The historian states that during the year of the Sultan's return to Kulbarga there was a grievous famine in the Dakhan, and "the next year also, no rain appearing, the people became seditious." These two years were probably A.H. 826, 827, extending from 15th December A.D. 1422 to 23rd November 1424. He continues, "In the year 828" the Sultan marched against Warangal. The last campaign began about December A.D. 1422; and since we must allow some months for Ahmad's blockade of Vijayanagar, which resulted in his reducing the inhabitants to a state of starvation so that the Râya was compelled to capitulate, the date for the end of the war cannot be safely placed earlier than the winter of the year A.D. 1423. During these twelve months, however, there was a famine and failure of rain, so that the Sultan may have been able to traverse the cotton plains lying between Vijayanagar and Kulbarga, plains quite impassable for troops in wet weather, somewhat earlier than would otherwise have been the case.

The Sultan's next war took place in A.H. 828, when

[1] This looks as if he was really paraded with ignominy as a vanquished inferior, and so displayed to the Muhammadan troops. If he had desired to do him honour, the Sultan himself would have met the prince and personally escorted him, as representing his father. Moreover, the prince was only permitted to sit at the *foot* of the throne, and was taken, almost as a prisoner, for many days with the army till it reached the Krishnâ river.

he advanced against Warangal over the undulating plains of the Dakhan, then rich in crop, and was completely successful. The Hindu kingdom was completely and for ever destroyed. The English date usually given for this event is A.D. 1424, but it is quite possible that a mistake has been made owing to the use of imperfect chronological tables by those who have written on the subject, and that Ahmad Shâh's capture of Warangal may have taken place in A.D. 1425. Briggs, for instance, calls A.H. 828 "A.D. 1424," but the year only began on November 23, 1424. The campaign, however, was very short, and may have been concluded before the end of December of that year.

We hear nothing more from Firishtah regarding the affairs of Vijayanagar till the early part of the reign of Ahmad's son and successor, Alâ-ud-dîn II., which began on Sunday, February 27, A.D. 1435,[1] the day of Sultan Ahmad's death.

Alâ-ud-dîn's first act was to despatch his brother Muhammad Khân with a powerful army against Deva Râya of Vijayanagar—

> "who had withheld his tribute for five years and refused to pay the arrears. They laid waste the country in such a manner that the Roy in a short time was glad to procure peace by giving twenty elephants, a great sum of money, and two hundred female slaves skilled in music and dancing, besides a valuable present to Mahummud Khan."

Flushed with this victory, and in command of a large force, Prince Muhammad rebelled against his brother, and Firishtah states that in doing so he obtained aid from Deva Râya. The prince took Mudkal, Raichûr, Sholapûr, Bîjapûr, and Naldirak from the Sultan's governors, but in a pitched battle with the royal forces was completely defeated and fled. Shortly afterwards,

[1] 8th Rajab A.H. 838 (Firishtah). The *Burhân-i Maâsir* says 22nd Rajab.

however, he was forgiven by his generous sovereign, and the fortress and territories of Raichûr were conferred on him.

About the year 1442 Deva Râya began to consider more seriously his situation in relation to his powerful neighbour at Kulbarga.

"He called[1] a general council of his nobility and principal bramins, observing to them that as his country of Carnatic in extent, population, and revenue far exceeded the territories of the house of Bahmenee; and in like manner his army was far more numerous, he wished therefore to explore the cause of the mussulmauns' successes, and his being reduced to pay them tribute. Some said . . . that the superiority of the mussulmauns arose from two circumstances: one, all their horses being strong, and able to bear more fatigue than the weak, lean animals of Carnatic; the other, a great body of excellent archers always kept up by the sultans of the house of Bahmenee, of whom the roy had but few in his army.

"Deo Roy upon this gave orders for the entertainment of mussulmauns in his service, allotted them jaghires,[2] erected a mosque for their use in the city of Beejanuggur, and commanded that no one should molest them in the exercise of their religion. He also ordered a koraun to be placed before his throne, on a rich desk, that the mussulmauns might perform the ceremony of obeisance in his presence, without sinning against their laws. He also made all the Hindoo soldiers learn the discipline of the bow; in which he and his officers used such exertions, that he had at length two thousand mussulmauns and sixty thousand Hindoos, well skilled in archery, besides eighty thousand horse and two hundred thousand foot, armed in the usual manner with pikes and lances."

On a day which must have been between November 1442 and April 1443 a desperate attempt was made on the life of King Deva Râya by one of his closest relatives—a brother, according to Abdur Razzâk, a nephew, according to Nuniz. Abdur Razzâk's story is without doubt the more reliable of the two, since he is a con-

[1] Firishtah (Scott), i. 118.

[2] Estates.

temporary witness. The story as told by Nuniz is given in the chronicle at the end of this volume.[1] Abdur Razzâk was ambassador from Persia to Calicut and Vijayanagar, and his account is particularly important as it definitely fixes the date.

"During the time that the author of this narrative was still sojourning at Calicut (November 1442 to April 1443) there happened in the city of Bidjanagar an extraordinary and most singular occurrence. . . .

"The king's brother, who had had a new house built for himself, invited thither the monarch and the principal personages of the empire. Now it is an established usage of the infidels never to eat in presence of each other. The men who were invited were assembled together in one grand hall. At short intervals the prince either came in person or sent some messenger to say that such or such great personage should come and eat his part of the banquet. Care had been taken to bring together all the drums, kettledrums, trumpets, and flutes that could be found in the city, and these instruments playing all at the same time, made a tremendous uproar. As soon as the individual who had been sent for entered the abovementioned house, two assassins, placed in ambush, sprang out upon him, pierced him with a poignard, and cut him in pieces. After having removed his limbs, or rather the fragments of his body, they sent for another guest, who, once having entered this place of carnage, disappeared. . . . In consequence of the noise of the drums, the clamour, and the tumult, no one was aware of what was going on. In this manner all those who had any name or rank in the state were slaughtered. The prince, leaving his house all reeking with the blood of his victims, betook himself to the king's palace, and addressing himself to the guards who were stationed in that royal residence, invited them with flattering words to go to his house, and caused them to follow the steps of the other victims. So that the palace was thus deprived of all its defenders. This villain then entered into the king's presence, holding in his hand a dish covered with betel-nut, under which was concealed a brilliant poignard. He said to the monarch, 'The hall is ready and they only wait your august presence.'

[1] Below, p. 303.

"The king, following the maxim which declares that eminent men receive an inspiration from heaven, said to him, 'I am not in good health to-day.'

"This unnatural brother, thus losing the hope of enticing the king to his house, drew his poignard, and struck him therewith several violent blows, so that the prince fell at the back of his throne. The traitor, thus believing that the king was dead, left there one of his confidants to cut off the monarch's head; then going out of the hall he ascended the portico of the palace, and thus addressed the people: 'I have slain the king, his brothers, and such and such emirs, Brahmins, and viziers; now I am king.'

"Meanwhile his emissary had approached the throne with the intention of cutting off the king's head, but that prince, seizing the seat behind which he had fallen, struck the wretch with it with so much violence on the chest that he fell upon his back. The king then, with the help of one of his guards, who at the sight of this horrible transaction had hidden himself in a corner, slew this assassin, and went out of the palace by way of the harem.

"His brother, still standing on the steps of the hall of council, invited the multitude to recognise him as their king. At that moment the monarch cried out, 'I am alive. I am well and safe. Seize that wretch.'

"The whole crowd assembled together threw themselves upon the guilty prince and put him to death.

"The only one who escaped was Danaik, the vizier, who previously to this sad event had gone on a voyage to the frontier of Ceylon. The king sent a courier to him to invite him to return, and informed him of what had just occurred. All those who had in any way aided in the conspiracy were put to death. Men in great numbers were slain, flayed, burnt alive, and their families entirely exterminated. The man who had brought the letters of invitation was put to the last degree of torture. . . ."

Nuniz states that the king died six months later and was succeeded by his son, but Abdur Razzâk declares that he was presented in person to Deva Râya about the month of December 1443. The name of Deva Râya's son is not given by Nuniz, nor yet the length of his reign ; he only states that he did nothing worth relating except to give enormous charities to temples. This king again was succeeded by a son called "Verupaca Rao," who must be identical with Virûpâksha, and Nuniz dates from his reign the commencement of the troubles that led to the usurpation of Narasimha and the downfall of the first dynasty.

But before putting together the confusing records of this period I must revert to the events of the year A.D. 1443.

"At this period," says Abdur Razzâk, referring to the second half of the year 1443, "Danaik[1] the vizier set out on an expedition into the kingdom of Kalbarga." The reasons which had led to this invasion were as follows : Sultan Alâ-ud-dîn had heard of the treacherous attempt to kill the king of Vijayanagar and the murder of the nobles and principal people, and he had sent a message to the king demanding payment of "seven lakhs of varâhas," as he thought the moment auspicious for an attempt to crush the kingdom. "Diou-rai, the king of Bidjanagar, was equally troubled and irritated by the receipt of such a message," but he sent a brave answer and prepared for war.

"Troops were sent out on both sides, which made great ravages on the frontiers of the two kingdoms. . . . Danaik, after having made an invasion upon the frontiers of the country of Kalbarga, and taken several unfortunate prisoners, had retraced his steps. . . ."

Firishtah also describes this war of A.D. 1443. He states that Deva Râya wantonly attacked the Bâhmanî princes—

"crossed the Tummedra suddenly, took the fortress of Mudkul, sent his sons to besiege Roijore and Beekapore, encamped him-

---

[1] *Danaik*, a word which the traveller apparently took for a proper name, is simply "the commander"—*Dhannâyaka.*

self along the bank of the Kistnah, and sent out detachments, who plundered the country as far as Saugher and Beejapore, laying waste by fire and sword.

"Sultan Alla ud Dien, upon intelligence of this invasion, prepared to repel it, and commanded all his forces from Telingana, Dowlutabad, and Berar to repair to the capital of Ahmedabad without delay. Upon their arrival he reviewed the whole, and found his army composed of fifty thousand horse, sixty thousand foot, and a considerable train of artillery. With this force he began to march against the enemy; and Deo Roy, upon his approach, shifted his ground, and encamped under the walls of the fortress of Mudkul, detaching a large body to harass the sultan.

"The sultan halted at the distance of twelve miles from Mudkul, and despatched Mallek al Tijar with the troops of Dowlutabad against the sons of Deo Roy;[1] also Khan Zummaun, governor of Beejapore, and Khan Azim, commander of the forces of Berar and Telingana, against the main body of the enemy. Mallek-al-Tijar, going first to Roijore, gave battle to the eldest son of Deo Roy, who was wounded in the action, and fled towards Beekapore, from whence he was joined by his younger brother, who quitted the siege of that fortress.

"In the space of two months, three actions happened near Mudkul between the two grand armies; in the first of which multitudes were slain on both sides, and the Hindoos having the advantage, the mussulmauns experienced great difficulties.[2] The sultan was successful in the others; and in the last, the eldest son of Deo Roy was killed by a spear thrown at him by Khan Zummaun, which event struck the Hindoos with a panic, and they fled with the greatest precipitation into the fortress of Mudkul."

Two chief Muhammadan officers, in the ardour of pursuit, entered the city with the fugitives, and were captured by the Hindus.

Deo Roy then sent a message to the Sultan that if he would promise never again to molest his territories he would pay the stipulated tribute annually, and return the two prisoners. This was accepted, a treaty was

[1] As to Deva Râya's age see above, p. 63. He had now been on the throne for twenty-four years.

[2] These words appear to confirm Abdur Razzâk's statement.

executed, and the prisoners returned with the tribute and added presents; and till the end of Deva Râya's reign both parties observed their agreement.

From the terms of the agreement we gather that, though Firishtah does not expressly mention it, tribute had been demanded by the Sultan, and this confirms the account given by Abdur Razzâk. It also shows why the "Danaik" in Abdur Razzâk's narrative had not returned covered with glory, but merely, having "taken several unfortunate prisoners, had retraced his steps."

The campaign must have been of short duration, since, while it began in A.H. 847 (May 1, A.D. 1443, to April 19, 1444) according to Firishtah, it was over before December 1443 when Abdur Razzâk left Vijayanagar.

The narrative being thus brought down to the close of the year 1443, let us, before passing on, turn to other records and see what they tell us about the reign of Deva Râya II. I have already stated that he appears to have been very young at his accession in A.D. 1419. In 1443 he had already reigned twenty-four years. Now the Hakluyt translation of Abdur Razzâk's chronicle states that Razzâk saw King Deva Râya II. in 1443, and the India Office copy contains the additional information that the king was then "exceedingly young." I am not aware which version is the more accurate. But even if these added words be accepted as part of the original, the difficulty is capable of being explained away by the supposition that perhaps the ambassador was presented to one of the princes and not to the king himself. The king appears to have been in doubt as to whether the traveller was not an impostor in representing himself as an envoy from Persia, and may have refrained from granting a personal interview.

Several inscriptions of the reign are extant. One

records a proclamation made in the king's name in A.D. 1426.[1] According to another bearing a date corresponding to Wednesday, October 16, in the same year,[2] he caused a Jain temple to be erected in the capital, in a street called the "Pân Supâri Bazaar." This temple is situated south-west of the temple marked as No. 35 on the Government map. It is within the enclosure of the royal palace, and close to the rear of the elephant stables still standing. The king is honoured in this inscription with the full imperial title of *Mahârâjâdhirâja Râjaparamesvara*. The site of this bazaar is thus definitely established. It lay on either side of the road which ran along the level dry ground direct from the palace gate, near the temple of *Hazâra Ramasvâmi*, in a north-easterly direction, to join the road which now runs to the Tungabhadra ferry through the fortified gate on the south side of the river immediately opposite Ânegundi. It passed along the north side of the Kallamma and Rangasvâmi temples, leaving the imperial office enclosure with its lofty walls and watch-towers, and the elephant stables, on the left, skirted the Jain temple and the temple numbered "35" on the plan, and passed along under the rocky hills that bound this plain on the north till it debouched on the main road above mentioned. This street would be the direct approach from the old city of Ânegundi to the king's palace.

In A.D. 1430 the king made a grant to a temple far in the south in the Tanjore district.[3] There are two inscriptions of his reign dated respectively in 1433–34

[1] Saka 1348 current; year Visvâvasu ("Asiatic Researches," xx. p. 22; Hultzsch's "South Indian Inscriptions," i. 82).

[2] *Op. cit.*, p. 160. Saka 1349 current, cyclic year Parâbhava, on the full moon day of the month Kârttika.

[3] Hultzsch's "South Indian Inscriptions," i. p. 79. Fifth Karkataka Sukla, Saka 1353 current, year Sâdhârana. The donor's name is given as Vîra Pratâpa Deva Râya Mahârâya and he is styled *Mahâmandalesvara*, "Lord of the four oceans."

and 1434–35 A.D. at Padavêdu in North Arcot.[1] If, as stated by Nuniz, King Deva Râya II. died a few months after his attempted assassination, and if Abdur Razzâk saw him in December 1443, we are led to the belief that he died early in 1444. Definite proof is, however, wanting. Other inscriptions must be carefully examined before we can arrive at any certain conclusion. Thus an inscription at Srâvana Belgola, of date corresponding to Tuesday, May 24 A.D. 1446, published by Professor Kielhorn,[2] relates to the death on that day of "Pratâpa Deva Râya;" and as it is couched in very curious and interesting terms, I give the translation in full :—

> "In the evil year Kshaya, in the wretched (month) second Vaisâkha, on a miserable Tuesday, in a fortnight which was the reverse of bright,[3] on the fourteenth day, the unequalled store of valour (*pratâpa*) Deva Râya, alas! met with death."

But since royal titles are not given to the deceased, he may have been only a prince of the blood. An inscription at Tanjore, also dated in A.D. 1446, mentions the name Deva Râya, but gives no further royal titles than the *biruda*—"Lord of the four oceans."[4] An inscription bearing date corresponding to Saturday, August 2 A.D. 1449, at Conjeeveram,[5] records a grant by a king called Vîra Pratâpa Prauḍha-Immaḍi-Deva Râya, to whom full royal titles are given.

It is provoking that Nuniz omits the name of the successor of Deva Râya II., as known to tradition in the

[1] *Op. cit.*, p. 109. They both give the king full royal titles.

[2] *Ind. Ant.*, xxv. 346.

[3] *I.e.* the second or dark half (*Krishna paksha*) of the month.

[4] Hultzsch's "South Indian Inscriptions," ii. 339. The date is Saka 1863 expired, year Kshaya, Wednesday the fifth day of the bright half of the month, on the day of the Nakshatra Pûrva Phalgunî.

[5] Hultzsch's "South Indian Inscriptions," i. 110. Saka 1371 expired, year Sukla, Saturday 13th Sukla of the month of Simha, on the day of the Nakshatra Uttarâshâdhâ.

sixteenth century, for this might have helped us to a decision. At present it looks as though there had been a Deva Râya III. reigning from A.D. 1444 to 1449; but this point cannot as yet be settled.

Mr. Rice has shown that one of the ministers of Deva Râya II. was named Nâganna; he had the title "Dhannâyaka," implying command of the army.

CHAPTER VII

THE CITY OF VIJAYANAGAR IN THE REIGN OF DEVA RÂYA II. (A.D. 1420 (?), 1443)

Description given by Nicolo to Bracciolini—The capital—Festivals—Immense population—Abdur Razzâk's description—His journey—The city walls—Palaces—The Mint—Bazaars—The great Mahânavamî festival.

It will be well to suspend our historical narrative for a time in order to acquire some idea of the appearance and condition of the great city of Vijayanagar in these days. We have already noticed that as early as 1375 A.D. Sultan Mujâhid of Kulbarga had heard so much of the beauty of this capital that he desired to see it, and it had grown in importance and grandeur during the succeeding half-century. About the year 1420 or 1421 A.D. there visited Vijayanagar one Nicolo, an Italian, commonly called Nicolo Conti or Nicolo dei Conti, and if he was not the earliest European visitor, he was at least the earliest that we know of whose description of the place has survived to this day. His visit must have taken place shortly after the accession of Deva Râya II. Nicolo never apparently wrote anything himself. His stories were recorded in Latin by Poggio Bracciolini, the Pope's secretary, for his master's information. Translated into Portuguese, they were re-translated from the Portuguese into Italian by Ramusio, who searched for but failed to obtain a copy of the original in Latin. This original was first published in 1723 by the Abbé Oliva of Paris under the title *P. Bracciolini, De Varietate Fortunæ, Liber quatuor*.

Nicolo, on reaching India, visited first the city of

Cambaya in Gujarât. After twenty days' sojourn there he passed down the coast to "Pacamuria," probably Barkûr, and "Helly," which is the "Mount d'Ely" or "Cabo d'Eli" of later writers. Thence he travelled inland and reached the Râya's capital, Vijayanagar, which he calls "Bizenegalia."[1] He begins his description thus :—

"The great city of Bizenegalia is situated near very steep mountains. The circumference of the city is sixty miles ; its walls are carried up to the mountains and enclose the valleys at their foot, so that its extent is thereby increased. In this city there are estimated to be ninety thousand men fit to bear arms."

I must here interpose a correction. There were no "mountains" properly so called at Vijayanagar ; only a confused and tumbled mass of rocky hills, some rising to considerable altitude. The extent of its lines of defences was extraordinary. Lofty and massive stone walls everywhere crossed the valleys, and led up to and mounted over the hillsides. The outer lines stretched unbroken across the level country for several miles. The hollows and valleys between the boulder-covered heights were filled with habitations, poor and squalid doubtless, in most instances, but interspersed with the stone-built dwellings of the nobles, merchants, and upper classes of the vast community ; except where the elaborately constructed water-channels of the Râyas enabled the land to be irrigated ; and in these parts rich gardens and woods, and luxurious crops of rice and sugar-cane, abounded. Here and there were wonderfully carved temples and fanes to Hindu deities, with Brahmanical colleges and schools attached to the more important amongst their number.

[1] The termination *ia* is appended to many Indian names by Bracciolini ; thus "Pacamuria" for Bacanor, the Portuguese way of spelling Barkûr, "Cenderghiria" for Chandragiri, "Odeschiria" for Udayagiri, and so on.

As to the appearance of the scenery, I cannot do better than quote the description given in 1845 by a distinguished South-Indian geologist, Lieutenant Newbold:[1]—

"The whole of the extensive site occupied by the ruins of Bijanugger on the south bank of the Tumbuddra, and of its suburb Annegundi on the northern bank, is occupied by great bare piles and bosses of granite and granitoidal gneiss, separated by rocky defiles and narrow rugged valleys encumbered by precipitated masses of rock. Some of the larger flat-bottomed valleys are irrigated by aqueducts from the river. . . . The peaks, tors, and logging-stones of Bijanugger and Annegundi indent the horizon in picturesque confusion, and are scarcely to be distinguished from the more artificial ruins of the ancient metropolis of the Deccan, which are usually constructed with blocks quarried from their sides, and vie in grotesqueness of outline and massiveness of character with the alternate airiness and solidity exhibited by nature in the nicely-poised logging stones and columnar piles, and in the walls of prodigious cuboidal blocks of granite which often crest and top her massive domes and ridges in natural cyclopean masonry."

The remains of palaces, temples, walls, and gateways are still to be seen, and these abound not only on the site of Vijayanagar proper, but also on the north side of the swiftly rushing river, where stood the stately citadel of Ânegundi, the mother of the empire-city. The population of this double city was immense, and the area occupied by it very extensive. From the last fortification to the south, beyond the present town of Hospett, to the extreme point of the defences of Ânegundi on the north, the distance is about twelve miles. From the extreme western line of walls in the plain to the last of the eastern works amongst the hills lying in the direction of Daroji and Kampli the interval measures about ten miles. Within this area we find the remains of the structures of which I have spoken. The

[1] *Journal of the Asiatic Society of Bengal*, vol. xiv. Part ii. p. 518.

hovels have disappeared, and the *débris* lies many feet thick over the old ground-level. But the channels are still in working order, and wherever they exist will be found rich crops, tall and stately trees, and a tangle of luxuriant vegetation. On the rocks above are the ruins of buildings and temples and walls, and in many places small shrines stand out, built on the jutting edges of great boulders or on the pinnacles of lofty crags, in places that would seem inaccessible to anything but monkeys and birds.

In the central enclosure are the remains of great structures that must once have been remarkable for their grandeur and dignity. These immediately surrounded the king's palace; but in 1565 the Muhammadans worked their savage will upon them with such effect that only the crumbling ruins of the more massive edifices amongst them still stand. The site of the palace itself is marked by a large area of ground covered with heaps of broken blocks, crushed masonry, and fragments of sculpture, not one stone being left upon another in its original position.

To return to Nicolo. He continues:—

"The inhabitants of this region marry as many wives as they please, who are burnt with their dead husbands. Their king is more powerful than all the other kings of India. He takes to himself 12.000 wives, of whom 4000 follow him on foot wherever he may go, and are employed solely in the service of the kitchen. A like number, more handsomely equipped, ride on horseback. The remainder are carried by men in litters, of whom 2000 or 3000 are selected as his wives on condition that at his death they should voluntarily burn themselves with him, which is considered to be a great honour for them. . . .

"At a certain time of the year their idol is carried through the city, placed between two chariots, in which are young women richly adorned, who sing hymns to the god, and accompanied by a great concourse of people. Many, carried away by the fervour of their faith, cast themselves on the ground before the wheels, in order that they may be crushed to death—a mode of death which they say is very acceptable to their god. Others, making an incision in their side, and inserting a rope thus through their body, hang themselves to the chariot by way of ornament, and thus suspended and half-dead accompany their idol. This kind of sacrifice they consider the best and most acceptable of all.

"Thrice in the year they keep festivals of especial solemnity. On one of these occasions the males and females of all ages, having bathed in the rivers or the sea, clothe themselves in new garments, and spend three entire days in singing, dancing, and feasting. On another of these festivals they fix up within their temples, and on the outside on the roofs, an innumerable number of lamps of oil of *susimanni*, which are kept burning day and night. On the third, which lasts nine days, they set up in all the highways large beams, like the masts of small ships, to the upper part of which are attached pieces of very beautiful cloth of various kinds, interwoven with gold. On the summit of each of these beams is each day placed a man of pious aspect, dedicated to religion, capable of enduring all things with equanimity, who is to pray for the favour of God. These men are assailed by the people, who pelt them with oranges, lemons, and other odoriferous fruits, all which they bear most patiently. There are also three other festival days, during which they sprinkle all passers-by, even the king and queen themselves, with saffron water, placed for that purpose by the wayside. This is received by all with much laughter."

The first of these festivals may be the Kanarese New Year's Day, which Domingo Paes in his chronicle asserts to have fallen, during his visit to Vijayanagar, on October 12—"*festas em que todos vestem panos novos e ricos e galantes, e cada hũu como o têm, e dão todos os capitãees panos a toda sua gente de muytas cores e galantes.*"[1] The second should be the *Dîpâvali* festival, which occurs about the month of October, when lamps are lighted by all the householders, and the temples

[1] Text of Paes, below, p. 281. I have discussed in full the dates given by the chronicler in considering the question as to the year of the battle of Raichûr (see pp. 140–147).

are illuminated. The description of the third answers to the nine-days' festival, called the *Mahânavamî*, at Vijayanagar, which, during the visit of Paes, took place on September 12. The other feast of three days' duration answers to the *Holi* festival.

Conti next describes the finding of diamonds on a mountain which he called "Albenigaras" and places fifteen days' journey beyond Vijayanagar "towards the north." He repeats the story which we know as that of "Sinbad the Sailor," saying that the diamonds lie in inaccessible valleys, into which lumps of flesh being thrown, to which the precious stones adhere, these are carried up to the summits by eagles, which are then driven off and the stones secured. The direction given, though it should rather be east than north, points to the mines on the Krishnâ river being those alluded to—mines which are often styled the "mines of Golkonda" by travellers. Marco Polo told the same tale of the same mines in the year 1296. Conti continues:—

"They divide the year into twelve months, which they name after the signs of the zodiac. The era is computed variously. . . ."

After having given a short account of the different coinages and currencies, which is interesting, but of which the various localities are left to the imagination, he writes:—

"The natives of Central India make use of the ballistæ,[1] and those machines which we call bombardas, also other warlike implements adapted for besieging cities.

"They call us Franks and say, 'While they call other nations blind, that they themselves have two eyes, and that we

[1] The stone balls, generally made of quartzose granite, which are so often found in the country about Vijayanagar on the sites of old forts, were probably intended to be projected from these weapons. They are often called "cannon-balls," but could hardly have been fired from guns, as they would have broken up under the discharge and have seriously injured the piece.

have but one, because they consider that they excel all others in prudence.'[1]

"The inhabitants of Cambay alone use paper; all other Indians write on the leaves of trees. They have a vast number of slaves, and the debtor who is insolvent is everywhere adjudged to be the property of his creditor. The numbers of these people and nations exceeds belief. Their armies consist of a million men and upwards."

Abdur Razzâk also visited the city during the reign of Deva Râya II., but about twenty years later than Conti. He was entrusted with an embassy from Persia, and set out on his mission on January 13, A.D. 1442. At the beginning of November that year he arrived at Calicut, where he resided till the beginning of April 1443. Being there he was summoned to Vijayanagar, travelled thither, and was in the great city from the end of April till the 5th December of the same year. The following passage explains why he left Calicut.

"On a sudden a man arrived who brought me the intelligence that the king of Bidjanagar, who holds a powerful empire and a mighty dominion under his sway, had sent him to the Sameri[2] as delegate, charged with a letter in which he desired that he would send on to him the ambassador of His Majesty, the happy Khakhan (*i.e.* the king of Persia). Although the Sameri is not subject to the laws of the king of Bidjanagar, he nevertheless pays him respect and stands extremely in fear of him, since, if what is said is true, this latter prince has in his dominions three hundred ports, each of which is equal to Calicut, and on *terra firma* his territories comprise a space of three months' journey."

In obedience to this request, Abdur Razzâk left

[1] About the same time, viz., 1436, Barbaro (Hakluyt Society, "Travels of Barbaro," p. 58), speaking of his sojourn in Tartary, wrote: "At which time, talking of Cataio, he tolde me howe the chief of that princes corte knewe well enough what the Franchi were. . . . We Cataini have twoo eyes, and yo[w] Franchi one, whereas yo[w] (torneing him towards the Tartares that were wth him) have never a one." The coincidence is curious.

[2] The Samuri of Calicut.

Calicut by sea and went to Mangalore, "which forms the frontier of the kingdom of Bidjanagar." He stayed there two or three days and then journeyed inland, passing many towns, and amongst them a place where he saw a small but wonderful temple made of bronze.

"At length I came to a mountain whose summit reached the skies. Having left this mountain and this forest behind me, I reached a town called Belour,[1] the houses of which were like palaces."

Here he saw a temple with exquisite sculpture.

"At the end of the month of Zoul'hidjah[2] we arrived at the city of Bidjanagar. The king sent a numerous cortège to meet us, and appointed us a very handsome house for our residence. His dominion extends from the frontier of Serendib to the extremities of the country of Kalbergah (*i.e.* from the Krishnâ River to Cape Comorin). One sees there more than a thousand elephants, in their size resembling mountains and in their form resembling devils. The troops amount in number to eleven *lak* (1,100,000). One might seek in vain throughout the whole of Hindustan to find a more absolute *raï*, for the monarchs of this country bear the title of *raï*.

"The city of Bidjanagar is such that the pupil of the eye has never seen a place like it, and the ear of intelligence has never been informed that there existed anything to equal it in the world. It is built in such a manner that seven citadels and the same number of walls enclose each other. Around the first citadel are stones of the height of a man, one half of which is sunk in the ground while the other half rises above it. These are fixed one beside the other in such a manner that no horse or foot soldier could boldly or with ease approach the citadel."

The position of these seven walls and gates have long been a puzzle to me, but I hazard the following explanation. The traveller approached from the south-west, and the first line of wall that he saw must have been that on the neck between the two hills

[1] Sir H. Elliot ("History," iv. 103, note) has "*Bidrûr*" as Abdur Razzâk's spelling. The place alluded to was probably Bednûr.

[2] This was in A.H. 846, and corresponds to the end of April A.D. 1443.

south-west of Hospett. Paes also describes this outer defence-work as that seen by all travellers on their first arrival from the coast. After being received at this entrance-gate Razzâk must have passed down the slope through "cultivated fields, houses, and gardens" to the entrance of Hospett, where the second line of fortification barred the way; and since that town was not then thickly populated, the same features would meet his eye till he passed a third line of wall on the north side of that town. From this point the houses became thicker, probably forming a long street, with shops on either side of the road, leading thence to the capital. The fourth line of wall, with a strong gateway, is to be seen on the south of the present village of Malpanagudi, where several remains of old buildings exist; and notably a handsome stone well, once probably belonging to the country-house of some noble or chief officer. The fifth line is on the north of Malpanagudi, and here the great gateway still stands, though the wall is much damaged and destroyed. The sixth line is passed just to the south of the Kâmalâpur tank. The seventh or inner line is the great wall still to be seen in fairly good repair north of that village. This last surrounded the palace and the government buildings, the space enclosed measuring roughly a mile from north to south, and two miles and a quarter from east to west. The remains of the upright stones alluded to by Razzâk were seen by Domingo Paes in A.D. 1520.[1] I believe that they have now disappeared.

Razzâk describes the outer citadel as a "fortress of round shape, built on the summit of a mountain, and constructed of stones and lime. It has very solid gates, the guards of which are constantly at their post, and examine everything with severe inspection." This passage must refer to the outer line of wall, since

[1] Below, p. 253.

Razzâk's "seventh fortress" is the innermost of all. The guards at the gates were doubtless the officers entrusted with the collection of the octroi duties. Sir Henry Elliot's translation (iv. 104) adds to the passage as quoted the words,—"they collect the *jizyât* or taxes." This system of collecting octroi dues at the gates of principal towns lasted till recent days, having only been abolished by the British Government.

"The seventh fortress is to the north, and is the palace of the king. The distance between the opposite gates of the outer fortress north and south is two parasangs,[1] and the same east to west.

"The space which separates the first fortress from the second, and up to the third fortress, is filled with cultivated fields and with houses and gardens. In the space from the third to the seventh one meets a numberless crowd of people, many shops, and a bazaar. By the king's palace are four bazaars, placed opposite each other. On the north is the portico of the palace of the *raï*. Above each bazaar is a lofty arcade with a magnificent gallery, but the audience-hall of the king's palace is elevated above all the rest. The bazaars are extremely long and broad.[2]

"Roses are sold everywhere. These people could not live without roses, and they look upon them as quite as necessary as food. . . . Each class of men belonging to each profession has shops contiguous the one to the other; the jewellers sell publicly in the bazaars pearls, rubies, emeralds, and diamonds.

---

[1] *I.e.* about seven miles. It is actually about eight miles if measured from the extreme south point of the first line of defence northwards to the river. Razzâk evidently did not include the walls of Ânegundi, the northern lines of which lie two miles farther still to the north.

[2] The descriptions are rather vague, but, if I am right in supposing that there was a long bazaar called the Pânsupâri bazaar, along the road leading from the palace gate to the Ânegundi gate on the river, it must certainly have been crossed by another road, and probably therefore a road lined with shops, leading from the Kâmalâpura gate of the inner enclosure northwards to the great Hampi temple. Close to the gate of the palace proper these roads would intersect at right angles, and would form four separate bazaars or streets. The galleries and porticoes are now not in existence, but the remains in the street running east from the Hampi temple will show what the galleries were like in those days. This last street alone is half a mile long.

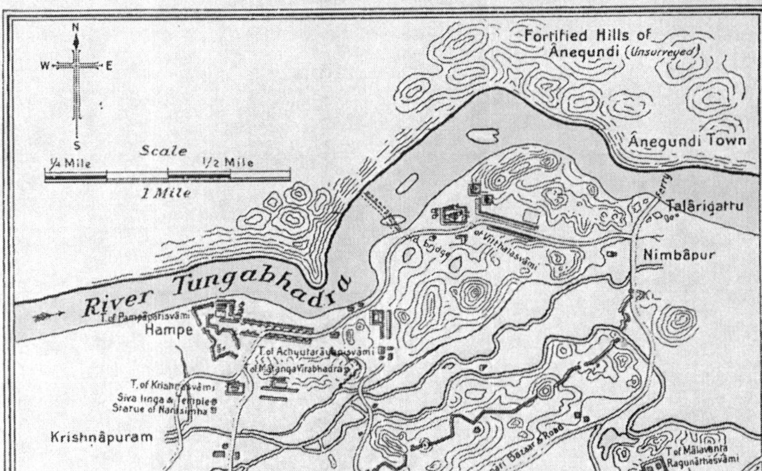

R. Sewell, del.

Swan Sonnenschein & Co., Ltd., London.

Plan of Central Portion of the

CITY OF VIJAYANAGAR.

shewing the principal remains.

In this agreeable locality, as well as in the king's palace, one sees numerous running streams and canals formed of chiselled stone, polished and smooth.[1]

On the left of the Sultan's portico rises the *Dewan-Khaneh*,[2] which is extremely large and looks like a palace. In front of it is a hall, the height of which is above the stature of a man, its length thirty ghez and its breadth ten.[3] In it is placed the *Defter-Khaneh* (court-house), and here sit the scribes. . . . . In the middle of this palace, upon an high estrade, is seated an eunuch called the Danaik,[4] who alone presides over the divan. At the end of the hall stand chobdars[5] drawn up in line. The Dewan or Danaik settles people's affairs and hears their petitions. There is no appeal. After concluding business the Danaik passes through seven doors into the palace, and entering the last alone, makes his report to the king.

"Behind the king's palace[6] are the house and hall allotted to the Danaik. To the left of the said palace is the Mint.

"This empire contains so great a population that it would

---

[1] Remains of these are still to be seen not far from the "Ladies' Bath." There was a long trough that conveyed the water, and on each side were depressions which may have been hollowed for the reception of round vessels of different sizes, intended to hold water for household use.

[2] "The *Dewañ Kḥanah* resembles a forty-pillared hall" (Sir H. Elliot's translation, "History," iv. 108). I am doubtful as to what building is referred to. The Hakluyt translator's rendering seems to point to the great enclosure west of the elephant stables, which has been called the "Zenana." I know of no hall exactly answering to Sir Henry Elliot's description. The lofty walls with watch-towers at the angles which surround the enclosure referred to would be just such as might be supposed to have been erected for the protection of the royal archives and offices of the kingdom—the "Dewân Khâna." If so, the "hall" in front would be the structure to which has been fancifully given the name of "the concert-hall." This hall, or *Daftar-Khâna*, would be the usual working office of the Minister and his colleagues—the office of daily work or courthouse, the necessary documents and records being brought to and from the central offices in the enclosure.

[3] Roughly, twenty yards by seven. It is difficult to understand the height mentioned.

[4] I give this word as in the India Office copy. The Hakluyt edition has *Daiang*, which seems incorrect.

[5] Officers with staves, generally covered with silver.

[6] Abdur Razzâk writes as if he was standing at the gate of the palace looking eastwards. Taken so, his description seems exact. Mr. A. Rea takes this view generally in a paper published in the *Madras Christian College Magazine* (December 1886).

be impossible to give an idea of it without entering into extensive details. In the king's palace are several cells, like basins, filled with bullion, forming one mass."

Opposite the *Divan-Khaneh*, he continues, is the house of the elephants.

"Each elephant has a separate compartment, the walls of which are extremely solid, and the roof composed of strong pieces of wood. . . . Opposite the Mint is the house of the Governor, where are stationed twelve thousand soldiers on guard. . . . Behind the Mint is a sort of bazaar, which is more than three hundred ghez in length, and more than twenty in breadth.[1] On two sides are ranged houses and forecourts; in front of them are erected, instead of benches (*kûrsi*), several lofty seats constructed of beautiful stones. On the two sides of the avenue formed by the chambers are represented figures of lions, panthers, tigers, and other animals.[2] Thrones and chairs are placed on the platforms, and the courtesans seat themselves thereon, bedecked in gems and fine raiment."

The author took up his abode in a lofty house which had been allotted to him, on the 1st Muharram (May 1, 1443).

"One day some messengers sent from the palace of the king came to see me, and at the close of the same day I presented myself at court. . . . The prince was seated in a hall, surrounded by the most imposing attributes of state. Right and left of him stood a numerous crowd of men arranged in a circle. The king was dressed in a robe of green satin, around his neck he wore a collar, composed of pearls of beautiful water, and other splendid gems. He had an olive complexion, his frame was thin, and he was rather tall; on his cheeks might be seen a slight down, but there was no beard on his chin. The expression of his countenance was extremely pleasing.[3] . . . .

---

[1] About two hundred yards by fifteen.

[2] All this seems to have disappeared, but the buildings may have stood on each side of what is now the main road from Kâmalâpura to Hampi—"behind the Mint," as the author stood.

[3] The India Office copy adds here: "He was exceedingly young." If so, the personage whom the ambassador interviewed could hardly have been Deva Râya II., who at this period (1443) had been on the throne for twenty-four years.

THE COUNCIL CHAMBER IN THE PALACE, VIJAYANAGAR

"If report speaks truly, the number of the princesses and concubines amounts to seven hundred."

Abdur Razzâk gives a glowing account of the brilliancy of a great festival of which he was a spectator while in the capital. He calls it the Mahânavamî[1] festival, but I have my doubts as to whether he was not mistaken, since he declares that it took place in the month Rajab (October 25 to November 23, 1443 A.D.). The Hindus celebrate the *Mahânavamî* by a nine days' festival beginning on Âsvina Sukla 1st in native reckoning, that is, on the day following the new moon which marks the beginning of the month Âsvina; while the New Year's Day at that period was the first day of the following month, Kârttika (if the year began, as it certainly did at Vijayanagar in the time of Paes, eighty years later, on 1st Kârttika). But the new moon of Rajab in A.D. 1443 corresponded to the new moon of *Kârttika*, not to that of *Âsvina*.[2] Either, therefore, the festival which he witnessed was the New Year's Day festival, or the traveller was in error in giving the month "Rajab." It seems most probable that the former was the case, because he apparently makes the festival one of only three days'

[1] *Mahanadi* (Hakluyt), *Mahânâwî* (Elliot). There can be little doubt as to the meaning.

[2] The actual moment of the new moon corresponding to the beginning of the month of Kârttika in Hindu reckoning was 7.40 A.M. on the morning of October 23, and the first Hindu day (*tithi*) of Kârttika began at 6 A.M. on October 24. The Muhammadan month begins with the heliacal rising of the moon, and this may have taken place on the 24th or 25th evening. At any rate, Razzâk could hardly have called a festival that took place a whole month earlier a festival which took place "during three days in the month Rajab." Hence I think that he must have been present at the New Year festivities in Kârttika, not at the Mahânavamî in Âsvina, a month previous. Note Paes' description of the festivals at which he was present. He states that the nine days' *Mahânavamî* took place on September 12, when he was at Vijayanagar, and the details correspond to the year A.D. 1520. September 12, 1520, was the first day of the month Âsvina. The New Year's festival that year took place on October 12, which corresponded to the first day of Kârttika, each of these being the day following the *new* moon, not the full moon.

duration, whereas the *Mahânavamı*, as its name implies, was a nine days' feast. But there is also another difficulty. The *Mahânavamî* celebrations began with the new moon, whereas Razzâk says that the festival he saw began with the "full moon." This, however, may have been due to a slip of the pen.

However that may be, he certainly was a spectator of a brilliant scene, and I append his account of it.

"In pursuance of orders issued by the king of Bidjanagar, the generals and principal personages from all parts of his empire . . . presented themselves at the palace. They brought with them a thousand elephants . . . which were covered with brilliant armour and with castles magnificently adorned. . . . During three consecutive days in the month of Redjeb the vast space of land magnificently decorated, in which the enormous elephants were congregated together, presented the appearance of the waves of the sea, or of that compact mass which will be assembled together at the day of the resurrection. Over this magnificent space were erected numerous pavilions, to the height of three, four, or even five storeys, covered from top to bottom with figures in relief. . . . Some of these pavilions were arranged in such a manner that they could turn rapidly round and present a new face: at each moment a new chamber or a new hall presented itself to the view.

"In the front of this place rose a palace with nine pavilions magnificently ornamented. In the ninth the king's throne was set up. In the seventh was allotted a place to the humble author of this narrative. . . . Between the palace and the pavilions . . . were musicians and storytellers."

Girls were there in magnificent dresses, dancing "behind a pretty curtain opposite the king." There were numberless performances given by jugglers, who displayed elephants marvellously trained.

During three consecutive days, from sunrise to sunset, the royal festival was prolonged in a style of the greatest magnificence. Fireworks, games, and amusements went on. On the third day the writer was presented to the king.

"The throne, which was of extraordinary size, was made of gold, and enriched with precious stones of extreme value. . . . Before the throne was a square cushion, on the edges of which were sown three rows of pearls. During the three days the king remained seated on this cushion. When the fête of Mahanawi was ended, at the hour of evening prayer, I was introduced into the middle of four *estrades*, which were about ten *ghez* both in length and breadth.[1] The roof and the walls were entirely formed of plates of gold enriched with precious stones. Each of these plates was as thick as the blade of a sword, and was fastened with golden nails. Upon the *estrade*, in the front, is placed the throne of the king, and the throne itself is of very great size."

The descriptions given by these travellers give us a good idea of the splendours of this great Hindu capital in the first half of the fifteenth century; and with this in our minds we return to the history of the period.

[1] About seven yards or twenty-one feet.

CHAPTER VIII

CLOSE OF THE FIRST DYNASTY (A.D. 1449 TO 1490)

Mallikârjuna and Virûpâksha I.—Râjasekhara and Virûpâksha II.—The Dakhan splits up into five independent kingdoms—The Bîjapûr king captures Goa and Belgaum—Fighting at Rajahmundry, Kondapalle, and other parts of Telingana—Death of Mahmûd Gawân—The Russian traveller Nikitin—Chaos at Vijayanagar—Narasimha seizes the throne.

I HAVE already stated that the period following the reign of Deva Râya II. is one very difficult to fill up satisfactorily from any source. It was a period of confusion in Vijayanagar—a fact that is clearly brought out by Nuniz in his chronicle.

A.D. 1449 is the last date in any known inscription containing mention of a Deva Râya, and Dr. Hultzsch[1] allots this to Deva Râya II. It may be, as already suggested, that there was a Deva Râya III. on the throne between A.D. 1444 and 1449, but this remains to be proved. Two sons of Deva Râya II., according to the inscriptions, were named Mallikârjuna and Virûpâksha I. respectively. There are inscriptions of the former dated in A.D. 1452–53 and 1464–65,[2] and one of the latter in 1470.[3] Mallikârjuna appears to have had two sons, Râjasekhara, of whom we have inscriptions in the years A.D. 1479–80 and 1486–87, and Virupâksha II., mentioned in an inscription dated A.D. 1483–84, three years earlier than the last of Râjasekhara.

[1] Genealogical table in *Epigraphia Indica*, iii. 36.

[2] Dr. Hultzsch (*Epig. Ind.*, iii. 36, and note ; *Ind. Ant.*, xxi. 321). The last is on a temple at Little Conjeeveram and is dated in Saka 1387 expired, year Pârthiva.

[3] Saka 1392 expired, year Vikriti, on the same temple (*Ind. Ant.*, xxi. 321–322).

Dr. Hultzsch, in the third volume of the *Epigraphia Indica*, p. 36, gives these dates, but in the fourth volume of the same work (p. 180) he notes that an inscription of Râjasekhara exists at Âmbûr in North Arcot, which is dated in the year corresponding to A.D. 1468–69. I have also been told of an inscription on stone to be seen at the village of Pârnapalle (or Paranapalle) in the Cuddapah district, of which a copy on copper-plate is said to be in the possession of one Nârâyana Reddi of Goddamari in the Tâdpatri Taluq of the Anantapur district. This is reported to bear date Saka 1398 (A.D. 1476–77), and to mention as sovereign "Praudha Deva Râya of Vijayanagar."

Râjasekhara's second inscription must have been engraved very shortly before the final fall of the old royal house, for the first certain date of the usurper Narasimha is A.D. 1490.

Amid this confusion of overlapping dates we turn for help to Nuniz; but though his story, gathered from tradition about the year 1535, is clear and consecutive, it clashes somewhat with the other records. According to him, Deva Râya II. had a son, Pina Râya, who died six months after his attempted assassination; but we have shown that Abdur Razzâk conclusively establishes that this unfortunate monarch was Deva Râya II. himself, and that the crime was committed before the month of April 1443. Pina Râya left a son unnamed, who did nothing in particular, and was succeeded by his son "Verupaca," by which name Virûpâksha is clearly meant. Virûpâksha was murdered by his eldest son, who in turn was slain by his younger brother, "Padea Rao," and this prince lost the kingdom to the usurper Narasimha.

The period was without doubt a troublous one, and all that can be definitely and safely stated at present is that for about forty years prior to the usurpation of

Narasimha the kingdom passed from one hand to the other, in the midst of much political agitation, discontent, and widespread antagonism to the representatives of the old royal family, several of whom appear to have met with violent deaths. The usurpation took place at some period between A.D. 1487 and 1490.

Leaving the Hindu and Portuguese records, we must turn to the Muhammadan historians in order to see what were the political relations existing at this time between Vijayanagar and its hereditary enemies to the north. Firishtah tells us of no event occurring between the year 1443 and 1458 A.D. to disturb the peaceful conditions then existing. Kulbarga was itself in too troubled a condition to venture on further national complications. Internal disputes and civil war raged in the Dakhan, and the country was divided against itself. The trouble had begun which ended only with the extinction of the Bâhmanî monarchy, and the establishment of five rival Muhammadan kingdoms in the place of one.

Alâ-ud-dîn died February 13, A.D. 1458, (?)[1] and was succeeded by his son Humâyun, a prince of "cruel and sanguinary temper." In the following year Ḥumâyun waged war against the country of the Telugus and besieged Devarakonda, which made so stout a resistance that the Dakhâni armies were baffled, and retired. He died on the 5th September 1461,[2] to the great relief of all his subjects. Mallikârjuna appears to have been then king of Vijayanagar.

Nizâm Shâh succeeded to the throne, being then only eight years old, but his reign was of short duration.

[1] Firishtah says that he reigned twenty-three years nine months and twenty days, which gives this date. The *Burhân-i Maâsir* fixes his decease at the end of Jumâda'l Awwal A.D. 862, which answers to April A.D. 1458. Major King states that another authority gives the date as four years later (*Ind. Ant.*, Sept. 1899, p. 242, note).

[2] 28th Zîl-kada A.H. 865.

He was succeeded by his brother Muhammad on July 30, A.D. 1463.[1]

In the middle of the year 1469, while either Râjasekhara or Virûpâksha I. was the king of Vijayanagar, Mahmûd Gawân, Muhammad's minister, marched towards the west, and after a fairly successful campaign attacked Goa, then in the possession of the Râya of Vijayanagar, both by sea and land. He was completely victorious and captured the place.

The war was probably undertaken in revenge for a cruel massacre of Muhammadans which took place in this year A.D. 1469, according to Barros.[2] At this period the coast trade was altogether in the hands of the Muhammadans, and they used to import large numbers of horses, principally for the use of the great contending armies in the Dakhan and Vijayanagar. The Hindu king depended on this supply to a large extent. In 1469 the Moors at Batecala (Bhatkal) having sold horses to the "Moors of Decan," the king of Vijayanagar ordered his vassal at Onor (Honawar) "to kill all those Moors as far as possible, and frighten the rest away." The result of this was a terrible massacre, in which 10,000 Musulmâns lost their lives. The survivors fled and settled themselves at Goa, thus founding the city that afterwards became the capital of Portuguese India. Nuniz alludes to the loss of "Goa, Chaull, and Dabull" by Vijayanagar in the reign of "Verupaca."[3] (Purchas states that the massacre took place in 1479 A.D.)

Shortly afterwards there arose to power under the Sultan Muhammad one Yusuf Âdil Khân, a slave, who before long grew to such power that he overthrew the Bâhmanî dynasty, and became himself the first independent sovereign of Bîjapur—the first "Âdil Shâh." In 1470, says the *Burhân-i Maâsir*, the Sultan took

[1] 13th Zîl-kada A.H. 867.

[2] Dec. l. viii. c. 10.

[3] Below, p. 305.

Rajahmundry and Kondavîd from the king of Orissa. An inscription at Kondapalle, a fine hill-fort beautifully situated on a range of hills, gives the date as 1470 or 1471; my copy is imperfect.

Firishtah tells us that—

"In the year 877 (A.D. 1472–73) Perkna, roy of the fortress of Balgoan, at the instigation of the prince of Beejanuggur, marched to retake the island of Goa. . . . Mahummud Shaw, immediately upon intelligence of this irruption, collected his forces and moved against Balgoan, a fortress of great strength, having round it a deep wet ditch, and near it a pass, the only approach, defended by redoubts."

The attack ended in the reduction of the place, when the Sultan returned to Kulbarga.

The *Burhân-i Maâsir* calls the chief of Belgaum "Parkatapah," and Major King, the translator of the work, gives a large variety of spellings of the name, viz.: "Birkanah," "Parkatabtah," "Parkatîyah," "Parkîtah," "Barkabtah."[1] Briggs gives it as "Birkana." It has been supposed that the real name was Vikrama.

About the year 1475 there was a terrible famine in the Dakhan and the country of the Telugus, which lasted for two years. At its close the Hindu population of Kondapalle revolted, murdered the Muhammadan governor, and invited aid from the king of Orissa. This monarch accordingly advanced and laid siege to Râjahmundry, which was then the governorship of Nizâm-ul-Mulkh, but on the Shâh marching in person to the relief of the place the army of Orissa retired. In the latter part of the year 882, which corresponds to March 1478 A.D., Muhammad penetrated to the capital of Orissa, "and used no mercy in slaughtering the inhabitants and laying waste the country of the enemy." The Râjah submitted, and purchased his immunity from further interference on

[1] *Ind. Ant.*, November 1899, p. 286, note.

the part of the Sultan by a present of some valuable elephants.

Firishtah and the *Burhân-i Maâsir* differ considerably as to what followed. The former states that, after his raid into Orissa, Muhammad Shâh reduced Kondapalle, where he destroyed a temple, slew the Brahman priests attached to it, and ordered a mosque to be erected on its site. He remained nearly three years at Rajahmundry, secured the Telingana country, expelled some refractory zamindars, and "resolved on the conquest of Nursing Râya."

"Nursing," says Firishtah, "was a powerful râja, possessing the country between Carnatic[1] and Telingana, extending along the sea-coast to Matchiliputtum,[2] and had added much of the Beejanuggur territory to his own by conquest, with several strong forts."

This was probably the powerful chief Narasimha Râya, a relation of the king of Vijayanagar, who, intrusted with the government of large tracts, was rising rapidly to independence under the weak and feeble monarch whom he finally supplanted. The Sultan went to Kondapalle,[3] and there was told that, at a distance of ten days' journey, "was the temple of Kunchy,[4] the walls and roof of which were plated with gold, ornamented with precious stones;" upon receipt of which intelligence the Sultan is said to have made a forced march thither, taking with him only 6000 cavalry, and to have sacked the place.

The account given by the *Burhân-i Maâsir* as to Muhammad Shah's proceedings at this period is that on going to Rajahmundry he found there Narasimha Râya

[1] Vijayanagar. [2] Masulipatam.

[3] Scott's translation has "Ghondpore" (i. 166); Briggs (ii. 500) says "Condapilly."

[4] This evidently means Kânchi or Conjeeveram; but the story is exceedingly improbable. The distance was 250 miles, and the way lay through the heart of a hostile country.

"with 700,000 cursed infantry, and 500 elephants like mountains of iron," who, in spite of all his pomp and power, fled like a craven on the approach of the army of Islâm. The Sultan then reduced Rajahmundry, which had been held by a *Hindu* force—not Muhammadan, as Firishtah declares. In November 1480[1] he marched from Rajahmundry to Kondavîd, going "towards the kingdom of Vijayanagar." After reducing that fortress, he proceeded after a while to Malur, which belonged to Narasimha, "who, owing to his numerous army and the extent of his dominions, was the greatest and most powerful of all the rulers of Telingana and Vijayanagar," and who "had established himself in the midst of the countries of Kanara and Telingana, and taken possession of most of the districts of the coast and interior of Vijayanagar."

While at Malur the Sultan was informed that "at a distance of fifty farsakhas from his camp was a city called Ganji," containing temples, &c., to which he promptly marched, arriving before the place on 13th March A.D. 1481.[2] He sacked the city and returned.

After this the Sultan went to Masulipatam, which he reduced, and thence returned to Kondapalle. This was his last success. His cold-blooded murder of the celebrated Mahmûd Gawân, his loyal and faithful servant, in 1481, so disgusted the nobles that in a short time the kingdom was dismembered, the chiefs revolted, the dynasty was overthrown, and five independent kingdoms were raised on its ruins.

Muhammad Shâh died on 21st March, A.D. 1482. Shortly before his death he planned an expedition to relieve Goa from a Vijayanagar army which "Sewaroy, Prince of Beejanuggur," had sent there (Firishtah); but the Sultan's death put a stop to this (*Burhân-i Maâsir*).

[1] Ramazân A.H. 885.
[2] 11th Muharram, A.H. 886.

We have some further information on the affairs of Kulbarga during the reign of Muhammad Shâh in the writings of the Russian traveller Athanasius Nikitin, but it is very difficult to fix the exact date of his sojourn there. Nikitin was a native of Twer, and set out on his wanderings by permission of the Grand Duke Michael Borissovitch, and his own bishop, Gennadius. This fixes the time of his start so far that it must have taken place subsequent to 1462, and the author of the "Bombay Gazetteer," *re* Poonah, assigns the period 1468 to 1474 as that of Nikitin's stay in India.

Nikitin first went to Chaul, and thence travelled by land to Junîr.

> "Here resides Asat, Khân of Indian Jooneer, a tributary of Meliktuchar. . . . He has been fighting the Kofars for twenty years, being sometimes beaten but mostly beating them."

By "Meliktuchar" is probably meant the celebrated minister Mahmud Gawân, who in 1457 A.D. received the title "Mallik-al-Tîjar," a title which was borne by the chief amongst the nobility at the Bâhmanî court. It meant literally "chief of the merchants." The "Kofars" are, of course, the Kaffirs or Hindus. Firishtah tells us of fighting having taken place in 1469 between the Mallik-al-Tîjar and "the roies of Songeer, Khalneh, and rebels in Kokun," when the troops of Junîr were under the Mallik's command. During the war he captured Goa, as already stated. There were campaigns also against the Hindus of Rajahmundry, Vinukonda, and other places, and in 1472 one against Belgaum, which has been already described. Firishtah tells us that the Daulatâbâd and Junîr troops were sent against the powerful Hindu Râja Narasimha on the east coast.[1] As to Kulbarga and his experiences there, Nikitin writes as follows:—

[1] Scott's translation, i. 167.

"The Hindus . . . are all naked and bare-footed. They carry a shield in one hand and a sword in the other. Some of the servants are armed with straight bows and arrows. Elephants are greatly used in battle. . . . Large scythes are attached to the trunks and tusks of the elephants, and the animals are clad in ornamental plates of steel. They carry a citadel, and in the citadel twelve men in armour with guns and arrows. . . . The land is overstocked with people; but those in the country are very miserable, whilst the nobles are extremely opulent and delight in luxury. They are wont to be carried on their silver beds, preceded by some twenty chargers caparisoned in gold, and followed by three hundred men on horseback and five hundred on foot, and by horn-men, ten torch-bearers, and ten musicians.

"There may be seen in the train of the Sultan about a thousand ordinary horses in gold trappings, one hundred camels with torch-bearers, three hundred trumpeters, three hundred dancers. . . . The Sultan, riding on a golden saddle, wears a habit embroidered with sapphires, and on his pointed head-dress a large diamond; he also carries a suit of gold armour inlaid with sapphires, and three swords mounted in gold. . . . The brother of the Sultan rides on a golden bed, the canopy of which is covered with velvet and ornamented with precious stones. . . . Mahmud sits on a golden bed, with a silken canopy to it and a golden top, drawn by four horses in gilt harness. Around him are crowds of people, and before him many singers and dancers. . . .

"Melikh Tuchar took two Indian towns whose ships pirated on the Indian Sea, captured seven princes with their treasures. . . . The town had been besieged for two years by an army of two hundred thousand men, a hundred elephants, and three hundred camels.[1] . . .

"Myza Mylk, Mek-Khan, and Farat Khan took three large cities, and captured an immense quantity of precious stones, the whole of which was brought to Melik Tuchar. . . . They came to Beder on the day of the Ascension."

The Sultan's brother "when in a campaign is followed by his mother and sister, and 2000 women on

[1] It is possible that one of these towns was Goa, which was taken in 1469.

horseback or on golden beds;[1] at the head of his train are 300 ordinary horses in gold equipment."

"Melik Tuchar moved from Beder with his army, 50,000 strong, against the Indians. . . . The Sultan sent 50,000 of his own army. . . . With this force Melik Tuchar went to fight against the great Indian dominion of *Chenudar*. But the king of *Binedar*[2] possessed 300 elephants, 100,000 men of his own troops, and 50,000 horse."

The writer then gives details as to the rest of the Sultan's forces, and the total comes to the enormous amount of over 900,000 foot, 190,000 horse, and 575 elephants.

"The Sultan moved out with his army . . . to join Melich Tuchar at Kalbarga. But their campaign was not successful, for they took only one Indian town, and that at the loss of many people and treasures.[3]

"The Hindu Sultan Kadam is a very powerful prince. He possesses a numerous army and resides on a mountain at *Bichenegher*. This vast city is surrounded by three forts and intersected by a river, bordering on one side on a dreadful jungle, and on the other on a dale; a wonderful place and to any purpose convenient. On one side it is quite inaccessible; a road gives right through the town, and as the mountain rises high with a ravine below, the town is impregnable.

"The enemy besieged it for a month and lost many people, owing to the want of water and food. Plenty of water was in sight but could not be got at.

"This Indian stronghold was ultimately taken by Melikh Khan Khoda, who stormed it, and fought day and night to reduce it. The army that made the siege with heavy guns had neither eaten nor drunk for twenty days. He lost 5000 of his best soldiers. On the capture of the town 20,000 inhabitants, men and women, had their heads cut off, 20,000 young and old were made prisoners and sold. . . . The treasury, however, having been found empty, the town was abandoned."

---

1 Meaning evidently palanquins.

2 "Chenudar" and "Binedar" appear to be variations of the name Vijayanagar, called "Bichenegher" farther on.

3 This may, perhaps, refer to Belgaum (A.D. 1471).

It is impossible to decide to what this refers, as we have no other information of any capture of Vijayanagar by the Sultan's forces at this period. But the traveller may have confused the place with Rajahmundry or one of the eastern cities of Telingana.

In 1482 A.D., as before stated, Mahmûd Shâh II. succeeded to the throne of Kulbarga, being then a boy of twelve, but his sovereignty was only nominal. Constant disturbances took place; the nobles in many tracts rose against the sovereign, and amongst others the governor of Goa attempted to assert his independence, seizing many important places on the coast; civil war raged at the capital; and before long the great chiefs threw off all semblance of obedience to the authority of the Bâhmanîs, and at length divided the kingdom amongst themselves.

At Vijayanagar, too, there seems to have been chaos, and about the time when the Dakhâni nobles finally revolted, Narasimha Râya had placed himself on the throne and established a new and powerful dynasty.

The five separate kingdoms which arose in the Dakhan were those of the Âdil Shâhs of Bîjapûr, with whom we have most to do; the Barîd Shâhs of Bîdr or Ahmadabad; the Imâd Shâhs of Bîrâr; the Nizâm Shâhs of Ahmadnagar; and the Qutb Shâhs of Golkonda.

Âdil Shâh was the first of his line at Bîjapûr, and he proclaimed his independence in A.D. 1489. The unhappy king Mahmûd II. lived in inglorious seclusion till December 18, A.D. 1517, and was nominally succeeded by his eldest son, Ahmad. Ahmad died after two years' reign, and was followed in rapid succession by his two brothers, Alâ-ud-dîn III. (deposed) and Wali (murdered), after whom Kalîm Ullah, son of Ahmad II., was nominally placed on the throne but was kept a close prisoner, and with his death the Bâhmanî dynasty fell for ever.

CHAPTER IX

THE FIRST KINGS OF THE SECOND DYNASTY

(A.D. 1490 to 1509)

Narasimha usurps the throne—Flight of the late king—Sâluva Timma—Vîra Narasimha—Bîjapûr again attacks Vijayanagar—The Portuguese in India—They seize Goa—Varthema's record—Albuquerque.

IN my "Sketch of the Dynasties of Southern India," published in 1883 (p. 106), the following passage occurs :—

"We now come to the second or Narasimha dynasty, whose scions became more powerful than any monarchs who had ever reigned over the south of India. Dr. Burnell fixes A.D. 1490 as the initial date of Narasimha's reign, and at present no inscription that I can be sure of appears to overthrow that statement. I observe, however, that Bishop Caldwell, in his 'History of Tinnevelly' (p. 48), fixes the date of the beginning of Narasimha's . . . reign as A.D. 1487. . . . *We have yet to learn the history of his acquiring the sovereignty of Vijayanagar and ousting the older dynasty.*"

Nothing has since transpired to throw light on this subject, and the whole matter has remained up to the present in its primeval darkness; but this newly-found chronicle of Nuniz gives us the entire story in most interesting form, though I can by no means vouch for its accuracy. It is, nevertheless, a *résumé* of the traditional history of the early sixteenth century, written within fifty or sixty years of the events with which it deals. He tells us that Virûpâksha Râya ("Verupacarao") was a weak and unworthy sovereign, in whose days large tracts of land were lost to the Muhammadans, including Goa, Chaul, and Dabhôl; and this statement, at least, is historically accurate. Virûpâksha was despotic, cruel, and sensuous, "caring for nothing but women and to fuddle himself with drink," so that the whole country was roused to indignation and rebellion. Eventually he was murdered by his eldest son, who in his turn was slain by his brother "Padearao," in whom the nation merely found repeated the crimes and follies of his dead sire. Disgusted with this line of sovereigns, the nobles rose, deposed their king, and placed on the throne one of their own number, Narasimha—"Narsymgua, *who was in some manner akin to him.*"

Nuniz gives us a graphic account of the last scenes; how Narasimha s captain arrived at the city gates and found them undefended; how he penetrated the palace and found no one to oppose him; how he even went as far as the harem, "slaying some of the women;" and how at last the craven king fled.

"After that, Narasymgua was raised to be king. . . . And as he had much power and was beloved by the people, thenceforward this kingdom of Bisnaga was called the kingdom of Narsymga."

The problem of Narasimha's relationship to the old royal line has never yet been satisfactorily solved. He belonged to a family called *Sâluva*, and we constantly hear, in the inscriptions and literary works of the time, of powerful lords who were relations or descendants of his. Thus our chronicle has much to say about the Sâluva Timma, whom Nuniz calls "Salvatinea," who was minister to King Krishna Deva Râya. An inscription of the Saka year 1395, which corresponds to A.D. 1472–73, speaks of Narasimha as a great lord, but a great lord *only*,[1] and so does another of A.D. 1482–83.[2]

[1] Mahâmandalesvara Medinîsvara Gandan Kattâri Sâluva Dharanivarâha Narasimha Râya Udaiyar. These are not the titles of a sovereign. (Hultzsch, "South Indian Inscriptions," i. 131, No. 116).

[2] *Op. cit.*, p. 132, No. 119.

In one of A.D. 1495–96, however,[1] he is called "*Mahâ-Râya*," or the "king." But although the exact date of the usurpation and the exact relationship of the usurper to the deposed king may be difficult to ascertain, the fact remains that Narasimha actually became sovereign about this time, that Muhammadan aggression was stayed by his power and the force of his arms, and that the empire of Vijayanagar was under him once more consolidated.

The account of this period as given by Firishtah differs altogether from that of Nuniz, and gives rise to much confusion and difficulty. And as to the relationship of the succeeding sovereigns, Narasa, Vîra Narasimha, Krishna Deva Râya, Achyuta, and Sadâsiva, the native inscriptions themselves are totally at variance with one another. Some few points, however, in the general scheme of history of the second dynasty are quite certain, and these may be shortly summarised. The last kings of the first dynasty were recognised down to *about* the year 1490 A.D. Narasimha and Vîra Narasimha ruled till the accession of Krishna Deva Râya in 1509; Achyuta succeeded Krishna in 1530, and Sadâsiva succeeded Achyuta in 1542. The latter was virtually a prisoner in the hands of Râma Râya, the eldest of three brothers, at first nominally his minister, but afterwards independent. The names of the other brothers were Tirumala and Venkatâdri. These three men held the government of the kingdom till 1565, when the empire was utterly overthrown by a confederation of the five Muhammadan kings of the Dakhan, already mentioned, at the battle of Talikota—so-called—and the magnificent capital was almost wiped out of existence.

With these few facts to guide us, we turn to the chronicles of Nuniz and Firishtah, trying in vain to

[1] *Op. cit.*, p. 131.

obtain some points of contact between them as to the origin of the second dynasty—some clue which will enable us to reconcile differences and arrive at the real truth. If we are to be guided purely by probabilities, it would seem that the history given by Nuniz is likely to be the more accurate of the two. His chronicle was written about the year 1535, during the reign of Achyuta; he lived at the Hindu capital itself, and he gained his information from Hindu sources not long subsequent to the events related. Firishtah did not write till about A.D. 1607, was not in any sense a contemporary recorder, and did not live amongst the Hindus, but at the court of Nizâm Shâh at Ahmadnagar. The lengths of reigns, however, as given by Nuniz do not tally with the dates which we obtain from sources undoubtedly reliable.

Nuniz has it that Virûpâksha's son "Padearao," the last of the old line, fled from the capital when the usurper Narasimha seized the throne; that the latter reigned forty-four years, and died leaving two sons. These youths being too young to govern, the dying king intrusted the kingdom to his minister, Narasa Naik, and both the princes were murdered. Narasa seized the throne, and held it till his death. The length of his reign is not given. His son, "Busbalrao" (? Basava Râya), succeeded, and reigned six years, being succeeded by his brother, the great Krishna Deva Râya. Now we know that Krishna Deva Râya began to reign in A.D. 1509. This gives 1503 for the date of the accession of his predecessor, "Busbal." If we allow five years for the reign of Narasa—a pure guess—we have his accession in 1498 A.D., and the forty-four years of Narasimha would begin in A.D. 1454; but this would apparently coincide with the reign of Mallikârjuna, son of Deva Râya II. It is perhaps possible that in after years the usurper Narasimha's reign was measured by the Hindus from the time when he began to attain power as minister or as a great noble, and not from the date when he actually became king; but this is pure conjecture.

Firishtah mentions a certain "Sewaroy" as being râja of Vijayanagar in 1482, shortly before the death of Muhammad Shâh Bahmanî. Speaking of the new sovereign of Bîjapûr, the first of the Âdil Shâhs, in 1489, the historian tells us that the Âdil's rival, Kâsim Barîd, asked the then minister of Vijayanagar for aid against the rising power of his enemy;[1] and that "the Roy being a child, his minister, Heemraaje,[2] sent an army" and seized the country as far as Mudkal and Raichûr. This occurred in A.H. 895, which embraces the period from November 1489 to November 1490. "*Heem*raaje," therefore, is probably for *Simha* or Narasimha Râja, or perhaps for Narasa, otherwise called Vîra Narasimha.

Firishtah also gives another account of the same event. According to this, the Âdil Shah, hearing of dissensions in the Hindu capital, marched, apparently in 1493, against Raichûr, when Heemraaje, having settled these dissensions, advanced "with the young Râya" to that city. A battle ensued, in which Heemraaje was defeated; and the young king being mortally wounded, and dying before he reached home, Heemraaje seized the government and the country.

There are, furthermore, two other passages in Firishtah dealing with the overthrow of the old dynasty and the accession of "Heemraaje." One[3] runs as follows:—

---

[1] Scott's "Firishtah," i. pp. 190, 210; Briggs, ii. 537, iii. 10.

[2] Briggs calls him "Timraj" (ii. 538) in all cases, whence I conclude that in this passage Scott's "Ramraaje" is a slip of the pen. It does not occur again. The former translator in the second of the two passages calls "Timraj" the general of the Roy of Beejanuggur.

[3] Scott, i. p. 228.

"Heemraaje was the first usurper. He had poisoned the young Raja of Beejanuggur, son of Sheoroy, and made his infant brother a tool to his designs, by degrees overthrowing the ancient nobility, and at length establishing his own absolute authority over the kingdom."

The other[1] states :—

"The government of Beejanuggur had remained in one family, in uninterrupted succession, for seven hundred years, when Seoroy dying, was succeeded by his son, a minor, who did not live long after him, and left the throne to a younger brother. He also had not long gathered the flowers of enjoyment from the garden of royalty before the cruel skies, proving their inconstancy, burned up the earth of his existence with the blasting wind of annihilation.[2] Being succeeded by an infant only three months old, Heemraaje, one of the principal ministers of the family, celebrated for great wisdom and experience, became sole regent, and was cheerfully obeyed by all the nobility and vassals of the kingdom for forty years; though, on the arrival of the young king at manhood, he had poisoned him, and put an infant of the family on the throne, in order to have a pretence for keeping the regency in his own hands.[3] Heemraaje at his death was succeeded in office by his son, Ramraaje, who having married a daughter of the son of Seoroy, by that alliance greatly added to his influence and power."

He then proceeds to describe an event that took place in 1535 or thereabouts, which will be considered in its place.

Writing of the events of the year 1530,[4] we find Firishtah stating that the affairs of Vijayanagar were then in confusion owing to the death of Heemraaje, who was newly succeeded by his son Ramraaje. And this passage helps us definitely to the conclusion that his Heemraaje, or Timma Râja, was the Muhammadan

[1] Scott, i. p. 262.

[2] This is very similar to the story told by Nuniz of the two sons of Virûpâksha.

[3] This again is similar to the tale Nuniz gives us of the minister Narasa and the two young princes.

[4] Scott, i. p. 252; Briggs, iii. 66.

name for the ruler of the state during the reigns of Narasimha, Narasa or Vîra Narasimha, and Krishna Deva Râya, the latter of whom died in 1530 Firishtah seems to have confused Narasa's and Krishna Deva Râya's powerful minister, Sâluva Timma, with Narasimha and Narasa, and made all three one person. "Ramraaje" is mentioned as king by Firishtah from the accession of Achyuta in 1530 down to the year 1565.

Though names and details differ, it will be observed that there is evidently a common basis of truth in the accounts given by Firishtah and Nuniz. Both relate the deaths of two young princes, brothers, the subsequent murder of two other heirs to the kingdom, and the usurpation of the throne by a minister.

With these remarks we turn to the more reliable portion of Firishtah's narrative.

Yusuf Âdil Khân proclaimed himself independent king of Bîjapûr in A.D. 1489. Shortly afterwards his rival, Kâsim Barîd, who ultimately became sovereign of the territories of Ahmadâbâd, in a fit of jealousy called in the aid of Vijayanagar against Bîjapûr, promising for reward the cession of Mudkal and Raichûr, or the country between the two rivers. Narasimha collected the forces of the Hindus, crossed the Tungabhadrâ with a large army, and after laying waste the country seized the two cities Mudkal and Raichûr, which thus once more passed into the possession of Vijayanagar.

Shortly after this, probably about the year 1493 A.D., Sultan Yusuf Âdil again marched to recover the lost territory and advanced to the Krishnâ, but falling ill he halted for two months; and Firishtah gives us the following account of what occurred. This has been already alluded to, but is now given in full:—

"In this interval Heemraaje, having settled his dissensions,[1] advanced with the young roy at the head of a great army to Roijore, which struck terror into the army of Adil Shaw, for whose recovery earnest prayers were offered up by his subjects." . . . (The prayers were answered and the Sultan recovered.)

"Intelligence arriving that Heemraaje had crossed the Tummedra and was advancing by hasty marches, Eusuff Adil Shaw ordered a general review of his army . . . (and advanced, entrenching his camp a short distance from the Hindus). Several days passed inactively, till on Saturday in Regib 898[2] both armies drew out, and in the beginning of the action near five hundred of Adil Shaw's troops being slain, the rest were disordered and fell back, but were rallied again by the sultan. One of the officers, who had been taken prisoner and made his escape, observed that the enemy were busily employed in plunder, and might be attacked with advantage. The sultan relished this advice and proceeded; when Heemraaje, not having time to collect his whole army, drew out with seven thousand horse and a considerable number of foot, also three hundred elephants. Adil Shaw charged his center with such fury, that Heemraaje was unable to stand the shock. Victory waved the royal standard, and the infidels fled, leaving two hundred elephants, a thousand horses, and sixty lacs of *oons*,[3] with many jewels and effects, to the conquerors. Heemraaje and the young roy fled to Beejanuggur, but the latter died on the road of a wound he had received by an arrow in the action. Heemraaje seized the government of the country; but some of the principal nobility opposing his usurpation, dissensions broke out, which gave Adil Shaw relief from war for some time from that quarter."

The disputed territory between the two rivers once more passed into the hands of the Muhammadans. Goa also remained in the Bîjapûr Sultan's possession.

The last historical event in the reign of Yusuf Âdil

[1] Firishtah has told us in a previous paragraph that "dissensions prevailed in Beejanuggur."

[2] April A.D. 1493.

[3] Scott's note to this is "about one million eight hundred thousand pounds sterling." Briggs (iii. p. 13) says two millions.

Shâh of Bîjapûr, as narrated by Firishtah, is as follows :—

"In the year 915,[1] the Christians surprised the town of Goa, and put to death the governor with many mussulmauns. Upon intelligence of which, Adil Shaw, with three thousand chosen men, Dekkanees and foreigners, marched with such expedition, that he came upon the Europeans unawares, retook the fort, and put many to death; but some made their escape in their ships out to sea."

These Christians were the Portuguese under Albuquerque, and the date of their entry into Goa was March 1, A.D. 1510.

At this period there was a complete change in the *personnel* of the chief actors on our Indian stage. Ahmad Nizâm Shâh, who had declared himself independent at Ahmadnagar in A.D. 1490, died in 1508, and was succeeded by his son, a boy of seven years of age named Burhân, with whom the traveller Garcia da Orta[2] afterwards became very friendly. Da Orta calls him "my friend."[3] Yusuf Âdil Shâh died in A.D. 1510, and his successor on the throne of Bîjapûr was his son Ismâîl. Krishna Deva Râya became Râya of Vijayanagar in 1509. The two last-mentioned monarchs were frequently in contact with one another, and in the end, according to our chronicles, the Hindu king was completely victorious. Even Firishtah admits that he dealt Ismâîl a crushing blow at the great battle of Raichûr, a full description of which is given by Nuniz.

But before dealing with the history of the reign of Krishna Deva Râya it is necessary that we should learn how it came about that these Portuguese Christians who

[1] April 1509 to April 1510.

[2] Da Orta was at Vijayanagar in 1534, at the same time as our chronicler Nuniz.

[3] Colloq., x.

seized Goa came to be living in India, and some of them even resident at the Hindu capital.

THE PORTUGUESE ARRIVE IN INDIA.

King John of Portugal had acquired some knowledge of India in A.D. 1484, and after causing inquiries to be made as to the possibility of discovering the rich and interesting country in the Far East, had begun to fit out three ships, but he died before they were ready. His successor, Dom Manuel, took up the matter warmly, and sent these ships out under Vasco da Gama and his brother Paulo, with orders to try and double the Cape of Good Hope. The full account of the extraordinary voyage made by them is given in the "Three Voyages of Vasco da Gama," translated and published in the Hakluyt edition; being a translation of certain portions of Correa's *Lendas da India.* Da Gama sailed on July 8, A.D. 1497, and arrived close to Calicut on August 26, 1498.[1] The Samuri, or king, of Calicut was at first friendly, but there were misunderstandings on the part of the Portuguese, and they made little or no progress either in trade or in establishing amicable relations with the Hindus. Da Gama returned shortly after to Portugal. Early in 1500 A.D. Cabral took out another and larger fleet, and arrived at Calicut on September 13th. He at once quarrelled with the Samuri, and instead of peaceful commerce we read of attacks and counter-attacks conducted in such sort by the Portuguese as irretrievably to alienate the natives of the country. A few Europeans, however, settled in that tract, and amongst them Duarte Barbosa, the celebrated chronicler of the time.

Da Gama returned to India in 1504, proclaiming

[1] May 20th, according to Barros.

the king of Portugal lord of the seas, and wantonly destroying with all hands a large vessel having several hundred people on board near the Indian coast. He reached Calicut on October 29th, and immediately bombarded the city, seizing the inoffensive native fishermen in the port, eight hundred of whom he massacred in cold blood under circumstances of brutal atrocity. In 1503 he again left for Europe, after establishing a factory at Cochin. In consequence of his violence a war ensued between Cochin and Calicut. In 1504 Lopo Soares came out with a fleet of fourteen caravels, and proclaimed a blockade of the port of Cochin, in spite of the fact that the Râjah of that place had always shown great kindness and hospitality to the Portuguese.

The next year, 1505, Almeida was appointed viceroy of the king of Portugal on the Indian coast, and took out with him a large fleet and 1500 soldiers. After some preliminary fighting at Honawar, Almeida began for the first time to perceive that the true interests of the Portuguese lay in peaceful commerce, and not in sanguinary and costly attacks on the natives; and he also learned from an influential native of the existence of the great kingdom of Vijayanagar and the power of its king, Narasimha (or Narasa). At Cannanore the viceroy's son, Lourenço, in 1506, received further information as to the state of the country from the Italian traveller Varthema, and in consequence of this Almeida asked King Narasa to allow him to erect a fortress at Bhatkal, but no answer was returned.

Varthema has left behind him a valuable account of his experiences[1] at this period. He speaks of Goa as being then under the "Savain," which is this writer's form of expressing the ruler known to the Portuguese

[1] Published by the Hakluyt Society in English.

as the "Sabayo,"[1] who was the governor of the place under the Âdil Shâh of Bîjapûr. The Sabayo was then at war with Narasimha of Vijayanagar.

He describes Vijayanagar as a great city, "very large and strongly walled. It is situated on the side of a mountain,[2] and is seven miles in circumference. It has a triple circlet of walls." It was very wealthy and well supplied, situated on a beautiful site, and enjoying an excellent climate. The king "keeps up constantly 40,000 horsemen" and 400 elephants. The elephants each carry six men, and have long swords fastened to their trunks in battle—a description which agrees with that of Nikitin and Paes. "The common people go quite naked, with the exception of a piece of cloth about their middle. The king wears a cap of gold brocade two spans long. . . His horse is worth more than some of our cities on account of the ornaments which it wears."[3] Calicut, he says, was ruined in consequence of its wars with the Portuguese.

Varthema saw forty-eight Portuguese traders massacred at Calicut by the "Moors," and in consequence of the dangerous state of things existing there he left the city and pursued his journey southwards round the coast. Here we may leave him.

[1] The origin of the name "Sabayo" has often been discussed, and never, I think, quite satisfactorily explained. Several of the old writers have exercised their ingenuity on the question. Barros (Dec. II. l. v. cap. 1) writes: "*Ao tempo que nos entramos na India, era Senhor desta Cidade Goa hum mouro per nome Soai, capitao d'el Rey do Decan, a que communamente chamamos Sabayo*"—"When we arrived in India, the lord of this city of Goa was a Moor, by name Soai, captain of the king of the Dakhan, whom we commonly call Sabayo." But Barros must not always be depended upon for Indian names. He explains "Sabayo" as derived from *Saba* or *Sava*—"Persian," and says that the Sabayo's son was Âdil Shâh. Garcia da Orta derives it from *Sahib*. Burton (*Lusiads*, iii. p. 290) thinks it was a corruption of *Sipahdar* or "military governor."

[2] I have not seen the original, and suspect an error of translation here.

[3] Compare the account given by Paes as to this horse, which he saw at the Mahânavamî festival, and at the review which followed (pp. 272, 278 below).

In March 1506 a Portuguese fleet destroyed, with immense loss of life, a large flotilla of small boats belonging to the Râjah of Calicut. In the next year an outrage committed by the Portuguese led to a siege of their factory at Cannanore, but the timely arrival of Tristan da Cunha with a new fleet from home relieved the beleaguered garrison. At the end of 1507 Almeida and Da Cunha joined forces and again attacked Calicut, with some measure of success.

Afonso d'Albuquerque was now in the Persian seas fighting with all the "Moors" he could meet. At the end of 1509 he became "Governor of India," *i.e.* of Portuguese India, in succession to Almeida; Diogo Lopes de Sequeira receiving the governorship under the king of Portugal of the seas east of Cape Comorin.

From the accession of Krishna Deva Râya to the throne of Vijayanagar in A.D. 1509 we once more enter a period when the history of the country becomes less confused, and we are able to trace the sequence of events without serious difficulty. This was the period of Vijayanagar's greatest successes, when its armies were everywhere victorious, and the city was most prosperous.

CHAPTER X

THE REIGN OF KRISHNA DEVA RÂYA

(A.D. 1509 TO 1530)

His character and person—Bankâpur—Almeida and Fr. Luis's mission—Duarte Barbosa—His description of the city—The king's early wars—Kondapalle—Rajahmundry—Kondavîd—Udayagiri—Wars of the Qutb Shâh of Golkonda in Telingana.

AN inscription in the Pampâpati temple at Hampe states that on the occasion of a festival in honour of the coronation of Krishna Deva Râya, the king built a hall of assembly and a *gopura* or tower there; and the date is given as the 14th of the first half of the lunar month Mâgha in the expired Saka year 1430, the year of the cycle being "Sukla."[1] It so happens that the cyclic year Sukla does not correspond to Saka 1430 expired, but to Saka 1431 expired; and this unfortunate error leaves us in doubt as to the true date of that important event. If we conceive the mistake as having occurred, not in the *name* of the year, which was perhaps in constant daily use, but in the number of the Saka year, then the date corresponds to 23rd or 24th January A.D. 1510; but if the number of the Saka year was correct and the name wrong, then the day must have been February 4, 1509, the cyclic year being properly "Vibhava." Even then it is not certain whether this festival took place on the coronation day itself, or on an anniversary of that event; and a considerable interval may have elapsed between the king's accession and coronation. Probably we shall not be wrong if we

[1] *Epig. Ind.*, i. 366; *Ind. Ant.*, xxiv. 205.

INTERIOR OF THE TEMPLE AT VITTHALASVÂMI

COMMENCED BY KRISHNA DEVA RÂYA

(*From a Photograph by* Col. W. Hooper)

consider that the new king succeeded to the throne in A.D. 1509.[1]

Krishna Râya seems to have possessed a very striking personality, to judge from the glowing description given us by Paes, who saw him about the year 1520. The account given by him is all the more interesting and valuable because without it the world would have remained justly in doubt as to whether this king really reigned at all, in the usual acceptation of the word—whether he was not a mere puppet, entirely in the hands of his minister, perhaps even an actual prisoner. For Firishtah never mentions him by name, and the inscriptions which relate his conquests prove nothing beyond the fact that they took place during a reign which, for all we know, might have been a reign only in name, the real power being in the hands of the nobles. But with the description of Paes in our hands there can be no longer a shadow of doubt. Krishna Deva was not only monarch *de jure*, but was in very practical fact an absolute sovereign, of extensive power and strong personal influence. He was the real ruler. He was physically strong in his best days, and kept his strength up to the highest pitch by hard bodily exercise. He rose early, and developed all his muscles by the use of Indian clubs and the use of the sword; he was a fine rider, and was blessed with a noble presence which favourably impressed all who came in contact with him. He commanded his immense armies in person, was able, brave, and statesmanlike, and was withal a man of much gentleness and generosity of character. He was beloved by all and respected by all. Paes writes of him that he was "gallant and perfect in all things." The only blot

[1] Henry VIII. of England succeeded to the throne on April 22nd of the same year. It is interesting, when reading the description of the splendours of Krishna Râya's court in the narrative of Nuniz, to remember that in Western Europe magnificence of display and personal adornment seems to have reached its highest pitch at the same period.

on his scutcheon is, that after his great success over the Muhammadan king he grew to be haughty and insolent in his demands. No monarch such as the Âdil Shâh could brook for a moment such a humiliation as was implied by a peace the condition of which was that he should kiss his triumphant enemy's foot; and it was beyond all doubt this and similar contemptuous arrogance on the part of successive Hindu rulers that finally led, forty years later, to the downfall of the Hindu empire.

All Southern India was under Krishna Deva's sway, and several quasi-independent chiefs were his vassals. These were, according to Nuniz, the chief of Seringapatam, and those of Bankâpur,[1] Garsopa, Calicut, Bhatkal, and Barkûr. The Portuguese treated these lesser

[1] The chief of Bankâpur seems to have been a Mahratta. Nuniz calls him the "Guym de Bengapor." Albuquerque styles him "King Vengapor" about A.D. 1512 (Hakluyt edit., iii. 187).

Osorio writes:—"*Est autem Vengapor Regio mediterranea, cum Zabaimi regione continens*" (p. 263).

Castanheda states that Albuquerque, then Governor-General of Goa, sent two embassies, one to Vijayanagar and one to "Vengapor," as if the latter were independent; and adds of the chief of Vengapor, "His kingdom is a veritable and safe road to Narsinga, and well supplied with provisions."

Barros speaks of the same event, calling the place "Bengapor" and stating explicitly that its king was "vassal of Narsinga" (or Vijayanagar) (Dec. II. l. v. cap. 3). Subsequently, writing of the chiefs in the same neighbourhood, Barros speaks of two brothers, "Comogij" and "Appagij" (Dec. III. l. iv. cap. 5), and describing Krishna Deva Râya's march towards Raichûr—recapitulating the story and details given by Nuniz—he speaks of "the Gim of the city of Bengapor." In l. v. cap. 3 of the same Decade Barros says that "Bengapor" was "on the road" to Vijayanagar. "Gim," "Guym" and other names appear to be renderings of the Mahratta honorific "Jî."

Bankâpur was one of the most important fortresses in the Karnâtaka country, situated forty miles south of Dhârwâr on the direct road from Honawar to Vijayanagar. The road from Bhatkal, a favourite landing-place, first went northwards to Honawar, then inland to Bankâpur, and thence to Banavâsi, Rânibennûr, and over the plains to Hospett and Vijayanagar. It was known as early as A.D. 848, and remained in possession of Hindu rulers down to 1573, when it was captured by Ali Âdil Shâh and its beautiful temple was destroyed. Firishtah calls the place "Beekapore" and "Binkapor" (Scott's edit., i. 47, 69, 85, 86, 119, 301, &c.).

TOWER OF THE HAMPE TEMPLE, ERECTED BY KRISHNA DEVA RÂYA

chiefs as if they were kings, called them so and sent embassies to them, no doubt much to their satisfaction.

The present head of the Brahmanical establishment at the Hampe temple informed me that Krishna Deva Râya celebrated his accession by erecting the great tower at the entrance of the temple, and the next largest tower shortly afterwards. Nuniz tells us that immediately on attaining power, the king, making Sâluva Timma his minister, sent his nephew, the son of the last sovereign, and his own three brothers, to the fortress of Chandragiri, 250 miles to the south-east, for his greater security, and himself remained for some time at the capital. This accords well with the writings of the other Portuguese, who relate that at least on two occasions, when missions were sent from Calicut and Goa, viz., those of Fr. Luis and Chanoca, the envoys saw the king in person at Vijayanagar.

At the beginning of Krishna's reign, Almeida, as stated above, was viceroy of the Portuguese settlements on the coast, but at the end of the year 1509 Albuquerque succeeded him under the title of governor. The latter suffered a severe reverse at Calicut, and from thence despatched Fr. Luis, of the Order of St. Francis, as ambassador to Vijayanagar, begging the Râya to come by land and reduce the Samuri of Calicut, promising himself to assault simultaneously by sea.[1] The governor declared that he had orders from his master, the king of Portugal, to war against the Moors, but not against the Hindus; that Calicut had been destroyed by the governor, and its king had fled into the interior; that he (the governor) offered his fleet to assist the king of Vijayanagar in his conquest of the place; that as soon as Calicut was captured the Moors would be driven

[1] "Commentaries of Afonso Dalboquerque" (Hakluyt edit., ii. p. 73). Fr. Luis left Cochin, travelled to Bhatkal, and thence to Vijayanagar.

therefrom, and that afterwards the Portuguese would assist the king of Vijayanagar against his enemies, the "Moors" of the Dakhan. He promised in future to supply Vijayanagar alone with Arab and Persian horses, and not to send any to Bîjapûr. No answer was returned.

Albuquerque next attacked Goa, then under the Âdil Shâh, and captured the place, making his triumphal entry into it on March 1, A.D. 1510. Immediately afterwards he despatched Gaspar Chanoca on a mission to Vijayanagar, renewing Almeida's request for a fort at Bhatkal for the protection of Portuguese trade. Barros[1] states that Chanoca reported that, though he was received "solemnly," Krishna Deva Râya only made a general answer in courteous terms, and did not specifically grant the governor's request; the reason being that the king had then made peace with the Âdil Shâh. Presumably this peace was made in order to enable the Âdil Shâh to retake Goa.[2]

Upon this a message was sent from Vijayanagar to Albuquerque congratulating the Portuguese on their conquest of Goa, and promising to aid them against the Âdil Shâh. This aid, however, does not appear to have been given. The Muhammadan troops attacked Goa in May and after a severe struggle were successful, Albuquerque evacuating the place after decapitating a hundred and fifty of the principal Muhammadans there, and slaughtering their wives and children.[3]

In November of the same year, Ismâîl Âdil's attention being called off by internal dissension at Bîjapûr, Albuquerque attacked Rasul Khân, Ismâîl's deputy at Goa, and the eight thousand men under his command, defeated them, retook the place on December 1, and

[1] Dec. II. l. v. cap. 3.

[2] See also Castanheda, who was in India in 1529 (Lib. iii. cap. 12).

[3] As before stated, Firishtah mentions this event (Scott, i. 225).

slew six thousand men, women, and children of the Muhammadans. Firishtah states that the young Âdil Shâh's minister, Kummal Khân, after this made peace with the Europeans, and left them securely established at Goa. This, however, is not quite correct, for Rasul Khân made a desperate attempt in 1512 to retake the place, but failed after severe fighting.[1]

As soon as the news reached Vijayanagar of Albuquerque's success in December 1510, Krishna Deva Râya sent ambassadors to Goa, and by them Fr. Luis sent letters to Albuquerque detailing the result of his mission. He "had been well received by all except the king," but the king had nevertheless granted permission for the Portuguese to build a fort at Bhatkal. Poor Fr. Luis never returned from his embassy. History is silent as to what happened or what led to the tragedy, but he was one day murdered in the city of Vijayanagar.[2]

His despatch is interesting as containing information regarding Vijayanagar and the Sultan of Bîjapûr, part of which is certainly accurate, while part tells us of Krishna Deva Râya's proceedings at this period regarding which we know nothing from any other source. Fr. Luis wrote to Albuquerque that the Âdil Shâh had attacked Bîjapûr, and had taken it after a siege of two months, while four lords had risen against him "since the latter had carried off the king of Decan as a prisoner." This king was the Bâhmanî king, while the Âdil Shâh and the "four lords"

[1] Purchas's summary of the Portuguese conquest of Goa runs as follows: "*Sabaius* (*i.e.* the "Sabayo") when he died, left his sonne *Idalcan* (Âdil Khân) very young; whereupon his Subjects rebelled, and the King of Narsinga warred upon him, to dispossesse him of his Dominion. Albuquerque, taking his opportunitie, besieged and . . . took Goa with the Iland. Which was soon after recovered by Idalcan, comming with a strong Armie thither, the Portugals flying away by night. But when the King of Narsinga again invaded Idalcan, He was forced to resist the more dangerous Enemy, leaving a strong Garrison at Goa, which yet *Albuquerk* overcame, and sacked the Citie." Purchas's work was published (folio) in 1626. He merely follows Barros (Dec. I. l. viii. cap. 10).

[2] "Commentaries of Afonso Dalboquerque" (Hakluyt edit., iii. 35).

were the revolting Muhammadan princes. He added that the people of Belgaum had revolted from the Âdil Shâh and submitted to the Hindu sovereign. As to Vijayanagar, he said that the king was getting ready a small expedition of seven thousand men to send against one of his vassals, who had risen up in rebellion and seized the city of Pergunda (? Pennakonda), saying that it belonged to himself by right; and that after he had taken the rebel the king would proceed to certain places on the sea-coast. Fr. Luis professed himself unable to understand the drift of this latter design, but warned Albuquerque to be careful. He advised him to keep up friendly communications with the king, and by no means to place any reliance on the man on whom, of all others, the Portuguese had pinned their faith—one Ṭimoja,[1] a Hindu who had befriended the new-comers. The priest declared that Timoja was a traitor to them, and had, in conjunction with the king of Garsopa, promised Krishna Deva Râya that he would deliver Goa to him before the Portuguese could fortify their possessions therein, if he should send a fully equipped army to seize the place.

After Albuquerque's second capture of Goa the chief of Bankâpur also sent messages of congratulation to the Portuguese, and asked for permission to import three hundred horses a year. The request was granted, as the place was on the road to Vijayanagar, and it was important that its chief should be on friendly terms with the Europeans. Moreover, Bankâpur contained a number of superior saddlers.[2]

Krishna Deva's anxiety was to secure horses. He must have thought little of this foreign settlement on the coast as a political power, but what he wanted was horses, and again horses, for his perpetual wars against the Âdil Shâh; and Albuquerque, after toying

[1] The name may represent "Timma Râja."

[2] "Commentaries of Dalboquerque," iii. pp. 246–247

a little with the Muhammadan, gratified the Hindu by sending him a message in which he declared that he would prefer to send cavalry mounts to him rather than to supply them to the Sultan of Bîjapûr.

About the year 1512 Krishna Deva Râya, who had taken advantage of the times to invade the Sultan's dominions, attacked the fortress of Raichûr, which at last was given up to him by the garrison; Ismâîl Âdil being too much employed in attending to the internal affairs of his government to afford it timely relief. So says Firishtah.[1] This event is not noticed by Nuniz, who writes as if the Râya's first campaign against the Âdil Shâh took place in 1520, when he advanced to attack Raichûr, it being then in the Shâh's possession; and here we see a difference between the story of Nuniz and the story of Firishtah, for the latter, writing of the same event, viz., the campaign of 1520, states that "Ismail Adil Shaw made preparations for marching to recover Mudkal and Roijore from the Roy of Beejanuggar," he having taken these cities about 1512, as narrated. Which account is correct I cannot say.

It appears[2] that in 1514 A.D. Krishna Deva offered Albuquerque £20,000 for the exclusive right to trade in horses, but the Portuguese governor, with a keen eye to business, refused. A little later the Hindu king renewed his proposal, declaring his intention of making war against the Âdil Shâh; and the Âdil Shâh, hearing of this message, himself sent an embassy to Goa. Albuquerque was now placed in a position of some political importance, and he wrote first to Vijayanagar saying that he would give the Râya the refusal of all his horses if he would pay him 30,000 cruzados per annum for the supply, and send his own servants to Goa to fetch away the animals, and also that he

[1] Firishtah (Scott), i. p. 236.

[2] "Commentaries of Dalboquerque," iv. 121.

would aid the king in his war if he was paid the expense of the troops; and he wrote afterwards to Bîjapûr promising the Sultan the refusal of all horses that came to Goa if he would surrender to the king of Portugal a certain portion of the mainland opposite the island. Before this matter was settled, however, Albuquerque died.

We learn from this narrative that Krishna Deva Râya was meditating a grand attack on the Muhammadans at least five years before his advance to Raichûr—a year even before his expedition against Udayagiri and the fortresses on the east, the story of which campaign is given in our chronicle.

We have an account of what Vijayanagar was like in A.D. 1504–14 in the narrative of Duarte Barbosa, a cousin of Magellan, who visited the city during that period.

Speaking of the "kingdom of Narsinga," by which name the Vijayanagar territories were always known to the Portuguese, Barbosa writes:[1] "It is very rich, and well supplied with provisions, and is very full of cities and large townships."

He describes the large trade of the seaport of Bhatkal on its western coast, the exports from which consisted of iron, spices, drugs, myrabolans, and the imports of horses and pearls; but as regards the last two items he says, "They now go to Goa, on account

[1] "East Africa and Malabar" (Hakluyt edit., pp. 78, &c.). Barbosa was son of Diego Barbosa, who sailed in the first fleet sent out under João de Nova in 1501. He gives no dates in his own writings except that he finished his work in 1516 (Preface), after "having navigated for a great part of his youth in the East Indies." It was probably begun about 1514. He was certainly in the Indian Ocean in 1508–9. The heading of the work is "Description of the East Indies and Countries on the sea-board of the Indian Ocean in 1514." It was published in Spanish (translated from the Portuguese) in 1524. The copy in the Library at Barcelona is said to be the oldest extant.

of the Portuguese." The governor of Bhatkal was a nephew of King Krishna Deva. "He lives in great state and calls himself king, but is in obedience to the king, his uncle."

Leaving the sea-coast and going inland, Barbosa passed upwards through the ghâts.

"Forty-five leagues from these mountains there is a very large city which is called *Bijanaguer*, very populous, and surrounded on one side by a very good wall, and on another by a river, and on the other by a mountain. This city is on level ground; the king of Narsinga always resides in it. He is a gentile, and is called Raheni.[1] He has in this place very large and handsome palaces, with numerous courts. . . . There are also in this city many other palaces of great lords, who live there. And all the other houses of the place are covered with thatch, and the streets and squares are very wide. They are constantly filled with an innumerable crowd of all nations and creeds. . . . There is an infinite trade in this city. . . . In this city there are many jewels which are brought from Pegu and Celani (Ceylon), and in the country itself many diamonds are found, because there is a mine of them in the kingdom of Narsinga and another in the kingdom of Decani. There are also many pearls and seed-pearls to be found there, which are brought from Ormuz and Cael . . . also silk-brocades, scarlet cloth, and coral. . . .

"The king constantly resides in the before-mentioned palaces, and very seldom goes out of them. . . .

"All the attendance on the king is done by women, who wait upon him within doors; and amongst them are all the employments of the king's household; and all these women live and find room within these palaces, which contain apartments for all. . . .

"This king has a house[2] in which he meets with the governors and his officers in council upon the affairs of the

[1] This name awaits explanation.

[2] This probably refers to the highly decorated building in the interior of what I believe to have been the Government offices, surrounded by a lofty wall with watch-towers, and often called "The Zenana." The elephant stables lie to the east of it. The building in question is "No. 29 Council Room" on the Government plan.

realm. . . . They come in very rich litters on men's shoulders. . . . Many litters and many horsemen always stand at the door of this palace, and the king keeps at all times nine hundred elephants and more than twenty thousand horses, all which elephants and horses are bought with his own money. . . . This king has more than a hundred thousand men, both horse and foot, to whom he gives pay. . . .

"When the king dies four or five hundred women burn themselves with him. . . . The king of Narsinga is frequently at war with the king of Dacani, who has taken from him much of his land; and with another gentile king of the country of Otira (apparently Orissa), which is the country in the interior."

Barbosa mentions that the lord of Goa, before the Portuguese attack on the place, was "Sabaym Delcani," meaning the king of the Dakhan, and he alludes to its first capture by Albuquerque on 25th February 1510, and the second on 25th November of the same year.

We learn from other sources that about this time Krishna Deva Râya was engaged with a refractory vassal in the Maisûr country, the Ganga Râjah of Ummatûr, and was completely successful. He captured the strong fortress of Sivasamudra and the fortress of Srirangapattana, or Seringapatam, reducing the whole country to obedience.

In 1513 A.D. he marched against Udayigiri, in the present district of Nellore, an exceedingly strong hill-fortress then under the king of Orissa,[1] and after the successful termination of the war he brought with him from a temple on the hill a statue of the god Krishna, which he set up at Vijayanagar and endowed with a grant of lands. This is commemorated by a long inscription still in existence at the capital. It was then that the great temple of Krishnasvâmi was built, which, though now in ruins, is still one of the most interesting objects in the city. This is also attested by a long

[1] Barbosa in A.D. 1514 mentions this expedition.

RUINS OF PALACE AT KONDAPALLE

inscription on stone, still in its place. The king further built the temple of Hazâra Râmasvâmi near, or in, his palace enclosure, at the same time.

Nuniz relates that at Udayagiri Krishna Râya captured an aunt of the king of Orissa and took her prisoner to Vijayanagar. He next proceeded against Kondavîd, another very strong hill-fortress also in possession of the king of Orissa, where he met and defeated the king in person in a pitched battle, and captured the citadel after a two months' siege. He left Sâluva Timma here as a governor of the conquered provinces, and went in pursuit of his enemy northwards. Nuniz says that Sâluva Timma appointed his own brother captain of Kondavîd, but an inscription at that place gives us the name of this man as Nâdendla Gopamantri, and calls him a nephew of Timma. Kondavîd seems to have been under the kings of Orissa since A.D. 1454; its capture by Krishna Deva took place in 1515.[1] To confirm our chronicler's account of the king's northward journey, I find that there is at the town of Mêdûru, twenty-two miles south-east of Bezvâda on the Krishnâ, an inscription which states that in 1516 a battle took place there between Krishna Deva and some enemy whose name is obliterated, in which the former was victorious.

The king advanced to Kondapalle, took the place after a three months' siege, and captured therein a wife and son of the king of Orissa. The unhappy fate of the latter is told in the chronicle. Thence he marched to Râjahmundry and halted six months. Peace was made shortly after, and Krishna Deva married a daughter of the Orissan king.[2] After this marriage

[1] An inscription at Kondavîd glorifying Sâluva Timma states that he took the fortress on Saturday, June 23, A.D. 1515 (Âshâdha Sukla Harivâsara Saurau, Saka 1437). This information was kindly supplied to me by Dr. Lüders.

[2] There is a long inscription in the temple of Varadarâjasvâmi at Conjeeveram exactly confirming this whole story. It relates that the king

King Krishna made an expedition against a place in the east which Nuniz calls "Catuir," on the Coromandel side, and took it. I have been unable to locate this place.

By these conquests the whole of his eastern dominions were brought into entire subjection to the sovereign.

Nuniz writes as though the attack on Raichûr immediately followed the campaign against Udayagiri, Kondavîd, and "Catuir," but, according to the evidence afforded by inscriptions, these expeditions were at an end in 1515, and the battle of Raichûr did not take place for at least five years later.

A long account of wars in the south-eastern Dakhan country between Sultan Qulî Qutb Shâh of Golkonda and his neighbours, both Mussulman and Hindu, is given in the third volume of Colonel Briggs' "Firishtah,"[1] translated from a Muhammadan historian—not Firishtah himself; and as this certainly covers the period of at least a portion of Krishna Deva's reign, it is well to give a summary of it. I cannot, however, as yet determine the exact dates referred to, and the story differs from that acquired from Hindu and Portuguese accounts, the dates of which are confirmed by epigraphical records.

Sultan Qulî proclaimed himself an independent sovereign in 1512. The historian referred to states that shortly after this Qulî attacked and took Râzukonda and Devarakonda, fortresses respectively south-east and south-south-east of Hyderâbad in Telingana. After the second of these places had fallen Krishna Râya of Vijayanagar marched against the Sultan with an immense army and invaded his dominions. This

first captured Udayagiri, Bellamkonda, Vinukonda, Kondavîd, and other places; then Bezvâda and Kondapalle, and finally Rajahmundry.

[1] Pp. 354 to 371.

must, I think, refer to about the year 1513. The Hindu army encamped at Pangul, in the angle of the Krishnâ river almost due east of Raichûr, and here a battle took place in which the Qutb Shâh was victorious. The place was then besieged; it capitulated, and the Muhammadans proceeded to Ghânpura, twenty miles to the north. This fort was captured after heavy loss, and the Sultan led his army to Kovilkonda, twenty miles to the north-west, on the borders of the country of Bîdar, the territory of Alâ-ud-dîn Imâd Shâh. This place also fell.

A war with the Imâd Shâh followed, in which Sultan Qulî was again victorious. Shortly afterwards there were disturbances on the east of the Golkonda territories. Sîtapati, Râjah of Kambampêta, on the Muniyêr river, who possessed extensive territories—including Warangal and Bellamkonda, a fortress south of the Krishnâ—rose against the Muhammadans, and the Sultan marched against Bellamkonda, which, after a long siege, he captured. Sîtapati then fought a pitched battle, was defeated, and fled, Qulî returning to Golkonda. The Râjah then stirred up a number of neighbouring chiefs and assembled large forces at Kambampeta. Hearing of this, the Golkonda forces marched to attack them, and met with complete success, Sîtapati flying to the protection of "Ramchunder Dew, the son of Gujputty, who held his court at Condapilly," and was king of Orissa. The Sultan advanced and attacked Kambampêta, where, after his capture of the place, he slew every man, woman, and child in the city, seizing the females of Sîtapati's household for his own seraglio. Meanwhile an immense Hindu host from all the countries about, under command of the king of Orissa, prepared to do battle for their country, and a decisive action took place near the river at Palinchinûr, in which the Hindus were completely defeated. Quli then seized Kondapalle, Ellore, and Rajahmundry, and a treaty was made between him and Orissa fixing the Godâvarî river as the eastern boundary of Golkonda. By this the Sultan added the districts of Ellore and Bezvâda to his own dominions.

Krishna Râya then advanced to the rescue and the Sultan marched to Kondavîd. He invested the place, but was forced to retreat owing to attacks made on him from Bellamkonda and Vinukonda, the first of which fortresses he succeeded in reducing after heavy loss. After this he retired towards Kondapalle. Krishna Râya now arrived and attacked the Muhammadan garrison in Bellamkonda, upon which the Sultan countermarched, and suddenly appeared in rear of the Hindu army. In the battle which ensued he was victorious and the siege was raised, after which he returned to Kondavîd and took it. On learning of the fall of Kondavîd, Krishna Râya detached "his general and son-in-law Seeva Ray"[1] with 100,000 foot and 8000 horse to march against the Muhammadans. The Sultan retreated and encamped on the banks of the Krishnâ, leaving Kondavîd to the Hindus.[2] After settling the place the Vijayanagar forces proceeded in pursuit of the Sultan, were attacked by him, defeated, and retired to Kondavîd, which was a second time invested by the army of Golkonda. The Hindus then submitted and agreed to become tributary.

On his return towards his capital the Sultan learned that Ismâîl Âdil Shâh of Bîjapûr was besieging Kovilkonda, "at the instance of the Raja of Beejanuggur."[3]

[1] Krishna Râya in 1515 was only about twenty-nine years old, but we must not forget the Hindu custom of the marriages of girls while infants.

[2] If this refers to Krishna Râya's capture of that place in 1515, it is to be noted here that Nuniz asserts that it was taken, not from the Muhammadans, but from the king of Orissa.

[3] Firishtah's account of this is that Ismâîl Âdil joined with Amîr Barîd in an attack on Telingana and laid siege to Kovilkonda. Vijayanagar had no part in the causes of the campaign.

He marched against him, and a series of actions ensued, the campaign lasting eleven months, at the end of which Ismâîl died of a fever, and was succeeded by his son Malu. In one of the fights Sultan Qulî was wounded severely by a sabre in the face, and disfigured for life.[1]

I have given the whole of this story in this place because it runs as a consecutive series of events in the original Muhammadan account. But it really covers a period of at least twenty-one years; for the narrative begins shortly after the beginning of Qulî's reign (1512), and ends with Ismâîl's death (1534). We are left, therefore, entirely in the dark as to the exact years referred to. But there are some points of agreement between our authorities. It is certain that Krishna Deva took Kondavîd in A.D. 1515, and fought battles in the neighbourhood in the following year; and though Nuniz asserts that he took Kondavîd from the king of Orissa, he also alludes to the presence of armed bodies of Muhammadans in that tract opposed to the Hindus.

With these remarks we return to Vijayanagar history.

From 1516 to 1520 we have no records from Hindu sources to guide us as to events at the capital.

The Portuguese traded on the coast, and there were some fights with the neighbouring Hindu chiefs, but they seem to have affected the capital but little; the foreigners were generally on friendly terms with the suzerain at Vijayanagar, and so far as he was concerned were welcome to consolidate their commerce, since he benefited largely by the import of horses and other requisites. The rest of his dominions were tranquil and the inhabitants obedient to his rule.

The whole country was divided out—so Nuniz tells us, and his account is confirmed by other evidence—into

[1] Firishtah tells this story of Jamshîd Qutb Shâh, Qulî's successor (1543–50).

governorships. Each chief was allowed entire independence in the territory allotted to him so long as he maintained the quota of horse, foot, and elephants, the maintenance of which was the price of his possession, in perfect readiness for immediate action, and paid his annual tribute to the sovereign. Failing these he was liable to instant ejection, as the king was lord of all and the nobles held only by his goodwill.

But during this period of peace the king made extensive preparations for a grand attack on the territory between the rivers, the ever-debatable land which for nearly two centuries had been the subject of dispute between his predecessors and their northern neighbours. His objective was the city of Raichûr, then under the Muhammadans,[1] and when all was ready he marched to the attack with an immense force.

This event requires a chapter to itself.

[1] So says Nuniz, but, as before stated, Firishtah differs. In my opinion we must accept the former as correct, for his account is so graphic and detailed that it is impossible to believe that he could have been mistaken. Firishtah did not write for many years later and was much more liable to error. Several Portuguese were present at the siege, and, if I am not mistaken, either Nuniz was there himself, or obtained his information from those who were so. The story bears all the marks of a personal narrative.

CHAPTER XI

THE SIEGE AND BATTLE OF RAICHÛR, AND CLOSE OF KRISHNA'S REIGN

(A.D. 1520 TO 1530)

The date of the siege—Evidence of Castanheda, Correa, Barros, Faria y Souza, Osorio, Lafitau, Firishtah—Ruy de Mello and the mainlands of Goa—Immense numbers engaged—Firishtah's story of the fight—Portuguese present—Christovão de Figueiredo—Political effects of the Hindu victory, and the events that followed it—The mainlands of Goa.

I SHALL ask my readers to turn for an account of the great battle and siege of Raichûr to the narrative of Nuniz,[1] whose description is so full and so vivid that it may well be allowed to stand by itself. It is only necessary for me to add a few notes.

The following is a short summary of the story:—

Krishna Deva Râya, having determined to attack the Âdil Shâh and once for all to capture the disputed fortress of Raichûr, collected all his forces, and marched with an immense host from Vijayanagar in a north-easterly direction. It was the dry season, and he probably set out in February or March. The weather must have been intensely hot during his advance, and still more so during the campaign; but the cotton plains that lay on his route out and home were then in the best condition for the passage of his troops, guns, and baggage. His enormous army consisted of about a million of men, if the camp-followers be included; for the fighting men alone, according to Nuniz, numbered about 736,000, with 550 elephants. The troops advanced in eleven great divisions or army corps, and other troops joined him before Raichûr.

[1] Pp. 323 to 347 below.

He pitched his camp on the eastern side of that citadel, invested the place, and began a regular siege. After an interval he received intelligence of the arrival of the Âdil Shâh from Bîjapûr, on the north side of the Krishnâ, with an army of 140,000 horse and foot to oppose him.

Having for a few days rested his troops, the Sultan crossed the river, advanced (according to Nuniz) to within nine miles of Raichûr, and there entrenched himself, leaving the river about five miles in his rear.[1] Firishtah, however, differs, and says that the Muhammadan forces crossed directly in face of the Hindu army encamped on the opposite bank.

On Saturday morning, May 19, in the year A.D. 1520, according to my deductions, the forces became engaged, and a decisive pitched battle was fought. Krishna Deva, making no attempt to outflank his adversary, ordered an advance to his immediate front of his two forward divisions. Their attack was so far successful that they drove the Muhammadans back to their trenches. The Sultan had apparently deployed his force over too wide an area, expecting that the Râya would do the same; but finding himself weak in the centre he opened fire from the guns that he had previously held in reserve, and by this means caused great loss in the close ranks of the Hindus. The Râya's troops fell back in face of this formidable bombardment, and at once their enemies charged them. The retreat was changed to a rout, and for a mile and a half to their direct front the Mussulman cavalry chased

[1] On the Ordnance Map I observe on the river-bank, thirteen miles N.N.E. of Raichûr, a plan of what appears to be a large fortified camp, with its base on the river, the average of its west, south, and east faces being about a mile each. It lies just below the junction of the Bhîma and Krishnâ rivers, and two miles west of the present railway station on the latter river. What this may be I know not, but it looks like the remains of an entrenched camp erected in some former year. Perhaps some one will examine the place.

the flying forces belonging to Krishna Deva's first line. The king himself, who commanded the second line, began to despair of victory, but rallied his troops, collected about him a number of his nobles, and determined to face death with the bravery that had always characterised him. Mounting his horse, he ordered a forward movement of the whole of his remaining divisions, and charged the now disordered ranks of the Mussulmans. This resulted in complete success, for the enemy, scattered and unable to form, fled before his impetuous onslaught. He drove them the whole way back to, and into, the river, where terrific slaughter took place, and their entire army was put to flight.

The Râya then crossed the river and seized the Shâh's camp, while the Shâh himself, by the counsel and help of Asada Khân, a man who afterwards became very famous, escaped only with his life, and fled from the field on an elephant.

While being driven back towards the river, Salâbat Khân, the Shâh's general, made a valiant attempt to retrieve the fortunes of the day. He had for his bodyguard 500 Portuguese "renegades," and with him these men threw themselves into the advancing ranks of the Hindus, where they "did such wonderful deeds" that ever after they were remembered. They penetrated the king's host, and cut their way forwards till they almost reached his person. Here Salâbat Khân lost his horse, but at once mounted another and pressed on. The little force was, however, surrounded and annihilated, and the general, being a second time overthrown, horse and all, was made prisoner.

The spoil was great and the result decisive. For years afterwards the "Moors" cherished a wholesome dread of Krishna Râya and his valiant troops, and the Sultan, panic-stricken, never again during his enemy's lifetime ventured to attack the dominions of Vijayanagar.

Krishna Deva, flushed with victory, returned at once to the attack of Raichûr, and the fortress was after a short time captured.

Its fall was due in great measure to the assistance rendered by some Portuguese, headed by Christovão de Figueiredo, who with their arquebusses picked off the defenders from the walls, and thus enabled the besiegers to approach close to the lines of fortification and pull down the stones of which they were formed. Driven to desperation, and their governor being slain, the garrison surrendered.

Date of the Battle.

Now as to the date of this battle.

I am bold enough to believe, and defend my belief, that when Nuniz fixed the day of the great fight as the new moon day of the month of May, A.D. 1522, he made a mistake in the year, and should have written "1520."

The chronicler states that Krishna Deva was prepared to give battle on a Friday, but was persuaded by his councillors to postpone his attack till the following day, Friday being unlucky. The battle accordingly took place on the Saturday, which was the new moon day.

Before proceeding to examine the month and day, let us consider the year A.D. of the battle.

Paes describes two grand festivals at the capital of which he was an eye-witness, and at which Christovão de Figueiredo was present. He fixes definitely the days on which these occurred. The first was the nine-days *Mahânavamî* festival, and the second was the festival of the New Year's Day. Paes states that on the occasion when he was present the *Mahânavamî* began on September 12 ("*estas festas se começão a doze dias de setêbro e durão nove dias*"[1]), and the latter began on October 12 ("*entramdo o mes d outubro a omze dias amdados d ele . . . neste dia começão o anno, e dia d anno bom . . . comecão o anno neste mes com a lua nova, e elles não contão o mes se não de lua a lua*").[2] Previously to this, when writing about Raichûr, Paes has described that place[3] as a city "that formerly belonged to the king of Narsymga (*i.e.* Vijayanagar); there has been much war over it, and *this king* took it from the Ydallcão" (Âdil Shâh). The chronicler, therefore, was present at these feasts on an occasion subsequent to the date of Krishna Deva's conquest of Raichûr.

Now the *Mahânavamî* festival begins in these tracts on the 1st of the month of Âsvina, and the New Year's Day in the time of Paes was evidently celebrated on the 1st of the month Kârttika, as was often the case in former years; both days being the days following the moment of new moon. In what year, then, during the reign of Krishna Deva Râya, did the 1st of Âsvina and the 1st of Kârttika fall respectively on September 12 and on October 12? I have worked these dates out for all the years of the reign, and I find that in no year except A.D. 1520 did this occur. In 1521 the *Mahânavamî* fell on September 2, and the New Year's Day on October 1; in 1522 the former fell on September 20, and the latter on October 20. This shows that Paes assisted at the festivals of A.D. 1520, and that therefore the battle and capture of Raichûr must have taken place before the month of September in that year.

This again throws fresh light on the magnificent

[1] Below, p. 263. "These feasts begin on the twelfth of September, and they last nine days."

[2] Below, p. 281. "At the beginning of the month of October when eleven of its days had passed. . . . On this day begins their year; it is their New Year's Day. . . . They begin the year in this month with the new moon, and they count the months always from moon to moon."

[3] Below, p. 243.

reception accorded to Christovão de Figueiredo by the king, and the latter's exceptional kindness to the Portuguese at the time of these feasts.[1] Krishna Râya cherished an especial fondness for Christovão on account of his invaluable aid at the siege of the city, and for the fact that but for him the war might have lasted much longer.

Let us now turn to the other Portuguese writers, and see whether they confirm our date, 1520, for the fall of Raichûr.

The decision of this question turns mainly on the date when the Portuguese obtained the mainlands opposite the island of Goa, consisting of the tracts called Salsette, Ponda, and Bardes. It seems certain that this capture of the mainlands took place by Krishna Deva's connivance shortly after the fall of Raichûr, at a time when Diogo Lopes de Sequeira, the governor-general, was away at the Red Sea, and when Ruy de Mello was governor of Goa. Now Sequeira left Goa for the Red Sea on February 13, A.D. 1520, and arrived again before Diu in India on February 9, 1521.

Castanheda tells us (and he is a good authority, since he was in India in 1529) that while Sequeira was absent at the Red Sea war broke out between the king of Vijayanagar and the Âdil Shâh,[2] at the close of which the latter was defeated and put to flight, while the Hindus took Raichûr and other places—

"so that many of the *Tanadâris*[3] near Goa on the mainland were left undefended. And since the king of Narsinga was

---

[1] "On the upper platform, close to the king, was Christovão de Figueiredo, with all of us who came with him, for the king commanded that he should be in such a place, so as best to see the feasts and magnificence." (Paes, p. 264 below.)

[2] Lib. v. c. 57.

[3] *Tanadaris* are small local divisions of the kingdom, each under its own petty official. A *thânâh* is a police-station in modern parlance. I can think of no English word exactly suitable, but, as far as area is concerned, perhaps the term "parish" would best express the meaning.

very rich, and had no need of these lands, and wanted that all the horses that came to Goa should come to him and none to the *Hidalcão*, he sent to say to Ruy de Mello, captain of Goa, that he had taken Belgaum by force of arms from the Hidalcão, with all the land appertaining to it as far as the sea, in which were *Tanadaris* yielding more than 500,000 gold pardaos, of which he desired to make a present to the king of Portugal . . . and that he wanted all the horses that came to Goa. He therefore said that the captain of Goa could enter and take possession of the *Tanadaris*."

This was immediately done, and Ruy de Mello took possession of the mainland of Goa, including Salsette, in ten days.

Correa, who was in India at the time, having gone thither in 1512 or 1514, mentions[1] that de Sequeira left Goa for the Red Sea in January 1520, and that "at that time" (*neste tempo*—the expression is unfortunately vague) war broke out between Vijayanagar and Bîjapûr. After its close the Hindu king sent a message to "Ruy de Mello, captain of Goa," in the absence of the governor-general, regarding the mainlands of Goa. Correa does not mention distinctly the year in which this occurred, but the edition of 1860 at the head of the page has the date "1521." This, however, must be an error on the part of the editor, for in May 1521 Sequeira was not absent, and therefore the year referred to cannot be 1521; while in May 1522 Dom Duarte de Menezes, and not Sequeira, was governor-general.[2] Sequeira sailed for Portugal January 22, A.D. 1522.

Barros relates the departure of de Sequeira from India for the Red Sea on February 13, 1520, and states

[1] *Lendas da India*, ii. 581.

[2] Menezes assumed charge of the Viceroyalty on January 22, 1522. A short summary of Sequeira's career is given in the interesting MS. volume called the *Livro das Fortalezas da India*, of which the text was written by Antonio Bocarro, and the numerous portraits and plans were drawn and coloured by Pero Barretto de Rezenda. The British Museum copy is in the Sloane Collection, and bears the number "197."

that in his absence Ruy de Mello was governor of Goa, under Sequeira's lieutenant, Aleixo de Menezes. Ruy de Mello seized the mainland of Goa after the battle of Raichûr,[1] and at that time de Sequeira was absent at the Red Sea. His description of the siege of Raichûr and the great battle in the vicinity clearly seems to have been taken from the chronicle of Nuniz. It follows the latter blindly, even in the misspelling of names, and therefore is really of no greater value. When, however, Barros comes to deal with the acquisition of the mainlands of Goa,[2] he is dependent on other information, and gives a much more detailed account. The time is clearly fixed. After the battle and flight of the Âdil Shâh the feeling between the two adversaries was naturally highly strained, and this "enabled Ruy de Mello, captain of Goa, to take the mainlands of Goa." Sequeira was at the Red Sea and Menezes at Cochin. A very important passage for my present purpose occurs a little later on in Barros's work:[3]—

> "Diogo Lopes de Sequeira, as soon as he arrived at Goa (from the Red Sea), all necessary arrangements having been made for the government of the city, *and principally of the mainlands, which he found that Ruy de Mello had taken* . . . went to Cochin;"

and thence to Diu, where he arrived on February 9, 1521.[4] Another passage farther on in the narrative of Barros also establishes the fact that Ruy de Mello took the lands during Sequeira's absence at the Red Sea.[5]

Faria y Souza, a Spanish writer, whose work was first published a century after these events, confirms the period, February 1520 to February 1521, as that of Sequeira's absence at the Red Sea, and he writes:—

---

[1] Dec. III. l. iv. cap. 4.
[2] *Idem*, cap. 5.
[3] *Idem*, cap. 8.
[4] *Idem*, cap. 9.
[5] *Idem*, cap. 10.

"While the governor[1] was in the Red Sea, the King Crisnao Rao of Bisnaga covered the plains and hills and stopped the flow of the rivers[2] with an army of thirty-five thousand horse, seven hundred and thirty-three thousand foot, and five hundred and eighty-six elephants carrying castles with four men in each, and twelve thousand watermen . . . and baggage in such quantities that the courtesans alone numbered more than twenty thousand."[3]

Souza also states, as does Nuniz, that after the defeat of the Âdil Shâh, Krishna Deva Râya demanded that, as the price of peace, the former should visit him and kiss his foot; and that, taking advantage of the Âdil Shâh's difficulties, Ruy de Mello seized the mainlands of Goa.[4] It is clear, therefore, that both authors are writing of the same event.

Osorio, a later writer, confirms the story in most of its details, stating that after the defeat of the Âdil Shâh, Krishna Râya sent to Ruy de Mello ("Roderigo Melos"), captain of Goa, offering the mainlands, and promising after the return of Sequeira to send a regular embassy to conclude a solemn treaty. De Mello accordingly took the mainlands.

Lafitau[5] also states that the war took place during Sequeira's absence at the Red Sea, and that the mainlands were taken after the Âdil Shâh's defeat.[6]

Turning to Firishtah, I find a difference. He states that the battle of Raichûr took place in Hijra 927

1 "Asia Portugueza" of Faria y Souza, I. Pt. iii. cap. 4 (Stevens' translation).

2 Compare Nuniz (text, p. 329).

3 These numbers are probably taken from Barros, who copied Nuniz.

4 "Asia Portugueza," I. Pt. iii. cap. 4, sec. 5. "Ruy de Mello, que estava a Goa, viendo al Hidalchan divertido con sus ruinas ó esperanças, ó todo junto, y a muchos en perciales remolinos robando la tierra firme de aquel contorno, ganóla facilmente con dozientos y sincuenta cavallos, y ochocientos peones Canaries."

5 "Histoire des Descouvertes et Conquestes des Portugais" (Paris, 1733).

6 Danvers, "The Portuguese in India," i. 347, gives us the same dates for Sequeira's absence, and mentions De Figueiredo's presence at the battle of Raichûr.

(December 12, 1520, to December 1, 1521, A.D.), which, if it was fought in May, as Nuniz declares, makes the date May 1521. That he is speaking of the same affair is obvious from the details given. He mentions, for instance, the vast host constituting the Hindu army, the Shâh's force advancing to the river Krishnâ, the too hasty crossing of the river, the gallant fight of the Muhammadans, their defeat and rout, the fact of the Âdil Shâh's forces being driven to the river and perishing in large numbers while attempting to re-cross it, the Shâh's narrow escape, and his dependence on Asada Khân. All this leaves no room for doubt. The only difference is that, whereas we learn from the other authorities that the fortress of Raichûr was in the hands of the Muhammadans, Firishtah states that the war arose because the Âdil Shâh "made preparations for marching to recover Mudkul and Roijore from the Roy of Beejanuggur," as if the latter were then in possession of those places. As to Firishtah's date, I believe it to be wrong by one year, for the reasons given above. It must be remembered that he wrote many years after the event.

Having thus, I hope satisfactorily, established the fact that the date given by Nuniz for the battle of Raichûr is wrong by two years, and should be 1520, I turn to examine the day and month. It was the new moon day of May, according to Nuniz, and a Saturday. Krishna Deva Râya was ready for battle on the Friday, but postponed his attack to the next day since Friday was considered an unlucky day.

The moment of the occurrence of new moon in May 1520 was 2.27 A.M. on the morning of Thursday, May 17. We do not know whether Nuniz ascertained his facts from native almanacks or the calculations of the astrologers, or whether he spoke from observations made by himself or by some one who was present; but Nuniz was an ordinary person, not a skilled astronomer, so far as we can tell, and he may well have called the day on which the crescent of the new moon first made its appearance just after sunset the "new moon day." This first appearance actually took place on the Saturday following. The first day of the Muhammadan month Jamâda' l âkhir, corresponding to the heliacal rising of the moon on that occasion, was Saturday, May 19.

I therefore believe that this great battle took place on Saturday, May 19, A.D. 1520,[1] a date almost synchronous with that of the "Field of the Cloth of Gold."

The Number of Troops Engaged.

When we total up the list given by Nuniz of the columns that marched from Vijayanagar for the campaign, the amount is so huge that we pause in natural doubt as to whether the story could by any possibility be true: 703,000 foot, 32,600 horse, and 551 elephants, *besides* the camp followers, merchants, &c., and "an infinitude of people" who joined him at a place close to Raichûr! It certainly demands a large strain on our credulity.

Let every one form his own opinion. I can only call attention to the fact that large armies seem to have always been the rule in India, and that certainly Krishna Râya had the power to raise immense numbers of troops,[2] though whether so many as is stated is another question. His power to do so lay in his mode of government. Allusion has already been made to this, and Nuniz gives us interesting details. The whole empire was divided into provinces and estates, held

[1] The corresponding actual new moon day in May 1521 was Monday, May 6, and the new moon was first visible on Wednesday. In 1522 the actual new moon day was Sunday, May 25, and it was first visible on Tuesday.

[2] Paes says that on an emergency he could raise even two millions.

by chiefs bound to keep up masses of troops fit for immediate service. It is, of course, natural to suppose that in this great war the king would have put forth all his strength.

To prove that immense armies were often employed by Indian kings, we have only to refer to a succession of writers. Barros notes the great power of the sovereign of Vijayanagar and his almost incredible richness, and is at pains to give an account of how these enormous forces were raised, "lest his tale should not be believed."

In the second volume of Scott's "History of the Dekhan" a translation is given of a journal kept by a Bondela officer in the reign of Aurangzîb, an officer who served under "Dulput Roy" in A.D. 1690. Writing about Vijayanagar in former days, at the height of its grandeur and importance, he says, "They kept an army of 30,000 horse, a million of infantry, and their wealth was beyond enumeration."

Conti, who was in India about a century earlier than the war in question, told Bracciolinî that the Vijayanagar army consisted of "a million of men and upwards."

Abdur Razzâk (1442 A.D.) tells the same story, putting the number at 1,100,000, with 1000 elephants.

Twenty years later Nikitin states that the Kulbarga forces marching to attack the Hindus amounted to 900,000 foot, 190,000 horse, and 575 elephants.

The Sultan himself, independently of his nobles, took the field with 300,000 men, and even when he only went out on a hunting expedition he took with him a train of 10,000 horse, 500,000 foot, and 200 elephants. He states that the Malik ul Tujâr alone had an army of 200,000 employed in the siege of one city. The Hindus fought almost nude, and were armed with shield and sword.

Even so far back as the time of Alexander the

Great (about B.C. 320) the army of Magadha was computed by the Greeks as consisting of 600,000 foot, 30,000 cavalry, and 9000 elephants, though Quintus Curtius makes a much more modest estimate.

Lord Egerton of Tatton states[1] that an army of Hindu confederated states, mustered for the defence of Northern India against the Muhammadan invasion in 1192 A.D., amounted, "according to the most moderate estimate," to 300,000 horse, 3000 elephants, and a great number of infantry.

In A.D. 1259 a Mogul embassy was received at Delhi by an *escort* of 50,000 horse, and was led past lines of infantry numbering as many as 200,000 in their ranks.

It will be remembered how Muhammad Taghlaq of Delhi[2] raised, according to Firishtah, an army of 370,000 men for the conquest of Persia, and when he wanted to destroy the inhabitants of a certain tract of country, he "ordered out his army as if he were going hunting," surrounded the tract, and then, pressing inwards towards the centre, slaughtered all the inhabitants therein. This implies that he took, when merely hunting, immense numbers of men with him. Shahab-ud-Dîn, indeed, declared that Muhammad Taghlaq had an army of 900,000 horse;[3] and Nuniz, on the opening page of his chronicle, says that this Sultan invaded the Bâlâghât with 800,000 horse.[4] This estimate was, of course, only according to the tradition extant in 1535.

Faria y Souza, writing in the seventeenth century, estimated the forces of Bahâdur, king of Cambay, in 1534, as 100,000 horse, 415,000 foot, and 600 elephants.

As late as 1762 the Mahrattas are said to have had an army of 100,000 horse.

1 "Handbook of Indian Arms," pp. 15-16.

2 Above, p. 12. 3 *Op. cit.*, p. 18. 4 Below, p. 292.

Nuniz[1] gives details of the provincial forces of Vijayanagar, compulsorily maintained by eleven out of a total of two hundred nobles amongst whom the empire was divided, and the total of the forces of these eleven amounts to 19,000 horse, 171,700 foot, and 633 elephants.

Castanheda confirms other writers in this matter, stating that the infantry of Vijayanagar were countless, the country being of large extent and thickly populated, so that the king could call upon a million, or even two millions, of men at will.[2] This writer visited India just at the close of the reign of Krishna Deva Râya. He states that the king kept up at his own cost an establishment of 100,000 horses and 4000 elephants.

As to all this, I repeat that every one is at liberty to form his own opinion; but at least it seems certain that all the chroniclers believed that the king of Vijayanagar could, if he so desired, put into the field immense masses of armed men. They were probably not all well armed, or well trained, or well disciplined, but as to large numbers there can be little reasonable doubt. A relic of this may be seen every year at modern Haidarâbâd, the capital city of H.H. the Nizâm, where, at the annual festival known as the "Langar," armed irregulars in very large numbers file through the principal streets. They are for the most part a mere mob of men with weapons, and are not maintained as State troops, but they are brought up by the various nobles in separate bodies, each chief mustering for the occasion all his hereditary retainers and forming them into rough regiments and brigades.

As to the description given by Nuniz of the offensive armour of the elephants, which are stated to have gone

[1] Below, pp. 384 to 389.

[2] Liv. ii. c. 16.

into battle with long swords like scythes attached to their trunks, the story is confirmed by many other writers.

Firishtah's Narrative.

Firishtah's account of the battle of Raichûr is interesting, as it gives a description of the affair from the enemy's point of view. Ismâîl Âdil Shâh marched

"to recover Mudkul and Roijore from the roy of Beejanugger, who, gaining early intelligence of his designs, moved with a great force, and stationed his camp on the bank of the Kistnah, where he was joined by many of his tributaries; so that the army amounted at least to 50,000 horse, besides a vast host of foot. The sultan would now have delayed his expedition, as the enemy possessed all the ferries of the Kistnah, but that his tents were pitched, and it would have been disgraceful to retract from his declarations. He therefore marched with 7000 horse, all foreign, and encamped on the bank of the river opposite to the enemy, waiting to prepare floats to cross and attack them.

"Some days after his arrival, as he was reposing in his tent, he heard one of the courtiers without the skreens reciting this verse:—'Rise and fill the golden goblet with the wine of mirth before the cup itself shall be laid in dust.' The sultan, inspired by the verse, called his favourites before him, and spreading the carpet of pleasure, amused himself with music and wine. When the banquet had lasted longer than was reasonable, and the fumes of the wine had exercised their power, a fancy seized the sultan to pass the river and attack the enemy. . . . Warm with wine he resolved to cross immediately, and mounting his elephant, without making his intentions known, proceeded to the river, as if to reconnoitre, but suddenly gave orders for as many of his troops as could to go upon the rafts, and others to follow him on elephants through the river. The officers represented the folly and danger of precipitation; but the sultan, without reply, plunged his own elephant into the stream, and was followed involuntarily by the amras and their followers, on about 250 elephants.

"By great good fortune, all reached the opposite shore in safety, and as many troops as could cross on the floats at two embarkations had time to arrive, when the enemv advanced to battle in so great force as excluded every probable hope of escape to the sultan, who had not more than 2000 men ready to oppose 30,000. The heroes of Islaam, animated with one soul, made so gallant a resistance that about a thousand of the infidels fell, among whom was Sunjeet Roy, the chief general of Beejanuggur; but at last, harassed beyond all power of opposition by cannon-shot, musquetry, and rockets, which destroyed near half their numbers, the survivors threw themselves into the river in hopes of escaping, and Nursoo Bahadur and Ibrahim Bey, who rode on the same elephant with Ismaeel Adil Shaw, drove the animal across the stream; but so great was the current, that except the royal elephant and seven soldiers, all the rest were drowned. The sultan's rashness was heavily punished by so great a loss. He took a solemn vow never to indulge in wine till he had revenged his defeat; and then, throwing away despair, busied his mind in repairing this unfortunate miscarriage.

"As Mirza Jehangeer had fallen in the action, the sultan consulted with Assud Khan on what measures would be best to take in the present crisis of his affairs. Assud Khan replied, that as his loss was great and the troops dispirited, it would be better for the present to retreat to Beejapore. The sultan approving the advice, marched from the Kistnah to Beejapore, and conferring the dignity of Sippeh Sallar[1] on Assud Khan, added several districts to his jaghire, and made him his principal adviser in all important affairs."

Comparison of Accounts.

Comparing this account with that given by Nuniz, there can, I think, be little doubt that both stories refer to the same event, though there are of course several discrepancies. The origin of the war is related differently. Firishtah states that on the arrival of the Sultan at the river-bank he found the Hindu army encamped on the opposite side; he crossed, after a few days' delay, with a small force, and was driven into the river. Nuniz says that Krishna Deva Râya heard of Ismâîl Âdil's

[1] Commander-in-chief.

arrival on the river-bank while he himself was in camp at Raichûr, fifteen miles away; and that he advanced and gave battle nine miles from the river, in the end driving the enemy across. But taking the two narratives as a whole, there are too many points of coincidence to leave any doubt in the mind that each chronicler is writing of the same event.

As to which of the two is more accurate it is impossible now to decide. But considering that Nuniz wrote only fifteen years afterwards, and that there were Portuguese present at the battle, some of whom Nuniz may have personally consulted as to what took place, it would seem more reasonable to trust in him rather than in a Muhammadan historian who did not compile his work till after an interval of sixty years. Moreover, there are some inherent improbabilities in Firishtah's narrative.

It is worthy of notice, too, that throughout the story of Nuniz at this part of his chronicle there is much that impels the belief that either himself or his informant was present at the Hindu camp while these events were taking place. The narrative of the campaign, in complete contrast to that of the remainder of the history, reads like the account of an eye-witness; especially in the passages describing the fortress of Raichûr [1] and the camp—where the supplies were so great that "you could find everything that you wanted," [2] where "you saw" [3] the goldsmiths and artisans at work as if in a city, where "you will find" [4] all kinds of precious stones offered for sale, and where "no one who did not understand the meaning of what he saw would ever dream that a war was going on, but would think that he was in a prosperous city." Note also the description given of the

[1] Below, p. 333.

[2] "*Omde achaveis . . . ho que avieis mister.*"

[3] "*Verieis.*"

[4] "*Achareis.*"

extraordinary noise made by the drums, trumpets, and shouts of the men; so that even the birds fell down into the soldiers' hands stricken with terror and "it seemed as if the sky would fall to the earth," and "if you asked anything, you could not hear yourself speak, and you had to ask by signs." Many such instances might be given, but not to be tedious I will invite attention to only three more, viz., the account given by Nuniz of how, when receiving the men of the city after its surrender, the king, "casting his eye on Christovão de Figueiredo, nodded his head, and turned to the people telling them to observe what great things could be effected by one good man;"[1] his description of the behaviour of the defeated citizens when Krishna Deva made his triumphant entry into the city· and his narrative of the ambassador's reception at Vijayanagar by the king after the conclusion of the campaign.[2] It may be remembered that our other chronicler, Domingo Paes, was at Vijayanagar with Christovão de Figueiredo some months after the battle, even if he were not personally present in the fighting at Raichûr.

The great interest of Nuniz's narrative lies in the fact that it is the only detailed account extant. Barros related the events in historical fashion, taking his facts from this very chronicle; but he was never in India, and his brief summary is altogether wanting in the power and force contained in the graphic story of Nuniz. The other Portuguese writers pass over the war very lightly. It appears as if it hardly concerned them, further than that at its close Ruy de Mello seized the mainlands near Goa.

[1] Below, pp. 346, 347. [2] Below, p. 351.

Political Effects of the Battle.

And yet it had far-reaching effects. The Hindu victory so weakened the power and prestige of the Âdil Shâh that he ceased altogether to dream of any present conquest in the south, and turned his attention to cementing alliances with the other Muhammadan sovereigns his neighbours. The victory also caused all the other Muhammadan Powers in the Dakhan seriously to consider the political condition of the country; and this eventually led to a combination without which nothing was possible, but by the aid of which the Vijayanagar Empire was finally overthrown and the way to the south opened. It furthermore greatly affected the Hindus by raising in them a spirit of pride and arrogance, which added fuel to the fire, caused them to become positively intolerable to their neighbours, and accelerated their own downfall.

It equally affected the fortunes of the Portuguese on the coast. Goa rose and fell simultaneously with the rise and fall of the second Vijayanagar dynasty; and necessarily so, considering that its entire trade depended on Hindu support; for the king of Portugal was never well disposed towards his hereditary enemies, the "Moors." This is a point frequently left unnoticed by writers on Portuguese colonial history. The two most recent authors of works on the subject, Mr. Danvers ("The Portuguese in India") and Mr. Whiteway ("The Rise of Portuguese Power in India"), pay very little attention to the internal politics of the great country on the fringe alone of which the Portuguese settled, and on the coast of which their vessels came and went. Mr. Danvers devotes one short paragraph to the battle of Raichûr,[1] and another[2] to the destruction of Vijayanagar. Mr. Whiteway does not even allude to

[1] Vol. i. p. 347. [2] Vol. i. p. 533.

the former event, and concludes his history before arriving at the date of the latter. Yet surely it is easy to see that the success or failure of maritime trade on any given coast must depend on the conditions prevailing in the empire for the supply of which that trade was established. When Vijayanagar, with its grandeur, luxury, and love of display, its great wealth and its enormous armies, was at the height of its power, the foreign traders were eminently successful; when Vijayanagar fell, and the city became desolate and depopulated, the foreign traders had no market for their goods, and trade decayed. So that this great Hindu victory at Raichûr deserved a better fate than to be passed over by the historians as if it had been an event of small importance.

The Events that followed the Battle.

Nuniz gives us in detail an account of the events that followed the victory of Krishna Deva Râya, and considering that he wrote only about fifteen years after their occurrence, we should do well to receive his account as probably true in the main. Firishtah, perhaps naturally, preserves a complete silence on the subject.

Nuniz tells us that when the city of Raichûr surrendered, the Hindu king made a triumphal entry into it, and treated the garrison with kindness and consideration; while the other Muhammadan kings sent envoys to Krishna Deva Rayâ on hearing of his success, and received a haughty and irritating reply. Krishna Deva then returned to Vijayanagar and held high festival. Shortly afterwards an ambassador arrived from the defeated Shâh, and was treated with scant courtesy for more than a month, after which he was received in audience; when the king sent answer by him to his enemy, that if the Âdil Shâh would come to him, do obeisance, and kiss his foot, his lands and fortresses should be restored to him. No attention being paid to this, the Râya set out to search for the Shâh, hoping that he would be induced to do homage in the manner demanded, and appearing to ignore altogether the effect which would necessarily be produced on the minds of the other kings of the Dakhan by this contemplated supreme humiliation of one of their number. The submission never took place. Krishna led his army as far north as Bîjapûr, the Âdil Shâh's capital, which for a time he occupied and left sadly injured. Then Asada Khân, the Shâh's wily courtier, successfully brought about the death of his personal enemy, Salâbat Khân, by inducing the Râya to order his execution; an act to which the king was led by the machinations of the arch-intriguer, who subordinated his chief's interests to his own selfish ends.

King Krishna had, in the city of Bîjapûr, taken prisoner three sons of a former king of the Bâhmanî dynasty, who had been held captive by the Âdil Shâhs, and he proclaimed the eldest as king of the Dakhan.[1] This abortive attempt to subvert the rule of the five kings who had established themselves on the ruins of the single Dakhan sovereignty naturally fell flat, and only resulted in stiffening the hostility which these sovereigns felt towards their common foe.

A little later Krishna Râya's son, a young prince on whom he desired to confer his crown, and in whose favour he had even gone so far as openly to abdicate, died suddenly of poison, and the king, then himself in a dying condition, arrested and imprisoned his own

[1] We hear nothing of this from Firishtah. But we know that the Bâhmanî Sultan Mahmûd II., who died in 1518, had three sons, Ahmad, Alâ-ud-Dîn, and Wali-Ullah, the first of whom became Sultan in December 1517, the second in 1521, the third in the same year; in all cases only nominally.

minister, Sâluva Timma, and his family. In this he was aided by some Portuguese who happened to be present at the Durbar. On Sâluva Timma's son escaping to a "mountain range"—perhaps Sandûr, on the south of the capital, where there are still to be seen the remains of a strong fortress built of cyclopean masonry on the summit of the highest hill, now known as Râmandrûg—the king summoned Timma and his brother and son, and had their eyes put out.

About this time the Âdil Shâh advanced again to retrieve his broken fortunes, but fled incontinently on hearing the news that Krishna Deva was advancing in person to meet him. That the king, though sorely ill, did indeed move in the manner stated, seems to be confirmed by the statement of Nuniz that on the way he bought six hundred horses from the Portuguese. Krishna began to make preparations for an attack on Belgaum, then in the Âdil Shâh's possession, and sent an envoy to invite the assistance in this enterprise of the Portuguese at Goa; but he fell too seriously ill to carry out his project, and died shortly afterwards at the age of from forty-two to forty-five years. It was then the year 1530 A.D.

He was succeeded by Achyuta.

So far Nuniz. We learn something more from other writers. Barros states that about the year 1523 Sâluva Timma, the king's minister, invaded the mainlands near Goa, which had been recently acquired by the Portuguese under Ruy de Mello; that he advanced towards Ponda with a small force, but that he was attacked and driven back.[1] Shortly after this, viz., in April 1524, the Muhammadans of Bîjapûr attacked these same mainlands with success, during the viceroyalty of Dom Duarte de Menezes. On October 31 of that year the Chamber of Goa wrote

[1] Dec. III. l. iv. c. 10.

a report to the king of Portugal in which occurs the following passage:—

"The mainland which Ruy de Mello, who was captain of this city, conquered, was entered by the Moors, who used to possess it, in the month of April of five hundred and twenty-four, and they hold it as theirs, and the first Thanadar's district which they took was that of Perna, which is by the seaside. There they captured two Portuguese, and one of them was the Thanadar; these are prisoners in the fortress of Bylgan (Belgaum), of which the Suffilarim is captain."[1]

It is evident, therefore, that "the Moors" were successful, and yet it is curious that very little mention is made of this circumstance by other historians. Firishtah does not mention it; and it may therefore be reasonably inferred that the "Moors" in question were not the royal troops acting under the orders of the Sultan, but belonged to the local levies of Asada Khân, then chief of Belgaum.

According to Firishtah, the defeat at Raichûr was followed by Ismâîl Âdil Shâh's marrying his sister to Burhân Nizâm Shâh of Ahmadnagar; quarrelling and fighting with him (A.D. 1523); again fighting with him (1528); marrying another sister to Alâ-ud-Dîn Ummad of Bîrâr; and fighting with and entirely defeating Sultan Amîr Barîd of Bîdar, then an old man, whom he captured. On the death of Krishna Deva, Ismâîl took advantage of the confusion of the Hindus to retake possession of Mudkal and Raichûr.

Firishtah gives no dates for the two last of the events above noted, but the submission of Amîr Barîd to the Âdil Shâh apparently did not take place till

[1] Correa, Stanley's translation (Hakluyt edition), p. 387, note; Danvers, "Portuguese in India," i. 363. The "Suffilarim" is Asada Khân.

Mr. Baden-Powell has published, in the *Journal of the Royal Asiatic Society* for April 1900, an interesting paper on the king of Portugal's regulations for, and record of customs in, the newly acquired tracts, dated at Goa in A.D. 1526, and called *Foral dos usos e costumes*.

1529, for Barros[1] implies that it occurred after an event which cannot have happened earlier than 1529 —namely, an attack on Ponda by three Hindu chiefs, which led to the inhabitants appealing for help to the then governor of Goa, Nuno da Cunha. Da Cunha was not governor till 1529. "*At this time*," writes the historian, "Melique Verido[2] submitted to the Hidalchan, by advice of Madre Maluco and Cota Maluco, and came to his camp in poor clothes, and flung himself at his feet." This evidently refers to what occurred after the Barîd's capture by the Âdil Shâh, if Firishtah's story is true.[3]

Let it be remembered, though the fact has no bearing on the history of Vijayanagar at this date, that in 1526 the Emperor Bâbar captured Delhi, and established himself as the first monarch of the great Moghul dynasty. He was succeeded in 1530 by Humâyun, and on the latter's death in 1556 the great Akbar attained the throne.

[1] Dec. IV. l. vii. c. 1.

[2] Mallik Barîd. The Hidalchan is the Âdil Khân or the Âdil Shâh; Madre Maluco is the Imâd Shâh, and Cota Maluco the Qutb Shâh.

[3] Perhaps this matter ought to find place under the reign of Achyuta Râya, but I mention it here as it may have occurred before the death of Krishna Deva.

Chinnâ dêviyammanavaru, Krishṇa-dêva-râyaru, Tirumala-
dêvi-yammanavaru. From a photograph
of this group of bronze statues
in the Venkatêsa
temple on Tiru-

CHAPTER XII

THE BUILDINGS, WORKS, AND INSCRIPTIONS OF KRISHNA DEVA

Temples—Irrigation works—Statue of Narasimha—Kâmalâpuram—Inscriptions.

Were it not that the description given us by Nuniz and Paes of the condition of the great city of Vijayanagar at this period is so graphic, so picturesque, and so detailed as positively to require no addition, I should have deemed it my duty to attempt to supply the want; but with their narrative before us in all its original freshness, it would be useless to attempt anything further. Both of these writers were on the spot at the time of the city's greatest grandeur and prosperity, though in the time of Nuniz the period of its political decay had set in. With their descriptions I shall not venture to interfere.

I cannot, however, pass on to the reign of Achyuta without calling attention to some of the works carried out at the capital by Krishna Deva, and to a few of the inscribed records of his reign.

At the beginning of his reign Krishna built a *gopura* or tower, and repaired another, at the Hampe temple, which had been built by the first kings in honour of Mâdhavâchârya, the founder of the fortunes of Vijayanagar. The great *Krishnasvâmi* temple was built by him in 1513, after his return from the successful campaign in the east. In the same year he commenced the temple of *Hazâra Râmasvâmi* at the palace, the architecture of which leads Mr. Rea[1] to think that it was not finished till a later period.

Later in his reign the king busied himself in improving the irrigation of the dry lands about Vijayanagar. He constructed in 1521 the great dam and channel at Korragal, and the Basavanna channel, both of which are still in use and of great value to the country.[2]

Another great work of his was the construction of an enormous tank or dammed-up lake at the capital, which he carried out with the aid of João de la Ponte, a Portuguese engineer, whose services were lent to him by the governor-general of Goa. Both Paes and Nuniz mention this lake, and as the former actually saw it under construction it may have been begun in A.D. 1520. I think that this is the large lake, now dry, to be seen at the north-western mouth of the valley entering into the Sandûr hills south-west of Hospett, the huge bank of which has been utilised for the conveyance of the highroad from Hospett to the southern taluqs. If so, the fact of its original failure is interesting to us, because for many years past this vast work has been entirely useless. The description given by Nuniz accords with the position of this tank, which was doubtless intended partly for irrigation purposes, and partly for the supply of water to the "new city," Nâgalâpura, the king's favourite residence, now known as Hospett. The chronicler mentions the existence of lofty ridges on each side, strong gates and towers guarding the entrance, and states that this was the principal approach to the capital from the south; all which data coincide with the position of the tank and road in question. It is through these gates that the Portuguese travellers entered Vijayanagar. This view is supported by the account given by Paes.

[1] Article "Vijayanagar" in the *Madras Christian College Magazine* for December 1886.

[2] "Bellary District Manual" (Kelsall), p. 231.

COLOSSAL STATUE OF UGRA NARASIMHA

(*From a Photograph by* F. DUNSTERVILLE, Esq.)

Writing of the approach to Vijayanagar from the western coast, and describing the "first range," *i.e.* the first that is seen on passing upwards from the plains, he states that in these hills was the principal entrance from that side. He alludes to the gates and wall, and the city, Nâgalâpur, constructed by King Krishna. Then he writes, "the king made a tank *there*," *i.e.* close to Hospett, at the mouth of two hills, and in order to this end "broke down a hill." He saw innumerable people at work on the tank. He confirms the story of Nuniz as to the sixty human beings offered in sacrifice to ensure the security of the dam. Both writers are therefore describing the same tank, and, taking the chronicles together, I can have no doubt as to the soundness of my identification.

Prior to 1520, Krishna Deva built the outlying town of Nâgalâpur, to which allusion has just been made. It was constructed in honour of his favourite wife, the quondam courtesan, Nâgalâ Devî, and the king made it his favourite residence.

He also appears to have begun the construction of the temple of Vitthalasvâmi on the river-bank, the most ornate of all the religious edifices of the kingdom. "It shows," writes Mr. Rea in the article already referred to, "the extreme limit in florid magnificence to which the style advanced." The work was continued during the reign of Krishna Deva's successors, Achyuta and Sadâsiva, and was probably stopped only by the destruction of the city in 1565. An inscription records a grant to the temple in 1561.

In 1528 was constructed one of the most curious and interesting monuments to be seen in the city. This is an enormous statue of the god Vishnu in his *avâtara* as Narasimha, the man-lion. It was hewn out of a single boulder of granite, which lay near the south-western angle of the Krishnasvâmi temple, and the king bestowed a grant of lands for its maintenance. Though it has been grievously injured, probably by the iconoclastic Muhammadans in or after the year 1565, it is still a most striking object.

I have already alluded to the grants made by Krishna Deva to the great Virûpâksha temple at Hampe, on the occasion of the festival of his coronation. There is an inscription of his reign on the base of the inner side of the front tower (*gopura*) of the temple at Virinchipuram, dated in the year A.D. 1513–14; and one dated Tuesday, September 20, 1513, at Sankalâpura, close to the capital, recording a grant of the lands of that village to the temple of Ganapati in the palace enclosure.[1] Mr. Fleet[2] mentions others of his reign in A.D. 1509–10, 1512–13, 1514–15, 1522–23, and 1527–28.

The last inscription of the reign at present known is one which bears a date corresponding to Friday, April 23, A.D. 1529.[3] It stands in front of the great statue of Ugra Narasimha, described above.

[1] "South Indian Inscriptions" (Hultzsch), p. 132; and *Epigraphia Indica*, by the same author, iv. 266.

[2] *Journal, Bombay Branch, Royal Asiatic Society*, xii. 336, &c.

[3] *Epig. Ind.*, i. 398; iv. p. 3, note 4.

CHAPTER XIII

THE REIGN OF ACHYUTA RÂYA

Achyuta Râya—Fall of Raichûr and Mudkal—Asada Khân and Goa—Disturbances at Bîjapûr—Ibrahim Shâh at the Hindu capital—Firishtah on Vijayanagar affairs—Rise of Râma Râya and his brothers—"Hoje" Tirumala—Varying legends—Venkatâdri defeated by Asada Khân near Adoni—Asada Khân's career—Belgâum and Goa—Asada's duplicity—Portuguese aggressions—Religious grants by, and inscriptions relating to, Achyuta.

ACHYUTA, according to Nuniz and some other authorities, was a brother of the late king,[1] and, in company with two other brothers and a nephew, had been confined by Krishna Deva in the fortress of Chandragiri, in order to prevent dissensions in the kingdom. The new monarch is said by Nuniz to have been specially selected by Krishna Deva. If so, the choice was singularly unfortunate, for Achyuta was a craven and under him the Hindu empire began to fall to pieces.

His minister was one of the powerful Sâluva family, to which also had belonged Timma, the minister of King Krishna. Nuniz calls him "Salvanay." The earliest known date of Achyuta's reign is gathered from an inscription bearing a date corresponding to Monday, August 15, A.D. 1530.[2]

The beginning of his reign was ominously signalised by the loss of the frontier fortresses Mudkal and Raichûr. Firishtah[3] states that the Âdil Shâh had, some time

[1] I have broadly declared this relationship, but, as a matter of fact, almost every inscription and literary work in the country differs as to the genealogy of the sovereigns who reigned from this time forward. Nuniz, however, as a contemporary writer residing at the capital, is an excellent authority.

[2] *Epig. Ind.*, iv. 3, note 4 (Professor Kielhorn).

[3] Scott's edition, i. 252.

before the death of Krishna Deva, made preparations to recover possession of these cities, and proceeds :—

> "The Sultan . . . put his army in motion, attended by Ummad Shaw and Ameer Bereed with their forces; and the affairs of Beejanuggur being in confusion owing to the death of Heemraaje, who was newly succeeded by his son Ramraaje,[1] against whom rebellions had arisen by several roies, met with no interruptions to his arms. Roijore and Mudkul were taken, after a siege of three months, by capitulation, after they had been in possession of the infidels for seventeen years."[2]

The relief and delight of the Âdil Shâh at these successes, and at the death of his mortal enemy Krishna, must have been great; and Firishtah relates that the Sultan, "who had vowed to refrain from wine till the reduction of these fortresses, at the request of his nobility now made a splendid festival, at which he drank wine and gave a full loose to mirth and pleasure." Raichûr and Mudkal were never again subject to Hindu princes.

Those who desire to obtain an insight into the character of the new king of Vijayanagar should turn to the chronicle of Nuniz. It will suffice here to say that he alienated his best friends by his violent despotism, and at the same time proved to the whole empire that he was a coward. His conduct and mode of government ruined the Hindu cause in Southern India and opened the whole country to the invader, though he himself did not live to see the end.

After the fall of Raichûr and the Doâb, Ismâîl Âdil had another fight (1531) with his rival at Ahmadnagar and defeated him; after which the two brothers-in-law consolidated a strong alliance. Three years later Ismâîl died, having contracted a fever while besieging a fortress belonging to the Qutb Shâh of Golkonda. His death occurred on Thursday, August 13, 1534,[3] and he was

[1] These names are discussed below.
[2] This is apparently an error. The period was only ten years.
[3] 16th Safar, A.H. 941 (Firishtah).

succeeded by his son Malû. Asada Khân was appointed regent of Bîjapûr, but immediately on his accession the new sovereign so offended his powerful subject that he retired to Belgaum, and Sultan Malû, giving himself up to all kinds of excesses, was deposed after a reign of only six months. Malû was blinded by the orders of his own grandmother, and Ibrahîm Âdil, his younger brother, was raised to the throne. It was now 1535.

Da Cunha, the Portuguese governor of Goa, took advantage of these events to erect a fortress at Diu, and early in 1536 to seize again the mainlands of Goa, which had been for ten years in the possession of Asada Khân. The Khân sent a force to recapture these lands, and in February an engagement took place in which the Portuguese were victorious. A second attack by the Moslems was similarly repulsed. A third fight took place in July, and again the Muhammadans were beaten; but Asada Khân then assembled a larger army, and the foreigners were compelled to retire after blowing up their fortress.

About this time[1] Qulî Qutb Shâh is said to have attacked Kondavîd on account of its withholding payment of tribute, to have taken it, and built a tower in the middle of the fort in commemoration of its reduction.

Two inscriptions at Conjeeveram, dated respectively in 1532 and 1533,[2] imply that at that period King Achyuta reduced the country about Tinnevelly; but apparently he was not present in person, and nothing further is known regarding this expedition.

We now enter upon a period very difficult to deal with satisfactorily, owing to the conflict of evidence in the works of the various writers.

"A year after his accession," writes Firishtah,[3] "Ibrahîm Âdil led his army to Beejanuggur on the

[1] Firishtah, Briggs, iii. 374–375.

[2] "Lists of Antiquities, Madras," vol. i. p. 181 (No. 86), and p. 182 (No. 115).

[3] Scott's translation, i. p. 262.

requisition of the roy." This would be the year 1536 A.D. But what led to such an extraordinary complication of affairs? Can it be true that King Achyuta was so humiliated and hard pressed as to be compelled to summon to his aid the hereditary enemies of his country?

Nuniz is silent as to the cause, though he admits the fact. It is quite possible that Firishtah is correct, that the public were not taken into confidence by their despotic rulers, and that the troops of Bîjapûr marched to the Hindu çapital at the request of King Achyuta. That they actually came there seems quite certain, and it is probable that Nuniz was in Vijayanagar at the time; but there is a *lacuna* in his story which can only be filled up by reference to Firishtah. Accepting Firishtah, we can readily understand why King Achyuta received the Sultan and his army without open opposition, as Nuniz declares that he did, and why the Muhammadan king received splendid presents before he retired. To Nuniz, however, this conduct was inexplicable except on the basis of Achyuta's craven spirit and utter unworthiness.[1] As to the assertion of Nuniz that the Sultan entered Nâgalâpur or Hospett and "razed it to the ground," we may remember the treatment of the city of Bîjapûr by Krishna Deva Râya,[2] and surmise that the houses of the Vijayanagar suburbs may have been pulled to pieces by the Mussalman soldiery in search for firewood. However all this may be, my readers have before them the story as given by Nuniz in Chapter XX. of his chronicle, and the following is Firishtah's account of the event.[3]

"Heem" Râjah, or, as Briggs renders the name, "Tim" Râjah—representing "Timma," and referring doubtless to Sâluva Timma, the great minister of Krishna Deva—had, forty years earlier, become *de facto* ruler of Vijayanagar on the death of the two sons of a

[1] Below, p. 367. [2] *Idem*, p. 354.
[3] Scott, i. pp. 262 ff.; Briggs, iii. p. 80.

former king, "Seo" Râya. He had poisoned the infant son of the younger of these sons, and had thus succeeded in becoming head of the state. During these forty years he had been obeyed by all. On his death his son Râma Râjah became ruler. Râma's marriage to "a daughter of the son of Seo" Râya[1] had greatly added to his dignity and power, and he now tried to secure the throne for himself and his family. He was, however, compelled by the nobles to recognise as king an "infant of the female line," whose person he committed to the care of the child's uncle, "Hoje" Tirumala Râya,[2] a man of weak intellect if not absolutely insane. In five or six years Rama cut off by treachery most of the chiefs who opposed him.[3] He then marched on an expedition into Malabar, and afterwards moved against a powerful zamindar to the south of Vijayanagar, who held out for six months and in the end beat off the troops of Râma Râya. Vijayanagar was at that time governed by a slave whom Râma had raised to high rank, and this man, on being applied to by the minister to send supplies from the capital, was so amazed at the wealth which he saw in the royal treasury that he resolved to attempt to gain possession of it. He therefore released the child-king, obtained the co-operation of Hoje Tirumala, assumed the office of minister, and began to raise troops. "Several tributary roies, who

[1] Briggs has it "a daughter of Shew Ray." Râma married a daughter of Krishna Deva, who was son of the first Narasimha.

[2] Inscriptions do not give us the name of any prince of the female line at this period. Briggs calls the uncle "Bhoj" Tirumala. Couto (Dec. VI. l. v. cap. 5) renders the name as "Uche Timma," and states that *uche* means "mad."

[3] Here we probably find an allusion to the reign of Achyuta. Râma was the elder of three brothers afterwards to become very famous. He and his brother Tirumala both married daughters of Krishna Deva Râya. Achyuta being, in Nuniz's belief, brother of the latter monarch, that chronicler calls these two brothers "brothers-in-law" of King Achyuta. (Below, p. 367.) Nuniz says that King Achyuta "destroyed the principal people in the kingdom and killed their sons" (p. 369).

were disgusted with Ramraaje, flew with speed to Beejanuggur to obey their lawful king; and in a short time thirty thousand horse and vast hosts of foot were assembled under his standard at the city." Tirumala then had the slave-governor assassinated. Râma Râjah at once returned to the capital, but was unable at that juncture to assert his authority. Finding himself deserted by many of the nobles he concluded a treaty with his lawful sovereign, and retired to his own province, which by agreement he was allowed to retain as his own independent state. Tirumala shortly afterwards strangled the king and seized the throne. The nobles submitted, since he was of royal blood, and better, in their opinion, than Râma Râjah; but when afterwards they found themselves unable to endure his tyranny and oppression, they rebelled and invited Râma Râjah to return.

Tirumala then found himself in great straits, and sent ambassadors with large presents to Ibrahîm Âdil Shâh, begging him to march to his assistance and promising that the Vijayanagar kingdom should be declared tributary to Bîjapûr. Ibrahîm, delighted beyond measure, after consulting Asada Khân accepted the terms, moved from his capital, and arrived before Vijayanagar "in the year 942," which corresponds to the period from July 2, A.D. 1535, to June 20, 1536.[1] "He was conducted into the city by Hoje Termul Roy, who seated him on the musnud of the raaje and made rejoicings for seven days." This conduct led to a change of front on the part of Râma Râjah and his supporters. They entreated Tirumala for the sake of the country to procure the retreat of the Sultan to his own dominions, promising submission and obedience if this should be done; and Tirumala, thinking that now he had no further use for his allies, requested the Sultan

[1] Achyuta had then been for about six years on the throne.

to return home. He paid over the subsidy agreed upon, which was assessed at something approaching two millions sterling, and made many other gifts. The story then ends with a tragedy.

"Ibrahim Adil Shaw had not yet recrossed the Kistnah, when Ramraaje and the confederates, who had bribed many of the troops in the city, broke their newly made vows, and hastened towards Beejanuggur, resolved to put the roy to death, on pretence of revenging the murder of his predecessor. Hoje Termul Roy, seeing he was betrayed, shut himself up in the palace, and, becoming mad from despair, blinded all the royal elephants and horses, also cutting off their tails, that they might be of no use to his enemy. All the diamonds, rubies, emeralds, other precious stones, and pearls, which had been collected in a course of many ages, he crushed to powder between heavy millstones, and scattered them on the ground. He then fixed a sword-blade into a pillar of his apartment, and ran his breast upon it with such force that it pierced through and came out at the back, thus putting an end to his existence, just as the gates of the palace were opened to his enemies. Ramraaje now became roy of Beejanuggur without a rival."

After this point in Firishtah's narrative we hear of no more "young Roies" or imprisoned sovereigns of the Second Dynasty. "Ramraaje" alone is spoken of as king, and Kings Achyuta and Sadâsiva—the latter of whom was undoubtedly recognised as king for some years though he was kept in custody—are not so much as mentioned.

Thus Firishtah and Nuniz both agree that Ibrahîm Âdil advanced as far as the city of Vijayanagar, and retired after payment of immense sums of money and the gift of many valuable presents. The date was A.D. 1535–36. With this date ends the historical portion of the chronicle of Nuniz.[1]

[1] If the Sultan's march towards Vijayanagar began in 1535–36, we shall perhaps not be far wrong in assigning Nuniz's chronicle to the year 1536–37, seeing that the author alludes to the dissatisfaction and disgust felt by the nobles and others for their rulers, which presupposes a certain interval to have passed since the departure of the Mussalman army.

We continue the narrative of events in Achyuta's reign as gathered from Firishtah.[1] As soon as he heard of the death of Hoje Tirumala and the seizure of the throne by "Ramraaje," Ibrahîm Âdil Shâh sent Asada Khân to reduce the important fortress of Adoni, which was undisputedly in Vijayanagar territory. Râma Râjah despatched his younger brother, Venkatâdri, to its relief, and the latter hastened thither with a large force.

"Assud Khan, upon his approach, raised the siege and moved towards him. A sharp engagement ensued, and Assud Khan, finding that he was likely to have the worst of the action, from the vast superiority in numbers of the enemy, retreated in good order, but was followed fourteen miles by the victors, when he encamped; and Venkatadry,[2] in order to be ready to harass the retreat the next day, halted in full security at a distance of only two miles from him. Assud Khan, who had ardently wished for such an event, towards the dawn of day, with four thousand chosen horse, surprized the camp of Venkatadry, whose self-confidence had left him wholly off his guard against such a manœuvre. Assud Khan penetrated to his tents before he received the alarm, and he had scarce time to make his escape, leaving his treasures, family, and elephants to the mercy of the victors. When the day had fully cleared up, Venkatadry collected his scattered troops, and drew up as if to engage; but seeing Assud Khan resolute to maintain his advantage, and fearing for the personal safety of his wife and children, he declined hazarding a battle, and, retiring some miles off, fixed his camp; from whence he wrote Ramraaje an account of his disaster, and requested reinforcements to enable him to repair it. Ramraaje immediately sent supplies of men and money, openly declaring his intentions of carrying on the war, but privately informed his brother that he had reason to imagine that Ibrahim Adil Shaw had not been led merely of his own will to besiege Oodnee; that he suspected the zemindars of that quarter had invited him to make war, and that many of the nobility with him were secretly in his interest;

[1] Scott's edit., i. 265.

[2] Scott spells the name "Negtaderee," but I have substituted the rendering given by Briggs, "Venkatadry," as less confusing.

therefore, he thought he would act prudently by making peace with the mussulmauns at present, and procuring the release of his wife and family from Assud Khan. Venkatadry, in consequence of the desires of his brother, having procured the mediation and influence of Assud Khan, addressed the sultan for peace, which being granted, and all affairs settled to the satisfaction of both states, Ibrahim Adil Shaw returned to Beejapore with Assud Khan and the rest of his nobility and army."

Asada Khân after this was greatly honoured by the Sultan, in spite of the intrigues which were fomented against him. Quarrels and disturbances, however, arose in the Bîjapûr dominions which lasted during the whole of the year 1542; in the course of which year King Achyuta died, and was succeeded nominally by Sadâsiva, during whose reign Vijayanagar was practically in the hands of Râma Râjah and of his two brothers, Tirumala and Venkatâdri.

Firishtah was a great admirer of Asada Khân and supports him in all that he did.[1] Asada was a Turk, who, beginning life under the simple name of Khusrû in the service of Ismâîl Âdil Shâh, distinguished himself in his sovereign's defence during the attack on Bîjapûr in 1511, a defence celebrated on account of the heroic conduct of the Sultan's aunt, Dilshâd Âgha. Khusrû was rewarded by Ismâîl with the title of "Asada Khân," a name which he bore for the rest of his life, and a grant of the jaghir of Belgaum. He

[1] Firishtah writes glowingly (Scott, i. 277) of the grandeur of Asada Khân. He "was famed for his judgment and wisdom. . . . For nearly forty years he was the patron and protector of the nobles and distinguished of the Dekhan. He lived in the highest respect and esteem, with a magnificence and grandeur surpassing all his cotemporary nobility. The sovereigns of Beejanuggur and every country observing a respect to his great abilities, frequently honoured him with letters and valuable presents. His household servants . . . amounted to 250. He had sixty of the largest elephants and 150 of a smaller size. In his stables he had 400 horses of Arabia and Persia, exclusive of those of mixed breed foaled in India. His treasures and riches were beyond amount," &c.

rose to be chief minister and commander-in-chief of the army of his master, and died full of years and honours in A.D. 1549.

The Portuguese at Goa had a very low opinion of Asada's character. They held him to be an inveterate intriguer, ready at every moment to betray his best friends, even his sovereign, if only by so doing he could advance his own personal and selfish interests; and in this, owing to his consummate skill and tortuous ways, he invariably succeeded. If space permitted, many interesting stories could be narrated of him, culled from the various writings of the day.[1]

Barros calls him "Sufo Larij,"[2] a name which some writers have derived from "Yusuf of Lar." Castanheda spells the name "Çufolarim."

Asada Khân is entitled to a chapter to himself, but, to avoid prolixity, I will only give one extract from the "Asia" of Barros.[3] Allusion has been made above to an attack on the mainlands of Goa by three Hindu chiefs, when Ponda was besieged. The inhabitants appealed to Nuno da Cunha, the governor-general, who hesitated to interfere for fear of bringing on a war with the Âdil Shâh. The principal danger was the lord of Belgaum, Asada Khân.

"Acadachan, like one who in a safe and lofty place watches some great fire spreading over the plains below, watched from his city of Belgaum the events that were passing;"—but did nothing till the Âdil Shâh wrote desiring him to return to Bîjapûr, which he had temporarily left owing to a disagreement, and to assist him in the government of the kingdom. Asada Khân replied craftily that he had done with the affairs of this life, and proposed to go and die at Mecca. At this Ismâîl flew

[1] Firishtah's story of Asada Khân's life is contained in Scott's edition, i. pp. 236–278; Briggs, iii. pp. 45–102.

[2] Dec. III. l. iv. cap. 5.

[3] Dec. IV. l. vii. cap. 6.

into a passion and vowed revenge against his powerful subject, who, to save himself, wrote to Da Cunha, professing his unalloyed friendship for the Portuguese, and inviting them to take possession of certain tracts on the mainland; declaring that his master, the Sultan, was powerless to defend himself against the armies of Vijayanagar. This was, it must be borne in mind, long after the Hindu victory at Raichûr. Da Cunha sent Christovão de Figueiredo, Krishna Deva's valiant friend, to bear his reply, since the latter was on friendly terms with the lord of Belgaum. A conversation took place, in which Asada Khân said that he was afraid of his master, who was of variable and inconstant character, and that he desired of all things to preserve friendship with the Portuguese. He therefore begged to be allowed to visit Goa and cement an alliance with the governor-general, to whom he faithfully promised that the lands in question should become for ever the property of the king of Portugal. Accordingly the lands were seized by Da Cunha.

Immediately afterwards Asada began to intrigue with the king of Vijayanagar, and being invited to visit that city on the occasion of one of the great *Mahânavamî* festivals, left Belgaum with 13,000 men and 200 elephants. Before starting he wrote to Da Cunha, asking that Figueiredo might be sent to accompany him, and promising to obtain for the Portuguese a definite cession of the lands from the Râya, since these had formerly been the latter's possession. Accordingly Figueiredo left for Vijayanagar, but learned that the Khân had already arrived there and had joined the king. The Râya received Asada favourably, and, as a present, gave him two towns, "Tunge and Turugel,"[1] since he hoped for his aid against the Sultan.

When the Sultan heard of Asada Khân's defection

[1] Turugel is probably Tirakhol, north of Goa.

he gave himself up for lost, but assembled an army and advanced to within twelve leagues of the king's camp, where Asada Khân had pitched his tents at some distance from those of the Hindu lords. The Sultan thence wrote to the Râya demanding the delivery to him of his recalcitrant "slave," and the Râya sent on the letter to Asada Khân, who told the king that he would never join the Muhammadans, but would remain faithful to Vijayanagar. A short pause ensued, during which the Râya learned that constant messages were passing between the camps of the Sultan and Asada Khân. Both armies then marched towards Raichûr, the Râya to retake the place from the Sultan, the Sultan watching for an opportunity to attack the Râya.

On the third day Asada Khân started with his forces two hours in advance of the royal troops, crossed the river first, and hastened to join the Sultan. Âdil Shâh received him with great apparent cordiality, and at length freely forgave him on the Khân's protestations that his intrigues with Vijayanagar and the Portuguese were only so many moves in a game undertaken for the advancement of the Sultan's interests. Previous to this move the Khân had held a conversation with Figueiredo, in which he succeeded in totally deceiving him as to his intentions, and reiterated his promises to obtain the cession of the mainlands from the Râya, for whom he professed the greatest friendship.

In the end, says Barros, the Âdil Shâh, secretly fearful of Asada Khân's duplicity, made a treaty of peace with the Râya, by which the Muhammadans retained Raichûr but gave up some other territory.

Though this story differs from Firishtah at almost every point, it is permissible to think that it may refer to the events of 1535, when the Sultan visited Vijayanagar; for in continuing his narrative, Barros a little later mentions the year 1536. It seems hopeless to try and reconcile the conflicting stories of Nuniz, Barros, and Firishtah, but enough has been said to afford insight into the character of Asada Khân. Nuniz echoes the general sentiment when he writes of the Khân's rescue of the Âdil Shâh, after his defeat at Raichûr in 1520 A.D., as being effected "by cunning" for his own purposes; and when he describes how, by a series of lies, Asada contrived the execution of Salâbat Khân at the hands of Krishna Râya.

During this reign the Portuguese were busy establishing themselves at various places on the coast, and they built several forts there for the protection of their trade. They had been constantly at war with the Samuri of Calicut and other feudatories of Vijayanagar; but with the Râya himself they were on terms of friendship, and in 1540 they ratified a treaty of peace with the sovereigns of Bîjapûr and Ahmadnagar as well as with the Samuri.

Throughout the whole of their dealings with the Portuguese I find not a single instance where the Hindu kings broke faith with the intruders,[1] but as much cannot, I fear, be said on the other side. The Europeans seemed to think that they had a divine right to the pillage, robbery, and massacre of the natives of India. Not to mince matters, their whole record is one of a series of atrocities. It is sad to turn from the description given us by Paes of the friendship felt for the Portuguese, and especially for Christovão de Figueiredo, by the "gallant and perfect" King Krishna Deva, and then to read of the treachery of the Viceroy towards the great Hindu Government; with which the Portuguese had

[1] Couto tells us (Dec. VII. l. vii. c. 1) that Râma Râya in 1555 made an expedition against the Christian inhabitants of San Thomé, near Madras, but retired without doing great harm; and it is quite possible that the king acknowledged no connection between San Thomé and Goa.

made alliances and treaties, and for which they openly professed friendship. Thus, to take one instance only, in 1545 the governor of Goa made ready a large fleet and a force of 3000 men, but kept all his preparations secret, for very good reason. His object was to sail round the coast to San Thomé, near Madras, land his troops, march inland and sack the great temple of Tirumala or Tirupati, purely for lust of gain. Luckily a severe storm prevented him from setting sail, but he plundered and destroyed some rich temples on the western coast, and enriched himself with the spoil. This was a mere wanton attack on property belonging to feudatories of the Vijayanagar empire, for there has never been any pretence that the peace-loving Brahmans attached to these temples had in any way offended or interfered with the Portuguese.

In the time of Achyuta a large number of grants were made by the nobles to temples throughout Southern India, and numerous inscriptions on stone and copper-plates are extant relating to these charitable and religious donations. One of the most important has been published by Professor Kielhorn.[1] It relates that the king, being on the banks of the Tungabhadrâ on the 12th October A.D. 1540, at the temple of Vitthalasvâmi or Vitthalêsvara—the splendidly sculptured pavilions of which remain to this day, even in their ruin and decay, an object of astonishment and admiration to all beholders—gave a grant of a village not far from Madras to the Brahmans learned in the Vêdas.

The last date of Achyuta known to epigraphists at present is found in an inscription[2] bearing a date corresponding to January 25, A.D. 1541; and the earliest date similarly available of his successor, Sadâsiva, is July 27, A.D. 1542.

[1] *Epigraphia Indica*, iii. 147.

[2] *Epigraphia Carnatica* (Rice), Part i. p. 176, No. 120.

THE STONE CAR IN THE TEMPLE OF VITTHALASVÁMI AT VIJAYANAGAR

CHAPTER XIV

THE BEGINNING OF THE END

Reign of Sadâsiva—The king a prisoner but acknowledged—Râma Râya—The Âdil Shâh again at Vijayanagar—Bîjapûr in danger—Saved by Asada Khân—Rebellion of Prince Abdullah—Royal gratitude—Death of Asada at Belgaum—The Portuguese support Abdullah—Treaties—Ain-ul-Mulkh—Fights near Goa—Râma Râya's threatened expedition to Mailâpur—He joins the Âdil Shâh and wastes the territories of Ahmadnagar—Portuguese violence on the Malabar coast—The Inquisition at Goa.

SADÂSIVA, then, began to reign in 1541 or 1542 A.D., but was only nominally king, the whole power of the state being in the hands of Râma Râya and his two brothers, Tirumala and Venkatâdri. That Sadâsiva was recognised by every one as the real sovereign is shown by a large number of inscriptions, ranging from 1542 to 1568;[1] most of which, however, have not yet been properly examined. A careful study has been made by Dr. Hultzsch[2] of one of these, dated in A.D. 1566-67, a year or so after the great defeat of the Hindus at Talikota and the destruction of the capital; and this is especially interesting as it bears out my assertion that even the three brothers themselves recognised Sadâsiva as king, though he had no power and was kept under constraint. In this document Râma Râjah's brother, Tirumala, is the important personage, but he submits to the minor title, *Mahâmandalêsvara*, while Sadâsiva is mentioned as sovereign. The inscription states that a certain person presented a petition to the "Mahâmandalêsvara Râma Râja Tirumala Râja,"

[1] I have published a rough list of eighty-eight of these, eighty-four of which are dated, in my "Lists of Antiquities, Madras" (vol. ii. p. 134 ff.).

[2] "South Indian Inscriptions," vol. i. p. 70.

who, *after obtaining sanction at the feet of Sadâsiva-deva Mahârâya*, granted a village to the great temple at Vellore. Râma Râjah and Venkatâdri were both at that time dead, and Tirumala was king *de facto*. Couto[1] even goes so far as to say that the three brothers "went on one day every year and prostrated themselves before their lawful sovereign in token of his rights over them." But as to the real relationship of Achyuta to Krishna, and Sadâsiva to both, we are still completely in doubt.

We saw that, according to Nuniz, Krishna Deva, immediately on his accession to the throne, imprisoned his three brothers and a nephew, then eight years old, son of the late king, "Busbalrao." This was in the year 1509 A.D., and Krishna was then over twenty years old. We hear of no king of the name of "Busbalrao," or anything like it, from other sources; nor are the names of Krishna's three brothers as given by Nuniz[2] at all like those of the two half-brothers mentioned in some of the inscriptions.

More than one epigraphical record contains the following genealogy:—

- TIMMA. (*m. Devakî.*)
  - ÎSVARA. (*m. Bukkamma.*)
    - NARASA OR NARASIMHA. (*Three wives.*) (*Usurped throne about* A.D. 1498.)
      - (*By Tippâjî.*) VÎRA NARASIMHA. (*King* [?] *for a few years till* 1509–10.)
      - (*By Nâgalâ.*) KRISHNA DEVA. (*King* 1509–10 *to* 1530.)
        - *A daughter.* (*m. Râma Râyà.*)
        - *A daughter.* (*m. Tirumala Râya.*)
      - (*By Ôbâmbikâ.*)
        - RANGA. (*m. Timmambâ.*)
          - SADÂSIVA. (*King in name* A.D. 1542–67).
        - ACHYUTA. (*King* A.D. 1530 *to* 1541–42.)
          - VENKATA.

---

[1] Dec. VI. l. v. cap. 5.

[2] "Tetarao," "Ramygupa," and "Ouamysyuaya" (text, below, p. 314).

Here we have two half-brothers of Krishna Deva named Ranga and Achyuta, the latter being chosen king; and a nephew, Sadâsiva.

Two inscriptions noted in my "Sketch of the Dynasties of Southern India"[1] state that Achyuta was the son of Krishna Deva; while a Telugu work, the *Manucharitram*, makes him son of the second Narasimha. Couto[2] says that he was nephew of Krishna Râya.

As to Sadâsiva, some authorities make him, as stated above, nephew of Krishna Deva and son of Ranga, while another says that he was the son of Achyuta.

An inscription at Conjeeveram[3] states that Achyuta had a wife named Varadâ Devî who bore him a son, Venkata. Venkata was actually raised to the throne, but lived only a short time, and then young Sadâsiva was crowned king.

If it is necessary to make any choice amid all this confusion, I recommend my readers to accept provisionally the pedigree given in the above table, leaving it for future research to finally settle the question.

As to Râma Râya, several inscriptions state that he and his two brothers were sons of one Ranga Râya, whose pedigree is given; and Professor Kielhorn considers it established that Râma married Krishna Deva's daughter.[4] She was probably a child at her marriage. She had a brother eighteen months old at the time of Krishna Deva's death—so Nuniz says—but we hear

[1] Page 108.

[2] Dec. VI. l. v. cap. 5.

[3] *Epig. Ind.*, iii. 236.

[4] Firishtah (Scott, i. 252) states that Râma Râya "married a daughter of the son of Seoroy, by that alliance greatly adding to his influence and power." If so, "Seoroy" must be the first Narasa. The historian says that "Seoroy dying was succeeded by his son, a minor, who did not live long after him, and left the throne to a younger brother." These brothers, then, were the second Narasa, called also Vîra Narasimha, and Krishna Deva. The rest of Firishtah's account does not tally with our other sources of information. As being son-in-law of Krishna Deva, Râma was called "Aliya," which means "son-in-law," and by this name he is constantly known.

nothing more about him, or what became of him. Another daughter of Krishna Deva Râya's is said to have been married to Râma Râya's brother, Tirumala. Some authorities state that Râma's wife was Sadâsiva's sister.[1]

That there were disturbances at the capital on the death of Achyuta in 1542 seems clear; and indeed it could hardly be otherwise, for he appears to have dislocated the whole empire, alienated the nobles, upon whom the defence of the country rested, and aroused in them a spirit of rebellion to the crown.

Gaspar Correa has left us an account of what took place at Vijayanagar at that time, and I repeat his story for what it is worth; though it certainly seems as if he had made a mistake and brought down to this year the affairs of 1535–36, the story of which has already been told. For he alludes to a visit of the Âdil Shâh to Vijayanagar, and unless there were two such visits, Correa would seem to be in error, since Firishtah's date is confirmed by Nuniz, in whose time King Achyuta was alive.

Correa[2] states that in 1542 Achyuta, king of Vijayanagar, died, leaving a young son in the power of his uncle, brother of the dead king, who had been king contrary to right.[3] The nobles wished to keep the boy at liberty, nominating two ministers to carry on the government; but the uncle disagreed, since in this way he would lose all power, and he contrived to gain over some partisans to his side. The nobles in disgust separated, returned to their estates, and, in despair of good government, began to assume independence each in his own province. The queen, mother of the boy, begged the Âdil Shâh to come to her aid and secure

[1] *Ind. Ant.*, xiii. 154.

[2] Vol. iv. pp. 247–249, 276–282.

[3] See the pedigree above. The young son would be Venkata, and the uncle, Ranga.

the kingdom for her son, promising him, in return for this favour, immense riches. The Sultan set out for this purpose, intending to visit Vijayanagar, but on the road he was met by emissaries from the minister, and bought off with lavish gifts. The king by real right (probably the uncle, Ranga), who had been detained in a fortress, was then liberated, and he also sought aid from the Sultan of Bîjapûr. The Sultan took advantage of the opportunity to set out afresh, nominally to aid the true king, but really to acquire the kingdom for himself. The Hindus, in fear for their safety, placed on the throne the brother of the dead king, and succeeded in defeating the Âdil Shâh close to Vijayanagar. The new king, in order to strengthen his position for the future, caused the boy, his rival, to be assassinated, as also two of the latter's uncles and a nephew of the dead king (Achyuta).[1] Then, in dread of the power of the principal nobles, he summoned them to court, and put out the eyes of those who arrived first; so that the rest returned in great anger to their homes and began to intrigue with the Sultan. They urged him to depose the tyrant, promising their aid, and offering him the kingdom for himself if only the country could be freed from this monster. The Âdil Shâh therefore advanced, entered the kingdom of Vijayanagar, and was received as sovereign by many; but he also assumed such intolerant and haughty airs that he aroused the hatred of all around him, and in the end was obliged, in fear for his own safety, to retire to Bîjapûr. "Meanwhile a new king had seized the throne of Vijayanagar, a great lord from Paleacate, married to a sister of the king that

[1] Who all these were we do not know. The boy Venkaṭa's uncles would be either brothers of Ranga or brothers of the queen-mother, widow of Achyuta. Achyuta's nephew referred to could not be Sadâsiva, because he survived. He may have been nephew of the Rânî. The assassination of the boy-king recalls to our minds the story of Firishtah of the murder of the infant prince by "Hoje" Tirumala.

preceded the dead king,[1] and in the end he secured the kingdom."[2]

It seems impossible, as Senhor Lopes justly observes, to get at the truth of all this at present, and I think it best to abandon the subject and pass on to consider the events of the reign of Sadâsiva, which lasted from 1542 to 1567. It is pretty evident that each chronicler acquired his knowledge "from stories transmitted from mouth to mouth and disfigured in the process."[3]

In 1543 Burhân Nizâm Shâh made an alliance with Râma Râjah and Jamshîd Qutb Shâh, Sultan of Golkonda, and attacked the Âdil Shâh, whereupon Râma Râjah, taking advantage of the latter's troubles, sent Venkatâdri to reduce Raichûr and the Doâb, "so that Beejapore, attacked at the same time by three powerful princes in three separate quarters, was full of danger and disorder."[4] True to the traditions of his predecessors, the new Sultan of Bîjapûr "called Assud Khân from Balgoan to his presence and demanded his advice on the alarming state of affairs," with the result that he patched up a peace with Burhân, making over to him the rich districts surrounding Sholâpur, and sent ambassadors to arrange terms with Vijayanagar. This done, and the allies having retired, Asada Khân marched against the Qutb Shâh of Golkonda, defeated

[1] Sister, that is, of Krishna Deva. As above stated, Râma Râya, for undoubtedly he is here referred to, married Krishna Deva's daughter, not sister, so far as we can gather.

[2] Cæsar Frederick states that Râma and his two brothers, of whom Tirumala was minister and Venkatâdri commander-in-chief, kept the rightful kings prisoners for thirty years prior to their downfall in 1565. If so, this would include the reign of Achyuta, and the story would differ from that of Nuniz, who represents King Achyuta as free but subject to the malign influence of his "two brothers-in-law." These two may, perhaps, represent Râma and Tirumala, who are said to have married two daughters of Krishna Deva. They would, however, not have been really brothers-in-law of Achyuta.

[3] Senhor Lopes, *Dos Reis de Bisnaga*, Introduction, p. lxix.

[4] Firishtah (Scott, i. 271).

him under the walls of his capital, and in a personal encounter grievously wounded him in the face with his sabre.[1]

The Portuguese at this period had been very active, and amongst other more or less successful enterprises the Governor, Affonso de Sousa, attacked the territory of the Rânî of Bhatkal on the pretext that she had withheld tribute due to the king of Portugal, and wasted her country with fire and sword. Her city was burnt, the Hindus were slain in large numbers, and the Râṇî reduced to submission.

About the year 1544—the date is somewhat uncertain—Sultan Burhân again attacked Ibrahîm Âdil at the instigation of Râma Râjah, but was completely defeated.

> "The sultan (Ibrahîm) after this victory growing haughty and imperious, treated the ambassadors of Nizam Shah in a contemptuous manner, and behaved tyrannically to his own subjects, putting to death many and severely punishing others of his principal nobility for slight offences, which occasioned disaffection to his government."

On Burhân again invading Bîjapûr territories, a party was formed to depose Ibrahîm and raise to the throne his brother Abdullah. This prince, finding that the conspiracy had been discovered, fled for safety to Goa, where he was well received. But when Ibrahîm promised certain provinces to the Portuguese if they would send Abdullah away to a place where he could no longer disturb the peace of the Bîjapûr territories, De Sousa accepted the conditions; receiving the gift of Salsette and Bardes for the crown of Portugal, and the whole of the vast treasures accumulated by Asada Khân at Belgaum as a personal

[1] So Firishtah. The Muhammadan historian of the Qutb Shâhi dynasty of Golkonda, translated by Briggs, tells this story of Qulî Qutb Shâh, Jamshîd's predecessor (Firishtah, Briggs, iii. 371).

present for himself. Having pocketed as much as he could of the bribe, however, he only took Abdullah as far as Cannanore and then brought him back to Goa; and when, at the end of the next year, De Castro succeeded De Sousa as Governor, the former refused to surrender the rebel prince. This duplicity placed the Sultan in great difficulty, and in February 1546 he executed a treaty of peace, one of the terms of which was that no person belonging either to the Dakhan, or to the territories of the Nizâm Shâh, or to those of the king of Vijayanagar, with certain others specially mentioned, should be permitted to have any communication with Abdullah or his family until the reply of the king of Portugal was received to an embassy which the Âdil Shâh proposed to send to him. There were other terms also, and these not being acted up to by the Portuguese, the Sultan in 1547 sent some troops into the provinces of Salsette and Bardes, which were driven out by the Viceroy after a stubborn fight.

De Castro then concluded treaties with Vijayanagar on the 19th September 1547, and with Ahmadnagar on the 6th October of the same year, by the former of which the Hindu king was secured in the monopoly of the Goa horse trade,[1] and by the latter a defensive alliance was cemented between the Portu-

[1] The terms of this treaty are interesting, as they throw much light on the political and commercial relations of the Portuguese at this period with the two great states their neighbours.

The contracting parties are stated to be the king of Portugal by his deputy, the captain-general and governor of Goa, Dom João de Castro, and the great and powerful King Sadâsiva, king of Bisnaga.

(*a*) Each party to be friends of the friends, and enemy of the enemies, of the other; and, when called on, to help the other with all their forces against all kings and lords in India, the Nizâm Shâh always excepted.

(*b*) The governor of Goa will allow all Arab and Persian horses landed at Goa to be purchased by the king of Vijayanagar on due notice and proper payment, none being permitted to be sent to Bîjapûr.

(*c*) The king of Vijayanagar will compel all merchants in his kingdom

guese and the Nizâm Shâh. This constituted a tripartite league against Bîjapûr.

Shortly afterwards a still more determined attack was made by the Bîjapûr troops against the mainlands of Goa, and in the battle which ensued one of the Âdil Shâh's principal generals was slain.

In 1548 the Viceroy concluded a more favourable arrangement with Bîjapûr and also with the Rânî of Bhatkal.

The Portuguese historians say that De Sousa and Asada Khân both joined the ranks of the supporters of Abdullah, and that Asada Khân promised to give the king of Portugal all the territories of the Konkan on the downfall of Ibrahîm, but the Viceroy changed his mind and withdrew, while Asada Khân's death put a stop to all intrigues in that quarter.

Firishtah's account, however, of the conduct of Asada at this period totally differs, as do his dates. He states that, although the Khân was much distressed at his master's neglect, his coldness towards him, and his attitude of suspicion, yet he himself was consistently loyal in his actions, and did his utmost to crush the conspiracy. As to the Portuguese, this historian avers that, so far from abjuring the cause of Abdullah, they actually marched with that prince from Goa towards Bîjapûr, supported by the Nizâm Shâh, and even reached the neighbourhood of Belgaum; but when it

trading with the coast to send their goods through ports where the Portuguese have factors, permitting none to proceed to Bîjapûr ports.

(*d*) The king of Vijayanagar will forbid the importation of saltpetre and iron into his kingdom from any Bîjapûr port, and will compel its purchase from Portuguese factors.

(*e*) The same with cloths, copper, tin, China silk, &c.

(*f*) The king of Vijayanagar will allow no Moorish ship or fleet to stop in his ports, and if any should come he will capture them and send them to Goa. Both parties agree to wage war on the Âdil Shâh, and all territory taken from the latter shall belong to Vijayanagar, except lands on the west of the Ghâts from Banda on the north to Cintacora on the south, which lands shall belong to the king of Portugal.

became evident that Asada could not be corrupted, the nobles of Bîjapûr returned to their allegiance to their sovereign, and the alliance broke up. Sultan Ibrahîm advanced to Belgaum in February 1549,[1] but on the road heard that Asada had died.

Firishtah's account of the Bîjapûr Sultan's conduct when he arrived at Belgaum is too suggestive to be omitted. The king, he says, "*comforted his (Asada Khân's) mourning family with khelauts and assurances of royal favour, but all his estates and treasures he took for his own use*"—though these treasures were the accumulated property of a man whom the historian declares to have been, during the whole of his long life, the most faithful, courageous, and devoted adherent of his royal master, whom on many occasions he had personally rescued from difficulties which appeared almost insurmountable! The Portuguese account as to the fate of the treasures accumulated by Asada Khân is given by Mr. Danvers, who, treating the Khân as an unprincipled rebel, writes:—

> "In addition to making over Salsette and Bardes to the Crown of Portugal, the Adil Khan had also given Martim Affonso (De Sousa, the Viceroy) the vast treasure which Acede Khan had collected for the purpose of carrying out his rebellion, and which is said to have amounted to ten millions of ducats, *of which, however, only one million came into the hands of Martim Affonso.* Some accounts state that he sent about half of this amount to Portugal for his own use, but others aver that he employed a great part of it in the public service in India, besides sending some home for the king's use in Portugal."[2]

It will be seen that the two accounts differ widely in details.

At this time Ibrahîm Qutb Shâh, younger brother of Jamshîd and heir presumptive to the throne of Gol-

[1] Muharram, A.H. 956. But the Portuguese records state that Asada Khân died in 1545 (Danvers, i. 465).

[2] Danvers' "Portuguese in India," i. 465, 466.

konda, was at Vijayanagar, whither he had fled in fear of Jamshîd's despotic and violent temper. Firishtah[1] relates a story of him which is worth repeating here, partly because the event occurred in the Hindu capital, partly because it illustrates the practice of duelling which, as Nuniz tells us, largely obtained at that time,[2] and partly because it confirms the assertions of Nuniz that the king of Vijayanagar was in the habit of disposing at will with the revenues of his provinces.

Râma Râya had despotically turned out of his estate an Abyssinian officer in his employ named Ambur Khân, and conferred the same on Prince Ibrahîm for his support.

"Ambur Khan, enraged at the alienation of his estate, and meeting Ibrahim Kootb Shah in the streets of Beejanuggur, accused him of depriving him of it. The latter replied that monarchs were at liberty to dispose of their own property, and that the king of Beejanuggur had chosen to give him the estate. Ibrahim Kootb Shah proceeded on his way; but the Abyssinian called him coward in refusing to dispute his title with the sword. Ibrahim warned him of his imprudence; but the Prince's mildness only added fury to the Abyssinian's anger, who proceeded to abuse him in grosser language. On this the Prince dismounted and drew. The Abyssinian rushed upon him, but the Prince's temper giving him the advantage, he killed his antagonist, whose brother, standing by, insisted on taking up the cause, and he also fell a victim to his temerity."

Prince Ibrahîm succeeded to the throne of Golkonda in A.D. 1550. In the previous year, says Firishtah, an alliance was cemented between Sultan Ibrahîm of Bîjapûr and the new sovereign of Bîdar, Ali Barîd, son of Amîr Barîd.

Râma Râjah having at this period accepted the presents and professions of regard sent to him by the Nizâm Shâh with an embassy, Sultan Ibrahîm, roused

[1] Briggs, iii. 328.   [2] Below, p. 383.

to indignation, treated the Vijayanagar ambassadors at Bîjapûr with such indignity that they fled in fear of their lives, and Râma Râjah, offended in his turn, induced Burhân Nizâm to attack Ibrahîm. He did so successfully, and captured the fortress of Kalliân; and on Ibrahîm's retaliating by seizing one of the Ahmadnagar forts, an open alliance was entered into between Burhân and Râma. The two kings met near Raichûr in 1551, laid siege to the place and took it. Mudkul also capitulated, and the Doâb was thus once more restored to the Hindu sovereign.

About this time,[1] so we are told by a Muhammadan historian, Râma Râya's two brothers rebelled against his authority during his absence from the capital, and seized the fortress of Adoni; upon which Râma begged aid from the Qutb Shâh Ibrahîm, and this being granted, Râma besieged Adoni for six months. The place eventually capitulated, and the brothers were then pardoned.

In 1553 Burhân died, and once more the two leading Muhammadan states became friendly for a short time; but the air was too full of intrigue and jealousy for this to last long. Sultan Ibrahîm negotiated an understanding with Vijayanagar, and this led to a renewal of the war, in the course of which a battle took place at Sholâpûr, where Ibrahîm was worsted.

But the most serious reverse which he suffered was at the hands of a chief named Ain-ul-Mulkh, whom by ingratitude and ill-treatment he had driven into open rebellion. At the end of a short campaign against this person the royal troops were completely beaten, and the Sultan was driven to take refuge at Bîjapûr. In a state of desperation he called on the Râya of Vijayanagar for aid, and Râma, as usual representing the puppet sovereign, sent his brother, Venkatâdri, with a large

[1] Briggs' "Firishtah," iii. 397, &c.

force to expel the enemy from the Sultan's dominions.[1] The story of the rebel "Ein-al-Moolk's" discomfiture at the hands of Venkatâdri is thus told by Firishtah:[2]—

"Syef Ein al Moolkh, imitating Assud Khan, resolved to surprize the infidels; but Venkatadry, having intelligence of his designs, ordered his troops to be on their guard; and having procured long faggots, with cloth steeped in oil bound round one end of each, commanded his followers upon the alarm being given to light them, and holding them up as high as possible, give the troops a full sight of the enemy. Ein al Moolk, agreeably to his intentions, having one night chosen two thousand men for the purpose, marched with Sullabut Khan to the enemy's camp, which he was allowed to enter unmolested; but upon a signal given, all the brands were instantly lighted up, and Venkatadry, who was prepared with his troops, rushed upon the surprizers, who expected no resistance, with such success that above five hundred of them were killed before the detachment could clear the camp. Ein al Moolk and Sullabut with the greatest difficulty made their escape; but, losing the road through the darkness of the night, a report spread in his camp on the return of some of the fugitives, that he was killed; and his troops being immediately struck with a panic, separated and fled to different quarters. Ein al Moolkh and Sullabut Khan, with two hundred horse, about daylight arriving at their ground, and seeing it deserted, fled in confusion by the route of Maan to the dominions of Nizam Shaw, where they sought protection, but were basely assassinated by his treachery."

In 1555 an attempt was made by the Portuguese under their new Viceroy, Pedro de Mascarenhas, to place Prince Abdullah on the throne of Bîjapûr, the foreigners being dazzled by the magnificent offers made to them, should the joint efforts of the conspirators be crowned with success. Abdullah was established at Ponda, and

[1] Senhor Lopes has recently found amongst the archives in the Torre do Tombo in Lisbon a paper, dated 1555 A.D., which states that the king of Vijayanagar had consented to aid Ibrahîm Âdil Shâh against Ain-ul-Mulkh and "the Meale" (*i.e.* Prince Abdullah, called "Meale Khan" by the Portuguese), in return for a present of 700,000 pardaos (*Corpo Chronologico*, Part i., packet 97, No. 40).

[2] Scott's edit., i. 284.

proclamation made of his accession to the throne. On the death of De Mascarenhas in 1555, Francisco Barreto succeeded him with the title of governor, and having installed the prince at Ponda he proceeded to collect the revenues of the country. He was, however, opposed by an officer of Ibrahîm Âdil who was backed by seven thousand troops, and several fights took place.

Meanwhile Ibrahîm himself had not been idle, and aided by fifteen thousand of Sadâsiva's troops from Vijayanagar he dethroned and captured the ambitious prince, following this up by several attacks on the Portuguese forces. The war lasted during the whole winter of 1556, but with no very decisive results. Next year a fresh relay of troops from Bîjapûr attacked Salsette and Bardes, but were beaten by a small force of Portuguese near Ponda, and hostilities were suspended for a time

Shortly after this, viz., in 1557, Sultan Ibrahîm died. "During his illness he put to death several physicians who had failed in cure, beheading some, and causing others to be trodden to death by elephants, so that all the surviving medical practitioners, alarmed, fled from his dominions." He was succeeded by his eldest son, Ali Âdil.

The new Sultan, immediately on his accession, cemented his father's alliance with Sadâsiva and Râma Râjah by the execution of a new treaty, and sent ambassadors on a similar errand to Husain Nizâm Shâh, the successor of Burhân at Ahmadnagar. These, however, were badly received, and Sultan Ali, whose envoys at the Hindu capital had been warmly welcomed and hospitably treated, determined to establish, if possible, a real and lasting friendship with Vijayanagar. To this end he adopted a most unusual course, the account of which will be best given in Firishtah's own words.

"Ali Adil Shaw, who was intent on extricating his dominions from the losses of his father by alliance with Ramraaje, on the death of a son of that monarch,[1] with uncommon prudence and resolution went, attended by one hundred horse, to Beejanuggur, to offer his condolence on the melancholy occasion. Ramraaje received him with the greatest respect,[2] and the sultan with the kindest persuasions prevailed upon him to lay aside his mourning. The wife of Ramraaje adopted the sultan as her son, and at the end of three days, which were spent in interchanges of friendly professions, he took his leave; but as Ramraaje did not attend him out of the city, he was disgusted, and treasured up the affront in his mind, though too prudent to show any signs of displeasure for the present."[3]

The incident thus entirely failed in its intended effect. It produced a lasting irritation in the mind of the Sultan, and a haughty arrogance on the part of Râma Râya, who conceived that the fortunes of his hereditary enemy must be at a very low ebb when he could condescend so far to humble himself.

In the next year, 1558, according to Couto,[4] Râma Râya made an expedition to "Meliapor," or Mailâpur, near Madras, where was an important establishment of Roman Catholic monks and the Church of St. Thomas. I quote the passage from the summary given by Senhor Lopes in his introduction to the *Chronica dos Reis de Bisnaga* (p. lxvi.). "The poor fathers of the glorious Order of St. Francis having seized all the coast from Negapatam to San Thomé, they being the first who had begun to preach there the light of the Holy Gospel, and

[1] The Muhammadans seem to have always treated Râma Râjah as king. Sadâsiva was perhaps too young at that period to have had a son, and the allusion is probably to a son of Râma.

[2] King Sadâsiva was apparently not shewn.

[3] That Ali Âdi actually made this visit is confirmed by the narrative of a Golkonda historian, whose work has been translated and published by Briggs (Firishtah, iii. 402). The story may be compared with that told above of the visit of Fîrûz Shâh Bâhmanî to King Deva Râya in A.D. 1406, which had a similar ending.

[4] Dec. VII. l. vii. c. 1.

having throughout that tract thrown down many temples and destroyed many pagodas, a thing which grieved excessively all the Brahmans, these latter reported the facts to Râma Râya, king of Bisnaga, whose vassals they were, and begged him that he would hasten to their assistance for the honour of their gods."

They succeeded in persuading him that the new-comers were possessed of enormous riches, and he proceeded against the place, but afterwards finding that this was not true, and that the inhabitants were loyal to him, he spared them and left them in peace.

On his return to Bîjapûr, Ali Âdil peremptorily demanded from Hussain Nizâm Shâh the restoration of the fortresses of Kalliân and Sholâpûr; and on the latter's contemptuous refusal (he "sent back a reply so indecent in expression as to be unfit to relate," says Firishtah) another war broke out.

> "In the year 966 (October 14, A.D. 1558 to October 3, 1559), Ali Adil Shaw having called Ramraaje to his assistance, they in concert divided the dominions of Houssein Nizam Shaw, and laid them waste in such a manner that from Porundeh to Khiber, and from Ahmednuggur to Dowlutabad, not a mark of population was to be seen. The infidels of Beejanuggur, who for many years had been wishing for such an event, left no cruelty unpractised. They insulted the honour of the mussulmaun women, destroyed the mosques, and did not even respect the sacred koraun." [1]

This behaviour on the part of the Hindus so incensed the followers of Islâm, not only the hostile subjects of Golkonda but even the allied troops and inhabitants of the Bîjapûr territories, that it laid the foundation for the final downfall and destruction of Vijayanagar.

In 1558 Dom Constantine de Braganza became Viceroy of Goa, and his period of government was

[1] See also Briggs' "Firishtah," iii. 403–405.

signalised by every kind of violence and aggression. In 1559 Luiz de Mello carried fire and sword into the towns along the Malabar coast. He attacked Mangalore, set fire to the town, and put all the inhabitants to death. Later in the year he destroyed in similar manner a number of towns and villages on the same coast, and desolated the whole seaboard.

In 1560 the See of Goa was elevated into an archbishopric, and the Inquisition, the horrors of which even excelled that of Spain, was established. The inhabitants of Goa and its dependencies were now forced to embrace Christianity, and on refusal or contumacy were imprisoned and tortured. In this year also, and those following, the predatory excursions of the Portuguese were continued. In 1564 the Viceroy sent Mesquita with three ships to destroy a number of ships belonging to the Malabarese. Mesquita captured twenty-four of these, by twos and threes at a time, sunk them, beheaded a large number of the sailors, and in the case of hundreds of others, sewed them up in sails and threw them overboard. In these ways he massacred 2000 men.

This resulted in a serious war in Malabar, as the wretched inhabitants of the country, driven to desperation, determined at all hazards to destroy the ruthless invaders of their land. The Portuguese were attacked at Cannanore, and a series of desperate struggles took place, in the course of which Noronha, the commandant, desolated the country and ruined many people by cutting down forty thousand palm trees. At last, however, peace was made.

CHAPTER XV

DESTRUCTION OF VIJAYANAGAR

(A.D. 1565)

Arrogance of Râma Râya—Ahmadnagar attacked—Muhammadans combine against Vijayanagar—The league of the five kings—Their advance to Talikota—Decisive battle, 1565, and total defeat of the Hindus —Death of Râma Râya—Panic at Vijayanagar—Flight of the royal family—Sack of the great city—Its total destruction—Evidence of Federici, 1567—Downfall of Portuguese trade, and decay of prosperity at Goa.

MEANWHILE affairs were advancing rapidly in the interior. After the Nizâm Shâh's dominions had been wasted, as already described, by the Âdil Shâh and Râma Râya, peace was made by the restoration of Kalliân to Bîjapûr;[1] but as soon as the allies had retired, Hussain entered into an alliance with Ibrahîm Qutb Shâh and again marched to attack Ali Âdil. Again Ali called in the aid of Vijayanagar, and again Râma Râya marched to his aid, this time with 50,000 horse and an immense force of infantry. The opposing forces met at Kalliân, when the Qutb Shâh deserted to Ali Âdil, and Hussain was compelled to

[1] Firishtah relates an interesting anecdote about this in his history of the Ahmadnagar Sultans. Hussain Nizâm Shâh desired to make peace with Vijayanagar, and Râma Râja offered to grant it on certain conditions, one of which was that Kalliân should be restored to Bîjapûr, and another that the Nizâm Shâh should submit to pay him a visit and receive betel from him. Hussain was in such straits that he accepted these severe terms and went to Râma Râja's camp, "who rose on his entering his tent (he did not go out to meet him) and kissed his hand. The Sultan, from foolish pride, called for a basin and ewer, and washed his hands, as if they had been polluted by the touch of Ramraaje, who, enraged at the affront, said in his own language, 'If he were not my guest he should repent this insult;' then calling for water, he also washed." Hussain then gave up the keys of Kalliân.

withdraw to Ahmadnagar. Attacked in his own capital, he retreated.

"The three sovereigns laid siege to Ahmednuggur, and despatched detachments various ways to lay waste the country round. The Hindoos of Beejanuggur committed the most outrageous devastations, burning and razing the buildings, putting up their horses in the mosques, and performing their idolatrous worship in the holy places; but, notwithstanding, the siege was pushed with the greatest vigour, the garrison held out with resolution, hoping that at the approach of the rainy season, the enemy would be necessitated to raise the siege.

"When the rains had set in, from the floods, damp, and want of provisions, distress began to prevail in the camp of the allies, and Kootub Shaw also secretly corresponded with the besieged, to whom he privately sent in grain."[1]

The siege was raised, therefore, and before long the allies separated, and the Hindu army returned home.

"In the first expedition on which Ali Adil Shaw, pressed by the behaviour of Houssein Nizam Shaw, had called Ramraaje to his assistance, the Hindoos at Ahmednuggur committed great outrages, and omitted no mark of disrespect to the holy religion of the faithful, singing and performing their superstitious worship in the mosques. The sultan was much hurt at this insult to the faith, but, as he had not the ability to prevent it, he did not seem to observe it. Ramraaje also, at the conclusion of this expedition, looking on the Islaam sultans as of little consequence, refused proper honours to their ambassadors. When he admitted them to his presence, he did not suffer them to sit, and treated them with the most contemptuous reserve and haughtiness. He made them attend when in publick in his train on foot, not allowing them to mount till he gave orders. On the return from the last expedition to Nuldirruk, the officers and soldiers of his army in general, treated the mussulmauns with insolence, scoffing, and contemptuous language; and Ramraaje, after taking leave, casting an eye of avidity on the countries of Koottub Shaw and Adil Shaw, dispatched armies to the frontiers of each."

---

[1] Scott's "Firishtah," i. 291; Briggs, iii. 406.

Both the great Shâhs, therefore, abandoned certain territories to the Hindus, and from Golkonda Râma obtained Ghânpura and Pangul. It was the last Hindu success.

"Ramraaje daily continuing to encroach on the dominions of the mussulmauns, Adil Shaw at length resolved, if possible, to punish his insolence and curtail his power by a general league of the faithful against him; for which purpose he convened an assembly of his friends and confidential advisers."

Some of these urged that the Râya was too wealthy and powerful, by reason of his immense revenues, which were collected from no less than sixty seaports in addition to very large territories and dependencies, and the number of his forces was too vast, for any single Muhammadan monarch to cope with him. They therefore pressed the Sultan to form a federation of all the kings of the Dakhan and wage a joint war. Ali Âdil heartily concurred in their opinion, and began by despatching a secret embassy to Ibrahîm Qutb Shâh.

Ibrahîm eagerly accepted, and offered his services as mediator between Ali Âdil and his great rival at Ahmadnagar. An envoy was sent to the latter capital, and the sovereign, Hussain Shâh, warned beforehand of the important proposals to be made, received him in private audience. The ambassador then laid before the king all the arguments in favour of the Bîjapûr plan.

"He represented to him that during the times of the Bhamenee princes, when the whole strength of the mussulmaun power was in one hand, the balance between it and the force of the roies of Beejanuggur was nearly equal; that now the mussulmaun authority was divided, policy demanded that all the faithful princes should unite as one, and observe the strictest friendship, that they might continue secure from the attacks of their powerful common enemy, and the authority of the roies of Beejanuggur, who had reduced all the rajas of Carnatic to their yoke, be diminished, and removed far from the countries of

Islaam; that the people of their several dominions, who ought to be considered the charge of the Almighty committed to their care, might repose free from the oppressions of the unbelievers, and their mosques and holy places be made no longer the dwellings of infidels."

These arguments had their full weight, and it was arranged that Hussain Nizâm Shâh should give his daughter Chand Bibi in marriage to Ali Âdil with the fortress of Sholâpûr as her *dot*, and that his eldest son, Murtiza, should espouse Ali's sister—the two kingdoms coalescing for the conquest and destruction of Vijayanagar. The marriages were celebrated in due course, and the Sultans began their preparations for the holy war.

"Ali Adil Shaw, preparatory to the war, and to afford himself a pretence for breaking with his ally, dispatched an ambassador to Ramraaje, demanding restitution of some districts that had been wrested from him. As he expected, Ramraaje expelled the ambassador in a very disgraceful manner from his court; and the united sultans now hastened the preparations to crush the common enemy of the Islaam faith."

Ibrahîm Qutb Shâh had also joined the coalition, and the four princes met on the plains of Bîjapûr, with their respective armies. Their march towards the south began on Monday, December 25, A.D. 1564.[1] Traversing the now dry plains of the Dakhan country, where the cavalry, numbering many thousands, could graze their horses on the young crops, the allied armies reached the neighbourhood of the Krishnâ near the small fortress and town of Talikota, a name destined to be for ever celebrated in the annals of South India.[2]

[1] 20th Jamâda 'l awwal, Hijra 972. Firishtah (Scott), i. 295; Briggs, iii. 413.

[2] Though, in fact, the battle did not take place there, but many miles to the south of the river. Talikota is twenty-five miles north of the Krishnâ. The battle took place ten miles from Râma Râya's camp south of the river, wherever that may have been. There is no available information on this point, but it was probably at Mudkal, the celebrated fortress. The ford

It is situated on the river Don, about sixteen miles above its junction with the Krishnâ, and sixty-five miles west of the point where the present railway between Bombay and Madras crosses the great river. The country at that time of the year was admirably adapted for the passage of large bodies of troops, and the season was one of bright sunny days coupled with cool refreshing breezes.

Here Ali Âdil, as lord of that country, entertained his allies in royal fashion, and they halted for several days, attending to the transport and commissariat arrangements of the armies, and sending out scouts to report on the best locality for forcing the passage of the river.

At Vijayanagar there was the utmost confidence. Remembering how often the Moslems had vainly attempted to injure the great capital, and how for over two centuries they had never succeeded in penetrating to the south, the inhabitants pursued their daily avocations with no shadow of dread or sense of danger; the strings of pack-bullocks laden with all kinds of merchandise wended their dusty way to and from the several seaports as if no sword of Damocles was hanging over the doomed city; Sadâsiva, the king, lived his profitless life in inglorious seclusion, and Râma Râya, king *de facto*, never for a moment relaxed his attitude of haughty indifference to the movements of his enemies. "He treated their ambassadors," says Firishtah, "with scornful language, and regarded their enmity as of little moment."[1]

Nevertheless he did not neglect common precau-

crossed by the allies would appear to be that at the bend of the river at Ingaligi, and the decisive battle seems to have been fought in the plains about the little village of Bâyapur or Bhôgapur, on the road leading directly from Ingaligi to Mudkal.

[1] Couto (Dec. VIII. c. 15) tells an incredible story that Râma Râya was utterly ignorant of any impending attack, and never even heard that the enemy had entered his territories till the news was brought one day while he was at dinner.

tions. His first action was to send his youngest brother, Tirumala, the "Yeltumraj" or "Eeltumraaje" of Firishtah, to the front with 20,000 horse, 100,000 foot, and 500 elephants, to block the passage of the Krishnâ at all points. Next he despatched his second brother, Venkatâdri, with another large army; and finally marched in person towards the point of attack with the whole power of the Vijayanagar empire. The forces were made up of large drafts from all the provinces—Canarese and Telugus of the frontier, Mysoreans and Malabarese from the west and centre, mixed with the Tamils from the remoter districts to the south; each detachment under its own local leaders, and forming part of the levies of the temporary provincial chieftain appointed by the crown. According to Couto, they numbered 600,000 foot and 100,000 horse. His adversaries had about half that number. As to their appearance and armament, we may turn for information to the description given us by Paes of the great review of which he was an eye-witness forty-five years earlier at Vijayanagar,[1] remembering always that the splendid troops between whose lines he then passed in the king's procession were probably the *élite* of the army, and that the common soldiers were clad in the lightest of working clothes, many perhaps with hardly any clothes at all, and armed only with spear or dagger.[2]

The allies had perhaps halted too long. At any rate, their scouts returned to their sovereigns with the

[1] Below, pp. 275 to 279.

[2] I have seen on several occasions bodies of men collected together at Vijayanagar and the neighbourhood, dressed and armed in a manner which they assured me was traditional. They wore rough tunics and short drawers of cotton, stained to a rather dark red-brown colour, admirably adapted for forest work, but of a deeper hue than our English khaki. They grimly assured me that the colour concealed to a great extent the stains of blood from wounds. Their weapons were for the most part spears. Some had old country swords and daggers.

news that all the passages of the river were defended, and that their only course was to force the ford immediately in their front. This was in possession of the Hindus, who had fortified the banks on the south side, had thrown up earthworks, and had stationed a number of cannon to dispute the crossing.

The defenders of the ford anxiously awaited intelligence of their enemy's movements, and learning that he had struck his camp and marched along the course of the river, they quitted their post and followed, keeping always to the south bank in readiness to repel any attempt to cross directly in their front. This manœuvre, a ruse on the part of the Mussulmans, was repeated on three successive days. On the third night the Sultans hastily left their camp, returned to the ford, and, finding it deserted, crossed with a large force. This movement covered the transit of the whole of their army, and enabled them to march southwards to the attack of Râma Râya's main body.

Râma Râya, though surprised, was not alarmed, and took all possible measures for defence. In the morning the enemy was within ten miles of his camp, and Venkatâdri and Tirumala succeeded in effecting a junction with their brother.

On the following day, Tuesday, January 23, 1565,[1] both sides having made their dispositions, a pitched battle took place[2] in which all the available forces of both sides were engaged. In one of his descriptions Firishtah estimates the Vijayanagar army alone as amounting to 900,000 infantry, 45,000 cavalry, and 2000 elephants, besides 15,000 auxiliaries; but he himself varies so greatly in the numbers he gives in

[1] Firishtah gives the date as "Friday the 20th of Jumad-oos-Sany," A.H. 972 (Briggs, iii. 414), but the day of the month given corresponds to Tuesday, not Friday.

[2] What follows is taken entirely from Firishtah (Scott, i. 296 ff.; Briggs, iii. 128, 247).

different parts of his narrative that there is no necessity to accept these figures as accurate. There can be little doubt, however, that the numbers were very large. The Hindu left, on the west, was entrusted to the command of Tirumala; Râma Râya in person was in the centre, and the right was composed of the troops of Venkatâdri. Opposed to Tirumala were the forces of Bîjapûr under their Sultan Ali Âdil; the Mussulman centre was under the command of Hussain Nizâm Shâh; and the left of the allied army, in Venkatâdri's front, consisted of the forces brought from Ahmadâbâd and Golkonda by the two Sultans, Ali Barîd and Ibrahîm Qutb. The allied forces drew up in a long line with their artillery in the centre, and awaited the enemy's attack, each division with the standards of the twelve Imâms waving in the van. The Nizâm Shâh's front was covered by six hundred pieces of ordnance disposed in three lines, in the first of which were heavy guns, then the smaller ones, with light swivel guns in the rear. In order to mask this disposition two thousand foreign archers were thrown out in front, who kept up a heavy discharge as the enemy's line came on. The archers fell back as the Hindus of Râma's division approached, and the batteries opened with such murderous effect that the assailants retreated in confusion and with great loss.

Râma Râjah was now a very old man — Couto says "he was ninety-six years old, but as brave as a man of thirty" — and, against the entreaties of his officers, he preferred to superintend operations from a litter rather than remain for a long time mounted — a dangerous proceeding, since in case of a reverse a rapid retreat was rendered impossible. But he could not be induced to change his mind, remarking that in spite of their brave show the enemy were children and would soon be put to flight. So confident was he of victory that it is said he had ordered his men to bring him the head of Hussain Nizâm, but to capture the Âdil Shâh and Ibrahîm of Golkonda alive, that he might keep them the rest of their lives in iron cages.

The battle becoming more general, the Hindus opened a desolating fire from a number of field-pieces and rocket-batteries. The left and right of the Muhammadan line were pressed back after destructive hand-to-hand fighting, many falling on both sides. At this juncture Râma Râya, thinking to encourage his men, descended from his litter and seated himself on a "rich throne set with jewels, under a canopy of crimson velvet, embroidered with gold and adorned with fringes of pearls," ordering his treasurer to place heaps of money all round him, so that he might confer rewards on such of his followers as deserved his attention. "There were also ornaments of gold and jewels placed for the same purpose." A second attack by the Hindus on the guns in the centre seemed likely to complete the overthrow of the whole Muhammadan line, when the front rank of pieces was fired at close quarters, charged with bags of copper money; and this proved so destructive that 5000 Hindus were left dead on the field in front of the batteries. This vigorous policy threw the Hindu centre into confusion, upon which 5000 Muhammadan cavalry charged through the intervals of the guns and cut their way into the midst of the disorganised masses, towards the spot where the Râya had taken post. He had again changed his position and ascended his litter; but hardly had he done so when an elephant belonging to the Nizâm Shâh, wild with the excitement of the battle, dashed forward towards him, and the litter-bearers let fall their precious burden in terror at the animal's approach. Before he had time to recover himself and mount a horse, a body of the allies was upon him, and he was seized and taken prisoner.

This event threw the Hindus into a panic, and they began to give way. Râma Râya was conducted by the officer who commanded the artillery of Hussain Nizâm to his Sultan, who immediately ordered his captive to be decapitated, and the head to be elevated on a long spear, so that it might be visible to the Hindu troops.

On seeing that their chief was dead, the Vijayanagar forces broke and fled. "They were pursued by the allies with such successful slaughter that the river which ran near the field was dyed red with their blood. It is computed on the best authorities that above one hundred thousand infidels were slain in fight and during the pursuit."

The Mussulmans were thus completely victorious, and the Hindus fled towards the capital; but so great was the confusion that there was not the slightest attempt made to take up a new and defensive position amongst the hills surrounding the city, or even to defend the walls or the approaches. The rout was complete.

> "The plunder was so great that every private man in the allied army became rich in gold, jewels, effects, tents, arms, horses, and slaves, as the sultans left every person in possession of what he had acquired, only taking elephants for their own use."

De Couto, describing the death of Râma Râya, states[1] that Hussain Nizâm Shâh cut off his enemy's head with his own hand, exclaiming, "Now I am avenged of thee! Let God do what he will to me!" The Âdil Shâh, on the contrary, was greatly distressed at Râma Râya's death.[2]

[1] Dec. VIII. c. 15.

[2] An interesting note by Colonel Briggs is appended to his translation of these passages of Firishtah (iii. 130). "It affords a striking example at once of the malignity of the Mahomedans towards this Hindoo prince, and

The story of this terrible disaster travelled apace to the city of Vijayanagar. The inhabitants, unconscious of danger, were living in utter ignorance that any serious reverse had taken place; for their leaders had marched out with countless numbers in their train, and had been full of confidence as to the result. Suddenly, however, came the bad news. The army was defeated; the chiefs slain; the troops in retreat. But still they did not grasp the magnitude of the reverse; on all previous occasions the enemy had been either driven back, or bought off with presents from the overstocked treasury of the kings. There was little fear, therefore, for the city itself. That surely was safe! But now came the dejected soldiers hurrying back from the fight, and amongst the foremost the panic-stricken princes of the royal house. Within a few hours these craven chiefs hastily left the palace, carrying with them all the treasures on which they could lay their hands. Five hundred and fifty elephants, laden with treasure in gold, diamonds, and precious stones valued at more than a hundred millions sterling, and carrying the state insignia and the celebrated jewelled throne of the kings, left the city under convoy of bodies of soldiers who remained true to the crown. King Sadâsiva was carried off by his jailor, Tirumala, now sole regent since the death of his brothers, and in long line the royal family and their followers fled southward towards the fortress of Penukonda.

Then a panic seized the city. The truth became at last apparent. This was not a defeat merely, it was a cataclysm. All hope was gone. The myriad dwellers

of the depraved taste of the times, when we see a sculptured representation of Ramraj's head, at the present day, serving as the opening of one of the sewers of the citadel of Beejapoor; and we know that the real head, annually covered with oil and red pigment, has been exhibited to the pious Mahomedans of Ahmudnuggur, on the anniversary of the battle, for the last two hundred and fifty years, by the descendants of the executioner, in whose hands it has remained till the present period." This was written in 1829.

in the city were left defenceless. No retreat, no flight was possible except to a few, for the pack-oxen and carts had almost all followed the forces to the war, and they had not returned. Nothing could be done but to bury all treasures, to arm the younger men, and to wait. Next day the place became a prey to the robber tribes and jungle people of the neighbourhood. Hordes of Brinjâris, Lambâdis, Kurubas, and the like,[1] pounced down on the hapless city and looted the stores and shops, carrying off great quantities of riches. Couto states that there were six concerted attacks by these people during the day.

The third day[2] saw the beginning of the end. The victorious Mussulmans had halted on the field of battle for rest and refreshment, but now they had reached the capital, and from that time forward for a space of five months Vijayanagar knew no rest. The enemy had come to destroy, and they carried out their object relentlessly. They slaughtered the people without mercy; broke down the temples and palaces; and wreaked such savage vengeance on the abode of the kings, that, with the exception of a few great stone-built temples and walls, nothing now remains but a heap of ruins to mark the spot where once the stately buildings stood. They demolished the statues, and even succeeded in breaking the limbs of the huge Narasimha monolith. Nothing seemed to escape them. They broke up the pavilions standing on the huge platform from which the kings used to watch the festivals, and overthrew all the carved work.

[1] Couto calls them "Beduês," probably for "Beduinos," "Bedouins" or wandering tribes.

[2] In this I follow Couto; but the Golkonda historian quoted by Briggs (Firishtah, iii. 414) states that the "allied armies halted for ten days on the field of action, and then proceeded to the capital of Beejanuggur." It is, however, quite possible that both accounts are correct. The advanced Muhammadan troops are almost certain to have been pushed on to the capital. The main body, after the sovereigns had received information that no opposition was offered, may have struck their camp on the tenth day.

They lit huge fires in the magnificently decorated buildings forming the temple of Vitthalasvâmi near the river, and smashed its exquisite stone sculptures. With fire and sword, with crowbars and axes, they carried on day after day their work of destruction. Never perhaps in the history of the world has such havoc been wrought, and wrought so suddenly, on so splendid a city; teeming with a wealthy and industrious population in the full plenitude of prosperity one day, and on the next seized, pillaged, and reduced to ruins, amid scenes of savage massacre and horrors beggaring description.

Cæsaro Federici, an Italian traveller—or "Cæsar Frederick," as he is often called by the English—visited the place two years later, in 1567. He relates that, after the sack, when the allied Muhammadans returned to their own country, Tirumala Râya tried to re-populate the city, but failed, though some few people were induced to take up their abode there.

> "The Citie of *Bezeneger* is not altogether destroyed, yet the houses stand still, but emptie, and there is dwelling in them nothing, as is reported, but Tygres and other wild beasts." [1]

The loot must have been enormous. Couto states that amongst other treasures was found a diamond as large as a hen's egg, which was kept by the Âdil Shâh.[2]

Such was the fate of this great and magnificent city. It never recovered, but remained for ever a scene of desolation and ruin. At the present day the remains of the larger and more durable structures rear themselves from amongst the scanty cultivation carried on by petty farmers, dwellers in tiny villages scattered over the area once so populous. The mud huts which constituted the dwelling-places of by far the greater portion of the inha-

[1] Purchas, edit. of 1625, ii. p. 1703.

[2] Couto states that this diamond was one which the king had affixed to the base of the plume on his horse's headdress (Dec. VIII. c. 15). (See Appendix A.)

bitants have disappeared, and their materials overlie the rocky plain and form the support of a scanty and sparse vegetation. But the old water-channels remain, and by their aid the hollows and low ground have been converted into rich gardens and fields, bearing full crops of waving rice and sugar-cane. Vijayanagar has disappeared as a city, and a congeries of small hamlets with an industrious and contented population has taken its place.

Here my sketch of Vijayanagar history might well end, but I have thought it advisable to add a few notes on succeeding events.

Tirumala took up his abode at Penukonda, and shortly afterwards sent word to the Portuguese traders at Goa that he was in need of horses. A large number were accordingly delivered, when the despotic ruler dismissed the men to return to Goa as best they could without payment. "He licensed the Merchants to depart," writes Federici, "without giving them anything for their Horses, which when the poore Men saw, they were desperate, and, as it were, mad with sorrow and griefe." There was no authority left in the land, and the traveller had to stay in Vijayanagar seven months, "for it was necessarie to rest there until the wayes were clear of Theeves, which at that time ranged up and downe." He had the greatest difficulty in making his way to Goa at all, for he and his companions were constantly seized by sets of marauders and made to pay heavy ransom for their liberty, and on one occasion they were attacked by dacoits and robbed.

Tirumala being now with King Sadâsiva in Penukonda, the nobles of the empire began to throw off their allegiance, and one after another to proclaim their independence. The country was in a state of anarchy. The empire, just now so solid and compact, became disintegrated, and from this time forward it fell rapidly to decay.

To the Portuguese the change was of vital importance. Federici has left us the following note on their trade with Vijayanagar, which I extract from "Purchas's Pilgrims:"—

"The Merchandize that went every yeere from Goa to Bezeneger were Arabian Horses, Velvets, Damaskes, and Sattens, Armesine[1] of Portugall, and pieces of China, Saffron, and Scarletts; and from Bezeneger they had in Turkie for their commodities, Jewels and Pagodas,[2] which be Ducats of Gold; the Apparell that they use in Bezeneger is Velvet, Satten, Damaske, Scarlet, or white Bumbast cloth, according to the estate of the person, with long Hats on their heads called Colae,[3] &c."

Sassetti, who was in India from 1578 to 1588, confirms the others as to Portuguese loss of trade on the ruin of the city:—

"The traffic was so large that it is impossible to imagine it; the place was immensely large; and it was inhabited by people rich, not with richness like ours, but with richness like that of the Crassi and the others of those old days. . . . And such merchandise! Diamonds, rubies, pearls . . . and besides all that, the horse trade. That alone produced a revenue in the city (Goa) of 120 to 150 thousand ducats, which now reaches only 6 thousand."

Couto tells the same story:[4]—

"By this destruction of the kingdom of Bisnaga India and our State were much shaken; for the bulk of the trade undertaken by all was for this kingdom, to which they carried horses, velvets, satins and other sorts of merchandize, by which they made great profits; and the Custom House of Goa suffered much in its Revenue, so that from that day till now the inhabitants of Goa began to live less well; for baizes and fine

---

[1] Portuguese *Armezim*, "a sort of Bengal taffeta" (Michaelis' Dict.).

[2] Gold coins of Vijayanagar.

[3] *Kullayi*. See below, p. 252, 273, 383, and notes.

[4] Dec. VIII. c. 15. I have taken this and the next paragraph from Lopes's *Chronica dos Reys de Bisnaga*, Introd., p. lxviii.

cloths were a trade of great importance for Persia and Portugal, and it then languished, and the gold pagodas, of which every year more than 500,000 were laden in the ships of the kingdom, were then worth 7½ Tangas, and to-day are worth 11½, and similarly every kind of coin."

Sassetti gives another reason, however, for the decay of Portuguese trade and influence at Goa, which cannot be passed over without notice. This was the terrible Inquisition. The fathers of the Church forbade the Hindus under terrible penalties the use of their own sacred books, and prevented them from all exercise of their religion. They destroyed their temples and mosques, and so harassed and interfered with the people that they abandoned the city in large numbers, refusing to remain any longer in a place where they had no liberty, and were liable to imprisonment, torture, and death if they worshipped after their own fashion the gods of their fathers.[1]

About this period, therefore (1567), the political condition of Southern India may be thus summed up:—The Muhammadans of the Dakhan were triumphant though still divided in interest, and their country was broken up into states each bitterly hostile to the other.

[1] Writing in 1675, the traveller Fryer relates what he saw of the Inquisition at Goa. I take the following from his Letter iv., chapter ii. "Going the next Morning to the Palace-Stairs, we saw their Sessions-House, the bloody Prison of the Inquisition; and in a principal Market-place was raised an Engine a great height, at top like a Gibbet, with a Pulley, with steppings to go upon, as on a Flagstaff, for the *Strapado*, which unhinges a Man's joints; a cruel Torture. Over against these Stairs is an Island where they burn . . . all those condemned by the Inquisitor, which are brought from the *Sancto Officio* dress'd up in most horrid Shapes of Imps and Devils, and so delivered to the executioner. . . . St. *Jago*, or St. James's Day, is the Day for the *Aucto de Fie*." And in chapter v. of the same Letter he states that, when he was at Goa, "all Butcher's Meat was forbidden, except Pork"—a regulation irksome enough even to the European residents, but worse for those Hindus allowed by their caste rules to eat meat, but to whom pork is always especially distasteful. Linschoten, who was in India from 1583 to 1589, mentions the imprisonments and tortures inflicted on the Hindus by the Inquisition (vol. ii. pp. 158–227).

The great empire of the south was sorely stricken, and its capital was for ever destroyed; the royal family were refugees at Pennakonda; King Sadâsiva was still a prisoner; and Tirumala, the only survivor of the "three brethren which were tyrants,"[1] was governing the kingdom as well as he could. The nobles were angry and despondent, each one seeking to be free; and the Portuguese on the coast were languishing, with their trade irretrievably injured.

Firishtah summarises the events immediately succeeding the great battle in the following words:—

"The sultans, a few days after the battle, marched onwards into the country of Ramraaje as far as Anicondeh,[2] and the advanced troops penetrated to Beejanuggur, which they plundered, razed the chief buildings, and committed all manner of excess. When the depredations of the allies had destroyed all the country round, Venkatâdri,[3] who had escaped from the battle to a distant fortress, sent humble entreaties of peace to the sultans, to whom he gave up all the places which his brothers had wrested from them; and the victors being satisfied, took leave of each other at Roijore (Raichûr), and returned to their several dominions. The raaje of Beejanuggur since this battle has never recovered its ancient splendour; and the city itself has been so destroyed that it is now totally in ruins and uninhabited,[4] while the country has been seized by the zemindars (petty chiefs), each of whom hath assumed an independent power in his own district."

In 1568 (so it is said) Tirumala murdered his sovereign, Sadâsiva, and seized the throne for himself; but

[1] Cæsar Frederick.

[2] *i.e.*, they advanced by way of Mudkal, Tâvurugiri, and Kanakagiri, a distance of about fifty-five miles, to Ânegundi on the north bank of the river at Vijayanagar.

[3] Other accounts say that Venkatâdri was killed in the battle, and that Tirumala alone of the three brothers survived. Firishtah only wrote from hearsay, and was perhaps misinformed. Probably for "Venkatâdri" should be read "Tirumala."

[4] Firishtah wrote this towards the close of the century.

up to that time he seems to have recognised the unfortunate prince as his liege lord, as we know from four inscriptions at Vellore bearing a date corresponding to 5th February 1567 A.D.[1]

And thus began the third dynasty, if dynasty it can be appropriately called.

[1] "South Indian Inscriptions," Hultzsch, i. 69; *Ind. Ant.*, xxii. 136.

CHAPTER XVI

THE THIRD DYNASTY

Genealogy—The Muhammadan States—Fall of Bankâpur, Kondavîd, Bellamkonda and Vinukonda—Haidarâbâd founded—Adoni under the Muhammadans—Subsequent history in brief.

THE following is the genealogy of this third family.[1] They came apparently of the old royal stock, but their exact relationship to it has never been conclusively settled. The dates appended are the dates of inscriptions, not necessarily the dates of reigns.

- RANGA I. (*m. Tirumalâmbâ*).
  - "ALIYA" RÂMA RÂYA II. (*killed* 1565). (*m. Tirumalamma, daughter of Krishna Deva Râya*).
    - RANGA IV. (*one of five brothers*).
      - PEDDA VENKATA II. (A.D. 1634 and 1636; *m. Bangâramma*).
      - CHINNA (or PINA) VENKATA III.
        - RANGA VI. (*adopted by Gopâla* A.D. 1644).
  - TIRUMALA I. (*king* A.D. 1567; *m. Vengalâ, daughter of Krishna Deva Râya*).
    - RAGHUNÂTHA.
    - RANGA II. (A.D. 1575 and 1584).
    - RÂMA III.
      - TIRUMALA II.
      - RANGA III.
        - RÂMA IV. (*one of several brothers*).
    - VENKATA I. (A.D. 1586 and 1614).
  - VENKATÂDRI (*killed* 1565).
    - RANGA V.
      - GOPÂLA (*adopted Ranga VI.*).

[1] The pedigree is taken from the *Epigraphia Indica*, iii. 238. I am not responsible for the numbers attached to the names. Thus I should prefer to call Râma Râya II. "Râma I.," since his ancestors do not appear to have reigned even in name. But I take the table as Dr. Hultzsch has given it. See

The present Râjah of Ânegundi, whose family name is Pampâpati, and who resides on the old family estate as a zamindar under H.H. the Nizâm of Haidarâbâd, has favoured me with a continuation of the family tree to the present day.

Ranga VI., or, as he is generally styled, Srî Ranga, is said to have been the youngest of three brothers, sons of Chinna Venkata III., Vîra Venkatapati Râya being the eldest. Gopâla, a junior member of the family, succeeded to the throne and adopted Ranga VI., who was thus a junior member of the eldest branch. The eldest brother of Ranga VI. was ousted.

I have no means of knowing whether this information is correct, but the succession of the eldest is given on the following page.

Pampâpati Râjah is recognised by his Government as head of the family for two reasons: first and foremost, because the elder line is extinct and he was adopted by his sister Kuppamma, wife of Krishna Deva of the elder line; secondly, because his two elder brothers are said to have resigned their claims in his favour. The title of the present chief is "Srî Ranga Deva Râya." Whether or no he has better title than his nephew, Kumâra Râghava, need not here be discussed. The interest to the readers of this history lies in the fact that these two are the only surviving male descendants of the ancient royal house.

To revert to the history, which need only be shortly summarised since we have seen Vijayanagar destroyed and its territories in a state of political confusion and disturbance.

I omit altogether the alternate political combinations and dissolutions, the treacheries, quarrels, and fights of

the Kondyâta grant of 1636 (*Ind. Ant.*, xiii. 125), the Vilapâka grant of 1601 (*id.* ii. 371), and the Kallakûrsi grant of 1644 (*id.* xiii. 153); also my "Lists of Antiquities, Madras," i. 35—an inscription of 1623 (No. 30) at Ellore.

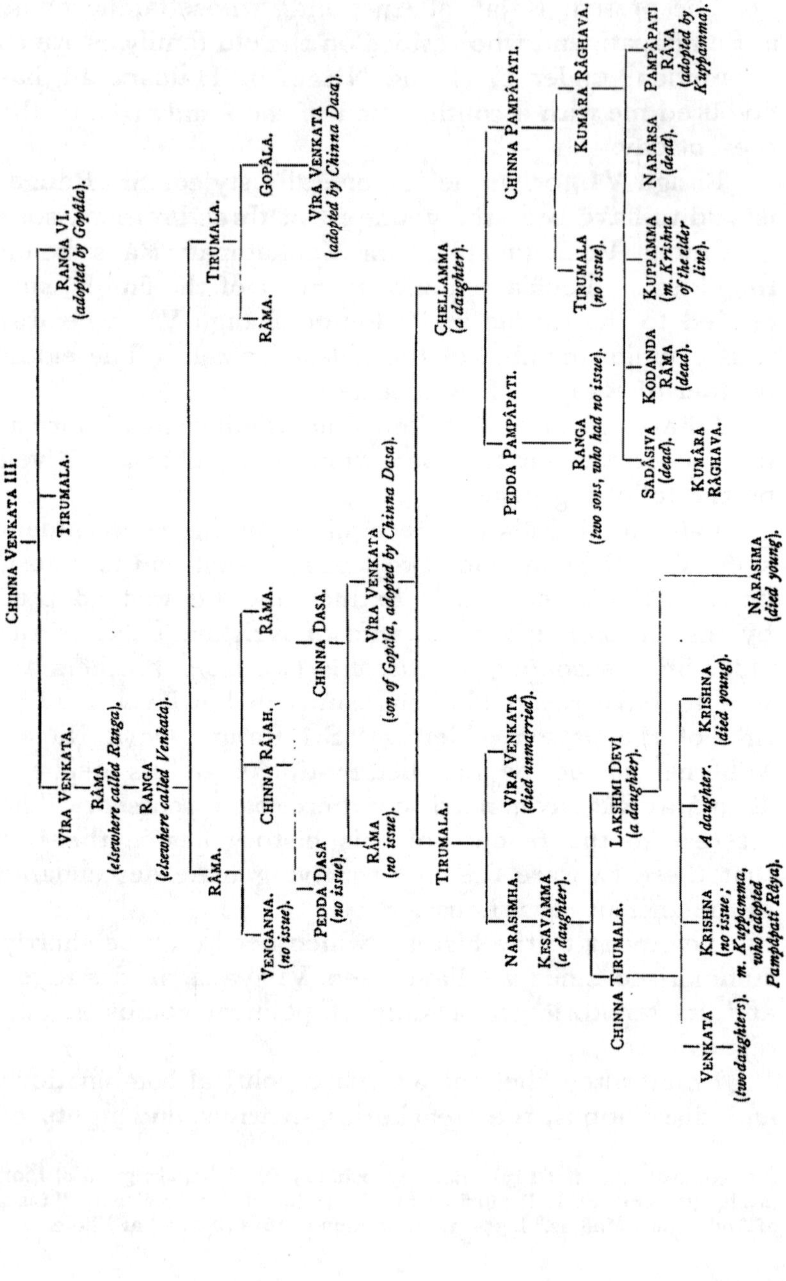
CHINNA VENKATA III.
VĪRA VENKATA.
TIRUMALA.
RANGA VI. (adopted by Gopāla).
RĀMA (elsewhere called Ranga).
RANGA (elsewhere called Venkata).
RĀMA.
TIRUMALA.
VENGANNA. (no issue).
CHINNA RĀJAH.
RĀMA.
RĀMA.
GOPĀLA.
VĪRA VENKATA (adopted by Chinna Dasa).
PEDDA DASA (no issue).
CHINNA DASA.
RĀMA (no issue).
VĪRA VENKATA (son of Gopāla, adopted by Chinna Dasa).
TIRUMALA.
CHELLAMMA (a daughter).
NARASIMHA.
VĪRA VENKATA (died unmarried).
PEDDA PAMPĀPATI.
CHINNA PAMPĀPATI.
KESAVAMMA (a daughter).
LAKSHMI DEVĪ (a daughter).
RANGA (two sons, who had no issue).
TIRUMALA (no issue).
KUMĀRA RĀGHAVA.
CHINNA TIRUMALA.
SADĀSIVA (dead).
KUMĀRA RĀGHAVA.
KODANDA RĀMA (dead).
KUPPAMMA (m. Krishna of the elder line).
NARARSA (dead).
PAMPĀPATI RĀYA (adopted by Kuppamma).
VENKATA
(two daughters).
KRISHNA (no issue; m. Kuppamma, who adopted Pampāpati Rāya).
A daughter.
KRISHNA (died young).
NARASIMA (died young).

the various Muhammadan states after 1565, as unnecessary for our purpose and in order to avoid prolixity, summarising only a few matters which more particularly concern the territories formerly under the great Hindu Empire.

According to Golkonda accounts, a year after the great battle which resulted in the destruction of Vijayanagar, a general of the Qutb Shâh, Raffat Khân Lâri, *alias* Malik Nâib, marched against Rajahmundry, which was finally captured from the Hindus in A.D. 1571–72 (A.H. 979).

Shortly after his return to Bîjapûr (so says Firishtah), Ali Âdil Shâh moved again with an army towards Vijayanagar, but retired on the Ahmadnagar Sultan advancing to oppose him; and not long afterwards he made an ineffectual attempt to reduce Goa. Retiring from the coast, he marched to attack Adoni, then under one of the vassal chiefs of Vijayanagar, who had made himself independent in that tract. The place was taken, and the Nizâm Shâh agreed with the king of Bîjapûr that he would not interfere with the latter's attempts to annex the territories south of the Krishnâ, if he on his part were left free to conquer Berar.

In 1573, therefore, Ali Âdil moved against Dhârwar and Bankâpur. The siege of the latter place under its chief, Velappa Nâik, now independent, lasted for a year and six months, when the garrison, reduced to great straits, surrendered. Firishtah[1] states that the Âdil Shâh destroyed a "superb temple" there, and himself laid the first stone of a mosque which was built on its foundation. More successes followed in the Konkan. Three years later Bellamkonda was similarly attacked, and the Râya in terror retired from Penukonda to Chandragiri. This campaign, however, resulted in failure, apparently owing to the Shâh of Golkonda

[1] Scott, i. 303.

assisting the Hindus. In 1579 the king of Golkonda, in breach of his contract, attacked and reduced the fortresses of Vinukonda and Kondavîd as well as Kacharlakota and Kammam,[1] thus occupying large tracts south of the Krishnâ.

In 1580 Ali Âdil was murdered. Firishtah in his history of the Qutb Shâhs gives the date as Thursday, 23rd Safar, A.H. 987, but the true day appears to have been Monday, 24th Safar, A.H. 988, corresponding to Monday, April 11, A.D. 1580. This at least is the date given by an eye-witness, one Rafî-ud-Dîn Shîrâzî, who held an important position at the court at the time. (The question is discussed by Major King in the *Indian Antiquary*, vol. xvii. p. 221.) Ibrahîm Qutb Shâh of Golkonda also died in 1580, and was succeeded by Muhammad Qulî, his third son, who in 1589 founded the city of Haidarâbâd, originally called Bhâgnagar. He carried on successful wars in the present Kurnool and Cuddapah districts, capturing Kurnool, Nandiâl, Dole, and Gandikota, following up these successes by inroads into the eastern districts of Nellore.

King Tirumala of Vijayanagar was in 1575 followed apparently by his second son, Ranga II., whose successor was his brother Venkata I.[2] (1586). The latter reigned for at least twenty-eight years, and died an old man in 1614. At his death there were widespread revolts, disturbances, and civil warfare, as we shall presently see from the account of Barradas given in the next chapter. An important inscription of his reign, dated in A.D. 1601–2, and recorded on copper-plates, has been published by Dr. Hultzsch.[3]

In 1593 the Bîjapûr Sultan, Ibrahîm Âdil, invaded

[1] Briggs, iii. pp. 435–438.

[2] According to the Kuniyûr plates (*Epig. Ind.*, iii. 236), Rama III., Tirumala's third son, was not king.

[3] *Epig. Ind.*, iv. 269—The Vilapâka Grant.

Mysore, which then belonged to the Râya, and reduced the place after a three months' siege. In the same year this Sultan's brother, Ismâîl, who had been kept prisoner at Belgaum, rose against his sovereign and declared himself independent king of the place. He was besieged there by the royal troops, but owing to treachery in the camp they failed to take the place, and the territories in the neighbourhood were for some time a prey to insurrections and disturbances. Eventually they were reduced to submission and the rebel was killed. Contemporaneously with these events, the Hindus again tried to obtain possession of Adoni, but without success;[1] and a war broke out between the rival kingdoms of Bîjapûr and Ahmadnagar.

With this period ends abruptly the narrative of Firishtah relating to the Sultans of Bîjapûr. The Golkonda history[2] appears to differ widely from it, but I have not thought it necessary here to compare the two stories.

The history of the seventeenth century in Southern

[1] Traditionary history at Adoni relates that the governor of the fortress appointed by Sultan Ali Âdil about A.D. 1566 was Malik Rahimân Khân, who resided there for nearly thirty-nine years. His tomb is still kept up by a grant annually made by the Government in continuation of the old custom, and is in good preservation, having an establishment with a priest and servants. Navâb Siddi Mâsûd Khân was governor when the great mosque, called the Jumma Musjîd, was completed (A.D. 1662). The Bîjapûr Sultan, the last of his line, sent to him a marble slab with an inscription and a grant of a thousand gold pieces. The slab is still to be seen on one of the arches in the interior, and the money was spent in gilding and decorating the building. Aurangzîb of Delhi annexed Bîjapûr in 1686, and appointed Navâb Ghâzi-ud-Dîn Khân governor of Adoni, who had to take the place from the Bîjapûr governor, Siddi Mâsûd Khân. This was done after a fight, in consequence of the Delhi troops firing (blank) on the great mosque from their guns; which so terrified the governor, who held the Jumma Musjîd dearer than his life, that he surrendered. The new governor's family ruled till 1752, when the country was given to Bassâlat Jung of Haidarâbâd. He died and was buried here in 1777, and his tomb is still maintained. The place was ceded to the English by the Nizâm in 1802 with the "Ceded Districts."

[2] Briggs, iii. 416, ff.

India is one of confusion and disturbance. The different governors became independent. The kings of the decadent empire wasted their wealth and lost their territories, so that at length they held a mere nominal sovereignty, and nothing remained but the shadow of the once great name—the prestige of family. And yet, even so late as the years 1792 and 1793, I find a loyal Reddi in the south, in recording on copper-plates some grants of land to temples, declaring that he did so by permission of "Venkatapati Mahârâya of Vijayanagar;"[1] while I know of eight other grants similarly recognising the old Hindu royal family, which were engraved in the eighteenth century.[2]

The Ikkeri or Bednûr chiefs styled themselves under-lords of Vijayanagar till 1650.[3] A Vijayanagar viceroy ruled over Mysore till 1610, after which the descendants of the former viceroys became Râjahs in their own right. In Madura and Tanjore the Nâyakkas became independent in 1602.

All the Muhammadan dynasties in the Dakhan fell under the power of the Mogul emperors of Delhi towards the close of the seventeenth century, and the whole of the south of India soon became practically theirs. But meanwhile another great power had arisen, and at one time threatened to conquer all India. This was the sovereignty of the Mahrattas. Sivajî conquered all the Konkan country by 1673, and four years later he had overthrown the last shreds of Vijayanagar authority in Kurnool, Gingi, and Vellore; while

[1] "Lists of Antiquities, Madras" (Sewell), ii. 6, 7, Nos. 45, 46.

[2] *Op. cit.*, ii. 139–140.

[3] The Italian traveller Pietro della Valle was at Ikkeri at the close of the year 1623, and gives an interesting account of all that he saw, and what befell him there. He went with an embassy from Goa to that place. "This Prince *Venktapa Naieka* was sometime Vassal and one of the ministers of the great King of *Vidiâ Nagâr* . . . but after the downfall of the king . . . Venktapâ Naieka . . . remain'd absolute Prince of the State of which he was Governour, which also, being a good souldier, he hath much enlarged."

his brother Ekojî had already, in 1674, captured Tanjore, and established a dynasty there which lasted for a century. But with this exception the Mahrattas established no real domination in the extreme south.

Mysore remained independent under its line of Hindu kings till the throne was usurped by Haidar Alî and his son and successor, "Tippoo," who together ruled for about forty years. After the latter's defeat and death at Seringapatam in 1799, the country was restored by the English to the Hindu line.

The site on which stands Fort St. George at Madras was granted to Mr. Francis Day, chief factor of the English there, by Srî Ranga Râya VI. in March 1639, the king being then resident in Chandragiri.

The first English factory at Madras had been established in 1620.

CHAPTER XVII

THE STORY OF BARRADAS (1614)

Chandragiri in 1614—Death of King Venkata—Rebellion of Jaga Râya and murder of the royal family—Loyalty of Echama Naik—The Portuguese independent at San Thomé—Actors in the drama—The affair at "Paleacate."—List of successors—Conclusion.

THE following note of occurrences which took place at Chandragiri in 1614 on the death of King Venkata I. will be found of singular interest, as it relates to events of which we in England have hitherto, I think, been in complete ignorance. In consists of an extract from a letter written at Cochin on December 12, A.D. 1616, by Manuel Barradas, and recently found by Senhor Lopes amongst a quantity of letters preserved in the National Archives at Lisbon.[1] He copied it from the original, and kindly sent it to me. The translation is my own.

"I will now tell you . . . about the death of the old King of Bisnaga, called Vencattapatti Rayalu,[2] and of his selection as his successor of a nephew by name Chica Rayalu; setting aside another who was commonly held to be his son, but who in reality was not so. The true fact was this. The

---

[1] *Cartario dos Jesuitos* (Bundle 36, packet 95, No. 22, in the National Archives at Lisbon, *Archivo da Torre do Tombo*). Compare Antonio Bocarro, *Decada* xiii. p. 296. Mr. Lopes also refers me to an as yet inedited MS., *Documentos remettidos da India*, or *Livros das monçoes*, t. i. 359, and t. ii. 370–371, as relating to the same tragic events.

[2] See the genealogical table on p. 214. Venkata I. was son of Tirumala, the first real king of the fourth dynasty. The nephew, "Chikka Raya," may have been Ranga III., "Chikka" (young) being, as Barradas tells us, a name usually given to the heir to the throne. In that case Ranga's son, Râma IV., "one of several brothers," would be the boy who survived the wholesale massacre related in the letter.

King was married to a daughter of Jaga Râya by name Bayamâ, and though she eagerly longed for a son she had none in spite of the means, legitimate or illegitimate, that she employed for that purpose. A Brahman woman of the household of the Queen's father, knowing how strong was the Queen's desire to have a son, and seeing that God had not granted her one, told her that she herself was pregnant for a month; and she advised her to tell the King, and to publish it abroad, that she (the Queen) had been pregnant for a month, and to feign to be in that state, and said that after she (the Brahman woman) had been delivered she would secretly send the child to the palace by some confidant, upon which the Queen could announce that this boy was her own son. The advice seemed good to the Queen, and she pretended that she was pregnant, and no sooner was the Brahman woman delivered of a son than she sent it to the palace, and the news was spread abroad that Queen Bayamâ had brought forth a son. The King, knowing all this, yet for the love he bore the Queen, and so that the matter should not come to light, dissembled and made feasts, giving the name 'Chica Râya' to the boy, which is the name always given to the heir to the throne.[1] Yet he never treated him as a son, but on the contrary kept him always shut up in the palace of Chandigri,[2] nor ever allowed him to go out of it without his especial permission, which indeed he never granted except when in company of the Queen. Withal, the boy arriving at the age of fourteen years, he married him to a niece of his, doing him much honour so as to satisfy Obo Râya, his brother-in-law.[3]

"Three days before his death, the King, leaving aside, as I say, this putative son, called for his nephew Chica Râya, in presence of several of the nobles of the kingdom, and extended towards him his right hand on which was the ring of state, and put it close to him, so that he should take it and should become his successor in the kingdom. With this the nephew, bursting into tears, begged the King to give it to whom he would, and that for himself he did not desire to be king, and he bent low, weeping at the feet of the old man. The King made a sign to those around him that they should raise

---

[1] The name "Chikka Râya" in Kanarese means "little" or "young" Râya.

[2] Chandragiri.

[3] It is not known to whom this refers. The name is perhaps "Obala."

the prince up, and they did so; and they then placed him on the King's right hand, and the King extended his own hand so that he might take the ring. But the prince lifted his hands above his head, as if he already had divined how much ill fortune the ring would bring him, and begged the King to pardon him if he wished not to take it. The old man then took the ring and held it on the point of his finger, offering it the second time to Chica Râya, who by the advice of the captains present took it, and placed it on his head and then on his finger, shedding many tears. Then the King sent for his robe, valued at 200,000 cruzados, the great diamond which was in his ear, which was worth more than 600,000 cruzados, his earrings, valued at more than 200,000, and his great pearls, which are of the highest price. All these royal insignia he gave to his nephew Chica Râya as being his successor, and as such he was at once proclaimed. While some rejoiced, others were displeased.

"Three days later the King died at the age of sixty-seven years. His body was burned in his own garden with sweet-scented woods, sandal, aloes, and such like; and immediately afterwards three queens burned themselves, one of whom was of the same age as the King, and the other two aged thirty-five years. They showed great courage. They went forth richly dressed with many jewels and gold ornaments and precious stones, and arriving at the funeral pyre they divided these, giving some to their relatives, some to the Brahmans to offer prayers for them, and throwing some to be scrambled for by the people. Then they took leave of all, mounted on to a lofty place, and threw themselves into the middle of the fire, which was very great. Thus they passed into eternity.

"Then the new King began to rule, compelling some of the captains to leave the fortress, but keeping others by his side; and all came to him to offer their allegiance except three. These were Jaga Râya, who has six hundred thousand cruzados of revenue and puts twenty thousand men into the field; Tima Naique, who has four hundred thousand cruzados of revenue and keeps up an army of twelve thousand men; and Maca Râya, who has a revenue of two hundred thousand cruzados and musters six thousand men. They swore never to do homage to the new King, but, on the contrary, to raise in his place the putative son of the dead King, the nephew of

PALACE OF THE RAJAHS AT CHANDRAGIRI

(*From a Photograph by* Messrs. Nicholas & Co.)

Jaga Râya,[1] who was the chief of this conspiracy. In a few days there occurred the following opportunity.

"The new King displeased three of his nobles; the first, the Dalavay, who is the commander of the army and pays a tribute of five hundred thousand cruzados, because he desired him to give up three fortresses which the King wished to confer on two of his own sons; the second, his minister, whom he asked to pay a hundred thousand cruzados, alleging that he had stolen them from the old King his uncle; the third, Narpa Râya, since he demanded the jewels which his sister, the wife of the old King, had given to Narpa. All these three answered the King that they would obey his commands within two days; but they secretly plotted with Jaga Râya to raise up the latter's nephew to be King. And this they did in manner following:—

"Jaga Râya sent to tell the King that he wished to do homage to him, and so also did Tima Naique and Maca Râya. The poor King allowed them to enter. Jaga Râya selected five thousand men, and leaving the rest outside the city he entered the fortress with these chosen followers. The two other conspirators did the same, each of them bringing with them two thousand selected men. The fortress has two walls. Arrived at these, Jaga Râya left at the first gate a thousand men, and at the second a thousand. The Dalavay seized two other gates of the fortress, on the other side. There being some tumult, and a cry of treason being raised, the King ordered the palace gates to be closed, but the conspirators as soon as they reached them began to break them down. Maca Râya was the first to succeed, crying out that he would deliver up the King to them; and he did so, sending the King a message that if he surrendered he would pledge his word to do him no ill, but that the nephew of Jaga Râya must be King, he being the son of the late King.

"The poor surrounded King, seeing himself without followers and without any remedy, accepted the promise, and with his wife and sons left the tower in which he was staying. He passed through the midst of the soldiers with a face grave and severe, and with eyes downcast. There was none to do him reverence with hands (as is the custom) joined over the head, nor did he salute any one.

---

[1] This youth was only a great-nephew of Jaga Râya's by a double marriage. His wife was niece of King Venkata, and therefore by marriage niece of Queen Bayamâ, who was Jaga Râya's daughter.

"The King having left, Jaga Râya called his nephew and crowned him, causing all the nobles present to do him homage; and he, finding himself now crowned King, entered the palace and took possession of it and of all the riches and precious stones that he found there. If report says truly, he found in diamonds alone three large chests full of fine stones. After this (Jaga Râya) placed the deposed King under the strictest guard, and he was deserted by all save by one captain alone whose name was Echama Naique, who stopped outside the fortress with eight thousand men and refused to join Jaga Râya. Indeed, hearing of the treason, he struck his camp and shut himself up in his own fortress and began to collect more troops.

"Jaga Râya sent a message to this man bidding him come and do homage to his nephew, and saying that if he refused he would destroy him. Echama Naique made answer that he was not the man to do reverence to a boy who was the son of no one knew whom, nor even what his caste was; and, so far as destroying him went, would Jaga Râya come out and meet him? If so, he would wait for him with such troops as he possessed!

"When this reply was received Jaga Râya made use of a thousand gentle expressions, and promised honours and revenues, but nothing could turn him. Nay, Echama took the field with his forces and offered battle to Jaga Râya; saying that, since the latter had all the captains on his side, let him come and fight and beat him if he could, and then the nephew would become King unopposed. In the end Jaga Râya despaired of securing Echama Naique's allegiance, but he won over many other nobles by gifts and promises.

"While Jaga Râya was so engaged, Echama Naique was attempting to obtain access to the imprisoned King by some way or other; but finding this not possible, he sought for a means of at least getting possession of one of his sons. And he did so in this manner. He sent and summoned the washerman who washed the imprisoned King's clothes, and promised him great things if he would bring him the King's middle son. The washerman gave his word that he would so do if the matter were kept secret. When the day arrived on which it was the custom for him to take the clean clothes to the King, he carried them (into the prison) and with them a palm-leaf letter from Echama Naique, who earnestly begged the King to send him one at least of the three sons whom he had with him, assuring him that the washerman could effect his escape. The

King did so, giving up his second son aged twelve years, for the washerman did not dare take the eldest, who was eighteen years old. He handed over the boy, and put him in amongst the dirty clothes, warning him to have no fear and not to cry out even if he felt any pain. In order more safely to pass the guards, the washerman placed on top of all some very foul clothes, such as every one would avoid; and went out crying '*Talla! talla!*' which means 'Keep at a distance! keep at a distance!' All therefore gave place to him, and he went out of the fortress to his own house. Here he kept the prince in hiding for three days, and at the end of them delivered him up to Echama Naique, whose camp was a league distant from the city, and the boy was received by that chief and by all his army with great rejoicing.

"The news then spread abroad and came to the ears of Jaga Râya, who commanded the palace to be searched, and found that it was true. He was so greatly affected that he kept to his house for several days; but he doubled the guards on the King, his prisoner, closed the gates, and commanded that no one should give aught to the King to eat but rice and coarse vegetables.[1]

"As soon as it was known that Echama Naique had possession of the King's son, there went over to him four of Jaga Râya's captains with eight thousand men; so that he had in all sixteen thousand, and now had good hope of defending the rightful King. He took, therefore, measures for effecting the latter's escape. He selected from amongst all his soldiers twenty men, who promised to attempt to dig an underground passage which should reach to where the King lay in prison. In pursuance of this resolve they went to the fortress, offered themselves to the Dalavay as entering into his service, received pay, and after some days began to dig the passage so as to gain entrance to the King's prison. The King, seeing soldiers enter thus into his apartment, was amazed, and even more so when he saw them prostrate themselves on the ground and deliver him a palm-leaf letter from Echama Naique, in which he begged the King to trust himself to these men, as they would escort him out of the fortress. The King consented. He took off his robes hastily and covered himself with a single cloth; and bidding farewell to his wife, his sons, and his daughters, told

[1] *Bredos.* See note, p. 245.

them to have no fear, for that he, when free, would save them all.

"But it so happened that at this very moment one of the soldiers who were guarding the palace by night with torches fell into a hole, and at his cries the rest ran up, and on digging they discovered the underground passage. They entered it and got as far as the palace, arriving there just when the unhappy King was descending into it in order to escape. He was seized and the alarm given to Jaga Râya, who sent the King to another place more confined and narrower, and with more guards, so that the poor prisoner despaired of ever escaping.

"Echama Naique, seeing that this stratagem had failed, bribed heavily a captain of five hundred men who were in the fortress to slay the guards as soon as some good occasion offered, and to rescue the King. This man, who was called Iteobleza,[1] finding one day that Jaga Râya was leaving the palace with all his men in order to receive a certain chief who had proffered his submission, and that there only remained in the fortress about five thousand men, in less than an hour slew the guards, seized three gates, and sent a message to Echama Naique telling him to come at once and seize the fortress. But Jaga Râya was the more expeditious; he returned with all his forces, entered by a postern gate, of the existence of which Iteobleza had not been warned, and put to death the captain and his five hundred followers.

"Enraged at this attempt, Jaga Râya, to strengthen the party of his nephew, resolved to slay the King and all his family. He entrusted this business to a brother of his named Chinaobraya,[2] ordering him to go to the palace and tell the poor King that he must slay himself, and that if he would not he himself would kill him with stabs of his dagger.

"The prisoner attempted to excuse himself, saying that he knew nothing of the attempted revolt. But seeing the determination of Chinaobraya, who told him that he must necessarily die, either by his own hand or by that of another—a most pitiful case, and one that I relate full of sorrow!—the poor King called his wife, and after he had spoken to her awhile he beheaded her. Then he sent for his youngest son and did the same to him. He put to death similarly his little daughter. Afterwards he sent for his eldest son, who was already married,

---

[1] Perhaps Ite Obalêsvara.

[2] Chinna Obala Râya.

and commanded him to slay his wife, which he did by beheading her. This done, the King took a long sword of four fingers' breadth, and, throwing himself upon it, breathed his last; and his son, heir to the throne, did the same to himself in imitation of his father. There remained only a little daughter whom the King could not bring himself to slay; but Chinaobraya killed her, so that none of the family should remain alive of the blood royal, and the throne should be secured for his nephew.

"Some of the chiefs were struck with horror at this dreadful deed, and were so enraged at its cruelty that they went over to Echama Naique, resolved to defend the prince who had been rescued by the washerman, and who alone remained of all the royal family. Echama Naique, furious at this shameful barbarity and confident in the justice of his cause, selected ten thousand of his best soldiers, and with them offered battle to Jaga Râya, who had more than sixty thousand men and a number of elephants and horses. Echama sent him a message in this form:—'Now that thou hast murdered thy king and all his family, and there alone remains this boy whom I rescued from thee and have in my keeping, come out and take the field with all thy troops; kill him and me, and then thy nephew will be secure on the throne!'

"Jaga Râya tried to evade this for some time; but finding that Echama Naique insisted, he decided to fight him, trusting that with so great a number of men he would easily not only be victorious, but would be able to capture both Echama Naique and the prince. He took the field, therefore, with all his troops. Echama Naique entrusted the prince to a force of ten thousand men who remained a league away, and with the other ten thousand he not only offered battle, but was the first to attack; and that with such fury and violence that Jaga Râya, with all the people surrounding his nephew, was driven to one side, leaving gaps open to the enemy, and many met their deaths in the fight. Echama Naique entered in triumph the tents of Jaga Râya, finding in them all the royal insignia belonging to the old King, and these he delivered to the young prince, the son of Chica Râya, proclaiming him rightful heir and King of all the empire of Bisnaga.

"The spoil which he took was very large, for in precious stones alone they say that he found two millions worth.

"After this victory many of the nobles joined themselves to Echama Naique. So much so, that in a short time he had with him fifty thousand fighting men in his camp; while Jaga Râya, with only fifteen thousand, fled to the jungles. Here, however, he was joined by more people, so that the war has continued these two years,[1] fortune favouring now one side now the other. But the party of the young prince has always been gaining strength; the more so because, although the great Naique of Madura[2]—a page of the betel to the King of Bisnaga, who pays a revenue every year of, some say, 600,000 pagodas, and has under him many kings and nobles as vassals, such as he of Travancor—took the side of Jaga Râya, and sustained him against the Naique of Tanjaor. Yet the latter, though not so powerful, is, with the aid of the young King, gradually getting the upper hand. Indeed there are now assembled in the field in the large open plains of Trinchenepalî[3] not only the hundred thousand men that each party has, but as many as a million of soldiers.

"Taking advantage of these civil wars, the city of San Thomé[4]—which up to now belonged to the King of Bisnaga, paying him revenues and customs which he used to make over to certain chiefs, by whom the Portuguese were often greatly troubled—determined to liberate itself, and become in everything and for everything the property of the King of Portugal. To this end she begged the Viceroy to send and take possession of her in the name of his Majesty, which he did, as I shall afterwards tell you. Meanwhile the captain who governed the town, by name Manuel de Frias, seeing that there was close to the town a fortress that commanded it, determined to seize it by

---

[1] Written in 1616.

[2] This was Muttu Vîrappa, Nayakka (or Naik) of Madura from 1609 to 1623. Mr. Nelson ("The Madura Country") mentions that in his reign there was a war with Tanjore. Nuniz, writing in 1535, does not mention Madura as amongst the great divisions of the Vijayanagar kingdom; and this coincides with the history as derived from other sources. But by 1614 the Naik of Madura had become very powerful, though the people still occasionally recognised their old sovereigns, the Pândiyans, one of whom is mentioned as late as 1623 ("Sketch of the Dynasties of Southern India," 85).

[3] Trichinopoly.

[4] Close to Madras, often called "Melliapor" by the Portuguese, its native name being Mailâpûr. Linschoten, writing at the end of the sixteenth century, a few years earlier than the date of the events described, says, "This towne . . . is now the chiefe cittie of Narsinga and of the coast of Choromandel."

force, seeing that its captain declined to surrender it. So he laid siege to it, surrounding it so closely that no one could get out."

In the end the Portuguese were successful. The fortress was taken, its garrison of 1500 men capitulated, and a fleet came round by sea to complete the conquest.

The foregoing story relates to events never before, I think, made known to English readers, and so far is of the highest interest. Let us, for the moment, grant its accuracy, and read it by the light of the genealogical table already given.[1]

King Venkata I. (1586–1614) had a sister who was married to a chief whom Barradas calls "Obo" (perhaps Obala) Râya. So far as we know, his only nephews were Tirumala II. and Ranga III., sons of his brother, Râma III. Since Tirumala II. appears to have had no sons, and Ranga III. had a son, Râma IV., who is asserted in the inscriptions to have been "one of several brothers," it is natural to suppose that the nephew mentioned by Barradas, who was raised to be king on the death of the old King Venkata I. in 1614, and who had three sons, was Ranga III., called "Chikka Râya" or "Crown-prince" in the text. He, then, succeeded in 1614, but was afterwards deposed, imprisoned, and compelled to take his own life. His eldest son at the same time followed his example, and his youngest son was slain by his father. The "middle son" escaped, and was raised to the throne by a friendly chief named Echama Naik. This second son was probably Ranga IV. Two of King Venkata's wives were Bayamâ, daughter of Jaga Râya, and a lady unnamed, sister of Narpa Râya. A niece of Venkata I. had been given in marriage to a Brahman boy, who had been surrep-

[1] See above, p. 214.

titiously introduced into the palace by Bayamâ and educated in the pretence that he was son of King Venkata. The plot to raise him to the throne was temporarily successful, and Ranga III. and all the royal family were killed, saving only Ranga IV., who afterwards came to the throne.

How much of the story told is true we cannot as yet decide; but it is extremely improbable that the whole is a pure invention, and we may for the present accept it, fixing the date of these occurrences as certainly between the years 1614 and 1616 A.D. — the date of Barradas's letter being December 12 in the latter year.

It will be observed that the inscriptions upon which the genealogical table given above, from the *Epigraphia Indica*, is founded do not yield any date between A.D. 1614 and 1634, when Pedda Venkata II. is named as king. In 1883 I published[1] a list of Vijayanagar names derived from reports of inscriptions which had then reached me. I am by no means certain of their accuracy, and it is clear that they must all be hereafter carefully examined. But so far as it goes the list runs thus:—

	A.D.
Ranga	1619
Râma	1620, 1622
Ranga	1623
Venkata	1623
Râma	1629
Venkata	1636

The last-mentioned name and date are apparently correct.

In 1633 the Portuguese, encouraged by the Vijayanagar king, still at Chandragiri, attempted to eject the Dutch from "Paleacate," or Pulicat. An arrangement was made by which the Portuguese were to attack by sea and the Rajah by land; but while the Viceroy sent

[1] "Sketch of the Dynasties of Southern India," p. 112.

his twelve ships as agreed on, the Rajah failed to attack, alleging in explanation that he was compelled to use his army to put down internal disturbances in the kingdom. A second expedition met with no better success, the plans of the Portuguese being again upset by the non-fulfilment of the king's part of the bargain. On the departure of the fleet the king did attack the Dutch settlement, but was bought off by a large payment, and the Hollanders remained subsequently undisturbed.

Senhor Lopes tells me that he has found in the National Archives in the Torre do Tombo, amongst the "Livros das Monçoes," a number of papers bearing on this subject. The most interesting are those contained in Volume xxxiv. (fol. 91–99). These were written by the Captain-General of Meliapor (St. Thomé), by Padre Pero Mexia of the Company of Jesus, and by the Bishop; and amongst the other documents are to be seen translations of two palm-leaf letters written by the king of Vijayanagar, then at Vellore. It appears from these that the king was devoid of energy, and that one Timma Râya had revolted against him.

We know that in 1639 the king of Vijayanagar was named Ranga or Srî-Ranga, and that he was at that time residing at Chandragiri; because in that year Mr. Day, the head of the English trading station at Madras, obtained from the king a grant of land at that place, one mile broad by five miles long, on which Fort St. George was afterwards constructed. The country about Madras was then ruled over by a governor or Naik, and so little heed did he pay to the wishes or commands of his titular sovereign, that although the Râya had directed that the name of the new town should be "Srîrangarâyalapatnam" ("city of Srî Ranga Râya"), the Naik christened it after the name of his own father, Chenna, and called it "Chenna-patnam," by which appellation it has ever since been known to the Hindus. Such, at least, is the local tradition. This king was probably the Ranga VI. of the *Epigraphia* list, mentioned as living in 1644 A.D.

After this date my (doubtful and unexamined) inscriptions yield the following names and dates :—

	A.D.
Ranga . . .	1643, 1647, 1655, 1662 1663, 1665, 1667, 1678
Venkata . .	1678, 1680
Ranga . . .	1692
Venkata . .	1706
Ranga . . .	1716
Mahâdeva . .	1724
Ranga . . .	1729
Venkata . .	1732
Râma . . .	1739 (?)
Venkata . .	1744
Venkata . .	1791, 1792, 1793

From Sir Thomas Munro's papers I gather that the territory about the old family estate of Ânegundi was early in the eighteenth century held by the Râyas from the Mogul emperor of Delhi as a tributary state. In 1749 it was seized by the Mahrattas, and in 1775 it was reduced by Haidar Alî of Mysore, but continued to exist as a tributary quasi-independent state till the time of Tîpu (Tippoo Sultan).

Tîpu, who never suffered from an excess of compunction or compassion when his own interests were at stake, annexed the estate bodily to his dominions in 1786. Thirteen years later he was killed at Seringapatam, and in the settlement that followed the little territory was made over to the Nizâm of Haidarâbâd, the English Government retaining all lands on their side of the Tungabhadrâ. Partly in compensation for this loss of land the Government has till very recently paid an annual pension to the head of the Ânegundi family. This has now been abolished.

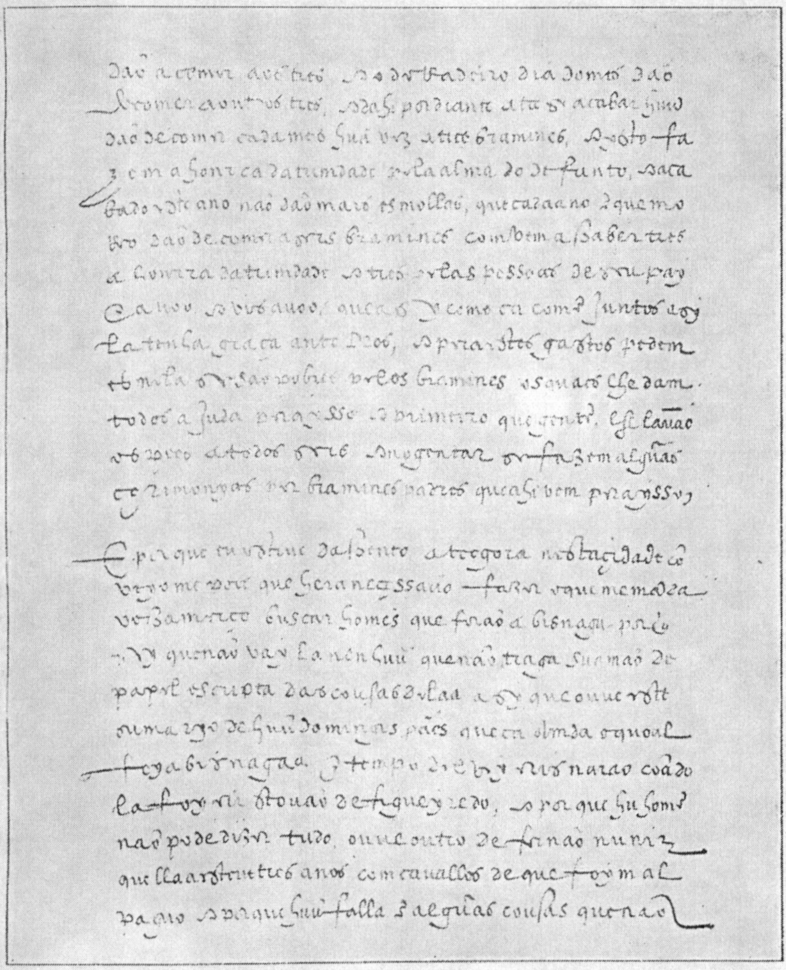

FACSIMILE OF MS. COPY (IN THE BIBLIOTHEQUE NATIONALE.

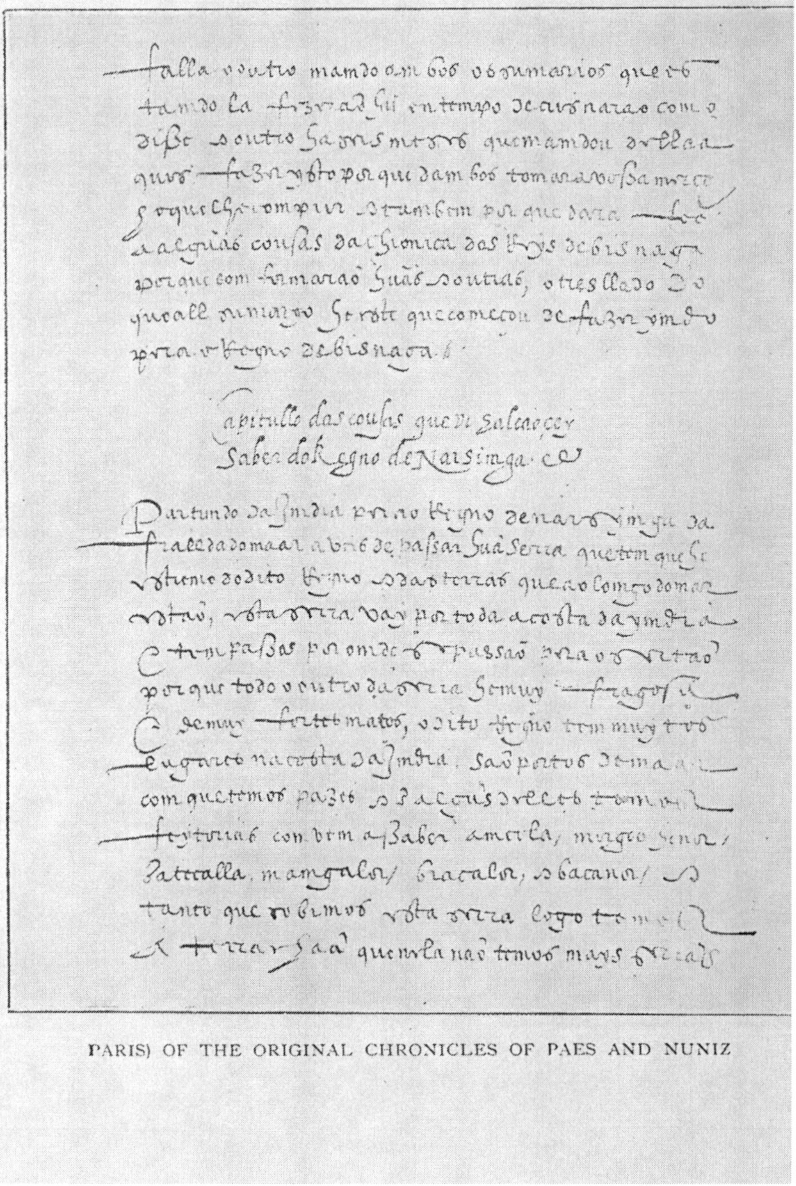

falla. E outro mamdo ambos os sumarios que es-
tamdo la fizera hũ em tempo de aver narao com o
diste e outro ha pouco tempo que mamdou e vellaa-
quy. fazy isto porque dambos tomara vosa merce
o que lhe comprir e tambem porque dara fee
a algũas cousas da chronica dos Reys de Bisnaga
porque com formarão hũas e outras, o tresllado do
qual sumario he este que começou de fazer yndo
pera o Reyno de Bisnaga.

Capitullo das cousas que vi e alcancei
saber do Reyno de Narsimga.

Partindo da India pera o Reyno de Narsymga da
fralda do mar avés de passar hũa serra que tem que he
o termo do dito Reyno e das terras que ao longo do mar
estão, esta serra vay por toda a costa da India
e tem passos per omde se passão pera o sertão
porque todo o outro da serra he muy fragosa
e de muy fortes matos, o dito Reyno tem muytos
lugares na costa da India, são portos de mar
com que temos pazes e em algũs delles temos
feytorias, convem a saber amcolla, mirgeo, honor,
batticalla, mamgalor, bracalor, e bacanor, e
tanto que sobimos esta serra logo temos
a terra chaã que nella não temos mays serras

PARIS) OF THE ORIGINAL CHRONICLES OF PAES AND NUNIZ

CHRONICLES OF PAES AND NUNIZ

LETTER

(? TO THE HISTORIAN BARROS) WHICH ACCOMPANIED THE CHRONICLES WHEN SENT FROM INDIA TO PORTUGAL ABOUT THE YEAR 1537 A.D.

SINCE I have lived till now in this city (? Goa), it seemed necessary to do what your Honour desired of me, namely, to search for men who had formerly been in Bisnaga; for I know that no one goes there without bringing away his quire of paper written about its affairs. Thus I obtained this summary from one Domingos Paes, who goes there, and who was at Bisnaga in the time of Crisnarão when Cristovão de Figueiredo was there. I obtained another from Fernão Nuniz, who was there three years trading in horses (which did not prove remunerative). Since one man cannot tell everything—one relating some things which another does not—I send both the summaries made by them, namely, one in the time of Crisnarão, as I have said, and the other sent from there six months since. I desire to do this because your honour can gather what is useful to you from both, and because you will thus give the more credit to some things in the chronicle of the kings of Bisnaga, since they conform one to the other. The copy of the summary which he began to make[1] when he first went to the kingdom of Bisnaga is as follows:—

[1] "He" here is Domingo Paes.

NARRATIVE OF DOMINGOS PAES

(WRITTEN PROBABLY A.D. 1520–22)

OF THE THINGS WHICH I SAW AND CONTRIVED TO LEARN CONCERNING THE KINGDOM OF NARSIMGA, ETC.[1]

ON leaving India[2] to travel towards the kingdom of Narsymga from the sea-coast, you have (first) to pass a range of hills (*serra*), the boundary of the said kingdom and of those territories which are by the sea. This *serra* runs along the whole of the coast of India, and has passes by which people enter the interior; for all the rest of the range is very rocky and is filled with thick forest. The said kingdom has many places on the coast of India; they are seaports with which we are at peace, and in some of them we have factories, namely, Amcola, Mirgeo, Honor, Batecalla, Mamgalor, Bracalor, and Bacanor. And as soon as we are above this *serra* we have a plain country in which there are no more ranges of hills, but only a few mountains, and these small ones; for all the rest is like the plains of Ssantarem.[3] Only on the road from Batecala[4] to a town called *Zambuja*,

[1] The "kingdom of Narsinga" is the name often given by the Portuguese and others to Vijayanagar.

[2] The term here is limited to the small territory of Portuguese India immediately round the city of Goa. Thus Linschoten (A.D. 1583) wrote, "At the end of Cambaya beginneth India, *and* the lands of Decam and Cuncam," meaning that immediately south of the territories of Cambay began those of Portuguese India, while other countries on the border were the Dakhan and the Konkan.

[3] In Portugal.

[4] This was apparently the usual route for travellers from the coast to Vijayanagar. Fr. Luis used it for his journey from Cochin to the capital in 1509 (above, p. 123, and note).

there are some ranges with forests; nevertheless the road is very even. From Batecala to this town of Zambur[1] is forty leagues; the road has many streams of water by its side, and because of this so much merchandise flows to Batecala that every year there come five or six thousand pack-oxen.

Now to tell of the aforesaid kingdom. It is a country sparsely wooded except along this *serra* on the east,[2] but in places you walk for two or three leagues under groves of trees; and behind cities and towns and villages they have plantations of mangoes, and jack-fruit trees, and tamarinds and other very large trees, which form resting-places where merchants halt with their merchandise. I saw in the city of Recalem[3] a tree under which we lodged three hundred and twenty horses, standing in order as in their stables, and all over the country you may see many small trees. These dominions are very well cultivated and very fertile, and are provided with quantities of cattle, such as cows, buffaloes, and sheep; also of birds, both those belonging to the hills and those reared at home, and this in greater abundance than in our tracts. The land has plenty of rice and Indian-corn, grains, beans, and other kind of crops which are not sown in our parts; also an infinity of cotton. Of the grains there is a great quantity, because, besides being used as food for men, it is also used for horses, since there is no other kind of barley; and this country has also much wheat, and that good. The whole country is thickly populated with cities and towns and villages; the king allows them to be surrounded only with earthen walls for fear of their becoming too strong. But if a city is situated at the

[1] Probably Sandûr, about 120 miles from the coast at Bhatkal. Sandûr is a small Mahratta state 25 miles from Vijayanagar.

[2] That is, on the east of Portuguese India, west of the territory of Vijayanagar.

[3] Unidentified. The great tree was of course a banyan.

extremity of his territory he gives his consent to its having stone walls, but never the towns; so that they may make fortresses of the cities but not of the towns.

And because this country is all flat, the winds blow here more than in other parts. The oil which it produces comes from seeds sown and afterwards reaped, and they obtain it by means of machines which they make. This country wants water because it is very great and has few streams; they make lakes in which water collects when it rains, and thereby they maintain themselves. They maintain themselves by means of some in which there are springs better than by others that have only the water from rain; for we find many quite dry, so that people go about walking in their beds, and dig holes to try and find enough water, even a little, for their maintenance. The failure of the water is because they have no winter, as in our parts and in (Portuguese) India, but only thunder-storms that are greater in one year than in another. The water in these lakes is for the most part muddy, especially in those where there are no springs, and the reason why it is so muddy is because of the strong wind and the dust that is in this country, which never allows the water to be clear; and also because of the numbers of cattle, buffaloes, cows, oxen, and other small cattle that drink in them. For you must know that in this land they do not slaughter oxen or cows; the oxen are beasts of burden and are like sumpter-mules; these carry all their goods. They worship the cows, and have them in their pagodas made in stone, and also bulls; they have many bulls that they present to these pagodas, and these bulls go about the city without any one causing them any harm or loss. Further, there are asses in this country, but they are small, and they use them only for little things; those that wash clothes lay the cloths on them, and use them for this more than for anything else. You must know that this kingdom of Narsymga has three hundred *graos* of coast, each *grao* being a league, along the hill-range (*serra*) of which I have spoken, until you arrive at Ballagate and Charamãodel,[1] which belong to this kingdom; and in breadth it is one hundred and sixty-four *graos;* each large *grao* measures two of our leagues, so that it has six hundred leagues of coast, and across it three hundred and forty-eight leagues . . . across from Batacalla to the kingdom of Orya.[2]

And this kingdom marches[3] with all the territory of Bengal, and on the other side with the kingdom of Orya, which is to the east, and on the other side to the north with the kingdom of Dakhan, belonging to which are the lands which the Ydallcão[4] has, and Ozemelluco.[5] Goa is at war with this Ydallcão, because that city was his, and we have taken it from him.

And this kingdom of Orya, of which I have spoken above, is said to be much larger than the kingdom of Narsymga, since it marches with all Bengal, and is at war with her; and it marches with all the kingdom of Pegu and with the *Mallaca* Sea. It reaches to the kingdom of Cambaya; and to the kingdom of Dakhan; and they told me with positive certainty that it extends

[1] Coromandel. This name was applied by the Portuguese to the Eastern Tamil and Southern Telugu countries. It had no well-defined limits, and often was held to extend even as far north as to the Krishnâ river, or even to Orissa. Yule and Burnell adhere to the now generally received definition of the name from *Chola-mandala*, the country of the Cholas (Glossary, *s.v.* Coromandel).

[2] Orissa.

[3] *Comquista com* is evidently an error for *confina com.* The same word is used three times in the next paragraph.

[4] The Âdil Khân, Sultan of Bîjapûr. The name is sometimes written by the Portuguese *Idalxa* (*xa* for *Shâh*). We have numberless spellings in the old chronicles, thus, *Ḥidalcan*, *Adelham*, &c.

[5] For Nizâm-ul-Mulkh, or the Nizâm Shâh, the Sultan of Ahmadnagar. Similarly the Qutb Shâh of Golkonda is called in these chronicles "Cotamaluco." The Imâd Shâh of Bîrâr is called the "Imademaluco," or even "Madremaluco," by the Dutch (Linschoten) and Portuguese. The Barîd Shâh of Bîdar is styled "Melique Verido."

as far as Persia. The population thereof is light coloured, and the men are of good physique. Its king has much treasure and many soldiers and many elephants, for there are numbers of these in this country. (My informants) know this well, and they say that there is no ruler greater than he. He is a heathen.

Coming back to our subject, I say that I will not mention here the situation of the cities, and towns, and villages in this kingdom of Narsymga, to avoid prolixity; only I shall speak of the city of Darcha,[1] which has a monument such as can seldom be seen elsewhere. This city of Darcha is very well fortified by a wall, though not of stone, for the reason that I have already stated. On the western side, which is towards (Portuguese) India, it is surrounded by a very beautiful river, and on the other, eastern, side the interior of the country is all one plain, and along the wall is its moat. This Darcha has a pagoda, which is the monument I speak of, so beautiful that another as good of its kind could not be found within a great distance. You must know that it is a round temple made of a single stone, the gateway all in the manner of joiners' work, with every art of perspective. There are many figures of the said work, standing out as much as a cubit from the stone, so that you see on every side of them, so well carved that they could not be better done—the faces as well as all the rest; and each one in its place stands as if embowered in leaves; and above it is in the Romanesque style, so well made that it could not be better. Besides this, it has a sort of lesser porch upon pillars, all of stone, and the pillars

[1] The spelling of this name in the original is very doubtful. First it reads *Archa*, on the next occasion it is undoubtedly *Darcha*. The third mention of the place calls it *Larcha*. But in each case the *r* is not very clear, and might be an *i* undotted. Moreover, the *c* may possibly be an *e*, and the name may be *Areha* or *Dareha*. If we should accept the latter, we may identify it with Dhárwár, and believe it to be the same as the *Duree* of Nuniz (below, p. 292).

with their pedestals[1] so well executed that they appear as if made in Italy; all the cross pieces and beams are of the same stone without any planks or timber being used in it, and in the same way all the ground is laid with the same stone, outside as well as in. And all this pagoda, as far round as the temple goes, is enclosed by a trellis made of the same stone, and this again is completely surrounded by a very strong wall, better even than the city has, since it is all of solid masonry. It has three entrance gates, which gates are very large and beautiful, and the entrance from one of these sides, being towards the east and facing the door of the pagoda, has some structures like verandahs, small and low, where sit some *Jogis*;[2] and inside this enclosure, which has other little pagodas of a reddish colour, there is a stone like the mast of a ship, with its pedestal four-sided, and from thence to the top eight-sided, standing in the open air. I was not astonished at it, because I have seen the needle of St. Peter's at Rome, which is as high, or more.[3]

These pagodas are buildings in which they pray and have their idols; the idols are of many sorts, namely, figures of men and women, of bulls, and apes, while others have nothing but a round stone which they worship. In this temple of Darcha is an idol in the figure of a man as to his body, and the face is that of an elephant with trunk and tusks,[4] and with three arms on each side and six hands, of which arms they say that already four are gone, and when all fall then the world will be destroyed; they are full of belief that this will be, and hold it as a prophecy. They feed the idol every day, for they say that he eats; and when he eats women dance before him who belong to that pagoda, and they give him food and all that is necessary, and all girls born of these

[1] *Pranhas* in original, probably for *pianhas* or *peanhas* (see below, p. 288).
[2] *Jogis*, Hindu ascetics.
[3] This probably refers to the Egyptian obelisk at St. Peter's.
[4] Evidently the god *Ganesa*.

women belong to the temple. These women are of loose character, and live in the best streets that there are in the city; it is the same in all their cities, their streets have the best rows of houses. They are very much esteemed, and are classed amongst those honoured ones who are the mistresses of the captains; any respectable man may go to their houses without any blame attaching thereto. These women (are allowed) even to enter the presence of the wives of the king, and they stay with them and eat betel with them, a thing which no other person may do, no matter what his rank may be. This betel is a herb which has a leaf like the leaf of the pepper, or the ivy of our country; they always eat this leaf, and carry it in their mouths with another fruit called areca. This is something like a medlar, but it is very hard, and it is very good for the breath and has many other virtues; it is the best provision for those who do not eat as we do. Some of them eat flesh; they eat all kinds except beef and pork, and yet, nevertheless, they cease not to eat this betel all day.

Afterwards, going from this city of Darcha towards the city of Bisnaga,[1] which is eighteen leagues distant, and is the capital of all the kingdom of Narsymga, where the king always resides, you have many cities and walled villages; and two leagues before you arrive at the city of Bisnaga you have a very lofty *serra* which has passes by which you enter the city. These are called "gates" (*portas*). You must enter by these, for you will have no means of entrance except by them. This range of hills surrounds the city with a circle of twenty-four leagues, and within this range there are others that encircle it

[1] "Bisnaga," the Portuguese rendering of *Vijayanagar*, the "city of victory." The spellings adopted by different writers have been endless. We have Beejanugger and Beejnugger in the translations of Firishtah; Bisnagar, Bidjanagar, Bijanagher, amongst the Portuguese; Bicheneger in the writings of the Russian Nikitin; Bizenegalia in those of the Italian Nicolo dei Conti.

closely. Wherever these ranges have any level ground they cross it with a very strong wall, in such a way that the hills remain all closed, except in the places where the roads come through from the gates in the first range, which are the entrance ways to the city. In such places there are some small pits (or caves?)[1] which could be defended by a few people; these *serras* continue as far as the interior of the city. Between all these enclosures are plains and valleys where rice is grown, and there are gardens with many orange-trees, limes, citrons, and radishes (*rabãos*), and other kinds of garden produce as in Portugal, only not lettuces or cabbages. Between these hill-ranges are many lakes by which they irrigate the crops mentioned, and amongst all these ranges there are no forests or patches of brushwood, except very small ones, nor anything that is green. For these hills are the strangest ever seen, they are of a white stone piled one block over another in manner most singular, so that it seems as if they stood in the air and were not connected one with another; and the city is situated in the middle of these hills and is entirely surrounded by them.

The *serras* reach as far as the kingdom of Daquem,[2] and border upon the territories belonging to the Ydallcão, and upon a city called Rachol that formerly belonged to the king of Narsymga; there has been much war over it, and this king took it from the Ydallcão. So that these ranges are in a way the cause (of the two kingdoms) never uniting and always being at war; and even on the side of Orya also there are ranges, but they are different from these, since like ours they have scrub and small patches of brushwood; these ranges are low and between them are great plains. On the extreme east of these two kingdoms you must know that the country is all covered with scrub, the densest possible to be seen, in

[1] *Buqueyrõis.* The word implies something dug out, as opposed to redoubts, which would be built up.

[2] Dakhan.

which there are great beasts, and (this) forms so strong a fortress for it that it protects both sides; it has its entrances by which they pass from one kingdom to the other. In these passes on the frontier the king of Narsymga has a captain with a quantity of troops, but on the side of (Portuguese) India he has none, except as I have said.

Now turning to the gates of the first range, I say that at the entrance of the gate where those pass who come from Goa, which is the principal entrance on the western side, this king has made within it a very strong city[1] fortified with walls and towers, and the gates at the entrances very strong, with towers at the gates; these walls are not like those of other cities, but are made of very strong masonry such as would be found in few other parts, and inside very beautiful rows of buildings made after their manner with flat roofs. There live in this many merchants, and it is filled with a large population because the king induces many honourable merchants to go there from his cities, and there is much water in it. Besides this the king made a tank[2] there, which, as it seems to me, has the width of a falcon-shot,[3] and it is at the mouth of two hills, so that all the water which comes from either one side or the other collects there; and, besides this, water comes to it from more than three leagues by pipes which run along the lower parts of the range outside. This water is brought from a lake which itself overflows into a little river. The tank has three large pillars handsomely carved with figures; these connect above with certain pipes by which they get water when they have to irrigate their gardens and rice-fields. In order to make this tank the said king broke down a hill which enclosed the

[1] This is Nâgalâpur, the modern Hospett (*Epig. Ind.*, iv. 267).
[2] This tank or lake is described by Nuniz (see p. 364).
[3] *Hũu tiro de fallcão*, a shot from a falcon, an old piece of artillery.

ground occupied by the said tank. In the tank I saw so many people at work that there must have been fifteen or twenty thousand men, looking like ants, so that you could not see the ground on which they walked, so many there were; this tank the king portioned out amongst his captains, each of whom had the duty of seeing that the people placed under him did their work, and that the tank was finished and brought to completion.

The tank burst two or three times, and the king asked his Brahmans to consult their idol as to the reason why it burst so often, and the Brahmans said that the idol was displeased, and desired that they should make a sacrifice, and should give him the blood of men and horses and buffaloes; and as soon as the king heard this he forthwith commanded that at the gate of the pagoda the heads of sixty men should be cut off, and of certain horses and buffaloes, which was at once done.

These Brahmans are like friars with us, and they count them as holy men—I speak of the Brahman priests and the lettered men of the pagodas—because although the king has many Brahmans, they are officers of the towns and cities and belong to the government of them; others are merchants, and others live by their own property and cultivation, and the fruits which grow in their inherited grounds. Those who have charge of the temples are learned men, and eat nothing which suffers death, neither flesh nor fish, nor anything which makes broth red, for they say that it is blood. Some of the other Brahmans whom I mentioned, who seek to serve God, and to do penance, and to live a life like that of the priests, do not eat flesh or fish or any other thing that suffers death, but only vegetables[1] and butter and other things which they make of fruit,[2] with their rice.

[1] *Bredos*, "blites," an insipid kitchen vegetable. But as the word is not common, and as Brahmans make use of most vegetables, I have preferred the more general term.

[2] *Maçaas*, literally "apples."

They are all married, and have very beautiful wives; the wives are very retiring, and very seldom leave the house. The women are of light colour, and in the caste of these Brahmans are the fairest men and women that there are in the land; for though there are men in other castes commonly of light complexion, yet these are few. There are many in this country who call themselves Brahmans, but they lead a life very different from those of whom I have spoken, for these last are men to whom the king pays much honour, and he holds them in great favour.

This new city that the king made bears the name of his wife for love of whom he made it,[1] and the said city stands in a plain, and round it the inhabitants make their gardens as the ground suits, each one being separate. In this city the king made a temple with many images. It is a thing very well made, and it has some wells very well made after their fashion; its houses are not built with stories like ours, but are of only one floor, with flat roofs and towers,[2] different from ours, for theirs go from storey to storey. They have pillars, and are all open, with verandahs inside and out, where they can easily put people if they desire, so that they seem like houses belonging to a king. These palaces have an enclosing wall which surrounds them all, and inside are many rows of houses. Before you enter the place where the king is there are two gates with many guards, who prevent any one from entering except the captains and men who have business there; and between these two gates is a very large court with its verandahs round it, where these captains and other honoured people wait till the king summons them to his presence.

This king is of medium height, and of fair com-

[1] It was generally called Nâgalâpur, but Nuniz says that the lady's name was Chinnadevî (below, p. 362).

[2] *Coruchees.* See p. 260, note 3.

plexion and good figure, rather fat than thin; he has on his face signs of small-pox. He is the most feared and perfect king that could possibly be, cheerful of disposition and very merry; he is one that seeks to honour foreigners, and receives them kindly, asking about all their affairs whatever their condition may be He is a great ruler and a man of much justice, but subject to sudden fits of rage,[1] and this is his title—"Crisnarão Macação,[2] king of kings, lord of the greater lords of India, lord of the three seas and of the land." He has this title[3] because he is by rank a greater lord than any, by reason of what he possesses in (?) armies and territories, but it seems that he has (in fact) nothing compared to what a man like him ought to have, so gallant and perfect is he in all things. This king was constantly at war with the king of Orya, and entered his kingdom, taking and destroying many cities and towns; he put to rout numbers of his soldiers and elephants, and took captive his son, whom he kept for a long time in this city of Bisnaga, where he died; and in order to make a treaty and (preserve) peace, the king of Orya gave him a daughter whom the king of Bisnaga married and has as his wife.

This king has twelve lawful wives, of whom there are three principal ones, the sons of each of these three being heirs of the kingdom, but not those of the others; this is (the case) when there are sons to all of them, but when there is only one son, whosesoever he may be, he is heir. One of these principal wives is the daughter of the king of Orya, and others daughters of a king his vassal who is king of Serimgapatão; another wife is a courtezan whom in his youth he had for mistress before he became king, and she made him

[1] *Grandes supitos.*

[2] A mixture, apparently, of *Mahâ*, "great," and "Shâh."

[3] The passage that follows is not very clear in the original.

promise that if he came to be king he would take her to wife, and thus it came to pass that this courtezan became his wife. For love of her he built this new city, and its name was . . . (*sic in orig.*) . . . Each one of these wives has her house to herself, with her maidens and women of the chamber, and women guards and all other women servants necessary; all these are women, and no man enters where they are, save only the eunuchs, who guard them. These women are never seen by any man, except perhaps by some old man of high rank by favour of the king. When they wish to go out they are carried in litters shut up and closed,[1] so that they cannot be seen, and all the eunuchs with them, fully three or four hundred; and all other people keep a long distance from them. They told us that each of these queens has a very large sum of money and treasure and personal ornaments, namely armlets, bracelets, seed-pearls,[2] pearls and diamonds, and that in great quantity: and they also say that each of them has sixty maidens adorned as richly as could possibly be with many jewels, and rubies and diamonds and pearls and seed-pearls. These we afterwards saw, and stood astonished; we saw them at certain festivals which I will afterwards speak of, and of the manner in which they came. Within, with these maidens, they say that there are twelve thousand women; for you must know that there are women who handle sword

[1] The word last used is *sellados*, literally "sealed."

[2] *Aljofar*. This word is constantly used in the chronicles. Garcia da Orta (*Colloq*. xxxv.) derives it from Cape Julfar in Arabia, near Ormuz. Cobarruvias says it is from Arabic *jauhar*, "jewel" (Yule and Burnell, Dict.). Da Orta writes: "*Chama-se* perla *em castelhano e* perola *em portuguez, e em latim* unio, *e isto no* aljofar *grande; porque o miudo chama-se em latim* margarita, *e em arabio* lulu, *e em persio e nest' outras gerações da India* moti, *e em malavar* mutu, *e em portuguez e castelhano* aljofar;" *i.e.* a large pearl is called *perla* in Spanish, *perola* in Portuguese, *unio* in Latin; a small pearl is called in Latin *margarita*, in Arabic *lulu*, in Persian and many Indian languages *moti*, in Malayâlam *mutu*, and in Portuguese and Spanish *aljofar*.

and shield, and others who wrestle, and others who blow trumpets, and others pipes, and others instruments which are different from ours; and in the same way they have women as bearers (*boois*) and washing-folk, and for other offices inside their gates, just as the king has the officers of his household. These three principal wives have each the same, one as much as the other, so that there may never be any discord or ill feeling between them; all of them are great friends, and each one lives by herself. It may be gathered from this what a large enclosure there must be for these houses where so many people live, and what streets and lanes they must have.

The king lives by himself inside the palace, and when he wishes to have with him one of his wives he orders a eunuch to go and call her. The eunuch does not enter where she is, but tells it to the female guards, who make known to the queen that there is a message from the king, and then comes one of her maidens or chamber-women and learns what is wanted, and then the queen goes where the king is, or the king comes where she is, and so passes the time as it seems good to him without any of the others knowing. Amongst these eunuchs the king has some who are great favourites, and who sleep where he sleeps; they receive a large salary.

This king is accustomed every day to drink a *quartilho* (three-quarter pint) of oil of *gingelly*[1] before daylight, and anoints himself all over with the said oil; he covers his loins with a small cloth, and takes in his arms great weights made of earthenware, and then, taking a sword, he exercises himself with it till he has sweated out all the oil, and then he wrestles with one of his wrestlers. After this labour he mounts a horse

[1] *Emgellym*, sesamum or gingelly, an oil seed.

and gallops about the plain in one direction and another till dawn, for he does all this before daybreak. Then he goes to wash himself, and a Brahman washes him whom he holds sacred, and who is a great favourite of his and is a man of great wealth; and after he is washed he goes to where his pagoda is inside the palace, and makes his orisons and ceremonies, according to custom. Thence he goes to a building made in the shape of a porch without walls, which has many pillars hung with cloths right up to the top, and with the walls handsomely painted; it has on each side two figures of women very well made. In such a building he despatches his work with those men who bear office in his kingdom, and govern his cities, and his favourites talk with them. The greatest favourite is an old man called Temersea;[1] he commands the whole household, and to him all the great lords act as to the king. After the king has talked with these men on subjects pleasing to him he bids enter the lords and captains who wait at the gate, and these at once enter to make their salaam to him. As soon as they appear they make their salaam to him, and place themselves along the walls far off from him; they do not speak one to another, nor do they chew betel before him, but they place their hands in the sleeves of their tunics (*cabayas*) and cast their eyes on the ground; and if the king desires to speak to any one it is done through a second person, and then he to whom the king desires to speak raises his eyes and replies to him who questions him, and then returns to his former position. So they remain till the king bids them go, and then they all turn to make the salaam to him and go out. The salaam,

[1] This was the great Sâluva Timma, Krishna Deva's minister. The termination *-rsea* probably represents *Arasa*, the Kanarese form for *Râjah*. *Temersea* = *Timmarasa* = *Timma Râjah*.

which is the greatest courtesy that exists among them, is that they put their hands joined above their head as high as they can. Every day they go to make the salaam to the king.

When we came to this country the king was in this new town, and there went to see him Christovão de Figueiredo[1] with all of us Portuguese that came with him, and all very handsomely dressed after our manner, with much finery; the king received him very well, and was very complacent to him. The king was as much pleased with him as if he had been one of his own people, so much attention did he evince towards him; and also towards those amongst us who went with him he showed much kindness. We were so close to the king that he touched us all and could not have enough of looking at us. Then Christovão de Figueiredo gave him the letters from the Captain-Major[2] and the things he had brought for him, with which he was greatly delighted; principally with certain organs[3] that the said Christovão de Figueiredo brought him, with many other things (*peças*). The king was clothed in certain white cloths embroidered with many roses in gold, and

[1] According to Correa, Christovão de Figueiredo had been sent by the governor, Lopo Soares, in 1517 to Vijayanagar as factor, with horses and elephants (*Lendas da India*, ii. 509–510); but Senhor Lopes points out (Introduction to his *Chronica*, lxxxii. note) that we do not know how far this assertion is true. He certainly lived at Goa, and not long after this battle was made chief *Tanedar* of the mainlands of Goa, with residence at the temple of Mardor. He was several times in peril at the hands of the Mussalmâns, and in 1536 was present at the battles which took place between the Portuguese and Asada Khân of Belgaum, with whom he was on terms of friendship. Mr. Danvers (ii. 507) states that he was also at one time attorney of the factory of Goa.

[2] This apparently refers to Ruy de Mello (see above, p. 142 ff.). If De Sequeira were meant he would have been called "Governor."

[3] *Horgãos*. Mr. Ferguson points out that these were undoubtedly musical instruments. Castanheda (v. xxviii.), describing the embassy to "Prester John" under Dom Roderigo de Lima in 1520 (the same year), states that among the presents sent to that potentate were "some organs and a clavichord, and a player for them." These organs are also mentioned in Father Alvares's account of their embassy (Hakluyt Society Trans., p. 10).

with a *pateca*[1] of diamonds on his neck of very great value, and on his head he had a cap of brocade in fashion like a Galician helmet, covered with a piece of fine stuff all of fine silk, and he was barefooted; for no one ever enters where the king is unless he has bare feet, and the majority of the people, or almost all, go about the country barefooted. The shoes have pointed ends, in the ancient manner, and there are other shoes that have nothing but soles, but on top are some straps which help to keep them on the feet. They are made like those which of old the Romans were wont to wear, as you will find on figures in some papers or antiquities which come from Italy. The king gave to Christovão de Figueiredo on dismissing him a *cabaya* (tunic) of brocade, with a cap of the same fashion as the king wore,[2] and to each one of the Portuguese he gave a cloth embroidered with many pretty figures, and this the king gives because it is customary; he gives it in token of friendship and love.

When Christovão de Figueiredo had been dismissed by the king we came to the city of Bisnaga, which is a league from this new city, and here he commanded us to be lodged in some very good houses; and Figueiredo was visited by many lords and captains, and other persons who came on behalf of the king. And the king sent him many sheep and fowls, and many vessels (*calõees*) full of butter and honey and many other things to eat, which he at once distributed amongst all the foot-soldiers and people whom he had brought with him. The king said many kind and pleasant things to him, and asked him concerning the kind of state which

[1] *Pateca*, something worn round the neck. There appears to be some mistake here, as *pateca* means "a sort of long robe or gown (worn) in India" (Michaelis' Dict.).

[2] Varthema says, "The king wears a cap of gold brocade two spans long." This was Krishna Deva's predecessor, Narasimha.

the king of Portugal kept up; and having been told about it all he seemed much pleased.

Returning then to the city of Bisnaga, you must know that from it to the new city goes a street as wide as a place of tourney, with both sides lined throughout with rows of houses and shops where they sell everything; and all along this road are many trees that the king commanded to be planted, so as to afford shade to those that pass along. On this road he commanded to be erected a very beautiful temple of stone,[1] and there are other pagodas that the captains and great lords caused to be erected.

So that, returning to the city of Bisnaga, you must know that before you arrive at the city gates there is a gate with a wall that encloses all the other enclosures of the city, and this wall is a very strong one and of massive stonework; but at the present time it is injured in some places. They do not fail to have citadels[2] in it. This wall has a moat of water in some places, and in the parts where it was constructed on low ground. And there is, separate from it, yet another (defence) made in the following manner. Certain pointed stones of great height are fixed in the ground as high as a man's breast; they are in breadth a lance-shaft and a half, with the same distance between them and the great wall. This wall rises in all the low ground till it reaches some hill or rocky land. From this first circuit until you enter the city there is a great distance, in which are fields in which they sow rice and have many gardens and much water, which water comes from two lakes. The water passes through this first line of wall, and there is much water in the lakes

[1] This may refer to the handsome temple of Anantasâyana, a mile or so from Hospett on the road to Kâmalâpur. The trees still stand in parts.

[2] *Fortalezas.* Probably the writer refers either to bastions or towers, or to strongly fortified places of refuge on the hilltops. The passage is obscure.

because of springs; and here there are orchards and a little grove of palms, and many houses.

Returning, then, to the first gate of the city, before you arrive at it you pass a little piece of water and then you arrive at the wall, which is very strong, all of stone-work, and it makes a bend before you arrive at the gate; and at the entrance of this gate are two towers, one on each side, which makes it very strong. It is large and beautiful. As soon as you pass inside there are two little temples; one of them has an enclosing wall with many trees, while the whole of the other consists of buildings; and this wall of the first gate encircles the whole city. Then going forward you have another gate with another line of wall, and it also encircles the city inside the first, and from here to the king's palace is all streets and rows of houses, very beautiful, and houses of captains and other rich and honourable men; you will see rows of houses with many figures and decorations pleasing to look at. Going along the principal street, you have one of the chief gateways,[1] which issues from a great open space[2] in front of the king's palace; opposite this is another which passes along to the other side of the city; and across this open space pass all the carts and conveyances carrying stores and everything else, and because it is in the middle of the city it cannot but be useful.

This palace of the king is surrounded by a very strong wall like some of the others, and encloses a greater space (*teraa moor cerca*) than all the castle of Lisbon.

Still going forward, passing to the other gate you see two temples connected with it, one on each side,

[1] Four words, *temdes hũa porta primcipal*, have been accidentally omitted in the printed copy.

[2] *Terreiro.* The gateway here spoken of is most probably the great entrance to the palace enclosure, just to the north of the village of Kâmalâpur.

CORNER OF A PAVILION, SHOWING REMAINS OF STREET AT VIJAYANAGAR

(*From a Photograph by* Col. W. Hooper)

and at the door of one of these they kill every day many sheep; for in all the city they do not kill any sheep for the use of the heathen (Hindus), or for sale in the markets, except at the gate of this pagoda. Of their blood they make sacrifices to the idol that is in the temple. They leave the heads to him, and for each sheep they give a *saco* (*chakram*), which is a coin like a *cartilha* (*quartilha*—a farthing).

There is present at the slaughter of these beasts a *jogi* (priest) who has charge of the temple, and as soon as they cut off the head of the sheep or goat this *jogi* blows a horn as a sign that the idol receives that sacrifice. Hereafter I shall tell of these *jogis*, what sort of men they are.[1]

Close to these pagodas is a triumphal car covered with carved work and images, and on one day in each year during a festival they drag this through the city in such streets as it can traverse. It is large and cannot turn corners.

Going forward, you have a broad and beautiful street, full of rows of fine houses and streets of the sort I have described, and it is to be understood that the houses belong to men rich enough to afford such. In this street live many merchants, and there you will find all sorts of rubies, and diamonds, and emeralds, and pearls, and seed-pearls, and cloths, and every other sort of thing there is on earth and that you may wish to buy. Then you have there every evening a fair where they sell many common horses and nags (*rocis e semdeiros*), and also many citrons, and limes, and oranges, and grapes, and every other kind of garden stuff, and wood; you have all in this street. At the end of it you have another gate with its wall, which wall goes to meet the wall of the second gate of which I have spoken, in such sort that

[1] The writer forgot to fulfil this promise.

this city has three fortresses, with another which is the king's palace. Then when this gate is passed you have another street where there are many craftsmen, and they sell many things; and in this street there are two small temples. There are temples in every street, for these appertain to institutions like the confraternities you know of in our parts,[1] of all the craftsmen and merchants; but the principal and greatest pagodas are outside the city. In this street lodged Christovão de Figueiredo. On every Friday you have a fair there, with many pigs and fowls and dried fish from the sea, and other things the produce of the country, of which I do not know the name; and in like manner a fair is held every day in different parts of the city. At the end of this street is the Moorish quarter, which is at the very end of the city, and of these Moors there are many who are natives of the country[2] and who are paid by the king and belong to his guard. In this city you will find men belonging to every nation and people, because of the great trade which it has, and the many precious stones there, principally diamonds.

The size of this city I do not write here, because it cannot all be seen from any one spot, but I climbed a hill whence I could see a great part of it; I could not see it all because it lies between several ranges of hills. What I saw from thence seemed to me as large as Rome, and very beautiful to the sight; there are many groves of trees within it, in the gardens of the houses, and many conduits of water which flow into the midst of it, and in places there are lakes (*tamques*); and the king has close to his palace a palm-grove and other rich-bearing fruit-trees. Below the Moorish quarter is a little river, and on this side are many

[1] *Por que são como as comfraryas que nas nossas partes haa.*

[2] *A muytos naturaes da terra.*

orchards and gardens with many fruit-trees, for the most part mangoes and areca-palms and jack-trees, and also many lime and orange trees, growing so closely one to another that it appears like a thick forest; and there are also white grapes. All the water which is in the city comes from the two tanks of which I have spoken, outside the first enclosing wall.

The people in this city are countless in number, so much so that I do not wish to write it down for fear it should be thought fabulous; but I declare that no troops, horse or foot, could break their way through any street or lane, so great are the numbers of the people and elephants.

This is the best provided city in the world, and is stocked with provisions such as rice, wheat, grains, Indian-corn, and a certain amount of barley and beans, *moong*,[1] pulses, horse-gram,[2] and many other seeds which grow in this country which are the food of the people, and there is large store of these and very cheap; but wheat is not so common as the other grains, since no one eats it except the Moors. But you will find what I have mentioned. The streets and markets are full of laden oxen without count, so that you cannot get along for them, and in many streets you come upon so many of them that you have to wait for them to pass, or else have to go by another way. There is much poultry; they give three fowls in the city for a coin worth a *vintem*,[3] which coins are called *favaos*;[4] outside the city they give four fowls for a *vintem*.

In this country there are many partridges, but

[1] *Munguo.* "Moong . . . green gram . . . a kind of vetch" (Yule and Burnell, Dict.).

[2] *Macharuỹ.*

[3] A *vintem* = 1 $\frac{7}{20}$ of a penny.

[4] Probably for *fanaos.* But the plural of *fanao* is usually given as *fanões.*

they are not of the same sort or quality as ours: they are like the *estarnas*[1] of Italy.

There are three sorts of these: one class has only a small spur such as those of Portugal have; another class has on each foot two very sharp spurs, almost as long and thick as one's finger; the other class is painted, and of these you will find the markets full; as also of quails, and hares, and all kinds of wild fowl, and other birds which live in the lakes and which look like geese. All these birds and game animals they sell alive, and they are very cheap, for they give six or eight partridges for a *vintem*, and of hares they give two and sometimes one. Of other birds they give more than you can count, for even of the large ones they give so many that you would hardly pay any attention to the little ones they give you, such as doves and pigeons and the common birds of the country. The doves are of two kinds; some are like those in Portugal, others are as large as thrushes; of the doves they give twelve or fourteen for a *favao;* the pigeons are the same price as the other birds. Then the sheep that they kill every day are countless, one could not number them, for in every street there are men who will sell you mutton, so clean and so fat that it looks like pork; and you also have pigs in some streets of butchers' houses so white and clean that you could never see better in any country; a pig is worth four or five *fanams*.[2] Then to see the many loads of limes that come each day, such that those of Povos are of no account,[3] and also loads of sweet and sour oranges, and wild *brinjals*, and other garden stuff in such abundance as to stupefy one. For the state of this city is not like

[1] *Estarna*. "A sort of small partridge with black feet" (Michaelis' Dict.).
[2] Here we have the plural *fanõees*.
[3] Povos is a place near Lisbon.

that of other cities, which often fail of supplies and provisions, for in this one everything abounds; and also the quantity of butter and oil and milk sold every day, that is a thing I cannot refrain from mentioning; and as for the rearing of cows and buffaloes which goes on in the city, there is so much that you will go very far before you find another like it. There are many pomegranates also; grapes are sold at three bunches a *fanam*, and pomegranates ten for a *fanam*.

On the north side of the city is a very great river with much water, in which are many fish, which fish are very unwholesome, and in this river there is that which passes for . . . (*sic. in orig.*); other streams flow into it, which make it very large.

Now as to the places on the bank of this river. There is a city built there which they call *Senagumdym*,[1] and they say that of old it was the capital of the kingdom, but there now live in it few people; it still has good walls and is very strong, and it lies between two hill-ranges which have only two entrances. A captain lives in this city for the king. People cross to this place by boats which are round like baskets;[2] inside they are made of cane, and outside are covered with leather; they are able to carry fifteen or twenty persons, and even horses and oxen can cross in them if necessary, but for the most part these animals swim across. Men row them with a sort of paddle, and the boats are always turning round, as they cannot go straight like others; in all the kingdom where there are streams there are no other boats but these.[3]

There are also in this city places where they sell live sheep; you will see the fields round the city full of them.

1 Ânegundi.

2 Below, pp. 292, 293.

3 The stone bridge, built on rows of rough monolithic uprights, the remains of which are still to be seen near the temple of Vitthalasvâmi, appears, from the absence of allusion to it, to have been constructed at a later date.

and also of cows and buffaloes — it is a very pretty sight to see,—and also the many she-goats and kids, and the he-goats so large that they are bridled and saddled. Many sheep are like that also, and boys ride them.

Outside the city walls on the north there are three very beautiful pagodas, one of which is called *Vitella*,[1] and it stands over against this city of Nagumdym; the other is called *Aõperadianar*,[2] and this is the one which they hold in most veneration, and to which they make great pilgrimages.

In this pagoda, opposite to its principal gate which is to the east, there is a very beautiful street of very beautiful houses with balconies and arcades, in which are sheltered the pilgrims that come to it, and there are also houses for the lodging of the upper classes; the king has a palace in the same street, in which he resides when he visits this pagoda. There is a pomegranate tree[3] above this first gate; the gate has a very lofty tower all covered with rows of men and women and hunting scenes and many other representations, and as the tower goes narrowing towards the top so the images diminish in size. Passing this first gate, you come at once into a large courtyard with another gate of the same sort as the first, except that it is rather smaller throughout; and passing this second gate, there is a large court with verandahs all round on pillars of

[1] This clearly alludes to the beautifully sculptured temple of Vitthalasvâmi, which is in the situation described.

[2] This word is a puzzle. If the temple be, as seems most probable from the description, the principal temple at Hampe, still in use, I suggest that *Aõpe* represents "Hampi" or "Hampe." *Radi* may be "râjah," or *radian* may be "râjyam." The name was perhaps given to Paes by some one who described it as "the royal Hampe temple," and this would accurately describe it. It was dedicated to Virûpâksha, and was the cathedral of the great city.

[3] The word used is *romeyra*, which may mean either a pomegranate tree or a female pilgrim. The allusion is to the plaster figures and designs on the tower (*corucheo*) above the gate.

ONE OF THE PAVILIONS IN THE TEMPLE OF VITTHALASVAMI

(*From a Photograph by* F. DUNSTERVILLE, Esq.)

stone, and in the middle of this court is the house of the idol.

Opposite the principal gate stand four columns, two gilded and the other two copper, from which, owing to their great age as it seems to me, the gold has worn off; and the other two are also of copper, for all are of copper. That which stands nearest the gate of the temple was given by this King Crisnarão who now reigns here, and the others by his predecessors. All the outer side of the gate of the temple up to the roof is covered with copper and gilded, and on each side of the roof on the top are certain great animals that look like tigers, all gilt. As soon as you enter this idol-shrine, you perceive from pillar to pillar on which it is supported many little holes in which stand oil lamps, which burn, so they tell me, every night, and they will be in number two thousand five hundred or three thousand lights. As soon as you pass this shrine you enter another small one like the crypt (*cinzeyro*)[1] of some church; it has two doors at the sides, and thence onward this building is like a chapel, where stands the idol which they adore. Before you get to it there are three doors; the shrine is vaulted and dark without any light from the sky; it is always lit with candles. At the first gate are doorkeepers who never allow any one to enter except the Brahmans that have charge of it, and I, because I gave something to them, was allowed to enter. Between gate and gate are images of little idols. The principal idol is a round stone without any shape; they have great devotion for it. This building outside is all covered with copper gilt. At the back of the temple outside, close to the verandahs of which I have spoken, there is a small idol of white

[1] *Cinzeyro* apparently means a place for ashes (*cinza*). *Cinzas* are "ashes of the dead." The reference may be to a place in a church where incense-burners are kept, or, as I think, equally well to the crypt, and this last sense seems better to suit the context.

alabaster with six arms;[1] in one it has a . . .[2] and in the other a sword, and in the others sacred emblems (*armas de casa*), and it has below its feet a buffalo, and a large animal which is helping to kill that buffalo. In this pagoda there burns continually a lamp of *ghee*, and around are other small temples for houses of devotion.

The other temples aforesaid are made in the same manner, but this one is the principal one and the oldest; they all have many buildings and gardens with many trees, in which the Brahmans cultivate their vegetables[3] and the other herbs that they eat. Whenever the festival of any of these temples occurs they drag along certain triumphal cars which run on wheels, and with it go dancing-girls and other women with music to the temple, (conducting) the idol along the said street with much pomp. I do not relate the manner in which these cars are taken, because in all the time that I was in this city none were taken round. There are many other temples in the city of which I do not here speak, to avoid prolixity.

You should know that among these heathen there are days when they celebrate their feasts as with us; and they have their days of fasting, when all day they eat nothing, and eat only at midnight. When the time of the principal festival arrives the king comes from the new city to this city of Bisnaga, since it is the capital of the kingdom and it is the custom there to make their feasts and to assemble. For these feasts are summoned all the dancing-women of the kingdom, in order that they should be present; and also the captains and kings and great lords with all their retinues,—except only those whom the king may have sent to make war, or those who are in other parts, or at the far end of the kingdom

[1] *Seus* for *seis*.

[2] The word is omitted in the original.

[3] *Bredos*. See above, pp. 227, 245, notes.

on the side where (an attack) is feared, such as the kingdom of Oria and the territories of the Ydallcão; and even if such captains are absent in such places, there appear for them at the feasts those whom I shall hereafter mention.

These feasts begin on the 12th of September,[1] and they last nine days, and take place at the king's palace.

The palace is on this fashion: it has a gate opening on to the open space[2] of which I have spoken, and over this gate is a tower of some height, made like the others with its verandahs; outside these gates begins the wall which I said encircled the palace. At the gate are many doorkeepers[3] with leather scourges in their hands, and sticks, and they let no one enter but the captains and chief people, and those about whom they receive orders from the Chief of the Guard. Passing this gate you have an open space, and then you have another gate like the first, also with its doorkeepers and guards; and as soon as you enter inside this you have a large open space, and on one side and the other are low verandahs where are seated the captains and chief people in order to witness the feasts, and on the left side of the north of this open space is a great one-storeyed building (*terrea*); all the rest are like it. This building stands on pillars shaped like elephants and with other figures, and all open in front, and they go up to it by staircases of stone; around it, underneath, is a terrace (*corredor*) paved with very good flagstones, where stand some of the people looking at the feast. This house is called the House of Victory, as it was made when the king came back from the war against Orya, as I have already told you. On the right side of the open space were some

[1] For a discussion as to the dates given in Paes, see p. 140 ff. above.

[2] *Terreyro.* See above, p. 254. Evidently the place of arms is referred to.

[3] *Porteyros, Porteyro moor.* These men are often mentioned in the chronicle. Their chief was one of the king's most important officers, and I give him the title "Chief of the Guard."

narrow scaffoldings, made of wood and so lofty that they could be seen over the top of the wall; they were covered at the top with crimson and green velvet and other handsome cloths, and adorned from top to bottom. Let no one fancy that these cloths were of wool, because there are none such in the country, but they are of very fine cotton. These scaffoldings are not always kept at that place, but they are specially made for these feasts; there are eleven of them. Against the gates there were two circles in which were the dancing-women, richly arrayed with many jewels of gold and diamonds and many pearls. Opposite the gate which is on the east side of the front of the open space, and in the middle of it, there are two buildings of the same sort as the House of Victory of which I have spoken; these buildings are served by a kind of staircase of stone beautifully wrought,—one is in the middle and the other at the end. This building was all hung with rich cloths, both the walls and the ceiling, as well as the supports, and the cloths of the walls were adorned with figures in the manner of embroidery; these buildings have two platforms one above the other, beautifully sculptured, with their sides well made and worked, to which platforms the sons of the king's favourites come for the feasts, and sometimes his eunuchs. On the upper platform, close to the king, was Christovão de Figueiredo, with all of us who came with him, for the king commanded that he should be put in such a place as best to see the feasts and magnificence. That I may not forget to tell of the streets that are in the palace I here mention them. You must know that inside the palace that I have spoken of is the dwelling of the king and of his wives and of the other women who serve them, as I have already said, who are twelve thousand in number; and they have an entrance to these rows of houses so that they can go inside. Between this palace and the House of Victory is a gate which serves as passage to it. Inside there are thirty-four streets.

Returning to the feasts, you must know that in this House of Victory the king has a room (*casa*) made of cloth, with its door closed, where the idol has a shrine; and in the other, in the middle (of the building), is placed a daïs opposite the staircase in the middle; on which daïs stands a throne of state made thus,—it is four-sided, and flat, with a round top, and a hollow in the middle for the seat. As regards the woodwork of it, you must know that it is all covered with silk cloths (? *soajes*),[1] and has lions all of gold, and in the spaces between the cloths (*soajes*) it has plates of gold with many rubies and seed-pearls, and pearls underneath; and round the sides it is all full of golden images of personages, and upon these is much work in gold, with many precious stones. In this chair is placed an idol, also of gold, embowered in roses and flowers. On one side of this chair, on the daïs below, stands a head-dress; this also is made in the same manner; it is upright and as high as a span, the top is rounded, it is all full of pearls and rubies and all other precious stones, and on the top of it is a pearl as large as a nut, which is not quite round. On the other side is an anklet for the foot made in the same fashion; it is another state jewel, and is full of large pearls and of many rubies, emeralds, and diamonds, and other stones of value; it will be of the thickness of a man's arm. In front of all this, at the edge[2] of the daïs, resting on a support were some cushions where the king was seated during all these feasts. The feasts commence thus:—

[1] I am doubtful about this translation. The word used has probably some technical meaning. Yule's Dictionary has *soosie* from Persian *súsí*. "Some kind of silk cloth, but we know not what kind." The original passage runs:—"Quoanto ao pao, sabereis que he toda chea de suas soajes, e de liõis todos d ouro, e no vão d estas soajes tem hũas chapas d ouro com muytos robis," &c.

[2] *Cabo.* I think this must mean the edge, the front, not the extreme end of the king's balcony.

You must know that when it is morning the king comes to this House of Victory, and betakes himself to that room where the idol is with its Brahmans, and he performs his prayers and ceremonies. Outside the house are some of his favourites, and on the square are many dancing-girls dancing. In their verandahs round the square are many captains and chief people who come there in order to see; and on the ground, near the platform of the house, are eleven horses with handsome and well-arranged trappings, and behind them are four beautiful elephants with many adornments. After the king has entered inside he comes out, and with him a Brahman who takes in his hand a basket full of white roses and approaches the king on the platform, and the king, taking three handfuls of these roses, throws them to the horses,[1] and after he has thrown them he takes a basket of perfumes and acts towards them as though he would cense them; and when he has finished doing this he reaches towards the elephants and does the same to them. And when the king has finished this, the Brahman takes the basket and descends to the platform,[2] and from thence puts those roses and other flowers on the heads of all the horses, and this done, returns to the king. Then the king goes again to where the idol is, and as soon as he is inside they lift the curtains[3] of the room, which are made like the purdahs of a tent, and the king seats himself there where these are, and they lift them all. Thence he witnesses the slaughter of twenty-four buffaloes and a hundred and fifty sheep, with which a sacrifice is made to that idol; you must know that they cut off the heads of these buffaloes and sheep at one blow with certain large sickles which are

[1] This is given in the singular number, probably by mistake, as the plural is used immediately afterwards—*ao cavallo . . . os encemça.*

[2] *Tavoleiro.*

[3] *Paredes*, probably for "purdahs" (Persian, *parda*), curtains or screens. The Portuguese word means a "wall."

wielded by a man who has charge of this slaughter; they are so sure of hand that no blow misses. When they have finished the slaughter of these cattle the king goes out and goes to the other large buildings, on the platforms of which is a crowd of Brahmans, and as soon as the king ascends to where they stand they throw to the king ten or twelve roses—those (that is) who are nearest to him. Then he passes all along the top of the buildings, and as soon as he is at the end he takes the cap from his head, and after placing it on the ground turns back (to the place) where the idol is; here he lies extended on the ground. When he has arisen he betakes himself to the interior of the building, and enters a garden (or walled enclosure—*quyntal*) where they say that a little fire has been made, and he throws into the fire a powder made up of many things, namely, rubies and pearls and all other kinds of precious stones, and aloes and other sweet-scented things. This done, he returns to the pagoda and goes inside and stays a little, at which time enter by the other door some of his favourites who are in the building, and they make their salaam. Then he goes back to the place whence he threw the flowers to the horses, and as soon as he is here all the captains and chief people come and make their salaam to him, and some, if they so desire, present some gifts to him; then as they came so they retire, and each one betakes himself to his own dwelling. And the king withdraws to the interior of his palace by that gate which I have already mentioned—that which stands between the two buildings that are in the arena (*terreyro*); the courtesans and bayadères[1] remain dancing in front of the temple and idol for a long time. This is what is done during the morning of each day of these nine days, with the ceremonies I have

[1] *Molheres solteiras e baylhadeiras, i.e.* the dancing-girls of the temple and palace.

mentioned, and each day more splendid (than the last).

Now, returning to the feasts. At three o'clock in the afternoon every one comes to the palace. They do not admit every one at once (they allowed us to go into the open part that is between the gates), but there go inside only the wrestlers and dancing-women, and the elephants, which go with their trappings and decorations, those that sit on them being armed with shields and javelins, and wearing quilted tunics.[1] As soon as these are inside they range themselves round the arena, each one in his place, and the wrestlers go close to the staircase which is in the middle of that building, where has been prepared a large space of ground for the dancing-women to wrestle. Many other people are then at the entrance-gate opposite to the building, namely Brahmans, and the sons of the king's favourites, and their relations; all these are noble youths who serve before the king. The officers of the household go about keeping order amongst all the people, and keep each one in his own place. The different pavilions are separated by doors, so that no one may enter unless he is invited.

Salvatinica,[2] who is the principal person that enters the building, supervises the whole, for he brought up the king and made him king, and so the king looks on him like a father. Whenever the king calls to him he addresses him as "Lord (*senhor*) Salvatinica," and all the captains and nobles of the realm make salaam to him. This Salvatinica stands inside the arena where the festivals go on, near one of the doors, and from there gives the word for the admission of all the things necessary for the festival.

[1] *Lavodes.* See below, p. 276, note regarding *laudes*.

[2] Sâluva Timma, the minister. The name is spelt in various ways in the chronicles of both Paes and Nuniz. Krishna Deva owed his throne to him (below, p. 315).

RUINS OF "HOUSE OF VICTORY" AT THE PALACE, VIJAYANAGAR

After all this is done and arranged the king goes forth and seats himself on the daïs I have mentioned, where is the throne and the other things, and all those that are inside make their salaam to him. As soon as they have done this the wrestlers seat themselves on the ground, for these are allowed to remain seated, but no other, howsoever great a lord he be, except the king so commands; and these also eat betel, though none else may eat it in his presence except the dancing-women, who may always eat it before him. As soon as the king is seated in his place he bids to sit with him three or four men who belong to his race, and who are themselves kings and the fathers of his wives; the principal of these is the king of Syrimgapatão and of all the territory bordering on Malabar, and this king is called Cumarvirya,[1] and he seats himself as far in front as the king on the other side of the daïs, the rest are behind.

There the king sits, dressed in white clothes all covered with (embroidery of) golden roses and wearing his jewels—he wears a quantity of these white garments, and I always saw him so dressed—and around him stand his pages with his betel, and his sword, and the other things which are his insignia of state. Many Brahmans stand round the throne on which rests the idol, fanning it with horsetail plumes, coloured, the handles of which

[1] The king of Seringapatam at this period was Bettâda Châma Râya, who ruled the Mysore country from 1513 to 1552. He had three sons. The two eldest received at his death portions of his estate, but both died without issue. The third son was called "Hîre" or "Vîra" Châma. He was apparently the most powerful, and the best beloved of his father, since he received as his portion on the latter's death the principal tract of Mysore, the town itself, and the neighbouring province. After the fall of Vijayanagar in 1565 he became practically independent, and ruled till the principal power was seized by his relative, Râja Udaiyâr, in 1578. The word *Kumâra* (= "son") is often applied in royal families in India to one of the reigning king's offspring, and I venture to think that *Cumarvirya* represents *Kumâra Vîrayya*, the king of Seringapatam being himself not present at these feasts, and the personage seen by Paes being his son Vîra.

are all overlaid with gold; these plumes are tokens of the highest dignity; they also fan the king with them.

As[1] soon as the king is seated, the captains who waited without make their entrance, each one by himself, attended by his chief people, and so on, all in order; they approach and make their salaams to the king, and then take their places in the pavilions (*veramdas*) which I have previously described. As soon as these nobles have finished entering, the captains of the troops approach with shields and spears, and afterwards the captains of the archers; these officers are all stationed on the ground around the arena in front of the elephants, and they constitute the king's guard, for into such a place no man may enter bearing arms, nor near to where the king is. As soon as these soldiers have all taken their places the women begin to dance, while some of them place themselves in the circular galleries that I have said were (erected) at their gate of entrance. Who can fitly describe to you the great riches these women carry on their persons?—collars of gold with so many diamonds and rubies and pearls, bracelets also on their arms and on their upper arms, girdles below, and of necessity anklets on the feet. The marvel should be otherwise, namely that women of such a profession should obtain such wealth; but there are women among them who have lands that have been given to them, and litters, and so many maid-servants that one cannot number all their things. There is a woman in this city who is said to have a hundred thousand *pardaos*,[2] and I believe this from what I have seen of them.

[1] The writer begins again, "But returning to the feasts." I have omitted the phrase here, as it has become rather monotonous.

[2] A small gold coin, of which it is very difficult to assess the exact value. Abdur Razzâk (1443) apparently makes it equal to the half pagoda; Varthema (1503–7) to the pagoda itself; and this latter is the sense in which we must take it. Varthema calls it a "gold ducat." Purchas says it was in

Then the wrestlers begin their play. Their wrestling does not seem like ours, but there are blows (given), so severe as to break teeth, and put out eyes, and disfigure faces, so much so that here and there men are carried off speechless by their friends; they give one another fine falls too. They have their captains and judges, who are there to put each one on an equal footing in the field, and also to adjust the honours to him who wins.

In all this portion of the day nothing more is done than this wrestling and the dancing of the women, but as soon as ever the sun is down many torches are lit and some great flambeaux made of cloth; and these are placed about the arena in such a way that the whole is as light as day, and even along the top of the walls, for on all the battlements are lighted lamps, and the place where the king sits is all full of torches. As soon as these are all lit up there are introduced many very graceful plays and contrivances, but these do not stop long; they only approach where the king is and then go out. Then there enter others in other fashion, with battles of people on horseback; these horses are like the hobby-horses made in Portugal for the feast of the Corpo de Dios; others come with casting-nets, fishing, and capturing the men that are in the arena. When these amusements are ended, they begin to throw up many rockets and many different sorts of fires, also castles that burn and fling out from themselves many bombs (*tiros*) and rockets.

When these fireworks are finished, there enter many triumphal cars which belong to the captains, some of

his day about the value of a Flemish dollar. The general value assigned in more recent days to the pagoda is 3½ rupees, or seven shillings when the rupee stands at par value. (See Yule and Burnell's Dictionary, "Hobson-Jobson," *s.v.* "pagoda" and "pardao." Yule apparently values it, at the period treated of, as about 4s. 6d.) Barros and Castanheda both agree with Paes that the pardao was worth 360 reis. (Below, p. 282.)

them sent by those captains who are waging war in foreign parts; and they enter thus. The first belongs to Salvatinica, and they come in one after the other. Some of the cars appear covered with many rich cloths, having on them many devices of dancing-girls and other human figures; there are other cars having tiers one on top of another, and others all of one kind; and so in their order they pass to where the king is. When the cars have gone out they are immediately followed by many horses covered with trappings and cloths of very fine stuff of the king's colours, and with many roses and flowers on their heads and necks, and with their bridles all gilded; and in front of these horses goes a horse with two state-umbrellas of the king, and with grander decorations than the others, and one of the lesser equerries leads it by the bridle. In front of this horse goes another caracoling and prancing, as do all horses here, being trained in that art. You must know that this horse that is conducted with all this state is a horse that the king keeps, on which they are sworn and received as kings, and on it must be sworn all those that shall come after them; and in case such a horse dies they put another in its place. If any king does not wish to be sworn on horseback, they swear him on an elephant, which they keep and treat with equal dignity.

These horses, then, going in the way I have stated, pass twice round the arena and place themselves in the middle of the arena in five or six lines, one before the other, and the king's horse in front of them, all facing the king; they stand in such a way that between them and the men there is an open space all round. As soon as they are arranged in this way and are all quiet there goes out from the inside of the palace a Brahman, the highest in rank of those about the king, and two others with him, and this chief Brahman carries in his hands a bowl with a cocoanut and some rice and flowers, while others carry a pot of water; and they pass round by the back of the horses, which all stand facing the king; and after performing his ceremonies there, he returns to the palace.

After this is over you will see issuing from inside twenty-five or thirty female doorkeepers, with canes in their hands and whips on their shoulders; and then close to these come many eunuchs, and after these eunuchs come many women playing many trumpets and drums and pipes (but not like ours) and viols, and many other kinds of music, and behind these women will come some twenty women-porters, with canes in their hands all covered with silver, and close to them come women clothed in the following manner. They have very rich and fine silk cloths; on the head they wear high caps which they call *collães*,[1] and on these caps they wear flowers made of large pearls; collars on the neck with jewels of gold very richly set with many emeralds and diamonds and rubies and pearls; and besides this many strings of pearls, and others for shoulder-belts; on the lower part of the arms many bracelets, with half of the upper arm all bare, having armlets in the same way all of precious stones; on the waist many girdles of gold and of precious stones, which girdles hang in order one below the other, almost as far down as half the thigh; besides these belts they have other jewels, and many strings of pearls round the ankles, for they wear very rich anklets even of greater value than the rest. They carry in their hands vessels of gold each as large as a small cask of water; inside these are some loops made of pearls fastened with wax, and inside all this a lighted lamp. They come in regular order one before the other, in all perhaps sixty women fair and young, from sixteen to twenty years of age. Who is he that

[1] *Kullāyi* in Telugu. See pp. 210, 252, note 2, and p. 383. These women appear to have worn men's head-dresses.

could tell of the costliness and the value of what each of these women carries on her person? So great is the weight of the bracelets and gold and jewels carried by them that many of them cannot support them, and women accompany them assisting them by supporting their arms. In this manner and in this array they proceed three times round the horses, and at the end retire into the palace. These women are maids of honour to the queens, and so are the others that go with them; on each day of these nine days of the feast one of the queens sends, each on her own day, her ladies with the others. The officials, in honour of the feast, have the days divided between them in accordance with their custom as already arranged by the king; and these women come every day most richly attired, taking pleasure in shewing themselves in such things, and in making a display each one of what she possesses.

When these women retire the horses also go, and then come the elephants, and after making their salaam they too retire. As soon as they are gone the king retires by a small door which is at the end of the building. Then the Brahmans go and take an idol, and carry it to the House of Victory, where is the room of cloth that I have spoken of; and the king at once comes from within, and goes to where the idol is, and offers his prayers and performs his ceremonies. Then they bring there more buffaloes and sheep, and kill them in the same way as before, and then come the professional women to dance. As soon as the slaughter of the buffaloes and sheep is over the king retires, and goes to his supper; for he fasts all these nine days, and (each day) they eat nothing until all is finished, and their hour for food is midnight. The bayadères remain dancing before the idol a long time after all this is done.

In this way are celebrated these festivals of nine days; on the last day there are slaughtered two hundred and fifty buffaloes and four thousand five hundred sheep.

When these days of festival are past, the king holds a review of all his forces, and the review is thus arranged. The king commands to pitch his tent of Mecca velvet a full league from the city, at a place already fixed for that purpose; and in this tent they place the idol in honour of which all these festivals are celebrated. From this tent to the king's palace the captains range themselves with their troops and array, each one in his place according to his rank in the king's household. Thus the soldiers stand in line; but it does not appear to you to be only one line but in some places two or three, one behind the other. Where there was a lake it was surrounded with troops, and where the road was narrow they were drawn up on the plain; and so on the slope of the hills and eminences, in such a way that you could see neither plain nor hill that was not entirely covered with troops. Those on foot stood in front of those on horses, and the elephants behind the horses; in this array was each captain with his troops. The captains who had their stations inside the city, since the soldiers could not be drawn up on the flat roofs of the houses, put up scaffoldings across the mouths of the streets to hold the troops, in such a way that all were full, both outside and in.

Now I should like to describe to you how they were armed, and their decorations. The cavalry were mounted on horses fully caparisoned, and on their foreheads plates, some of silver but most of them gilded, with fringes of twisted silk of all colours, and reins of the same;[1] others had trappings of Mecca velvet, which is velvet of many colours with fringes and ornaments; others had them of other silks, such as satins and damask, and others of brocade from China and

[1] The reins were not of leather, but of silk twisted into ropes.

Persia.[1] Some of the men with the gilded plates had them set with many large precious stones, and on the borders lace-work of small stones. Some of these horses had on their foreheads heads of serpents and of other large animals of various kinds, made in such a strange manner that they were a sight to see for the perfection of their make. The horsemen were dressed in quilted tunics,[2] also of brocade and velvet and every kind of silk. These tunics are made of layers of very strong raw leather, and furnished with other iron (plates) that make them strong; some have these plates gilded both inside and out, and some are made of silver. Their headpieces are in the manner of helmets with borders covering the neck, and each has its piece to protect the face; they are of the same fashion as the tunics. They wear on the neck gorgets (*cofos*) all gilded, others made of silk with plates of gold and silver, others of steel as bright as a mirror. At the waists they have swords and small battle-axes, and in their hands javelins with the shafts covered with gold and silver. All have their umbrellas of state made of

[1] I read the word in the MS. *Xismael*, and Mr. Lopes suggests that this stands for Sheik (*Xeque*) Ismâîl. If so, undoubtedly Persia is meant.

[2] *Laudeis*. This word, variously spelt, is constantly used. It appears to refer to the thick quilted tunics, strengthened by leather or metal pieces, which were so often worn in India in old days. They were in many cases richly ornamented, and formed a good defence against sword-cuts. The pillars of the elaborately ornamented *Kalyâna Mandapa* of the temple in the fort at Vellore in North Arcot, which was built during the Vijayanagar period, are carved with rearing horses, whose riders wear jerkins, apparently of leather, fastened with buttons and loops. It is possible that this was the body-clothing referred to by the chronicler. I can give no clue to the origin of the word, unless it be connected with the Kanarese *lôdu*, "a stuffed cloth or cushion." Barros, describing the dress of the Hindu cavalry in the Raichûr campaign of 1520, says that they wore *laudees* of cotton (*embutidos*, whatever that may mean in this context—lit. "inlaid"), on body, head, and arms, strong enough to protect them against lance-thrusts or sword-cuts; the horses and elephants were similarly protected. Foot-soldiers carried no defensive armour "but only the *laudees*."—Dec. III. l. iv. c. 4.

embroidered velvet and damask, with many coloured silks on the horses. They wave many (standards with) white and coloured tails, and hold them in much esteem —which tails are horses' tails. The elephants in the same way are covered with caparison of velvet and gold with fringes, and rich cloths of many colours, and with bells so that the earth resounds; and on their heads are painted faces of giants and other kinds of great beasts. On the back of each one of them are three or four men, dressed in their quilted tunics, and armed with shields and javelins, and they are arrayed as if for a foray. Then, turning to the troops on foot, there are so many that they surround all the valleys and hills in a way with which nothing in the world can compare. You will see amongst them dresses of such rich cloths that I do not know where they came from, nor could any one tell how many colours they have; shield-men with their shields, with many flowers of gold and silver on them, others with figures of tigers and other great beasts, others all covered with silver leaf-work beautifully wrought, others with painted colours, others black and (so polished that) you can see into them as into a mirror, and their swords so richly ornamented that they could not possibly be more so. Of the archers, I must tell you that they have bows plated with gold and silver, and others have them polished, and their arrows very neat, and so feathered that they could not be better; daggers at their waists and battle-axes, with the shafts and ends of gold and silver; then you see musqueteers with their musquets and blunderbusses and their thick tunics, all in their order, with their . . .[1] in all their bravery; it was indeed a thing to see. Then the Moors —one must not forget them—for they were there also in the review with their shields, javelins, and Turkish bows, with many bombs and spears and fire-missiles;

[1] *Liões*. The meaning is not clear.

and I was much astonished to find amongst them men who knew so well how to work these weapons.

The king leaves his palace riding on the horse of which I have already told you, clothed in the many rich white cloths I have mentioned, with two umbrellas of state all gilded and covered with crimson velvet, and with the jewels and adornments which they keep for the purpose of wearing at such times: he who ever wears such jewels can understand the sort of things so great a lord would wear. Then to see the grandeur of the nobles and men of rank, I cannot possibly describe it all, nor should I be believed if I tried to do so; then to see the horses and the armour that they wear, you would see them so covered with metal plates that I have no words to express what I saw, and some hid from me the sight of others; and to try and tell of all I saw is hopeless, for I went along with my head so often turned from one side to the other that I was almost falling backwards off my horse with my senses lost. The cost of it all is not so much to be wondered at, as there is so much money in the land, and the chiefs are so wealthy.

There went in front of the king many elephants with their coverings and ornaments, as I have said; the king had before him some twenty horses fully caparisoned and saddled, with embroideries of gold and precious stones, that showed off well the grandeur and state of their lord. Close to the king went a cage such as is seen at Lisbon on the day of the Corpo de Dios festival, and it was gilded and very large; it seemed to me to be made of copper or silver; it was carried by sixteen men, eight on each side, besides others who took their turns, and in it is carried the idol of which I have already spoken. Thus accompanied the king passed along gazing at his soldiers, who gave great shouts and cries and struck their shields;

the horses neighed, the elephants screamed, so that it seemed as if the city would be overturned, the hills and valleys and all the ground trembled with the discharges of arms and musquets; and to see the bombs and fire-missiles over the plains, this was indeed wonderful. Truly it seemed as if the whole world were collected there.

In this way it went on till the king arrived at the place where the tent was that I have already mentioned, and he entered this and performed his usual ceremonies and prayers. You must not think that when the king passed the troops moved from their positions, on the contrary they stood motionless in their places till the king returned. As soon as the king had finished his ceremonies he again took horse and returned to the city in the same way as he had come, the troops never wearying of their shouting; as soon as he passed by them they began to march. Then to see those who were on the hills and slopes, and the descent of them with their shouts and beating of shields and shaking of arrows and bows that were without count. Truly, I was so carried out with myself that it seemed as if what I saw was a vision, and that I was in a dream. Then the troops began to march to their tents and pavilions in the plains, which were in great number; and all the captains accompanied the king as far as the palace, and thence departed to rest themselves from their labour.

Now I desire you to know that this king has continually a million fighting troops,[1] in which are included 35,000 cavalry in armour; all these are in his pay, and he has these troops always together and ready to be despatched to any quarter whenever such may be necessary. I saw, being in this city of Bisnaga, the king despatch a force against a place, one of those which

[1] As to this large number see p. 147 ff. above.

he has by the sea-coast; and he sent fifty captains with 150,000 soldiers, amongst whom were many cavalry. He has many elephants, and when the king wishes to show the strength of his power to any of his adversaries amongst the three kings bordering on his kingdom, they say that he puts into the field two million soldiers; in consequence of which he is the most feared king of any in these parts. And although he takes away so many men from his kingdom, it must not be thought that the kingdom remains devoid of men; it is so full that it would seem to you as if he had never taken away a man, and this by reason of the many and great merchants that are in it. There are working people and all other kinds of men who are employed in business, besides those who are obliged to go into the field; there are also a great number of Brahmans. In all the land of the heathen there are these Brahmans; they are men who do not eat anything that suffers death; they have little stomach for the use of arms.

Should any one ask what revenues this king possesses, and what his treasure is that enables him to pay so many troops, since he has so many and such great lords in his kingdom, who, the greater part of them, have themselves revenues, I answer thus: These captains whom he has over these troops of his are the nobles of his kingdom; they are lords, and they hold the city, and the towns and villages of the kingdom; there are captains amongst them who have a revenue of a million and a million a half of *pardaos*, others a hundred thousand *pardaos*, others two hundred, three hundred or five hundred thousand *pardaos*, and as each one has revenue so the king fixes for him the number of troops he must maintain, in foot, horse, and elephants.[1] These troops are always ready for duty,

[1] Some details are given by Nuniz (below, p. 384 f.).

THE ELEPHANT STABLES AT VIJAYANAGAR

From a Photograph by Col. W. Hooper)

whenever they may be called out and wherever they may have to go; and in this way he has this million of fighting men always ready. Each of these captains labours to turn out the best troops he can get because he pays them their salaries; and in this review there were the finest young men possible to be seen or that ever could be seen, for in all this array I did not see a man that would act the coward. Besides maintaining these troops, each captain has to make his annual payments to the king, and the king has his own salaried troops to whom he gives pay. He has eight hundred elephants attached to his person, and five hundred horses always in his stables, and for the expenses of these horses and elephants he has devoted the revenues that he receives from this city of Bisnaga. You may well imagine how great these expenses may be, and besides these that of the servants who have the care of the horses and elephants; and by this you will be able to judge what will be the revenue of this city.

This king of Bisnaga has five kings his subjects and vassals,[1] besides other captains and lords having large territories and great revenues; whenever a son happens to be born to this king, or a daughter, all the nobles of the kingdom offer him great presents of money and jewels of price, and so they do to him every year on the day of his birth.

You must know that when these feasts of which I have spoken are ended, at the beginning of the month of October, when eleven of its days are past, they make great feasts, during which every one puts on new, and rich, and handsome cloths, each one according to his liking, and all the captains give their

[1] According to the quite independent testimony of Nuniz (below, p. 374) these were the "kings" of Bankâpur, Gersoppa, Bakanûr Calicut, and Bhatkal.

men handsome cloths of many colours, each one having his own colour and device. On the same day they give great gifts of money to the king, it is even said that they give on that day to the king in money a million and five hundred thousand gold *pardaos*, and each *pardao* is worth three hundred and sixty *reis*, and from this you will be able to know how many *reis* there will be. I wish you to know that on this day begins their year; it is their New Year's Day, and for this they make the feast and give the gifts; and it is not to be wondered at, for we also do the same on New Year's Day. They begin the year in this month with the new moon, and they count the months always from moon to moon.[1]

And now I wish you to know that the previous kings of this place for many years past have held it a custom to maintain a treasury, which treasury, after the death of each, is kept locked and sealed in such a way that it cannot be seen by any one, nor opened, nor do the kings who succeed to the kingdom open them or know what is in them. They are not opened except when the kings have great need, and thus the kingdom has great supplies to meet its needs. This king has made his treasury different from those of the previous kings, and he puts in it every year ten million *pardaos*, without taking from them one *pardao* more than for the expenses of his house. The rest remains for him, over and above these expenses and of the expenses in the houses of his wives, of whom I have already told you that he keeps near him twelve thousand women; from this you will be able to judge how great is the richness of this kingdom, and how great the treasure that this king has amassed.

And if any one does not know what a *pardao* is,

[1] For a full note as to these chronological details see above, p. 140 ff.

let him know that it is a round gold coin, which coin is not struck anywhere in India except in this kingdom; it bears impressed on it on one side two images and on the other the name of the king who commanded it to be struck; those which this king ordered to be struck have only one image. This coin is current all over India. Each *pardao*, as already said, is worth three hundred and sixty *reis*.

After all these things (feasts) had passed the king betook himself to the new city, of which I have already told you that he delights in it much because it was made and peopled by him, of which I have already told you. In two years the king built this city. The king was received by the citizens with great feasts, and the streets were hung with rich cloths, and with many triumphal arches under which he passed. In this city the king held another review of the troops of his guard, and he distributed pay to all because it was the beginning of the year, and it is their custom to pay salaries year by year. An inspection is held by the officers of his house, and they write down the name of each one, and the marks that he has on his face or body. There are men of the guard who have a thousand *pardaos* pay, and others eight hundred, others six hundred and more, and a little more or less; there is a difference, and also a difference in the persons. Some men of them who are of higher rank than others have two horses or three, and others have no more than one. These troops have their captains, and each captain goes with his guard to mount guard at the palace according to order and custom; the king has in his guard five hundred horse, and these watch outside the palace armed with their weapons. There are two watches inside, and people with swords and shields.

The king, then, being in his new city, as I have said, Christovão de Figueiredo begged him of his kindness that he would permit him to be shown the palace of the city of Bisnaga, forasmuch as there had come with him many Portuguese who had never been in Bisnaga, and they would rejoice to see it, in order to have somewhat to tell of on their return to their own lands, whenever God should take them there. The king at once commanded that they should be shown certain of his residences, for that of his wives no one ever sees. As soon as we had returned to the city of Bisnaga, the governor of that place, who is called Gamdarajo, and is brother of Salvatinica,[1] showed us the palace.

You must know that on entering that gate of which I have spoken, by which the ladies serving the king's wives make their exit when they come to the feast, opposite to it there is another of the same kind. Here they bade us stand still, and they counted us how many we were, and as they counted they admitted us one by one to a small courtyard with a smoothly plastered floor, and with very white walls around it.[2] At the end of this courtyard, opposite this gate by which we entered, is another close to it on the left hand, and another which was closed; the door opposite belongs to the king's residence. At the entrance of this door outside are two images painted like life and drawn in their manner, which are these; the one on the right hand

[1] The "Guandaja" of Nuniz (below, p. 361).

[2] All these buildings are utterly destroyed, but there is no doubt that careful and systematic excavations would disclose the whole plan of the palace, and that in the ruins and débris would be found the remains of the beautiful sculptures described. Close behind the great decorated pavilion, from which the king and his court witnessed the feasts described by Paes, and therefore close to the gate just alluded to, are to be seen, half-buried in earth and débris, two large stone doors, each made of a single slab. The stone has been cut in panels to imitàte woodwork, and has large staples carved from the same block.

is of the father of this king, and the one on the left is of this king. The father was dark and a gentleman of fine form, stouter than the son is; they stand with all their apparel and such raiment as they wear or used to wear when alive. Afterwards, wishing to pass in at this door, they again counted us, and after they had finished counting us we entered a little house which contained what I shall now relate.

As soon as you are inside, on the left hand, are two chambers one above the other, which are in this manner: the lower one is below the level of the ground, with two little steps which are covered with copper gilded, and from there to the top is all lined with gold (I do not say "gilded," but "lined" inside), and outside it is dome-shaped. It has a four-sided porch made of cane-work[1] over which is a work of rubies and diamonds and all other kinds of precious stones, and pearls, and above the porch are two pendants of gold; all the precious stone-work is in heart-shapes, and, interweaved between one and another, is a twist of thick seed-pearl work; on the dome are pendants of the same. In this chamber was a bed which had feet similar to the porch, the cross-bars covered with gold, and there was on it a mattress of black satin; it had all round it a railing of pearls a span wide; on it were two cushions and no other covering. Of the chamber above it I shall not say if it held anything because I did not see it, but only the one below on the right side. In this house there is a room with pillars of carved stone; this room is all of ivory, as well the chamber as the walls, from top to bottom, and the pillars of the cross-timbers at the top had roses and flowers of lotuses all of ivory, and all well executed, so that there

[1] *Feyto de huas meyas canas.* I am doubtful as to the meaning of this. Examination of the mass of ruins now remaining would settle all these points. Stone sculptures were broken up and left. They were not removed. (See also p. 288 below.)

could not be better,—it is so rich and beautiful that you would hardly find anywhere another such. On this same side is designed in painting all the ways of life of the men who have been here even down to the Portuguese, from which the king's wives can understand the manner in which each one lives in his own country, even to the blind and the beggars. In this house are two thrones covered with gold, and a cot of silver with its curtains. Here I saw a little slab of green jasper, which is held for a great thing in this house. Close to where this jasper is, *i.e.* underneath some arches where is the entrance into the palace, there is a little door closed with some padlocks: they told us that inside it there was a treasury of one of the former kings.

As soon as we left this house we entered a courtyard as large as an arena for beast-fights, very well plastered, and almost in the middle are some pillars of wood, with a cross beam at the top all covered with copper gilt, and in the middle four chains of silver links with hooks which are caught one into the other; this serves for a swing for the wives of the king. At the entrance of this courtyard on the right hand we mounted four or five steps and entered some beautiful houses made in the way I have already told you—for their houses are single-storeyed houses with flat roofs on top, although on top there may be other houses; the plan is good, and they are like terraces. There is a building there built on many pillars, which are of stone-work, and so also is all the work of the roof, with all the rest of wood (*maneria*), and all the pillars (with all the other work) are gilded so that they seem as if covered with gold.

Then at the entrance of this building in the middle nave, there is, standing on four pillars, a canopy covered with many figures of dancing-women, besides other small figures[1] which are placed in the stone-work. All this is also gilded, and has some red colour on the under-sides of the leaves which stand out from the sculpture. You must know that they make no use of this building because it belongs to their idol and to the temple. At the end of this is a little closed door where the idol is. Whenever they celebrate any festival of this idol, they carry it on a golden throne and put it underneath that canopy which is made for that purpose; and then come the Brahmans to perform their ceremonies there, and the dancing-girls come to dance.

Descending from this building, we passed on the left side of the courtyard, and we entered a corridor which runs the whole length of it, in which we saw some things. On entering the corridor was a cot suspended in the air by silver chains; the cot had feet made of bars of gold, so well made that they could not be better, and the cross-bars of the cot were covered with gold. In front of this cot was a chamber where was another cot suspended in the air by chains of gold; this cot had feet of gold with much setting of precious stones, and the cross-bars were covered with gold. Above this chamber was another, smaller, and with nothing in it save only that it was gilt and painted. Passing this chamber, along the same corridor in front was a chamber which this king commanded to be made; on the outside were figures of women with bows and arrows like amazons. They had begun to paint this chamber, and they told us that it had to be finer than the others, and that it was to be all plated with gold, as well the ground below as all the rest. Passing this corridor and mounting up into another which is higher, we saw at one end three caldrons of gold, so large that in each one they could

[1] Mr. Ferguson has ingeniously emendated Senhor Lopes's reading, from *yinagees por que nas que estão metidas* to *ymagees pequenas que*, &c. . . . The MS., however, which is itself a copy, has *por que nas*.

cook half a cow, and with them were others, very large ones, of silver, and also little pots of gold and some large ones. Thence we went up by a little staircase, and entered by a little door into a building which is in this manner. This hall is where the king sends his women to be taught to dance. It is a long hall and not very wide, all of stone sculpture on pillars, which are at a distance of quite an arm's length from the wall; between one and another is an arm's length and a half, perhaps a little more. These pillars stand in that manner all around the building; they are half-pillars (?)[1] made with other hollows (?) all gilt.[2] In the supports (or pedestals) on the top[3] are many great beasts like elephants, and of other shapes; it is open so that the interior is seen, and there are on the inner side of these beasts other images, each placed according to its character; there are also figures of men turned back to back, and other beasts of different sorts. In each case from pillar to pillar is a cross-bar (the architrave) which is like a panel, and from pillar to pillar are many such panels; there are images of old men, too, gilded and of the size of a cubit. Each of the panels has one placed in this way. These images are over all the building. And on the pillars are other images, smaller, with other images yet more subordinate, and other figures again, in such a way that I saw this work gradually diminishing in size on these pillars with their designs, from pillar to pillar,

[1] *São de meas canas* (see above, p. 285). Meaning not understood, unless it be as rendered.

[2] This description deserves special notice. The writer is evidently describing a *mandapa* richly sculptured, of which so many examples are still to be seen in temples, and he states that the whole of the stone carving was richly coloured and gilded. This probably was always the case. Traces of colour still remain on many of these buildings at Vijayanagar.

[3] *Pranhus* (see above, p. 241). Probably the sculptures were like many still to be seen in the temples of that date in Southern India, where the base of the pillar is elaborately carved with grotesque figures of elephants, horses, and monsters.

and each time smaller by the size of a span as it went on, becoming lost; so it went dwindling gradually away till there remained of all the sculptured work only the dome, the most beautiful I ever saw. Between these images and pillars runs a design of foliage, like plates (*a maneyra de lamines*), all gilt, with the reverses of the leaves in red and blue, the images that are on the pillars are stags and other animals, they are painted in colours with the pink on their faces; but the other images seated on the elephants, as well as those on the panels, are all dancing women having little drums (tom-toms).

The designs of these panels show the positions at the ends of dances in such a way that on each panel there is a dancer in the proper position at the end of the dance; this is to teach the women, so that if they forget the position in which they have to remain when the dance is done, they may look at one of the panels where is the end of that dance. By that they keep in mind what they have to do.

At the end of this house on the left hand is a painted recess where the women cling on with their hands in order better to stretch and loosen their bodies and legs; there they teach them to make the whole body supple, in order to make their dancing more graceful. At the other end, on the right, in the place where the king places himself to watch them dancing, all the floors and walls where he sits are covered with gold, and in the middle of the wall is a golden image of a woman of the size of a girl of twelve years, with her arms in the position which she occupies in the end of a dance.

They did not show us more than this. The residence of the women no one may see except the eunuchs, of whom I have already told you. From here we returned by the way we had entered to the second gate, and there they again counted us.

Of the city of Bisnaga they say that there are more than a hundred thousand dwelling-houses in it, all one-storeyed and flat-roofed, to each of which there is a low surrounding wall, and in this city the king lives most of the time. On the north side are rocky hills; a river runs between them, and the wall runs along the top of them, and on the farther side is a city called Nagumdym; and it has only three gates, namely one by the river, which they cross in boats embarking just at this gate;[1] one on the other side which is to the north, this is a stronger gate; and one on the north-west side, a little gate between two very high ridges; and it is such a bad road that only one horseman can pass out a time.

And on the north-west side (of Bisnaga) is another city called Crisnapor[2] connected with Bisnaga, in which are all their pagodas, those in which they most worship, and all the revenue of this city is granted to them; and they say that they have a revenue of a hundred thousand *pardaos* of gold. The pagodas are high and have great buildings with many figures of men and women, all in lascivious attitudes.

On the south side is the other city called Nagalapor in a plain; in it the Ydalcão stopped with all his forces when he besieged Bisnaga, and he razed it to the ground; but already it is again rebuilt, and this is a league from Bisnaga.[3]

On the east side is another city called Ardegema,[4] which is the name of the principal wife of this king, and it is new, and he built it for love of her.

[1] The gate still exists opposite the Ânegundi ferry.

[2] Krishnâpura, where are the ruins of a fine temple.

[3] It seems clear that this sentence must be interpolated, and perhaps also the whole of the last four paragraphs. For the penultimate sentence could not have formed part of the original chronicle of Paes, written perhaps in 1522, or thereabouts, as it refers to an event that took place in 1535–36.

[4] Elsewhere called "Ondegema." Its other name was Nâgalâpur. It is the modern Hospett. (See below, Nuniz, p. 387.)

CHRONICLE OF FERNÃO NUNIZ

(WRITTEN, PROBABLY, A.D. 1535-37)

CHAPTER I

Copy and Summary of a Chronicle of the Kings of Bisnaga, who reigned (orig. *were*) *from the era one thousand two hundred and thirty, which was after the general destruction of the kingdom of Bisnaga.*[1]

IN the year twelve hundred and thirty[2] these parts of India were ruled by a greater monarch than had ever reigned. This was the King of Dili,[3] who by force of arms and soldiers made war on Cambaya for many years, taking and destroying in that period the land of Guzarate which belongs to Cambaya,[4] and in the end he became its lord.

And this taken, not being content with the victory which he had already gained, he made ready a large army of foot and horse, and determined to make war on the King of Bisnaga, leaving his captains in his lands and fortresses to defend themselves against his enemies, of whom there were many; for this King[5] was at that time at war with Bemgalla, and with the Turkomans on the confines of the country of Sheikh Ismael.[6] These men are fair and large of body; in their lands are

[1] This "general destruction" evidently refers to the conquest of Ânegundi by Muhammad Taghlaq.

[2] (See above, p. 8.) The date should be about 1330. Nuniz was here about a century wrong.

[3] Delhi.

[4] A common error with the foreigners. Properly speaking it was Cambaya which belonged to Gujarât.

[5] Muhammad Taghlaq of Delhi.

[6] Persia (above, p. 10).

many horses with which this King of Delly made war on Cambaya and laid it waste; and after the country was taken and he lord of it, there still remained to him as many as eight hundred thousand horsemen with whom he passed on to Bisnaga; of the number of people on foot nothing is said here because no one counted them.

And, determining to make war on the King of Bisnaga and to reduce him under his rule, he passed out of the lands which he had newly gained, entering into those of the King of Bisnaga, which at that time were many; and quitting the kingdom of Cambaya, he began to invade and make war on the Ballagate,[1] whose lands now belong to the Idalcão,[2] taking and destroying many towns and places in such a way that the people of the country surrendered to him their persons and property, though he left to them their weapons which he could not prevent their carrying.

And after he had become lord of all the country of the Ballagate, he passed the river of Duree,[3] which forms the boundary of the territories of the Ballagate and of those of the King of Bisnaga, which river he passed in basket-boats without finding any one to oppose the passage. Up to that time, in all that was (afterwards) the kingdom of Bisnaga, no place was populated save only the city of Nagumdym,[4] in which the King of Bisnaga[5] then was, awaiting his

[1] *i.e.* the Bâlâghât, or country above the ghâts. "The high land on the top is very flatte and good to build upon, called Ballagatte and Decan, and is inhabited and divided among divers kings and governors" (Linschoten, i. 65). Correa divides this part of India into "Bisnega, Balagate, and Cambay."

[2] This is the Portuguese rendering of the Âdil Khân, or Âdil Shâh of Bîjapûr. "Idalxa" represents the latter title.

[3] The description applies best to the Mâlprabha River, and perhaps "Duree" represents Dhârwâr.

[4] Ânegundi.

[5] He was at that time only chief or king of Ânegundi, Vijayanagar not having been yet founded.

destruction, since it was strong, and because he possessed no other citadel but that, which was his Lisbon.

And from the river which that King of Delly passed in basket-boats,[1] to that city was twenty-five leagues, all being open country (*campos*); and in them it seemed good to him to pitch his camp, so that his people might drink of the water in the plain (*campos*) along the length of the river. At that time there was great drought by reason of the summer season, and the waters of the few little lakes that were in the plain would not suffice for ten days for his troops, horses, and elephants, without drying up; and for that reason he halted some days by the banks of that river, till rain fell in the fields and lakes, enough for such a large army as he had brought with him.

And when the time came he raised his camp and brought his array to a halt in sight of that city of Nagundy.

And the King of Bisnaga, seeing his great power and how many troops he had brought with him, determined to abandon the city, which was very difficult to enter; close to which was, and now is, a river which is called Nagundy, whence the city is called Nagundy, and they say the city had its name because of it. And he fled for shelter to a fortress called Crynamata,[2] which was by the bank of the river, and which contained much provision and water; but not enough for the sustenance of so many people as he had with him, as many as fifty thousand men. Therefore the King chose five thousand men with their property and took refuge in the fortress; and for the

[1] These basket-boats are described by Paes (see above, p. 259).

[2] I have not been able to identify this name. It is possible that the first syllable represents the word *Srí*, and that the whole may have been a special appellation of the upper fortress or citadel, on the rocky heights above the town of Ânegundi.

rest he bade them betake themselves to another fortress of his in another part of his kingdom.

And being sheltered in the fortress, after he had taken order about his provisions, he was beset on all sides by the King of the people of Dely, who had already up to this time been at war with him[1] for twelve years; over which siege little time was spent, because the people that were inside the fortress were numerous, and in a little space had consumed their provisions.

Then the King of Bisnaga, seeing the determination of the soldiers of the King of Delly that they would never leave the place without making an end of those whom he had with him in the fortress, made a speech to them all, laying before them the destruction that the King of the troops of Dely had caused in his own kingdoms;[2] and how, not content with that, he had besieged this fortress, so that now there was nothing for them to look to but death, since already there was no water in the fortress nor anything left to eat. And (he said) that of the fifty thousand men who had been in the city of Nagundy he had chosen them alone as his companions and true friends, and he begged of them that they would hold fast in death to the loyalty which they had borne him in their lives; for he hoped that day to give battle to the King of Delly. Then he said that already there remained to him of his kingdom and lordship nothing but that fortress and the people that were in it, and so he asked them to arm themselves and die with him in battle, giving their lives to the enemy who had deprived them of all their lands.

[1] There had been no special war with Ânegundi that we know of; but the Râjah of that place had very possibly been directly affected by, if not actually engaged in, the wars between the Hindu Hoysala Ballâlas and the rulers of Warangal and Gujarât on the one hand, and the Muhammadan invaders from Delhi on the other.

[2] See Introduction, p. 13. "His kingdoms" (*seus reynos*) refers to the territories of Muhammad Taghlaq, whose barbarities had resulted in the wasting and depopulation of large tracts.

All of them were very content and glad at this, and in a short space were all armed; and after they were so the King made them another speech, saying, "Before we join battle we have to wage another war with our sons and daughters and wives, for it will not be good that we should allow them to be taken for the use of our enemies." And the King said, "I will be the first to deal with my wife and sons." At this time they were all standing in a large open space which was before the citadel, and there by the hand of the King were slain over fifty of his wives and some sons and little daughters; and the same was done with their own hands by all who had wives and sons that could not fight.

When these nuptial feasts, so abhorred of all, were fulfilled, they opened the gates of the fortress, and their enemies forthwith entered, and slew all of them except six old men who withdrew to a house. These were made captive and were taken before the King (of Delhi), and the King asked them who they were and how they had escaped, and they told them who they were; at which the King greatly rejoiced, because one of them was the minister of the kingdom and another the treasurer, and the others were leading officers in it. They were questioned by the King concerning the treasures of the King of Bisnaga, and such riches as were buried in the vaults of the fortress were delivered up to him; they also gave him an account of the revenues of the kingdom of Bisnaga at that time. When all was known to the King he delivered them to one of his captains, and commanded to make over the bodies of the dead to another captain, and gave orders that the bodies should be burned; and the body of the King, at the request of those six men, was conveyed very honourably to the city of Nagundy. From that time forward that place became a burying-place of the kings. Amongst themselves they still worship this King as a saint.

CHAPTER II

Of what the King (of Delhi) did after he had slain the King of Bisnaga, and entirely overthrown him, and seized his lands for himself, none being left to defend them.

As soon as the King had thus fulfilled all his desires, he bade his captains destroy some villages and towns which had risen against him, and give security to those who sought it of him. After the death of the (Hindu) King he stayed in that fortress two years, having already for twelve waged war on the kingdom.[1] He was far from his home, which was more than five hundred leagues distant; and, his forces being all scattered, news came to him how that all the land which was first gained by him had rebelled. As soon as this was known to the King he sent to collect his people, leaving in this fortress, which was the strongest in the kingdom, abundant provisions for its defence in all circumstances; and he left, for captain and governor of the kingdom, Enybiquymelly,[2] a Moor, and with him he left many troops, showing much kindness to each one of them separately, giving to each lavish gifts and lands in such a way that all were content, and, abandoning forthwith all hope of returning to their own country, made there their homes.

CHAPTER III

How the King of Dily departed with his troops, and took to his kingdom the six captives that he had taken in the fortress, &c.

THE King having departed to his own kingdom in consequence of the news that had been brought to him, leaving the kingdom of Bisnaga in the power of Meli-

[1] See above, p. 294, note 1.

[2] Spelt below "Meliquy niby" and "Mileque neby;" evidently for *Mallik Naib*, the king's deputy.

quy niby, when it was known throughout the country how he was out of it, those who had escaped to the mountains, with others who, against their will and through fear had taken oaths of fealty for their towns and villages, rose against the captain Mileque neby, and came to besiege him in the fortress, allowing no provisions to go in to him, nor paying him the taxes that had been forced on them. And Meliquy niby, seeing how little profit he could get in this country, and how badly he was obeyed, and how far off was the succour sent by his lord the King, sent quickly to him to tell him how all the land was risen against him, and how every one was lord of what he pleased, and no one was on his side; and that His Highness should decide what he thought best to be done in such case. And when the King heard this news he took counsel, telling the great people of the realm of the letter and message which he had from Melinebiquy, his captain and governor of the kingdom of Bisnaga, and how badly the lords of the land obeyed him; so that each one was king and lord over whomsoever he pleased, as soon as he acquired any power, there being no justice amongst them, nor any one whom they wished to obey. What was it seemed best to them (he asked), and what in such case ought they, and could they, do, so that he should not lose so fair a territory and one so rich, the seizure of which had cost such labour, so much money, and the lives of so many of their fellows? All the councillors decided that the King should command the presence of the six men whom he held captive, and that he should learn from them who was at that time the nearest of kin, or in any way related to the Kings of Bisnaga; and, this questioning done, no one was found to whom by right the kingdom could come, save to one of the six whom he held captive, and this one he who at the time of the destruction of Bisnaga had been minister of the kingdom. He was not related by blood to the kings, but only was the principal judge; but (it seemed) good that His Highness should give the kingdom to that one. And this advice pleased the King and them all.

At once the six captives were released and set at liberty, and many kindnesses and honours were done them, and the governor was raised to be King and the treasurer to be governor;[1] and he took from them oaths and pledges of their fealty as vassals; and they were at once despatched and sent to their lands with a large following to defend them from any one who should desire to do them an injury. And when these six men had thus finished their journey to the city of Nagundy, they found only the ruined basements of the houses, and places peopled by a few poor folk.

In a short time the arrival of Deoráo[2] (for so he was called) was known in all the country, and how he had been exalted to be King, with which the people were well content, as men who had felt so deeply their subjection to a lord not of their own faith; and from this man have descended all those who have reigned up to now. And they made great feasts for him, and delivered up to him the lands taken by former kings and lost to them, and he was obeyed as King. And when the captain Meliquy niby became aware of this, he was very pleased and contented, and delivered up to him the fortress and kingdom as the King his lord had commanded; and making himself ready with all speed he departed, leaving the land to its proper owner. And after he had gone, King Deoráo, entering on his rule, strove to pacify the people and those who had

[1] Above, p. 19 ff.

[2] Deva Râya. This was the general title of the Vijayanagar kings; thus, Harihara Deva Râya, Bukka Deva Râya, Krishna Deva Râya, &c. This first king is given no personal name by Nuniz. There were afterwards two kings who are known to history by the names Deva Râya I. and Deva Râya II., with no personal name prefixed.

revolted, and to make them safe, and he did them many kindnesses so as to secure their good-will, and travelled about their fortresses and towns. He abandoned the lost lands since he knew that he could not regain them, having no army or forces for such a work, nor any cause for which he could make war; and also because he was very old.

CHAPTER IV

How the City of Bisnaga was built by that King Dehorão.

THE King going one day a-hunting, as was often his wont, to a mountain on the other side of the river of Nagumdym, where now is the city of Bisnaga,—which at that time was a desert place in which much hunting took place, and which the King had reserved for his own amusement,—being in it with his dogs and appurtenances of the chase, a hare rose up before him, which, instead of fleeing from the dogs, ran towards them and bit them all, so that none of them dared go near it for the harm that it did them.[1] And seeing this, the King, astonished at so feeble a thing biting dogs which had already caught for him a tiger and a lion, judged it to be not really a hare but (more likely) some prodigy; and he at once turned back to the city of Nagumdym.

And arriving at the river, he met a hermit who was walking along the bank, a man holy among them, to whom he told what had happened concerning the hare. And the hermit, wondering at it, said to the King that he should turn back with him and shew him the place where so marvellous a thing had happened; and being

[1] This same tale is told of many kings and chiefs in Southern India. The "Tazkarat-ul-Mulûk" (*Ind. Ant.*, May 1899, p. 129) also relates it of the Bahmanî Sultan Ahmad Shah (1422–35), alleging that it was the behaviour of a hunted hare that induced him to make Bîdar his capital.

there, the hermit said that the King ought in that place to erect houses in which he could dwell, and build a city, for the prodigy meant that this would be the strongest city in the world, and that it would never be captured by his enemies, and would be the chief city in the kingdom. And so the King did, and on that very day began work on his houses, and he enclosed the city round about; and that done he left Nagumdym and soon filled the new city with people. And he gave it the name Vydiajuna, for so the hermit called himself[1] who had bidden him construct it; but in course of time this name has become corrupted, and it is now called Bisnaga. And after that hermit was dead the King raised a very grand temple[2] in honour of him and gave much revenue to it. And ever since, in his memory, the Kings of Bisnaga, on the day when they are raised to be kings, have, in honour of the hermit, to enter this house before they enter their own; and they offer many prayers in it, and celebrate many feasts there every year.

This King Dehoráo reigned seven years, and did nothing therein but pacify the kingdom, which he left in complete tranquillity.

By his death one called Bucaráo[3] inherited the kingdom, and he conquered many lands which at the time of the destruction of that kingdom remained rebellious, and by him they were taken and turned to his power and lordship; and he took the kingdom of Orya, which is very great; it touches on Bemgalla. He reigned thirty-seven years, being not less feared than esteemed, and obeyed by all in his kingdom.

On the death of that King Bucaráo there came to

[1] This was the great Sringêri Guru, Mâdhavâchârya, surnamed *Vidyâranya*, or "Forest of Learning." This derivation of the name of the city is very common, but is believed to be erroneous.

[2] The large temple of Virûpâksha at Hampe.

[3] Bukka Râya.

the throne his son called Pureoyre Deoráo,[1] which in Canara means "powerful lord," and he coined a money of *pardaos* which even now they call "*puroure deoráo;*" and from that time forward it has become a custom to call coins by the names of the kings that made them; and it is because of this that there are so many names of *pardaos* in the kingdom of Bisnaga. And this King in his time did nothing more than leave at his death as much conquered country as his father had done.

This King had a son who by his death inherited the kingdom, who was called Ajaráo;[2] and he reigned forty-three years, in which time he was always at war with the Moors; and he took Goa, and Chaul, and Dabull, and Ceillão,[3] and all the country of Charamamdell,[4] which had also rebelled after the first destruction of this kingdom, and he did many other things which are not recorded here.

This King made in the city of Bisnaga many walls and towers and enclosed it anew. Now the city at that time was of no use, there being no water in it by which could be raised gardens and orchards, except the water of the Nagumdym which was far from it, for what water there was in the country was all brackish and allowed nothing to grow; and the King, desiring to increase that city and make it the best in the kingdom, determined to bring to it a very large river which was at a distance of five leagues away, believing that it would cause much profit if brought inside the city. And so he did, damming the river itself with great boulders; and according to story he threw in a stone so great that it alone made the river follow the King's will. It was dragged thither

[1] *Pureoyre* probably represents "Harihara." This king was not the first to coin *pardaos* or pagodas. A pagoda of Bukka I. is known (*Ind. Ant.*, xx. 302).

[2] See above, p. 51. There is no name amongst those of this dynasty with which this can be at present connected.

[3] Ceylon.

[4] Coromandel (note, p. 239 above).

by a number of elephants of which there are many in the kingdom; and the water so brought he carried through such parts of the city as he pleased. This water proved of such use to the city that it increased his revenue by more than three hundred and fifty thousand *pardaos*. By means of this water they made round about the city a quantity of gardens and orchards and great groves of trees and vineyards, of which this country has many, and many plantations of lemons and oranges and roses, and other trees which in this country bear very good fruit. But on this turning of the river they say the King spent all the treasure that had come to him from the king his father, which was a very great sum of money.

This King left a son at his death called Visaráo,[1] who inherited the kingdom on the death of his father; and he lived six years, and during this time did nothing worth relating.

At his death he left a son called Deoráo, who reigned twenty-five years. He determined to collect great treasures, but owing to constant warfare he could not gain more than eight hundred and fifty millions of gold, not counting precious stones. This was no great sum, seeing that in his time the King of Coullão,[2] and Ceyllão, and Paleacate,[3] and Peguu, and Tanaçary[4] and many other countries, paid tribute to him.

At his death this King left a son who inherited the kingdom, who was called Pinaráo,[5] he reigned twelve years, and was a great astrologer; he was given much to letters, and made many books and (promulgated) ordinances in his land and kingdom. As long as he

[1] Vijaya Rao. [2] Quilon.

[3] Pulicat, near Madras. This was an important province of Vijayanagar in later years. [4] Tenasserim.

[5] *Pina*=*Chinna* in Telugu, *Chikka* in Kanarese, and means "little." Pina Râya or Chikka Râya was the title applied to the Crown Prince (above, p. 223). The derivation given by Nuniz is plainly wrong.

reigned he had twenty ministers, which is an office that amongst these (people) is (generally) held only by one person. This King was very wise; he was well versed in all his duties, and possessed such good talents and qualities that they called him Pinaráo, which amongst them, in the language of Canara, means a very wise man. This King was killed by treason by the hand of a nephew whom he had brought up in his house like a son, who thus caused the death of the King.[1] The nephew resolved to marry, and for the feasts at his wedding he prayed the King, his uncle, that he would command that he should be attended and honoured at his wedding by the King's own son; and the King, for the love that he bore him and the pleasure that he had in honouring him, bade his son make ready with his following, and sent him with the ministers and captains of his court to attend and honour the wedding of his nephew. And he, making all ready, as soon as they were in his house, being at table, they were all slain by daggers thrust by men kept in readiness for that deed. This was done without any one suspecting it, because the custom there is to place on the table all that there is to eat and drink, no man being present to serve those who are seated, nor being kept outside, but only those who are going to eat; and because of their thus being alone at table, nothing of what passed could be known to the people they had brought with them. And after he had killed the King's son with all the captains, the minister[2] set out to ride as if he were going to bear a present to the King, and as soon as he arrived at the gates of the palace he sent a message to the King saying that he was there, and had brought

[1] Abdur Razzák relates the same story, and fixes the event as having taken place between November 1442 and April 1443 A.D., "while he was at Calicut" (above, p. 73).

[2] This seems to imply that the nephew of the king had been one of the twenty ministers (*regedores*) mentioned in the chronicle.

him a present according to custom. And the King, being at that time at leisure and amusing himself with his wives, bade him enter; and as soon as he was come to where he stood, he presented to the King a golden bowl in which he had placed a dagger steeped in poison, with which he wounded him in many places; but the King, as he was a man who knew how to use both sword and dagger better than any one in his kingdom, avoided by twists and turns of his body the thrusts aimed at him, freed himself from him, and slew him with a short sword that he had. And this done he ordered a horse to be saddled, and mounted it, and rode holding his nephew's head in his hand; and he took the road to the latter's house, apprehending that treason might have been wrought and fearing that his son might be dead. And as soon as he arrived he beheld the treason in very deed, and how wicked a deed his nephew had done; seeing that his son and his principal captains were dead, and that the traitor might have prevailed against himself had he had the power. In great wrath the King commanded his men to inflict dreadful punishments on all found guilty of this treason, and indeed many who were not so. He himself remained grievously wounded with the poisoned wounds and he lasted only six months, and these ended, died of the poison carried on the dagger.

After his death a son remained to him who inherited the kingdom and was called . . . [1], and this King, as soon as he began to reign, sent to call his treasurers and the minister and the scribes of his household, and inquired of them the revenue of his kingdom, and learned how much revenue came in yearly; and His Highness had every year thirteen millions of gold. This King granted to the pagodas a fifth part of the revenue of his kingdom; no law is possible in the

[1] *Sic* in orig.

country where these pagodas are, save only the law of the Brahmans, which is that of the priests; and so the people suffer.

On the death of this King succeeded a son named Verupacarao.[1] As long as he reigned he was given over to vice, caring for nothing but women, and to fuddle himself with drink and amuse himself, and never showed himself either to his captains or to his people; so that in a short time he lost that which his forefathers had won and left to him. And the nobles of the kingdom, seeing the habits and life of this king, rebelled, every one of them, each holding to what he possessed, so that in his time the King lost Goa, and Chaull, and Dabull, and the other chief lands of the realm. This King in mere sottishness slew many of his captains. Because he dreamed one night that one of his captains entered his chamber, on the next day he had him called, telling him that he had dreamed that night that the captain had entered his room to kill him; and for that alone he had him put to death. This King had two sons already grown up, who, seeing the wickedness of their father and how he had lost his kingdom, determined to kill him, as in fact was done by one of them, the elder, who was his heir; and after he had killed him, when they besought him to be King, he said, "Although this kingdom may be mine by right, I do not want it because I killed my father, and did therein that which I ought not to have done, and have committed a mortal sin, and for that reason it is not well that such an unworthy son should inherit the kingdom. Take my brother and let him govern it since he did not stain his hands with his father's blood;" which was done, and the younger brother was raised to the throne. And when they had entrusted the kingdom to him he was advised by his minister and captains that he should slay

[1] Virûpâksha Râya.

his brother, because, as the latter had killed his father so he would kill him if desirous of so doing; and as it appeared to the King that such a thing might well be, he determined to kill him, and this was at once carried out, and he slew him with his own hand. So that this man truly met the end that those meet with who do such ill deeds. This King was called Padearáo; and after this was done he gave himself up to the habits of his father, and, abandoning himself to his women, and not seeking to know ought regarding his realm save only the vices in which he delighted, he remained for the most part in the city.

One of his captains who was called Narsymgua,[1] who was in some manner akin to him, seeing his mode of life, and knowing how ill it was for the kingdom that he should live and reign, though all was not yet lost, determined to attack him and seize on his lands; which scheme he at once put into force.

He wrote, therefore, and addressed the captains and chiefs of the kingdom, saying how bad it was for them not to have a King over them who could govern properly, and how it would be no wonder, seeing the manner of his life, if the King soon lost by his bad government even more than his father had done.

He made great presents to all of them so as to gain their goodwill, and when he had thus attached many people to himself he made ready to attack Bisnaga where the King dwelt. When the King was told of the uprising of this captain Narsymgua, how he was approaching and seizing his lands and how many people were joining him, he seemed unmindful of the loss he had suffered, he gave no heed to it nor made ready, but, instead, he only ill-treated him who had brought the

[1] *Narasimha.* He had apparently large tracts of country under his charge to the east of the capital towards the east coast. His relationship to the sovereign has always been a matter of doubt.

news. So that a captain of the army of this Narsymgua arrived at the gates of Bisnaga, and there was not a single man defending the place; and when the King was told of his arrival he only said that it could not be. Then the captain entered the city, and the King only said that it could not be. Then he even entered his palace and came as far as the doors of his chamber, slaying some of the women. At last the King believed, and seeing now how great was the danger, he resolved to flee by the gates on the other side; and so he left his city and palaces, and fled.

When it was known by the captain that the King had fled he did not trouble to go after him, but took possession of the city and of the treasures which he found there; and he sent to acquaint his lord, Narsymgua. And after that Narsymgua was raised to be king. And as he had much power and was beloved by the people, thenceforward this kingdom of Bisnaga was called the kingdom of Narsymga.

After he was raised to be king and was obeyed he came to Bisnaga, where he did many acts of justice; and he took the territories from whomsoever had, contrary to right, taken them from the king. This King reigned forty-four years, and at his death left all the kingdom in peace, and he regained all the lands which the kings his predecessors had lost. He caused horses to be brought from Oromuz and Adeem [1] into his kingdom and thereby gave great profit to the merchants, paying them for the horses just as they asked. He took them dead or alive at three for a thousand *pardaos*, and of those that died at sea they brought him the tail only, and he paid for it just as if it had been alive.

At the death of that King there remained three fortresses which had revolted from his rule, and which

[1] Persia (Ormuz) and Aden. The latter were Arabs.

he was never able to take, which were these—Rachol, and Odegary and Conadolgi,[1] which have large and rich territories and are the principal forts in the kingdom. At his death he left two sons, and the governor of the kingdom was Nasenaque, who was father of the king that afterwards was king of Bisnaga;[2] and this king (Narsymgua), before he died, sent to call Narsenaque his minister, and held converse with him, telling him that at his death he would by testament leave him to govern the kingdom until the princes should be of an age to rule; also he said that all the royal treasures were his alone, and he reminded him that he had won this kingdom of Narsymgua at the point of the sword; adding that now there remained only three fortresses to be taken, but that for him the time for their capture was passed; and the King begged him to keep good guard over the kingdom and to deliver it up to the princes, to whichever of them should prove himself most fitted for it. And after the King's death this Narsenaque remained as governor, and soon he raised up the prince to be king, retaining in his own hands the treasures and revenues and the government of the country.

At that time a captain who wished him ill, determined to kill the prince, with a view afterwards to say that Narsenaque had bidden him commit the murder, he being the minister to whom the government of the kingdom had been entrusted, and he thought that for this act of treason Narsenaque would be put to death. And he soon so arranged it that the prince was killed one night by one of his pages who had been bribed

[1] "Rachol" is Raichûr; "Odegary" represents Udayagiri; "Conadolgi" probably is Kondavîd, *dolgi* for *drûg*, a mountain fortress.

[2] This account of the second Narasa and the family relationship differs altogether from the results obtained from epigraphical study, according to which the second Narasa was elder son of the first Narasa or Narasimha Krishna Deva being the latter's younger son.

for that purpose, and who slew the prince with a sword. As soon as Narsenaque heard that he was dead, and learned that he himself (was supposed to have) sent to kill him, he raised up another brother of the late King's to be king, not being able further to punish this captain, because he had many relations, until after he had raised this younger brother to be king, who was called Tamarao. He (Narsenaque) went out one day from the city of Bisnaga towards Nagumdym, saying that he was going hunting, leaving all his household in the city. And after he had arrived at this city of Nagumdym he betook himself to another called Penagumdim,[1] which is four-and-twenty leagues from that place, where he at once made ready large forces and many horses and elephants, and then sent to tell the King Tamarao of the cause of his going; relating to him the treason that that captain by name Tymarsaa[2] had carried out slaying his brother the king, and by whose death he (the prince) had inherited the kingdom. He told him how that the kingdom had been entrusted to him by his father, as well as the care of himself and his brother, that as this man had killed his brother, so he would do to him in the same way, for he was a traitor; and he urged that for that reason it was necessary to punish him. But the king at that time was very fond of that captain, since by reason of him he had become King, and in place of punishing him he bestowed favour on him and took his part against the minister. And, seeing this, Narsenaque went against him with large forces, and besieged him, threatening him for four or five days, until the King, seeing his determination, commanded Timarsaa to be put to death; after which he (the King) sent the (traitor's) head to be shown to the minister, who greatly rejoiced. Narsenaque sent away all

[1] Pennakonda.

[2] *Cf.* "Temersea," p. 250, and note. This, however, was not the man there alluded to, though he bore the same name.

the troops and entered the city, where he was very well received by all the people, by whom he was much loved as being a man of much justice.

And after some days and years had passed, Narsenaque, seeing the age of the king how young he was, determined to keep him in the city of Penagumdy, with large guards to make safe his person, and to give him 20,000 cruzados of gold every year for his food and expenses, and himself to govern the kingdom—for it had been entrusted to him by the king his lord so to do. After this had been done he told the King that he desired to go to Bisnaga to do certain things that would tend to the benefit of the kingdom, and the King, pleased at that, told him that so it should be; thinking that now he himself would be more his own master and not be so liable to be checked by him. And after he had departed and arrived at Bisnaga, Narsenaque sent the King 20,000 men for his guard, as he had arranged, and he sent as their captain Timapanarque, a man in whom he much confided; (commanding him) that he should not allow the King to leave the city, and that he should carefully guard his person against treachery.

And after this was done Narsenaque began to make war on several places, taking them and demolishing them because they had revolted. At that time it was proposed by some captains that they should kill the King, as he was not a man fitted to govern, but to this Narsenaque would answer nothing. After some days had passed, however, Narsenaque, pondering on the treason about which they had spoken to him, how it would increase his greatness and more easily make him lord of the kingdom of which he was (only) minister, called one day those same captains who had often proposed it to him, and asked them by what means the King could be slain without its being known that he had had a hand in his death. Then one man[1] told him that a very good way would be that he (the minister) should appear to be annoyed with him and should send to command his presence, which mandate he would not obey, and on account of this act of disrespect he (the minister) should ordain that some punishment be inflicted, and at this aggravation he would leave the city and fly to Penagundy to stir up the King against the minister. He said that after he had gained the goodwill of the King he would so plot against him that he would render him disobedient; and that to give the King greater encouragement he would forge letters as if from captains which should contain the same counsel—namely, that he should leave that city where he was more prisoner than free—and would point out to him that he alone was king and lord, and yet that the land was under the power of Narasenaque his vassal, who had made himself very strong and powerful in the kingdom and held him (the King) prisoner, and had rebelled. He would urge the King to secretly quit the city and betake himself to a fortress belonging to the captain who had sent him that letter, and that there he should prepare himself, getting together a large following. And he would tell him that when the lords and captains came to know of his wish and determination they would act according to it, and would help him, and would come with him to fall upon Narsenayque, and would bestow upon him (Narsenaque) the prison in which he (the King) was now kept. So he would be king. (The captain further said) that after he had persuaded the King to this he would cause him to (leave the city), and while going out he would kill him, and that in this way Narsenaque should become king.

Narsenayque was well pleased to listen to this treason and to hear of the evil deed which this captain planned,

[1] Later on we learn that this man's name was Codemerade (p. 360).

and he showed him much favour. The captain disappeared after some days from where Narsenayque was, feigning to have fled; and he came to Penagumdy, where in a few days his arrival was known; and he set about and put in hand all those things that had been arranged. Every day he showed the King a letter, one day from a captain of one fortress, the next day another from another captain; and the King, understanding the plots contained in the letters so shown, replied that the counsel and advice seemed good, and yet how could he resist the power of Narsenayque, who, besides being minister of the kingdom, had (possession of) all the horses and elephants and treasure, so that he could at once make war against him? "True it is, Sire, that which thou sayest," answered the traitor, "and yet he is much misliked by all the captains who raised thee to be king, and as soon as they shall see thee in Chãodagary"[1] (which was a fortress whither he had advised him to flee, being one which up to that time was independent), "all will flock to thine aid, since they esteem it a just cause." Said the King,—"Since this is so, how dost thou propose that I should leave this place, so that my going should not be known to the guards and to the 20,000 men who surround me in this city?" "Sire," he replied, "I will disclose to thee a very good plan; thou and I will go forth by this thy garden, and from thence by a postern gate which is in the city (wall), and which I know well; and the guards, seeing thee alone without any following, will not know that it is thou, the King, and thus we shall pass to the outside of the city, where I will have horses ready that will take us whithersoever it seemeth good to thee." All this pleased the King well, and he placed everything in his hands; and, seeing fulfilled all his desire, the captain spoke with those men who

[1] Chandragiri, the capital of the kingdom in its decadent days.

guarded that part of the garden by which he wished that the King should fly, and which was near the King's own houses, (for into this garden the King often went to amuse himself with his wives, which garden was at that part guarded by a matter of 300 armed men) and to these men he spoke thus, saying to them :—"If ye shall happen to see me pass by here on such a night and at such an hour, and if ye shall see a man coming with me, slay him, for he well deserves it of me, and I will reward ye;" and they all said that that would be a very small service to do for him. When that day had passed the traitor went to the King and said to him :—"Sire, do not put off till to-morrow that which thou hast to do to-day; for I have the horses ready for thy escape, and have planned so to escort thee forth that even thy ladies shall not be aware of thy departure, nor any other person. Come, Sire, to the garden, where I will await thee." The King replied that his words were good and so he would do, and as soon as night was come and the hour arrived, the King went carefully out, and still more careful was he who for some time had awaited him; and he gave signal to the armed men, and as soon as he was come to the garden he passed between two of them who were the guards, and they threw themselves on the King and slew him, and forthwith buried him at the foot of a tree in the same garden. And this being accomplished without their knowing whom they had slain, the traitor gave them his thanks, and returned to his inn to make ready to leave the city, and also so as not to give cause for talk therein. And the next morning it was found that the King was missing; and though searched for throughout all the city no news of him could be heard, all the people thinking that he had fled somewhere, whence he would make war on Narsenayque. And to Narsenayque the news was straightway brought, and he, feigning much sorrow at it, yet made ready all his horses and elephants in case the kingdom should be plunged into some revolution by the death of the king; although as yet he knew not for certain how the matter stood, save that the King had disappeared. And afterwards the man came who had killed the King, and told him how it had been done and how secretly he had been slain, so that even the very men who had killed him knew not who it was; and Narsenayque bestowed upon him rich reward. And since there was no news of the King, and he holding everything now under his hand, he was raised to be king over all the land of Narsymga.

And this king left at his death five sons, one was called Busbalrao, and another Crismarao, and another Tetarao, and another Ramygupa and another Ouamysyuaya.[1]

And this Busbalrao inherited the kingdom at the death of his father Narsenayque and reigned six years, during which he was always at war, for as soon as his father was dead the whole land revolted under its captains; who in a short time were destroyed by that King, and their lands taken and reduced under his rule. During these six years the King spent, in restoring the country to its former condition, eight million gold *pardaos*. This King died of his sickness in the city of Bisnaga; and before he died he sent for Salvatimya, his minister,[2] and commanded to be brought to him his (the King's) son, eight years old, and said to Sallvatina that as soon as he was dead he must raise up this son to be

[1] Inscriptions do not give us the names of any sons having names like these. "Crismarao" probably represents Krishna Deva Râya, son of the first Narasa or Narasimha, and brother of the second Narasa, often called Vîra Narasimha.

[2] Sâluva Timma. This man belonged apparently to the new royal family, whose family name was Sâluva. He was the powerful minister of Krishna Deva Râya, but died disgraced, imprisoned, and blinded. He is constantly mentioned in inscriptions of the period.

king (though he was not of an age for that, and though the kingdom ought perhaps to belong to his brother Crisnarao) and that he must put out the eyes of the latter and must bring them to show him; in order that after his death there should be no differences in the kingdom. Salvatina said that he would do so and departed, and sent to call for Crisnarao, and took him aside to a stable, and told him how his brother had bade him put out his eyes and make his son king. When he heard this, Crisnarao said that he did not seek to be king, nor to be anything in the kingdom, even though it should come to him by right; that his desire was to pass through this world as a *jogi* (ascetic, recluse), and that he should not put his eyes out, seeing that he had not deserved that of his brother. Sallvatina, hearing this, and seeing that Crisnarao was a man of over twenty years and therefore more fit to be king, as you will see farther on, than the son of Busbalrao who was only eight years old, commanded to bring a she-goat, and he put out its eyes, and took them to show the King, for already he was at the last hour of his life; and he presented them to him, and as soon as the King was dead his brother Crisnarao was raised to be king, whose eyes the late King had ordered to be torn out.

CHAPTER V

Of the things done by King Crisnarao after he was raised to the throne.

As soon as Crisnarao was raised to be King and was obeyed throughout all his kingdom,—Salvatine being his minister, who had been the same for his brother Busbalrao,[1]—he without delay sent his nephew, son of

[1] Perhaps "Basava Râya," but as yet no brother of Krishna Deva is known bearing that name.

Busbalrao his brother, together with his own three brothers, to a fortress called Chãodegary; the nephew remained there till he died. And after the King had done this for his own safety he stayed in the city of Bisnaga for a year and a half without going outside of it, learning the affairs of the kingdom and looking at the testaments of past kings. Amongst these he found one of king Narsymga, whose minister his father Narsenayque had been, in which that King desired that his sons, or whoever should inherit this kingdom of Narsymga which he had gained by force of arms, should capture three fortresses that at his death remained in revolt against him, the which he had not himself taken because time failed him; one of them was called Rracholl,[1] and another Medegulla.[2]

Crisnarao, seeing this testament and seeing how badly the kings his predecessors had acted in what had been enjoined on them, determined at once to prepare armies and to go against these places; and one of these fortresses was called Odigair, and it belonged to the King of Orya. And, determining to go first against this, he collected (an army of) thirty-four thousand foot and eight hundred elephants, and arrived with this force at the city of Digary,[3] in which there were ten thousand foot soldiers and four hundred horse; for the fortress had no necessity for more by reason of its great strength, because it could not be taken except by being starved out.

And the King laid siege to it for a year and a half, in which time he made many paths across rocky hills, breaking up many great boulders in order to make a road for his soldiers to approach the towers of the fortress. The place at this time was so strong that they could not approach it except by one way which was so narrow that men could only pass along it one

[1] Raichûr. [2] Mudkal. [3] Udayagiri.

at a time; and in this place he made a broad road, and many others also, so that he could come close to the fortress.

And he took it by force of arms, and in it captured an aunt[1] of the King of Orya, who was taken captive and carried off with all the courtesy that he could show her, having her liberty; and he took her along with himself.

And after this was done he called Salvatinya and bade him see how well he had performed that which king Narsymga had by his testament enjoined on him, and yet he said he was not content with such a trivial victory, for[2] he desired to go forward a hundred leagues into the kingdom of Orya; and he ordered him to make ready provisions and pay fully the salaries of the forces.

And after this fortress was taken he departed and went against Comdovy,[3] which was one of the principal cities of the kingdom of Orya, and besieged it; and, learning this, the King of Orya came against him to defend his territories, and brought with him one thousand three hundred elephants, and twenty thousand horsemen, and he brought five hundred thousand foot-soldiers. Crisnarao, being aware of the approach of the king of Orya, left the city without assaulting it, saying that he preferred to fight the King in person and his army rather than to attack the city, and that there would be plenty of time afterwards to take it; and he went forward four leagues from it, leaving a force to prevent the escape of the people from the city if they should seek to flee to the coast. And he arrived at a large river of salt water crossed by a ford,[4] and on the other side of the river

[1] Some say uncle.

[2] In the MS. *em que avia* is evidently a mistake for *e que avia.*

[3] Kondavîd.

[4] I cannot identify this river. There is none such, to my knowledge, twelve miles or thereabouts from Kondavîd. "Salt" may perhaps mean brackish.

was the King of Orya with his army. King Crisnarao halted his army on this side of the river, and sent the King a message that if he desired to fight with him he would retire from the river two leagues, so that he (the king of Orya) might pass the river unmolested, and as soon as he had passed he would join battle; to which message the King of Orya gave no reply, but on the contrary made ready to give battle. And King Crisnarao, seeing his determination, crossed the river with all his forces and elephants, and in the crossing of the river there were heavy encounters on both sides, and many were slain. Notwithstanding this, King Crisnarao crossed the river, and on the bank fought so bravely that he defeated the King of Oria and put him to flight, in which defeat he took many horses and elephants.

And after the King had done this he told Salvatinea his minister that he purposed to turn back to the fortress, which had not yet experienced his strength, and he went against it, and stopped there two months besieging it; and he took it.

And he gave the command of it to Salvatinea, who left in it, from his army, for captain one of his brothers, in order that he himself might go forward with the King through the kingdom of Orya. And the King, passing the river once more in pursuit of the King of Orya, and taking and ravaging all the country which had no reason for expecting him, arrived at a city called Comdepallyr,[1] where were all the chiefs of the kingdom, it being the chief city in that kingdom. And he laid siege to it, and remained there three months without being able to capture it, and in the end he took it more by reason of his numbers than by force of arms; in which fortress he found many people of high rank whom he made captive, amongst whom was a wife of the King, and one of

[1] Kondapalle.

his sons who was a prince, and seven principal captains of the kingdom, all of whom he sent by road to Bysnaga.

And he went forward a hundred leagues into the kingdom, finding no one to bar his progress till he got to Symamdary,[1] which was a very large city, in which he halted for six months, waiting for the King of Orya. He sent many messages to say that he was waiting for him in the field, but he never came. And in this city he did many works, and gave alms to the temples, and erected therein a very grand temple to which he gave much revenue. And he commanded to engrave on it an inscription which says:—"Perhaps when these letters are decayed, the king of Orya will give battle to the King of Bisnaga. If the King of Orya erases them, his wife shall be given to the smiths who shoe the horses of the King of Bisnaga."

And after this was done he returned, leaving the greater part of those lands to the temples, and came to Bisnaga where he rested some days. And he sent to call the son of the king of Orya who was taken captive in the first fortress, and told him that as people said that he was a very active man and was very dexterous with both sword and dagger, he would be pleased to see him fence.

The young man said that since His Highness summoned him he would do what he could, and asked that this might be put off till next day. And when the next day came the King sent to call him, and also sent for one of his own men who at that time was very expert in the art,[2] that he should fence with him.

[1] Rajahmundry. The first syllable has been accidentally dropped, perhaps by the copyist.

[2] Senhor Lopes's "Chronica" has "*hũ homẽ seu que aquelle tempo d aquelle tempo muito sabia.*" Mr. Ferguson suggests, and with good reason, that for the second *tempo* we should read *jogo*. I have translated the passage accordingly. Senhor Lopes concurs.

And when the son of the King of Orya saw him, being offended with the King for sending a man to fight with him who was not the son of a King but only a man of humble birth, he cried out to the King:—"God forbid that I should soil my hands by touching a man not of the blood royal," and saying this he slew himself. And his father, hearing how his son was dead, wrote to Salvatinea (asking) by what means he could ransom his wife who remained in the power of the King, since his son was dead; to which he made answer that he should arrange the marriage of his daughter with the King, and that afterwards the King would restore him his wife and lands (or, would take only his lands).[1] This counsel he accepted, and he sent ambassadors to Bisnaga to arrange a marriage with his daughter, with which King Crisnarao was well content; and when the King of Orya knew his will (in the matter) he sent him his daughter; and with the coming of her they were friends. And Crisnarao restored the lands on the other side of the river, and kept those on the hither side for himself.

CHAPTER VI

How Crisnarao, after he had made peace with the King of Oria, determined to go against the land of Catuir.

AFTER Crisnarao had made peace, and had married the daughter of the King of Oria, and had restored to him his wife and the lands beyond the river, as has been narrated above, he made ready a large army

[1] The original MS. has *tomaria suas terras*—"would take his lands." Possibly the first of these words should have been *tornaria*, in which case the sentence would mean that the King "would restore the lands" to his enemy.

and prepared to attack Catuir,[1] which is the land of a lord who had been in revolt for fifty years; this land is on the Charamãodel side. And he went against it, and laid siege to one of the principal cities where the lord of the land was; and it is called . . .[2] and is surrounded with water.

Now at the time when Crisnarao attacked this city it was winter, for which cause the river that surrounded it was so swollen, and carried down so much water, that the king could do no harm to the place. And King Crisnarao, seeing this, and seeing that time was passing away without his attaining his desire, commanded his men to cut many new channels in order to be able to attack that principal (river) which had opposed itself to the fulfilment of his wishes. And this was done in a short time, since he had many soldiers; and after the (new) watercourses were finished and brought to where the water should go he opened mouths in the river, the water of which very soon flowed out so that the bottom could be seen, and it was left so shallow that it enabled him to reach the walls of the city; and the river was thus diverted into fifty different beds. Inside the city were one hundred thousand foot-soldiers and three thousand cavalry, who defended themselves and fought very bravely, but this availed little to prevent Crisnarao from entering in a few days and slaughtering all of them. He found large treasures in this city, amongst others in ready money a million and six hundred thousand golden *pardaos*, besides jewels, and horses, which were numerous, and elephants. And after he had finished the capture of this land Crisnarao divided

[1] I am unable to identify this country. The description of the town answers to Vellore in North Arcot, the fine old fort at which place is surrounded with a deep moat. According to tradition, this place was captured by Krishna Deva Râya from a Reddi chief.

[2] Blank in the original.

it amongst many of his captains, giving to each one what was necessary for him; and the chief who lived in the city and who was lord of the land was taken away captive and carried to Bisnaga, where he died in the King's prison.

And after the King had settled the country he came to Bisnaga, whence he sent Salvatinea to the city of Comdovy, since he was chief of it, by whom his brother was placed in it so as to see directly to the land and its government; for after the King returned from Orya he never went again thither.

And Salvatinea, having departed on his journey to Comdovy, before he arrived there, met, opposing his path, a Muhammadan named Madarmeluquo, who was a captain of the King on this side,[1] and who was awaiting him with sixty thousand men. Salvatinea had two hundred thousand men, and had very little fear of him; and with these he went against him, and took and defeated him, and took prisoners himself and his wife and son and horses and elephants and much money and store of jewels, and sent them all to King Crisnarao. The king commanded to put (the captives) in prison, and there they died. And Sallvatinea went to his territories, and after he had stayed there some months and seen to its government and decided matters in dispute, he returned to the King at Bisnaga, by whom he was well received as being the principal person in the kingdom.

[1] *Elrey Daquem.* This may be "the king on this side" or "the king of the Dakhan." The former seems most probable, and I think that the reference is to the forces of Sultan Qulî Qutb Shâh of Golkonda (see the Muhammadan account of affairs at this time, given above, pp. 132–135.)

CHAPTER VII

How Crisnarao, on the arrival of Salvatinia, determined to attack Rachol, a city of the Ydalcão, and to break the peace that had lasted so long; and the reason why.

AFTER Salvatinia had arrived and had been well received by the King, and after the lapse of some days, the King told him that he desired to fulfil all the wishes expressed in the testament of King Narsynga, one of which was to capture Rachol, which was a very strong city and amongst the principal ones of the Ydallcão, who had taken it from the kings his ancestors; and because there was now peace between both parties, and had been so for forty years, he knew not how he could manage to break it. But Salvatinia said that since the peace had been made under certain conditions—one of which was that if on either one side or the other any land-owners, captains in revolt, or other evil-doers should be harboured and their surrender should be demanded, they should forthwith be given up—there was now great reason for breaking the peace, since many land-owners and debtors to His Highness had fled into the kingdom of the Ydallcão. He counselled therefore that the King should send to demand the surrender of these men, and that on refusal to give them up there would be good ground for breaking the peace. Many, however, disagreed with this advice. Now it happened at this time that the King (of Bisnaga) sent Cide Mercar with forty thousand *pardaos* to Goa to buy horses, which Cide Mercar was a Moor in whom the King of Bisnaga confided on account of various affairs with which he had already been entrusted; and this man, when he arrived at a place where the Moors lived which was called Pomdaa and is two leagues from Goa, fled from that place, Pomdaa, to the Ydallcão, carrying with him all the treasure. Some say that the Ydallcão wrote to him a letter as soon as he got there. As soon as they gave to the King this news of the flight of Cide, and how he had carried off all the money, he said that he would write to the Ydallcão to send the man back to him with all the money, since he was his friend. Then the King caused a letter to be written, in which he spoke of the friendship that had existed for so many years so that nothing could shake it, and that he hoped that a traitor would not be the cause of breaking a peace of such long standing as had been between them; and he begged that he would send Cide back at once.

As soon as the letter was read to the Ydallcão he sent to summon his kazis and the men of his council, and he bade them read the letter which had come from the King, as to which letter there were many suggestions made. At the end of all they agreed that he should not send him (Cide) to him (the King of Bisnaga), for they said that he (Cide) was one learned in the law and related to Mafumdo.[1] And the Ydallcão, as a cloak to his action, gave Dabull to that Cide, by way of showing that he was not near his person nor knew he aught of him; from which town of Dabull Cide fled, nor had they any further news of him. When those who had come from the King returned bearing the Ydallcão's answer, the King showed great indignation at it, and held that the peace was broken; he at once ordered to appear before him the great lords of his Council, and had the letter read aloud so that all might hear. As soon as it was read he said that without more ado they should make ready, since he was determined to take full vengeance. But the councillors advised the King, saying that for such a small sum of money as this it was not well so to act; that he should think of what would be said and talked of throughout the world; and that if he

[1] Muhammad, Mahomet, *i.e.* he was of the Prophet's kindred.

was bent on breaking so prolonged a peace for such a trifling cause, he should call to mind that there never was any honesty in a Moor; that others were to blame in that which Cide had done; and that if Cide should dare to come to that war which was waged in order to take vengeance on him,[1] then it would be well that those who accompanied him should die, but that they knew that Cide would keep well away from the army.[2]

The councillors, however, saw that the King remained unmoved from his determination to make war, and they then counselled him, saying:—"Sire, do not go to war by that route (Dabull), but go against Rachol, which now belongs to the Ydallcão but of old was part of this kingdom; then the Ydallcão will be forced to come to defend it, and thus thou wilt take vengeance jointly both on one and the other." The King held this advice to be good and prepared for his departure, sending letters to Madre Maluco, and Demellyno, and Desturvirido,[3] and other superior lords, giving them an account of what had taken place in the matter of the Ydallcão, and how he had

[1] The text is confused here.

[2] The following is Barros's account of this affair of "Cide Mercar." After mentioning the terms of the treaty between Vijayanagar and Bîjapûr, one of which provided for the reciprocal extradition of criminals and debtors, he writes:—

"Crisnarao, knowing that he could catch the Hidalcão in this trap, called a Moor by name Cide Mercar, who had been in his service for many years, and bade him take forty thousand pardaos and go to Goa to buy horses of those that had come from Persia. Crisnaro wrote letters to our Captain . . . on purpose so that the affair might become widely known to all. Cide Mercar, either tempted by the large sum of money in his charge, or swayed by a letter which they say was sent to him by the Hidalcão, when he arrived at a *Tanadaria* called Pondâ, three leagues from Goa, fled to the Hidalcão from there. The Hidalcão as soon as he arrived sent him to Chaul, saying that he bestowed on him this *Tanadaria* as he was an honourable man of the family of Mahamed . . . ; but in a few days he disappeared from there, and they say that the king ordered his murder after he had taken from him the forty thousand pardaos."

[3] "Madre" stands for Imâd, the Bîrâr Sultan; "Virido" for the Barîd Sultan of Bîdar. I cannot explain *Demellyno* or *Destur*, unless the former be an error of the copyist for "Zemelluco" as written below, which certainly

determined to make war on him; from which lords he received answer that he was doing rightly, and that they would assist him as far as they were able. As to the Zemelluco, at the time when the messengers returned this answer he could find no excuse for not sending some troops to the aid of his sister who was wedded to the Ydallcão.

The King had sent the letters to those lords out of his great craftiness, for he told them of what he was about to do in order to seduce them to his side,—so far at least as concerned their goodwill, seeing that in the matter of troops he had no need of them—because if they had joined the Ydallcão he (the King) would never have conquered as he did; but because the Ydallcão was hated by them all as being a more powerful chief than they, (for there is little faith amongst the Moors, and they bite one another like dogs and like to see one after the other destroyed) he was conquered, as you will see hereafter, in the month of May, on the new moon day, in the year one thousand five hundred and twenty-two.[1]

After the King had made his offerings and performed sacrifices to his idols he left the city of Bisnaga with all his troops; and they marched in the following order. The chief of the guard (*o porteiro moor*)[2] led the advance with thirty thousand infantry—archers, men with shields, and musqueteers, and spearmen—and a thousand horse, and his[3] elephants. After him went Trimbicara with fifty thousand foot and two thousand horse and twenty elephants. After him went Timapanayque; he had

refers to the Nizâm Shâh. Several Portuguese writers omit the first syllable of "Nizâm" in their chronicles. On p. 348 below, these names are given as Madremalluco, Zemelluco, "Destuy" and "Virido;" and therefore "Destur" and "Destuy" must mean the Qutb Shâh of Golkonda, at that period Sultan Qulî. On p. 349 we have the form "Descar."

[1] For a full discussion of this date see above, p. 140.

[2] See above, p. 263, note. His name was Kâma Naik (p. 329).

[3] *Seus allyfantes.* Perhaps *seus* is a clerical error for *seis*, "six." Barros, in describing the same event, says "sixteen elephants."

with him sixty thousand foot and three thousand five hundred horse and thirty elephants; and after him went Adapanayque with one hundred thousand foot and five thousand horse and fifty elephants. After him came Comdamara,[1] and he had one hundred and twenty thousand foot six thousand horse and sixty elephants; after him went Comara, and he had eighty thousand foot and of horse two thousand five hundred, and forty elephants; after him the forces of Ogemdraho,[2] the governor of the city of Bisnaga, with one of his captains, who had one thousand horse and thirty thousand foot and ten elephants. After him went three eunuchs, favourites of the King, who had forty thousand foot and one thousand horse and fifteen elephants. The page who served the King with betel[3] had fifteen thousand foot and two hundred horse, but he had no elephants. Comarberca[4] had eight thousand foot and four hundred horse and twenty elephants. The people of the chief of Bengapor[5] went by another route with the people of Domar, who were very numerous; and in the same way went other captains of ten or twelve thousand men, of whom I make no mention, not knowing their names. The King took of his guard six thousand horse and forty thousand foot, the pick of all his kingdom, men with shields, archers, and three hundred elephants.

All were equally well armed, each after his own fashion, the archers and musqueteers with their quilted tunics,[6]

[1] See below, p. 360, note.

[2] Probably Ganda Râjah, brother of Sâluva Timma, the minister. (See p. 284, and note to p. 361.) The initial "O" may be the article "The."

[3] The great vassal lords of Madura, who after the fall of the kingdom established themselves as a dynasty of independent sovereigns, descended, so Barradas tells us, from the "Page of the betel" (above, p. 230).

[4] I think that the second *c* in this name is an error for *e*, and that "Comarberea" represents Kumâra Virayya of Mysore (above, p. 269). Later on Nuniz spells the name "Comarberya" (below, p. 336).

[5] Above, pp. 40, 60, 122.

[6] *Lades*, for *laudeis*, quilted tunics, doublets. The word is spelt in other places *laydes*, *lamdes*, *landys*, *lamdys*, and *landeis*. See note, p. 276, above.

and the shieldmen with their swords and poignards[1] in their girdles; the shields are so large that there is no need for armour to protect the body, which is completely covered; the horses in full clothing, and the men with doublets,[2] and weapons in their hands, and on their heads headpieces after the manner of their doublets, quilted with cotton. The war-elephants go with their howdahs (*castellos*) from which four men fight on each side of them, and the elephants are completely clothed, and on their tusks they have knives fastened, much ground and sharpened, with which they do great harm. Several cannon were also taken. I do not speak here of the washermen, who are numberless here—they wash clothes—nor of the public women who accompanied the army; there were twenty thousand of them with the king during his journey. Any one can imagine the amount of baggage that such a large number of people would take. In the rear with the king, but always on the road in front of him, some ten or twelve thousand men with water-skins who go seeking water, and place themselves along the road to give water to those who have no one to bring it to them; this is done so that none of the people should die of thirst. Three or four leagues in front of all this multitude go some fifty thousand men who are like scouts; they have to spy out the country in front, and always keep that distance; and on their flanks there are two thousand horse of the cavalry of that country. These are all bowmen, and they always advance on the flanks of the scouts.

In this order, as I have stated, they left the city of Bisnaga, and with them a great number of merchants,

[1] *Gomedares*, probably the modern *agomia* or *gomia*, "a poignard." Senhor Lopes refers me to Barros, Mendes, Pinto, &c., where the form used is *gumia;* the word being derived from the Arabic *kummiya*, which properly means a curved dagger—"*um punhal em meo arco*" (MS. in Portuguese, on Morocco, in Senhor Lopes's possession).

[2] See above, p. 276.

besides many others who were already in advance with all supplies; so that wherever you may be you will at once find all you want. Every captain has his merchants who are compelled to give him all supplies requisite for all his people, and in the same way they carry all other necessaries.

According to the King's custom, when he wishes to lie down and sleep, they make for him a hedge of brushwood and of thorns behind which his tent is pitched, which was done for him all along this route; on which route was seen a wonderful thing, namely that on passing a river which, when they reached it, came half-way up to the knee, before half the people had passed it was totally dry without a drop of water; and they went about in the sand of it making pits to find some water. In this order the King proceeded till he arrived at the town of Mollabamdym,[1] which is a league from the city of Rachol, where he pitched his camp so as to give a rest to the people after the fatigues of the march.

And the King being in the city of Mollabamdyn, settling all that was necessary for the siege of Rachol, there came to him people of the King of Bisnaga, and the people of Domaar, and also many other captains with an infinitude of people. As soon as they had joined and everything was put in order, and after his Brahmans had finished their ceremonies and sacrifices, they told the King that it was now time, that the pagodas had given sign of conquest, and that he should advance.

Then he sent the Moors in the royal service to lead the van, and Camanayque, the chief of the guard, pitched the camp very near the ditches of the city of Rachol, and every captain halted his people according to the commands given. The people of the city received them

[1] Malliâbâd, as now called, close to Raichûr. The name given by Nuniz I take to represent "Mallia (or Malliya) Banda," probably the Hindu name. *Banda* = "rock." "Malliâbâd" is the name given by the Musalmâns.

with many shots from heavy cannon that they had, and from many firelocks, and many arrows and musket-shots, so that those of the besiegers who arrived close to the ditches suffered heavily and wanted to retreat. But the King would not permit this, saying that he would not have sent them there were it not that he would soon effect an entry into the city, and if not, that they should all die; wherefore his men were compelled to attack the city, and did so in many brave and severe fights. In these many of them lost their lives, since those of the city were in very strong position and well acquainted with everything that was necessary for their defence, while the King's troops never ceased their attacks on the city. The captains, seeing how badly the attack was going in consequence of the number of soldiers killed, had recourse to lavish gifts and stratagems, as thus:—They began to buy (from the soldiers) the stones which they took from the walls and towers, and they paid them according to the value of the stone; so that the stones were worth ten, twenty, thirty, forty, and fifty *fanams*.[1] By this device they contrived to dismantle the wall in many places, and laid the city open; but since the city was in itself so strong, and the soldiers who were in it were such chosen men and so used to warfare, they killed many of the King's people. Yet not for that did they cease fighting, but every day and at every attack they became bolder, in consequence of their greed for what the captains gave them; for the money had the power of taking from them the terror of death which had inspired them before. They also gave them something for dragging away a dead man from the foot of the wall. So the fight dragged on for a space of three months till the Ydallcão came up with reinforcements.

Now I wish you to know more of the situation, and

[1] A small copper coin.

of the city, and the people which it held. This city of Rachol lies between two great rivers, and in the midst of a great plain where there are no trees except very small ones, and there are great boulders there; from each river to the city is three leagues. One of these rivers is the northern boundary, and beyond it the country belongs to the Ydallcão, and the other is the boundary to the south which is the boundary of Narsymga. This plain lies in the middle of these two rivers, and there are large lakes therein and wells and some little streams where the city is situated, and a hill which looks like a woman's breast and is of natural formation. The city has three lines of strong walls of heavy masonry made without lime; the walls are packed with earth inside, and it has on the highest point a fortress like a tower, very high and strong; at the top where the fortress stands is a spring of water which runs all the year round. It is held to be a holy and mysterious thing that a spring which is in a lofty situation should in some way never be without water. Besides this spring there are several tanks of water and wells, so that the citizens had no fear of being ever taken for lack of water; and there were in the city supplies for five years. There were eight thousand men as garrison and four hundred horse and twenty elephants, and thirty catapults (*trabucos*) which hurled heavy stones and did great damage. The towers which are on the walls are so close together that one can hear words spoken from one to the other. Between these and all around they posted their artillery, which consisted of two hundred heavy pieces, not to mention small ones. As soon as the people of the city knew of the arrival of the King's troops, and after they had received a captain of the Ydallcão who came with some soldiers to the city, they closed the gates with stone and mortar. The chief fight which takes place is on the east side, because on the north and south sides it stands on huge rocks which make it very strong; and, the city being besieged on all sides, the camp of the King was on the east side, and so was the strength of the attack.

CHAPTER VIII

Of the manner in which the King had his camp, &c.

THE tent of the King was surrounded by a great hedge of thorns with only one entrance, and with a gate at which stood his guards. Inside this hedge lodged the Brahman who washes him and has charge of the idol that he always carries about with him, and also other persons who hold offices about the King's person, and eunuchs who are always to be found in his chamber. And outside this circle all around are his guards, who watch all night at fixed spots; with this guard are quartered the officers of the household; and from thence to the front were all the other captains in their appointed posts, according as each one was entrusted and ordered. Outside of all these people, in a camp by themselves, were the scouts of whom I have already spoken, whose duty it is to patrol all night through the camp and watch to see if they can catch any spies. On the other side the washermen, (who are those that wash clothes) were in a camp by themselves, and they were near to the place where they could best wash clothes.

All the camp was divided into regular streets. Each captain's division has its market, where you found all kinds of meat, such as sheep, goats, pigs, fowls, hares, partridges and other birds, and this in great abundance; so much so that it would seem as if you were in the city of Bisnaga. And you found many endless kinds of rice, grains, Indian-corn, vetches (*minguo*),[1] and other seeds that they eat. Besides these things, which are necessaries, they had another (market) where you could find in great abundance everything that you wanted; for in these markets they sell things that in our parts are sold by professional hucksters.[2] There were craftsmen, also, working in their streets, so that you saw made there golden jewels and gewgaws, and you will find all kinds of rubies and diamonds and pearls, with every other kind of precious stone for sale. There also were to be seen sellers of cloths, and these were without number as that is a thing so many want, they being of cotton. There were also to be seen grass and straw in infinite abundance. I do not know who could describe it so as to be believed, so barren a country is this Rachol and so sandy. It is a mystery how there should be an abundance of everything therein. Any one can imagine what grass and straw would be required each day for the consumption of thirty-two thousand four hundred horses and five hundred and fifty-one elephants,[3] to say nothing of the sumpter-mules and asses, and the great numbers of oxen which carry all the supplies and many other burdens, such as tents and other things. Indeed no one who did not understand the meaning of what he saw would ever dream that a war was going on, but would think that he was in a prosperous city. Then to see the numbers of drums and trumpets, and other musical instruments that they use. When they strike up their music as sign that they are about to give battle it would seem as if the heavens must fall; and if it happened that a bird came flying along at the time when they made such a terrific noise, it used to come

[1] *Minguo*, probably *moong* or green grain ("Hobson-Jobson"). Ibn Batuta calls it *munj*, others *mungo*.

[2] *Regatoẽs d arte.*

[3] The total cavalry and elephants of the different columns enumerated above comes to 32,600 and 551 respectively.

down through terror of not being able to get clear of the camp, and so they would catch it in their hands; principally kites, of which they caught many.

But I cease to speak more of this because I should never finish; and so I turn to tell of the battle.

CHAPTER IX

How the King attacked the city of Rachol.

THE King, being as I have said at the siege of the city of Rachol, there came to him sure news that the Ydallcão had arrived at the river on the northern side, and that there he had pitched his camp. The King therefore sent his spies to keep watch over the foe, to see what he was doing and to send word of his every movement. With the coming of this news a tumult broke out in the camp, principally among the common soldiers, in whose minds suspicion was never wanting, and they still suffered under the terror inspired from old time by the Moors. There the Ydallcão halted some days so as to see what the King was doing and whether he would march to attack him there in his camp; for it was thought by him and by his people that as soon as the King should learn of his arrival he would at once march to meet him, and they decided that he could defend himself from the King in the place where he was better than in any other, by help of the river. For there was no other ford than the one close at hand; and this they proposed to guard so well that none should take it, least of all, they thought, men who (in their eyes) were only blacks.

Although the King heard that the enemy was on the opposite bank of the river, he yet made no move, nor did he do anything; and the Ydallcão, seeing that he made no advance, took counsel with his officers, and at this council the advice given greatly differed, as each had his own opinion regarding the non-movement of the King. Many said that this was because the King held his foe to be of little account, and wished to show his people how great was his power; and they said that he was only waiting for them to cross the river to at once fall upon them. The principal person who said this was Amcostam,[1] who was captain of Pomdaa at the time that Dom Guterre was captain of Goa.[2] Others said no, but that the King was afraid, thinking of times past and the many conquests that the Moors had gained over the Hindus, and that he had brought with him some veteran soldiers that had taken part in those wars. The advice of these was to push forward and pass the river. It was not well (they said) for the Ydallcão to show weakness, and the longer he stayed where he was the less would he benefit himself and harm the enemy; and although they were not so many in number as the Hindus, yet they had the advantage in the remembrance of the former battles that had been fought between them.[3] In the end the Ydallcão ordered that they should muster the forces, and said that after this was ended he would decide what was best to be done. When the muster was made, he found that he had one hundred and twenty thousand men on foot, archers and musqueteers and men with shields and spearmen, and eighteen

[1] Barros has *Ancostão*, and Correa *Ancoscão*. The latter termination seems the most natural—*cão* for *Khân*. The name appears to be "Ankus Khân." "Pomdaa" is Pomdâ or Pondâ, close to Goa.

[2] Dom Guterre de Monroy sailed from Portugal to India in 1515 in command of a fleet (Albuquerque, Hakluyt edition, iv. 194). In 1516 he was in command at Goa during the absence of Governor Lopo Soares at the Red Sea, between the months of February and September, and during that period attacked the Bîjapûr troops at Pondâ, which were commanded by Ankus Khân, with some success (Barros, Dec. III. l. i. c. 8). Osorio (Gibbs' translation, ii. 235) represents De Monroy as a man of a very cruel and licentious disposition. He was married to a niece of the governor.

[3] They believed, that is, that their prestige would give them great moral superiority over the Hindus.

thousand cavalry, and one hundred and fifty elephants; and when the muster was over and he had seen his forces for himself, seeing also the great strength of artillery that he had, he said that with his artillery he would seek to defeat the Rao of Narsymga. He therefore ordered them to make ready, since he desired to cross the river at once and advance to the attack; for the Ydallcão believed that his best course was to halt on the farther side and thence send his troops to charge the camp of the King, and that in so doing he would not be beaten and would not lose Rachol.[1]

In this greedy resolve he passed the ford and advanced to within three leagues of the King's camp, and he caused his own camp to be strengthened by large trenches, and commanded all his artillery to take post in front, and he arranged the order of his positions and the manner in which they should behave if they were attacked by the enemy. His camp extended along the length of the river for the sake of the water, that he might not be cut off from it by the enemy.

As soon as they brought news to the King that the Ydallcão had passed the river, he commanded all to make ready, but that no movement should take place in his army till he should see how the enemy acted; and when they brought him further news that the enemy had pitched his camp and strengthened his position, he ordered a general advance of all his forces. He divided his army into seven wings. Comarberya[2] begged from him (the command) of the van, he being the king's father-in-law and a great lord; he is King of Serigapatão and lord of a large state; he brought with him thirty grown-up sons. The King bade him pitch his camp a league from the Ydallcão and ordered all to arm themselves at dawn, as he intended then to give

[1] This passage is obscure.

[2] See above, p. 327 and note.

battle to the enemy; but the men of the Council said that that day was an unlucky day, and begged him not to attack, as it was a Friday, and they asked him not to attack till Saturday, which they hold for a lucky day.

When the King had left Rachol, those inside opened a gate, and one of the captains who was inside, a eunuch, made a sally with two hundred horse, certain foot-soldiers and elephants; he kept entirely along the river-bank on the King's flank. The object of this no one could guess, each one having his own opinion. As soon as the King halted he also did the same, keeping always his spies in the King's camp to see what passed and (what would be) the end of the battle. Since both armies were so close, each to his foe, they never put aside their weapons but watched all the night through.

Seeing that the dawn of Saturday was now breaking, the drums and trumpets and other music in the King's camp began to sound and the men to shout, so that it seemed as if the sky would fall to the earth; then the neighing and excitement of the horses, and the trumpeting of the elephants, it is impossible for any one to describe how it was. But even if told in simple truth it would hardly be believed the great fear and terror that struck those who heard it, so that even those very men that caused the noise were themselves frightened at it. And the enemy on their part made no less noise, so that if you asked anything you could not hear yourself speak and you had to ask by signs, since in no other manner could you make yourself understood. When all in the camp had gone to the front it was already two hours after sunrise, and the King ordered an advance of his two forward divisions, with command so to strike home that they should leave not one of the enemy alive; and this was forthwith done. They attacked the enemy so hotly that many of the King's troops found themselves on the tops of the trenches[1] that the Moors had constructed in the fields. The Moors were disposed as if they expected that the King would engage them all at once with all his forces, and so it appeared to the Ydallcão and to his officers; and for that reason he held ready all his artillery, waiting for the time when, owing to the adventurousness of their main body, his men must of necessity cause much slaughter in their ranks. Then he intended to bring up his artillery and destroy them. But as soon as he saw the manner of their attack the Ydallcão had to abandon the plan that had seemed to him best for their safety, and he commanded the whole of the artillery at once to open fire; which discharge, as it was very great, did much damage to the enemy, killing many of the horse and foot and many elephants, and it compelled the King's troops to retire. As soon as the Moors saw their enemies beginning to leave the field they charged all amongst them, so that there did not remain one man in the saddle nor one who kept his face to the foe; but all the King's troops began to fly, and the Moors after them, slaughtering them for about half a league. When the King saw the way in which his troops fled he began to cry out that they were traitors, and that he would see who was on his side; and that since they all had to die they should meet their fate boldly according to custom.[2] "Who ranges himself with me?" he cried. Immediately there thronged about him all those lords and captains that were ready to side with him, and the King said that the day had arrived in which the Ydallcão would boast that he had slain in it the greatest lord in

[1] The original has *cavas e baudes*. The meaning of the last word is not clear.

[2] *Avyão de morrer pedido ausa da morte*. *Ausa* is perhaps for *ousadia*, "boldness;" and the passage would then mean that since death appeared inevitable they should meet it half-way, and not lazily await it; they should die like soldiers in a charge, not stupidly standing still to be slaughtered.

the world, but that he should never boast that he had vanquished him. Then he took a ring from his finger and gave it to one of his pages, so that he might show it to his queens in token of his death, that they might burn themselves according to custom. Then he mounted a horse and moved forward with all his remaining divisions, commanding to slay without mercy every man of those who had fled. As soon as these last saw what a reception they received at the hand of their fellows they felt compelled to turn and charge the enemy, and their attack was such that not one amongst the Moors was found to face them; for the Moors met them as men engaged in a pursuit, all in great disorder. The confusion was so great amongst the Moors and such havoc was wrought (in their ranks) that they did not even try to defend the camp they had made so strong and enclosed so well; but like lost men they leaped into the river to save themselves. Then after them came large numbers of the King's troops and elephants, which latter worked amongst them mischief without end, for they seized men with their trunks and tore them into small pieces, whilst those who rode in the castles (howdahs) killed countless numbers.

The troops advanced thus, pursuing the foe, till the King reached the river, where, seeing the death of so many—for here you would see women and boys who had left the camp, there horses and men who through clinging one to another could not escape as there was so much water in the river—and the King's troops stood on the bank, so that whenever a man appeared he was killed, and the horses that tried to clamber up by the bank of the river, unable to do so, fell back on the men, so that neither one nor the other escaped, and the elephants went into the stream, and those that they could seize were cruelly killed by them. Seeing what passed, I say, the King out of compassion commanded the troops to retire, saying that numbers had died who did not deserve death nor were at all in fault; which order was at once obeyed by all the captains, so that each one withdrew all his forces.

The King then advanced to the camp of the Ydallcão and rested himself in his tent, but many of the captains spoke against his action in thus taking repose, saying that he ought rather to complete the destruction of all his enemies, and they would secure this for him; and that if he did not wish himself to do this he should at least command some of them to do it, and that it was not wise to cease from pursuit so long as daylight should last. To whom the King answered that many had died who were not to blame; that if the Ydallcão had done him wrong, he had already suffered enough; and moreover, that it did not seem to him good, since Rachol remained behind them to be taken, that they should go forward, but rather they should make themselves ready for its capture; for that the siege had to be conducted henceforth in a new and better manner. For the King was persuaded throughout that, since the Ydallcão had lost so many men and so much honour, and had lost indeed all his power, he would not wish to live any longer, and that he must be dead on the field. Which, however, was not so, seeing that the Ydallcão had not even entered into the fight, but had all the time remained under guard of Sefallarym[1]—he who now calls himself Açadacão and is lord of Belgaum—who, fearing the event, contrived by cunning that the Ydallcão should select him for his guard with all his troops, among whom he had four hundred cavalry; and when he saw how the soldiers fled, and how completely they

[1] "Sufo Larij," Barros, Dec. III. l. iv. cap. 5. Asada Khân's love of intrigue was proverbial amongst the Portuguese of that day.

had been defeated, he said to the Ydallcão, "Sire, if thou seekest to live follow me!" and the Ydallcão took refuge on an elephant and followed him, leaving his camp and all that he possessed. And as Açadacão wished him to travel by land,[1] he took no care to search for the ford, but skirting the range of hills on the south he went by that way.[2]

As it may be asked what became of the captain who sallied out of Rachol with the two hundred horsemen and elephants and foot-soldiers, I say that he ever kept himself advised of what passed in the field; and as soon as he learned that the Ydallcão was defeated he turned back to take refuge again in the citadel. But those within were not of a mind to receive him, there being a quarrel between him and another captain who was in the city; and he, seeing that they would not admit him, was forced to think how he could save himself, and he did so by passing the river by another ford farther down, and so saved himself. The belief of many was that he who was inside thought that he would now possess the city for his own, and that he would thereby become rich, and for that reason refused to receive the captain.

CHAPTER X

Of the spoil taken from the Moors, of how the King burned all the dead, and of what Christovão de Figueiredo did.

THE King being thus in the camp, he commanded the spoil that remained of the Moors to be collected, and there were found five captains who were taken prisoners (those of highest rank were found amongst

[1] *Como quer que Açadacão trazia quem hia a terra.* A doubtful passage.

[2] *Tomamdo a falldra da serra da bamda do sul.* It would be interesting to learn which range of hills is referred to.

the dead); the chiefest of them was Salabatacão,[1] who was captain-general of all the troops of the Ydallcão. He had taken for his guard in the battle five hundred Portuguese of the renegades who were with the Moors; and as soon as this Salabatacão saw that his army was defeated, he strove to collect and form a body of men, but could not do it because there was not one amongst them who thought of aught but to save himself. And thinking it worse to be conquered than to die, he threw himself amongst the King's troops, slaughtering them, and doing such wonderful deeds that ever after he and his Portuguese were remembered, so much were their terrible strokes feared, and the deeds they did; so that they let them pass on, and they penetrated so far amongst the troops that they found themselves close to the King's bodyguard. There the horse of Salabatacão was killed. In order to succour him the Portuguese did great deeds, and killed so many men that they left a broad road behind them which no one dared to enter, and they fought so well that they got another horse for Salabatacão. As soon as he was on its back he seemed like nothing but a furious wolf amongst sheep; but since already they were all so exhausted, so wounded all over, and so encircled by the enemy (for they were attacked at every point), Salabatacão was at length overthrown, and his horse with him. And as the Portuguese who tried to succour him were all killed, not one escaping, and he himself was wounded in many places, he was taken prisoner.

The spoil was four thousand horses of Ormuz, and a hundred elephants, and four hundred heavy cannon, besides small ones; the number of gun-carriages for them was nine hundred, and there were many tents and pavilions. I take no account of the sumpter-

[1] Salâbat Khân.

horses and oxen and other beasts, for they were numberless, nor of the numbers of men and boys, nor yet of some women, whom the King ordered to be released.

Here the King stayed till all the dead had been burned, and the customary honours had been paid to them; and here he gave much alms for the souls of those who had been killed in battle on his side. These numbered sixteen thousand and odd. These things done, he turned again upon Rachol and pitched his camp as he had done before.

During this return of the King there came to meet him Christovão de Figueiredo,[1] who was at that time in the city of Bisnaga with horses, and he took with him twenty Portuguese musqueteers, he also himself having his musquet. The King took much pleasure in his company, glad that he should see the war and his great power; and he ordered some tents to be given to him of those taken from the Ydallcão, and commanded that he should be lodged close to his own quarters. One day Christovão de Figueiredo told the King that he wanted to go and see the city, but the King said that he should not set his heart upon that because he did not want any disaster to befall him. But Christovão de Figueiredo replied that the whole business of the Portuguese was war, and that this would be the greatest favour that he could do him, namely that His Highness should permit him to go and see the Moors. So the King gave him leave and sent some people with him. Christovão de Figueiredo went close to the trench before the walls, keeping himself as much concealed as possible, and seeing how fearlessly the Moors exposed themselves on the wall, began, with the musqueteers whom he had brought, to open fire on them in such a way that he slew many,

[1] See above, p. 251, note.

the Moors being careless and free from fear, as men who up to then had never seen men killed with fire-arms nor with other such weapons. So they began to forsake the wall (at this point), and the king's troops found an opportunity of coming in safety to it, and they began to destroy much of the masonry; and so many people collected on this side that all the camp was put in commotion, saying that Christovão de Figueiredo had entered the city with his Portuguese. This was told to the King. Those in the city could not understand what was going on, nor how these people came to be in the King's service, until they recollected how on the day of the other fight the Portuguese had come, and then they considered themselves lost. For by the aid of those men the King's people came without fear to the wall, where already it was damaged in many places, because the city had its cannon so high up that these could do no injury to the men who were at the foot of the wall. The wall also was filled up inside with earth, and there were no cannon in the breaches. The people of the city whom up to that time they had killed had been supplied with stones which they had flung on the besiegers from the top of the wall, and with musquets and arrows, so that even if the King's men were able to reach the wall at all they were at least wounded; but as Christovão de Figueiredo with the Portuguese prevented the enemy from appearing at all on the wall, the Hindus were enabled to reach it at their ease.

Here you would have seen how the King's captains begged Christovão de Figueiredo to permit them one day to attack the Moors in his company, and he, in order to content the more honourable of them, went with them on those days. One day he divided his musqueteers into three companies and began to kill several amongst the Moors who showed themselves,

RAICHUR FORT

(*From a Photograph by* F. DUNSTERVILLE, Esq.)

insomuch that none durst be seen; and then the King's troops began, in these three divisions, to attack the wall with many pickaxes and crowbars,[1] and he sent to tell the rest that they should attack on their own account; and such was the result that the defenders of the city began to abandon the first line of fortification, and the women and children took refuge in the citadel. The captain of the city, seeing the dismay that had spread amongst his people, began to turn them back with encouraging words, and with some of them betook himself to that part of the wall which he saw was most severely pressed, begging them that they would come back to the wall and not be afraid. He was answered by some that at that point were those Franks[2] who were helping, and that as soon as any one showed himself he was a dead man; and he, wishing to see for himself where the Portuguese were, reached over with his body in front one of the embrasures and was killed with a musquet-shot that struck him in the middle of his forehead. It was said by the Moors that Christovão de Figueyredo had killed him, and they took notice of him (*derão sygnaes d elle*). As soon as the captain was thus killed there was great lamentation in the city, and soon the wall was deserted, so that the men from the King's camp were left to do as they pleased with it; and they noticed the outcry that arose within and saw that there was no one defending the wall. They therefore retired to see what should happen, and left off fighting for that day.

[1] *Llavãocas*, for *alavanca*, a Portuguese word for crowbar still used everywhere in Ceylon.

[2] *Framges*, *i.e.* Feringhees, Franks, or Europeans.

CHAPTER XI

How those in the city asked for terms, and the king granted them quarter.

NEXT day, which was twenty days since the battle had taken place in which the Ydallcão had been defeated, the men of the city opened a gate, and with a white flag carried in front of them went the way of the King's camp with their hands uplifted, begging the King's mercy.

When the King was advised of their coming, he commanded Solestema,[1] his minister, to receive them; and when they saw that he came out to receive them they began to hope that they should experience kindness at the King's hands.

Thus they came to the place where he was, and there they prostrated themselves on the ground with much groaning and tears, and besought his pity and benevolence.

The King commanded them to rise, saying that he would save all their persons and property, and that they need have no fear but should return to the city, and that on the next day he would enter it; and he bade a captain take possession of the city.

Whilst the Moors were thus in presence of the King (the soldiers looking on), they saw Christovão de Figueiredo, and told the King that the conquest and capture of the city was due to that foreigner, that he had slain their captain, and with his people had killed many Moors, which caused the city's destruction. The King, casting his eyes on Christovão de Figueiredo, nodded his head, and turned to the people telling them to observe what great things could be

[1] Sâluva Timma.

effected by one good man. He then retired to his tent and the men of the city to the city, and the king's troops made great feasting and rejoicing.

CHAPTER XII

How the King entered the city, and of the feast that was made for him, and of the regulations and arrangements he made there.

As soon as the next day dawned, the King, after he had performed both his customary prayers and others which it is their wont to offer after victories, giving thanks to God (for indeed the principal thing they pray for is a conquest such as this), rode in company with the other great lords and his captains, and with his guard took the way to the city. There the citizens were standing awaiting his arrival, with more cheerful countenances than their real feelings warranted, yet striving to take courage, and they followed him with much loud shouting; crying,—"God be praised who has sent to save us after so many years!" and with these and other such words they begged him to spare them and have pity on them. So he proceeded till he arrived close to the citadel, when he sent to call the most honoured men in the city, and to these the King said that he would spare all their property, that they might freely act as they wished regarding both that and their persons, and those who wished to stay in the city might remain in their old state as before; and as for those who wished to depart they might do so at once with all that they possessed. They all raised their hands to Heaven, and threw themselves on the ground in thankfulness for such gentle treatment. While the King was thus engaged there came men to tell him that his troops were robbing the city, and he at once took measures to prevent this, and everything was returned to its owner; but as in such cases as these the conquered are content merely with their own liberty, laying little store by anything they may get back, great robberies took place; and some of these afterwards came to the ears of the King, and those who had done it were soundly chastised.

In a short time the defeat of the Ydallcão was known all over India, and also in other regions of the interior, he being a great lord in these parts; and as soon as the news was carried to Zemelluco and Madremalluco and Destuy and Virido, and also to other lords who were like slaves to the king Daquym,[1] although in some measure they rejoiced since they wished him ill, yet on the other hand they began to be fearful for their own safety.[2] So they all took measures to send their envoys, and these found the King still inside the city of Rachol. Astonished though they were to see that the King had captured so strong a city, they were much more surprised to see how great was his power and how numerous his troops. Having arrived where he was they gave him the letters they had brought, and these were forthwith read. In these the chiefs told the King that he ought to content himself with having defeated the Ydallcão as he had done, and ought not to wage further war; they begged him of his goodness to return to the Ydallcão that which he had so taken from him, and that if he did so they would always obey whatever he commanded; but if he was not of a mind to this, then he must know for certain that they would be compelled to turn against him and forthwith

[1] Rey Daquym, *i.e.* King of the Dakhan. This evidently refers to the Bâhmanî king, who was still recognised as titular sovereign, though the whole country had revolted and broken up into five independent kingdoms. For the names that precede this see note to p. 325 above.

[2] *Começarão deitar as barbes em remolho.* This refers to the Portuguese proverb—"Quando vires arder as barbas do teu vizinho, põe (or deita) as tuas em remolho"—"When you see your neighbour's beard on fire, steep your own in water;" or guard against like treatment.—D. F.

join the Ydallcão, for whom they would speedily recover that which he had now lost. The King, seeing what was contained in the letters, answered them in the following manner by one single letter to them all;—"Honoured Madremalluco, and Zemelluco, Descar, and Veride, and all others of the kingdom of Daquym, I have seen your letters; and thank you much for what you have sent to say. As regards the Ydallcão, what I have done to him and taken from him he has richly deserved; as regards returning it to him that does not seem to me reasonable, nor am I going to do it; and as for your further statement that ye will all turn against me in aid of him if I do not do as ye ask, I pray you do not take the trouble to come hither, for I will myself go to seek ye if ye dare to await me in your lands;—and this I send you for answer." And he commanded to give many gifts to the messengers, and giving his letter to them sent them away.

CHAPTER XIII.

How a number of people left the city, and the King did much kindness to them.

MANY people left the city, and to many who had nothing wherewith to depart the king commanded to give all that was required for their journey. Here the King stayed some days, after having made all the arrangements that were necessary for the government of the city; and after repairing the walls he left behind him sufficient troops to guard the place, and took the road to the city of Bisnaga, where he was received with great triumphs, and great feasts were made and he bestowed bountiful rewards on his troops.

As soon as the festivals were ended he went to the new city; and, being there, they told him how there was entered an ambassador of the Ydallcão. Already he knew that an ambassador had come but he pretended that he did not know, since it is not customary for the King to send out to receive any ambassador (on his arrival). Since this ambassador was in the city of Bisnaga, knowing that the King was in the new city, which is two leagues from Bisnaga, he betook himself thither; and close to the city bade the people pitch his tent, which was the best and most beautiful and rich that up to that time had ever been seen in those parts. This ambassador was called Matucotam; he brought with him one hundred and fifty horse and much people to serve him and many pack animals, among which were certain camels. He brought also two of the scribes of the chamber of the Ydallcão, so that indeed you would believe that he had brought all the power of the Ydallcão "pera segumdo elle ficou desbaratado."[1]

As soon as he had thus settled himself the ambassador sent to inform the King of his arrival, and begged that His Highness would grant him an audience and despatch him without delay. The King replied that he would see him,[2] but told him that he should not be impatient since he himself had but now arrived, and that he would give him leave to depart as soon as the time had arrived. And with this the ambassador stayed there a month without the King having sought to see him, nor having asked to know why he had come; he went every day to the palace, and seeing the way in which the King acted towards him he determined to speak no more but to wait till the King summoned him. Still he never ceased to go every day to the palace and to speak with the nobles. One day the King sent to tell the ambassador that the following day was an auspi-

[1] This passage appears to be corrupt, and I have been unable to guess at its meaning. Senhor Lopes, whom I have consulted, is equally at fault about it.

[2] *Elrey o mamdou ver.*

cious day, and that he wished to hear him and learn wherefore he had come, and the ambassador made ready as it behoved him to present himself before so great a lord. As was fitting, considering his mission and the request he had to make, he was accompanied by many Moors whom the city contained, and had with him all his people with their trumpets and drums as was customary; and so he went to the palace, where he was received very honourably by the nobles and officers of the household. They seated themselves inside the first gate, awaiting there a message from the King giving permission to enter where he was, and there was no long delay before the command to admit him was given. His obeisance to the King having been made according to his mode and custom, the men of the council standing by the King's side, he was bidden to announce the terms of his embassy, the King being ready graciously to listen; and the ambassador, seeing that the King so commanded, delivered himself of his message in manner following, with the awed demeanour assumed by such envoys when they find themselves in presence of such great kings.

CHAPTER XIV

How the Captain acquitted himself of his embassy before the King.

"SIRE! the Ydallcão, my master, sends me to thee; and by my mouth he begs thee that thou wouldest be pleased to do justice. He bids me say that he bears very good will towards thee[1] as towards the most true and powerful prince in all the world, and one possessed of most justice and truth; that thou without reason hast broken the friendship and peace which thou hast had

[1] *Que elle te ama a ty diante de ty.* The latter words may be an emphatic expression, akin to *diante de Deus e de todo o mundo*, "In the face of God and all the world."

towards him, and not only so but a peace which was made so many years ago and maintained by all the kings so truthfully; that he does not know why thou hast left thy kingdom and made such war on him; that he was without suspicion when they brought him the news how thou hadst besieged the city of Rachol, and hadst robbed and destroyed the country round about, which news caused him to move and come to its rescue; that then all the members of his court were slain by thee, and his camp all plundered and destroyed, thou thyself being good witness of what was done, and that he begs thee to make amends therefor, and to send back to him his artillery and tents, his horses and elephants, with the rest that was taken from him, and also to restore his city of Rachol; that if thou wilt give him the satisfaction for which he prays as to this property and all other things thou wilt have him always for a loyal friend; but if not, thy action will be evil, even though pleasing to thyself." Thus he ended, without saying more. The King said that he might retire and repose, and that next day he would give him leave to depart, and the King gave him a robe of silk and the cloths that are customary.

CHAPTER XV

How the King sent to call the ambassador, and of the answer which he gave to him.

NEXT day the King sent to call the ambassador, and after other things had been spoken of between[1] them, the King said that he would be content to restore everything to the Ydallcão according to his wish, and would be pleased at once to release Salabetacão, provided the Ydallcão would come and kiss his foot. When the

[1] *Ante elles* should be "*antre elles.*"

ambassador heard the King's answer he took leave of him and went to his tent; and he wrote to the Ydallcão and told him what had passed, sending to him one of the scribes that had come with him. And much time had not passed when the Ydallcão sent him a reply, saying: How could it be possible for him to meet the King, seeing that he could not go to Bisnaga? and yet that he was of full mind joyfully to do that which the King wished. With this answer the ambassador went to the King, and since the King would have set higher value on the Ydallcão's coming to kiss his feet than on all that he had taken from him, he said to the ambassador, "Do thou cause the Ydallcão to come to the confines of my kingdom, for I shall be soon there." Agreeing to this, the ambassador departed, so as to persuade the Ydallcão to come to the boundary. The King on his part went forthwith to a city called Mudugal[1] which is close to the boundary, and there he waited until they told him that the Ydallcão was coming and was already near at hand. Forthwith the King set out to meet him, and entered the kingdom of Daquem, so desirous was he to meet the Ydallcão; but the Ydallcão, after all, dared not meet the King. And the King journeyed so far, whilst they kept saying to him, "Lo! he is here close at hand," that he even went as far as Bizapor,[2] which is the best city in all the kingdom of Daquem. It has numbers of beautiful houses built according to our own fashion, with many gardens and bowers made of grape-vines, and pomegranates, and oranges and lemons, and all other kinds of garden produce.

Hither went the King, for it seemed well for him to await the coming of the Ydallcão in so goodly a city; and he formed the determination that if he got him here he would seize him or command him to be put

[1] Mudkal. [2] Bîjapûr.

to death, to avenge the affront that had been put upon him; and seeing that his enemy did not dare to come he remained in the city several days. Then he turned away because water failed him; for since this city lies in a plain and has no water save that which it receives from rainfall into two lakes, of which there are two large ones, the Moors had opened these in order to drain them, so that the King should not be able to stay in their country. For this reason it behoved the King to depart. But the city was left almost in ruins—not that the King had commanded it to be destroyed, but that his troops, in order to make fires for cooking, had torn down so many houses that it was a great grief to see —and this was occasioned by there being in the country a dearth of firewood, which comes to them from a great distance. The Ydallcão sent to ask the King what wrong the houses of his captains had done that he had commanded to destroy them; for there remained no other houses standing save only the palaces of the Ydallcão, the King himself being therein. The King sent answer that it was not he who had done it, but that he could not control his people.

When the King went to the town of Modogal the Ydallcão returned to Bigapor, where, seeing the great havoc that had been wrought in it, he took to himself the blame for such damage having been done,[1] saying that if he had gone to the King such destruction would not have taken place, and that at least he could do this in future; he said that he had been badly advised since for his own part he had been prepared to do it. Thus he took counsel with his advisers, putting before them how secure his position was if he had the friendship of the King, that if allied to him he might be able to still further increase (the greatness of) his State, and that

[1] *Todo a cullpa de tall ser feyto por asy.* Lit. "all on account of his having acted thus."

with the King's favour he would be able to carry out all his wishes. Concerning these things and others similar to these he continued constantly speaking with his advisers. Wherefore Açadacão the lord of Bilgao, he who had fled with him in the battle, and who was a man sagacious and cunning in such matters, addressed the Ydallcão begging permission to go himself to the King, and saying that he would remedy everything and would cause everything to take place just as his lord wished; and the Ydallcão listened to him readily.

Now Açadacão did not trouble himself to make this journey because he desired to serve the Ydallcão, for another would have done it as well, but he did it with a villanous motive and from the ill-will he bore to Salebatacão whom the King held in prison at Bisnaga; and the reason that he had this wicked motive was because Salebatacão knew that Açadacão was the man that had caused the Ydalcão to flee, and that the cowardice of such an act was enough to destroy an army. Salebatacão had spoken angrily about this to all those who went to see him or who were sent to visit him, and he always said that he did not desire to be released from his captivity save for one reason only, namely that he might ruin Açadacão and war against him as against a mortal enemy. These things were all known to Açadacão, and he knew that if they released him it would come to pass as he had said, and therefore he determined to prevent this by contriving his enemy's death, as will be mentioned in its place. It was for this reason that Açadacão asked to be sent as ambassador to the King; and this was done.

CHAPTER XVI

How Açadacão went as ambassador for his King and compassed the death of Sallabatecão.

Açadacão, being despatched by the Ydallcão, accompanied by certain horsemen with some servants took the road to the city of Mudogal where the King was, and the Ydallcão went with him as far as the river. When Açadacão had arrived, being allowed inside the city by command of the King, he remained several days without seeing the King until he was summoned by his order; then he was admitted and spoke with the King, giving him, with the manner of one who in such negotiations is both wise and bold, an excuse for the mistake which the Ydallcão had committed. He knew how to speak to the King so well that he removed all the King's wrath and fury against the Ydallcão, and he told the King that the principal cause why the Ydallcão did not meet him was the conduct of Salebatacão whom he had captured, and that this man had written to the Ydallcão telling him not to do so, and giving for reason that the King desired to slay him. By these and other similar sayings he sought to set the King's mind against Salebatacão, even to the death, and the King, seeing what Açadacão wanted, and believing that a man of such great fame would not be guilty of saying anything that was not perfectly true, angrily commanded that Salebatacão, who was then in Bisnaga, should be beheaded; and this was at once done as soon as the message arrived.

As soon as Açadacão had accomplished this business he thought himself unsafe, and at once asked leave of the King, saying that he wished to go and get the Ydallcão to come to the river, so that when His Highness arrived he might meet him there. But the King told him not to be impatient but to amuse himself there some days, and added that he wished to show him some things, and that he had somewhat about which to speak to him. Açadacão, however, being afraid that his treason would be discovered, did not feel safe, and behaved in such a manner that what he had done concerning Salebatacão was found out; wherefore the King sent to seize him, but when they went to look for him he was already gone. For he fled one night and betook himself to the Ydalcão, telling him that the King had commanded Salebatacão to be put to death, and that he wanted to do the same to him, and so he had escaped; and it seemed to him that he (the Ydalcão) ought not to trust the King, who after all was nothing but a black. After he had spoken in this way he went to Bilgao, where he strengthened his position, and when the Ydallcão sent afterwards to summon him he never obeyed, because he knew that the wickedness that he had done had been found out.

CHAPTER XVII

How the King went to the extremity of his territory to meet the Ydalcão, and what he did on not finding him.

THE King did not fail to go to the extremity of his territory, and since he did not find the Ydalcão there, nor his mother, as Açadacão had told him, he at once perceived that this was due to trickery on the part of Açadacão, and that he had done it all in order to compass the death of Salebatacão. Full of fury at this he entered the kingdom of Daquem and marched against the city of Culbergura[1] and destroyed it and razed the fortress to the ground, and the same with many other places.

Thence he wanted to press forward, but his council-

[1] Kulbarga, the ancient Bahmanî capital.

lors did not agree to this, saying that water would fail him by that road and that it did not seem to them that those Moorish lords whom they counted as friends would be otherwise than afraid that the King would take their lands as he had taken those of the others, since they all served one sovereign, and that for this reason these lords would probably make friends with the Ydalcão, and together they would come against the King; and although there was no reason to be afraid of them, yet the King must needs fear the want of water, of which they had none. And the King agreed that this counsel was good.

In this city of Calbergara, in the fortress belonging to it, the King took three sons of the King of Daquem. He made the eldest King of the kingdom of Daquem, his father being dead, though the Ydallcão wanted to make King one of his brothers-in-law, who was a bastard son of the King of Daquem, and had married one of the Ydallcão's sisters; for this reason he had kept these three brothers prisoners in that fortress. He whom he thus made King was received by all the realm as such, and obeyed by all the great lords, and even by the Ydallcão owing to his fear of the King.[1] The other two brothers he took with him, and gave them each one an allowance, to each one every year fifty thousand gold *pardaos;* and he holds them and treats them as princes and great lords, as indeed they are. After the return of the King to Bisnaga, which took place in the same year in which he had left, nothing more passed between him and the Ydalcão worthy of record, relating either to peace or war.

[1] This passage does not seem very exact from an historical standpoint (see above, p. 157, and note).

CHAPTER XVIII

How this King, during his own lifetime, raised to be King his son, being of the age of six years.

AFTER the King had made an end of this, and had obtained so great a victory over his enemies, perceiving that he was already advanced in years, desiring to rest in his old age and wishing his son to become King when he died, he determined to make him King during his lifetime, the boy being six years old and the King not knowing what would happen after his death. Wherefore he abdicated his throne and all his power and name, and gave it all to his son, and himself became his minister, and Salvatinica[1] who had held that office became his counsellor, and he made one of the latter's sons a great lord among them. And so far did King Crisnarao go that after he had given the kingdom to his son, he himself did obeisance to him. With these changes the King made great festivals which lasted eight months, during which time the son of the King fell sick of a disease of which he died.

After his death Crisnarao learned that his son had died by poison given him by the son of Sallvatinica, and in his anger, being certain that this was so, he sent to call Salvatinica and his son and Guandaja, brother of Ssallvatinica, and many other captains relatives of Ssallvatinica, and made them a speech at the time of the salaam, there being present many chiefs and principal persons of the kingdom, and relations of Ssallvatinica; he addressed him thus:—"I held thee always as my great friend, and now for these forty years thou hast been governor in this kingdom, which thou gavest me; yet I am under no obligation to thee for that, because in doing so thou didst act in a way contrary to thy duty. Thou

[1] Sâluva Timma.

wert bound, since thy lord the King my brother commanded so, to put out mine eyes; yet thou didst not carry out his will nor obey him, but instead thou didst cheat him and the eyes of a goat were put out, wherefore, since thou didst not fulfil his command, thou wert a traitor, and thy sons with thee for whom I have done so much. Now I have learnt that my son died of poison given to him by thee and thy sons, and for that ye are all here made prisoners." With these words he arose and laid hands on them and seized them, and in doing so called for aid from many Portuguese who were then in the country with horses, asking them to come to his aid; and after he had seized the men, father and sons, they remained three years in prison. And he made minister a son of Codemerade, the same who had killed the son of King Narsymga in the city of Penagundy in the garden by treachery, by command of the King his father, as has already been told in this history.[1]

And soon afterwards Danayque, son of Salvatinica, escaped from prison and betook himself to a mountain range in which dwelt nobody but robbers and highwaymen, and in this there was a fortress where dwelt a captain, his relative, who received him and helped him in all that he could, and from there he made such war on the King Crisnarao that he was driven to send against him much people, and as captain of the army

[1] (Above, p. 310 f.) The original text has "*e fez regedor hũu filho Codemerade*," but I cannot identify the name with any ordinary Hindu name or title; and if "son of Codemerade" be meant, as I suppose, the *de* has been omitted accidentally. If, however, there has been a confusion of syllables and the original reading was "*filho de Codemera*," then I would point to the list given above of powerful nobles (p. 327) who commanded the forces of the king in the great Râchol campaign, one of whom was called *Comdamara*. In the concluding paragraph of this chapter we have this new minister's name given as "Ajaboissa," and in the list of provincial lords (p. 385 below) as "Ajaparcatimapa." The latter name sounds more probable than the former. The first half would be the family name, the last, "Timmappa,' his own personal name.

he sent his minister Ajaboissa, who invested the place on all sides and took him therein and brought him prisoner to the King. After he had so come the King commanded him to be brought before him, with Sallvatinica his father and another brother of his who was kept in the prison, and he sent them to the place of executions and there had their eyes put out, for in this country they do not put Brahmans to death but only inflict some punishment so that they remain alive. So he put them in prison again, and there Timadanayque died, and Salvatinica his father remained in the prison with his other son Gamdarja.[1]

CHAPTER XIX

How the Ydallcão came against Rachol, and did not dare to await the King, and fled.

AT this time the Ydallcão collected his army and formed afresh his forces of cavalry and elephants, and marched upon Rachol which remained under the king of Bisnaga. Hearing this news, Crisnarao, without even telling any one, ordered to saddle a horse, and he rode at full speed in the direction of Rachol where already the Ydallcão was; but as soon as his enemy was aware of the coming of the King he fled. On the road King Crisnarao bought six hundred horses from the Portuguese at the rate of 4¾ for 1000 *pardaos*.[2] And from Rachol he sent a message to the Ydallcão saying that

[1] In the passage earlier in this chapter Sâluva Timma is said to have had a brother "Guandaja." Putting the two together, it would seem that his brother and son both bore the same name, probably Ganda Râjah. Paes refers to the brother as being in his day governor of the capital (above, p. 284). He calls him "Gamdarâjo." See also p. 327, note 2.

[2] *Cymco menos huũ quoarto por mil pardaos*, or nineteen for four thousand pardaos. The chronicler was a trader in horses at Vijayanagar. Later on he mentions the usual price as twelve or fifteen horses for a thousand *pardaos* (below, p. 381).

he had already twice broken his oath and his word, and that as he had not fulfilled the promise he had made he would make war on him in such fashion as that by force he should become his vassal, and that he would not let him alone till he had taken from him Billgao.[1]

As the winter had now begun the King could not then go forward, and so he went to Bisnaga to make ready for this war; and he commanded to prepare a large force of artillery, and sent an ambassador to Goa to ask for the help of the Governor. He promised him that after taking Billgao he would give him the mainland; for this city of Billgao is fifteen leagues from Goa, and its captain is lord of the mainland of Goa. Goa is the frontier or boundary of his city of Billgao, and there is one of his captains at a fortress called Pomda which is three leagues from Goa by the mainland, who also receives the revenues and has command over several villages; and in like manner these and others have captains appointed by the Ydalcão, who is lord of the whole land.[2]

While Crisnarao was thus making ready he presently fell sick of the same illness of which all his ancestors had died, with pains in the groin, of which die all the kings of Bisnaga.

Now this King Crisnarao, when he was young and growing up in this city of Bisnaga, had an intrigue with a courtezan for whom he had much affection, and who was called Chinadevidy, and for the great love he bore her he promised many times that if ever he became King he would marry her; and though he said this in jest, it afterwards became true, so the history records. For when raised to the throne and taken away from the things he had done when a young man, he still did not forget the affection he felt for this woman, but used

[1] Belgaum.

[2] The captain of Pondâ was Ankus Khân (above, p. 335, notes 1, 2).

A GATEWAY IN THE FORT OF VIJAYANAGAR

secretly to leave his palace and go to her house. And this was discovered one night by his minister Sallvatinica, who watched him until he had got into the woman's house, and he rebuked him much for it and brought him back to the palace. Then the King told him how well he loved her, and that he had promised to marry this woman and was determined to do so in any case; and the minister, seeing how he was bent on it, gave way to his wish, saying that he would accomplish it in such a way that His Highness would not be blamed for it. In order to do this he sought for him a very beautiful woman of the family of the kings of Narsymga, and after he had married him to her, at the end of the wedding ceremonies, he put this woman and the other in a house, to which he had added a tower very lofty and large, and in which he lodged her. Afterwards the King married many other wives, for these kings hold it as a very honourable thing to have many wives; and this King Crisnarao married four, and yet he loved this one better than any of the others. This King built a city in honour of this woman, for the love he bore her, and called its name Nagallapor and surrounded it with a new wall which is one of the best works that he has in his kingdom, and he made in it a street very long and large with houses all of masonry. In order to people this town he ordered all the chiefs of his kingdom to build themselves palaces therein, and so they did. This town has one principal street, of length four thousand and seven hundred paces [1] and of breadth forty, which is certainly the most beautiful street it is possible to see; and he made and finished this town without stinting any expense on it. It now yields forty-two thousand *pardaos* of duties for things which enter into it, the duties in

[1] About a mile and a quarter. Nágalapúr is the modern Hospett. If the measurement is accurate, this street, leading, no doubt, towards the capital, is now non-existent.

this land being very great; since nothing comes through the gates that does not pay duty, even men and women, as well as head-loads and all merchandise.

This King also made in his time a lake for water, which lies between two very lofty *serras*. But since he had no means in the country for making it, nor any one who could do it, he sent to Goa to ask the Governor to send some Portuguese masons, and the Governor sent him João della Ponte,[1] a great worker in stone,

[1] The Della Pontes are more than once mentioned in the history of the sixteenth century. They were probably an Italian family, or Italian in origin, and engineers by profession, the Rialto at Venice having been constructed by Antonio della Ponte in 1588. This, however, may be a fanciful connection. It is possible that both in Portugal and in Italy families may have received that surname in consequence of their skill in bridge-building, or of one of the family having in former days distinguished himself by the construction of a particular bridge. The engineer mentioned in the text is probably the individual who at the end of April 1520 was sent by the king of Portugal to examine into the possibility of building a fortress at Tetuan in Morocco. Dom Pedro de Mascarenhas (afterwards, in 1554, Viceroy at Goa) sailed on this mission from Ceuta, and "João Nunes del Pont" is mentioned as accompanying him. The king and the Emperor Charles V. were both at this time anxious to prevent the Moorish corsairs from using Tetuan in future, as they had done in the past, as a base for their piratical attacks on Spain and Portugal. (Damião de Goes, *Chronica de Dom Manuel*, edit. of Coimbra, 1790, vol. i. Part IV. p. 532; *Alguns documentos do Archivo Nacional da Torre do Tombo*, Lisbon, 1892, pp. 445–446.)

In 1521, some time after the month of March, when Dom Diogo Lopes de Sequeira, the governor of Goa, had returned from his expedition to the Red Sea, he was urged by his counsellors to build a fortress at Madrefabâ near Goa, as the place contained an anchorage sufficient for an entire fleet. (Correa, *Lendas da India*, ii. p. 622.) Correa continues: "The governor, however, thought better to send in a *cotia* Antonio Correa and Pero de Coimbra, his chief pilot, to inspect the river of Madrefabâ and measure the water on the bar, and Manuel da Ponte, Overseer of Works, and João de la Ponte, his brother, who understood it well, to view the land, and if there were stone, and if lime could be made for the work, and to bring him certitude of all."

If this man were the same as he who went with Mascarenhas to Tetuan, he had, in all probability, not been long in India when he went to Madrefabâ. This seems to show that the great tank of Krishna Deva Râya, seen in process of construction by the chronicler Paes (see p. 244), and mentioned in the text by Nunez, was not begun till at least the autumn of 1521. If so, Paes did not *write* his description of Vijayanagar till after that date (say 1522). (See above, p. 162.)

to whom the King told how he wanted the tank built. Though it seemed to this man (*mestre*, modern *maistry*) impossible to be made, nevertheless he told the King he would do it and asked him to have lime prepared, at which the King laughed much, for in his country when they build a house they do not understand how to use lime. The King commanded to throw down quantities of stone and cast down many great rocks into the valley, but everything fell to pieces, so that all the work done in the day was destroyed each night, and the King, amazed at this, sent to call his wise men and sorcerers and asked them what they thought of this thing. They told him that his idols were not pleased with this work, it being so great and he giving them nothing, and that unless he spilled there the blood of men or women or buffaloes that work would never be finished. So the King sent to bring hither all the men who were his prisoners, and who deserved death, and ordered them there to be beheaded; and with this the work advanced. He made a bank across the middle of the valley so lofty and wide that it was a crossbow-shot in breadth and length, and had large openings;[1] and below it he put pipes by which the water escaped, and when they wish so to do they close these. By means of this water they made many improvements in the city, and many channels by which they irrigated rice-fields and gardens, and in order that they might improve their lands he gave the people the lands which are irrigated by this water free for nine years,[2] until they had made their improvements, so that the revenue already amounts to 20,000 *pardaos*.

Above this tank is a very large ridge all enclosed, and in the middle some very strong gates with two towers, one on one side and one on the other; and

[1] *Espaços.* This probably means sluices or weirs.

[2] *Por nove anos de graça.*

within are always posted 1000 men on guard. For through this gate all things must enter that come into the two cities, since in order to enter the city of Bisnaga there is no other road but this, all other roads meeting there. This gate is rented out for 12,000 *pardaos* each year, and no man can enter it without paying just what the renters ask, country folk as well as strangers. In both these cities there is no provision or merchandise whatever,[1] for all comes from outside on pack-oxen, since in this country they always use beasts for burdens;[2] and every day there enter by these gates 2000 oxen, and every one of these pays three *vintẽes*,[3] except certain polled oxen without horns, which never pay anything in any part of the realm.

Outside these two cities are fields and places richly cultivated with wheat and gram and rice and millet, for this last is the grain which is most consumed in the land; and next to it betel (*betre*), which is a thing that in the greater part of the country they always eat and carry in the mouth.

CHAPTER XX

How on the death of Crisnarao his brother Achetarao was raised to be king.

BEFORE[4] the death of King Crisnarao from his disease as has been before recounted, being sick and already

[1] *Não ha nenhũ manimẽto nem mercadaryas.*

[2] The original (itself a copy) has "*nesta terra não se servem de bestas pera carreguas.*" I think that the words *se não* must have been accidentally omitted before *de bestas*, and have ventured so to render the passage.

[3] About 3½d. (?). A *vintem* is about $1\frac{7}{20}$d.

[4] I have given the meaning here, not a literal translation. The writer begins: "After the death of King Crisnarao from his disease, as has been already recounted." Then he inserts a long parenthesis which might be read: "While he was sick . . . he had made a will . . . &c. . . ." down to . . . "but only one of the age of eighteen months." Then he continues: "After his death (as I have said) Salvanay became minister," &c. . . .

despairing of his life, he made a will, saying that of his three brothers whom, at the time when they raised him to be King, he had sent to be confined in the fortress of Chamdegary[1] with his nephew, son of the King Busbalrao,[2] they should make King his brother Achetarao[3] who now reigns; for the latter seemed to him to be better fitted for that than any of the others, for the reason that he himself had no son of fit age for the throne, but only one of the age of eighteen months. After his death Salvanay became minister of the kingdom, and governed it till the coming of King Achitarao from the fortress of Chamdegary where he was detained. And he further left in his will that he should take Billgao,[4] and should make war on the Ydallcão.

Which King Chytarao, after he ascended the throne, gave himself over to vice and tyranny. He is a man of very little honesty, and on account of this the people and the captains are much discontented with his evil life and inclinations; for he has never done anything except those things that are desired by his two brothers-in-law,[5] who are men very evilly disposed and great Jews. By reason of this the Ydalcão, learning of how little weight he was, determined to make war on him, believing that he would easily succeed since the King was not inclined to war; so he made his forces ready, and began to invade the King's territory, and arrived within a league of the city of Bisnaga. Chetarao was in the city with such great forces and power that he could easily have captured him if his heart had allowed him to take action, since the Ydallcão had with him

[1] Chandragiri.

[2] See above, p. 315.

[3] Achyuta.

[4] Belgaum.

[5] These two may perhaps be two of the three powerful brothers Râma, Tirumala, and Venkatâdri, of whom the two first married two daughters of Krishna Deva. In such case, however, they would not have been actually brothers-in-law of King Achyuta, but of his brother the late king.

only 12,000 foot and 30,000 horse; yet with this small force the Ydallcão entered Nagallapor a league from Bisnaga and razed it to the ground. The King never tried to go out against him, nor had he the stomach for a fight, and there were only small skirmishes by some captains, good horsemen. These spoke to the King, asking that His Highness would give them leave to attack, and saying that his own presence was unnecessary for so slight an affair; but the King was terrified, and by the advice of his brothers-in-law (of which they gave not a little) decided to send and make peace with the Ydallcão. The Ydallcão was very glad and made a peace with him which was to last for a hundred years, on condition that the King should give him ten *lakhs* of gold *pardaos*, each *lakh* being 100,000 *pardaos*, and further should yield up to him the city of Rachol which the King Crisnarao had taken from him, and which had a revenue with its lands of 150,000 *pardaos*, as well as jewels which could easily be valued at a *lakh*. The King accepted these terms, and the Ydallcão departed well pleased with this money; and after all was done the King sent to him a diamond stone weighing 130 *mangellinis*,[1] with fifteen other similar ones worth fully a *lakh*. This money he soon afterwards recovered and put in his treasury, exacting payments from his captains and people so ruthlessly that they say that in six months he had recovered and put the whole in his treasury.

Wherefore the captains and troops, both because he made this peace and because he exacted this sum of money contrary to the wishes of them all, have lived greatly discontented, and have held that if this kingdom should ever be brought to destruction, it

[1] A mangelin is roughly equivalent to a carat, but actually the difference is one-fifth; 4 mangelins = 5 carats. So that 130 mangelins = 162 carats. The *Koh-i-nur*, when brought to England, weighed 186 carats. (See Appendix A.)

must take place in the lifetime of King Chitarao; for he had destroyed the principal people of his kingdom and killed their sons and taken their goods, all owing to the bad counsel of his brothers-in-law, by whom he was dominated.

I will tell you of one who was called Crisnaranarque whom he seized one night, and who, before he surrendered himself, killed all his wives, in number two hundred, and then killed himself with poison in presence of the King. This was because the King wanted to kill his son in his presence. By sale of the captain's arms, namely daggers, swords, spears, battle-axes and other things, which were all ornamented with gold and silver, the King realised more than 3000 *pardaos*. In this way the kingdom has been deprived of its principal men and of those who sustain it, wherefore the Ydalcão holds it in so little esteem that he puts upon it every day a thousand affronts and requisitions. Of this King there is nothing more so far to recount, save that he is a man that they hold to be of little force of character, and very negligent of the things which most concern the welfare of his kingdom and State.

CHAPTER XXI

Of the manner of attendance on these kings, which is as follows.

[What follows concerns the reign of Achyuta Râya.]

ALL the service of this house, with the things which they make use of, is of silver and gold, that is to say basins and bowls, stools, ewers, and other vessels of that sort. The bedsteads[1] in which his wives sleep are covered and adorned with silver plates. Every wife has her bed in which she sleeps, and

[1] The word used is *catre*, a light bedstead, probably the origin of the modern South Indian word "cot," for a camp bedstead.

that of the King is plated and lined and has all its legs of gold, its mattress of silk, and its round bolster worked round the ends with large seed pearls. It has four pillows of the same pattern for the feet, and has no other sheet than a silk cloth on top. He always carries with him a mosquito curtain with a frame of silver,[1] and he has a house made of pieces of iron in which is contained a very large bed, which is intended for such time as he takes the field.

He has five hundred wives and as many less or more as he wants, with whom he sleeps; and all of these burn themselves at his death. When he journeys to any place he takes twenty-five or thirty of his most favourite wives, who go with him, each one in her palanqueen with poles. The palanqueen of the principal wife is all covered with scarlet cloth tasselled with large and heavy work in seed-pearls and pearls, and the pole itself is ornamented with gold. The palanqueens of the other wives are ornamented only with silver, but another palanqueen, which is for his own person, always goes on the right side, and is in the same way decorated with gold. For a son or a daughter, if such an one goes with him, he takes another bedstead of ivory inlaid with gold; and when he takes the field, wherever he pitches his camp there they make for him houses of stone and clay, for he does not stay in a tent, and he always has these decorated with cloths.[2]

[1] *Arquelha de prata. Arquelha* is a mosquito-net. Since manifestly the net itself could not be made of silver, the allusion is probably to its supports. Senhor Lopes, in a letter to me, suggests that it means the upper portion of the canopy, "*le ciel du lit*," or the framework that holds the curtains, *arquelha* being a diminutive of *arco*, a "bow" or "arch." In this case it might mean the domed ceiling of a canopy made in Muhammadan fashion, and the curtains may have been of silk or brocade, and not of mosquito-netting.

[2] The word used is *armadas*. It may mean "furnished" or "hung round with cloths," or possibly "fenced" or "fortified."

In his palace within the gates he is served by women and eunuchs and servants numbering fully five or six hundred; and these wives of the King all have their own officials for their service, each for herself, just as the King has within the gates, but these are all women. The palaces of the King are large and with large rooms; they have cloisters like monasteries, with cells, and in each one is one of his wives, and with each of these ladies is her maid-servant; and when the King retires to rest he passes through these cloisters, and his wives stand at the doors and call him in; but these are not the principal wives, they are the daughters of captains and nobles of the country. Inside the gates of the palace they say that there are over two hundred milch-cows, from the milk of which they make butter for these ladies to eat.

The King has no expense in connection with his food, because the nobles send it to him every day to his house, namely rice and wheat and meat and fowls with all other necessary things. In the kitchen there are some two hundred inferior guards, and four over it, and two chief officers of the guard; and those who are now captains of the guard of this king are called, one Pedanayque and the other Ajanaique, they are also captains of soldiers; these porters do not go further inside than through four or five doors, because inside of these are none but eunuchs and women.

When the King rides out there go with him usually two hundred horsemen of his guard whom he pays, and a hundred elephants, and this in addition to the captains, forty or fifty in number, who are always in attendance with their soldiers. He takes with him two thousand men with shields, all men of good position, ranged in order on the flanks, and in front goes the chief *alcaid* with about thirty horsemen having canes in their hands like porters; the chief *alcaid* bears a different wand; he who is now the chief *alcaid* of this King is called Chinapanaique. Behind with the rearguard goes the Master of the Horse with two hundred horsemen, and behind the cavalry go a hundred elephants, and on their backs ride men of high estate. He has in front of him twelve destriers, saddled, and in front of these horses go five elephants, specially for the King's person, and in front of these elephants go about five-and-twenty horsemen with banners in their hands, and with drums and trumpets and other music playing so loudly that you can hear nothing. Before these goes a great drum carried by men at the sides, and they go now and then striking it; the sound of this is heard a long distance off; and this drum they call *picha*. After the King has mounted he counts the two hundred horsemen and the hundred elephants and the shield-bearers of the guard, and whoever is missing is severely punished and his property confiscated.

CHAPTER XXII

Of the manner in which obeisance is done to the King, &c.

THE manner of the salaam which the nobles make to the King every day is this:—In the morning the nobles go to the palace at ten or eleven o'clock, at which hour the King comes out from within where his wives are, and after he has taken his seat they open to the nobles, and each one comes by himself and bows his head and raises his hands. This is what they call the "salaam" (*salema*). With the king are about ten or twelve men who have the duty, on the entrance of each captain, of saying to the King: "See, your Highness, your captain so-and-so, who makes salaam to you."

The Kings of Bisnaga have always liked, for show, to have many horses in their stables, and they always had eight or nine hundred horses and four or five hundred elephants, on account of which, and on account of the people that looked after them, they were put to great expense; and this King that now is (Achyuta Râya) has in his stable seven hundred and odd horses and four hundred elephants. He spends on account of them and for their attendants, to whom he gives food, two thousand gold *pardaos* per day. And of horsemen whom the King pays he has six thousand, and all of them are on the stables establishment (?) (*comem da estrebarya*); and those who serve them are paid each year, some a thousand *pardaos*, some five hundred, some three hundred, and those who have less pay receive not less than a hundred. Of these six thousand, two hundred are obliged to ride with the King.

The kings of this country are able to assemble as many soldiers as they want, as they have them there in their kingdom and have much wealth wherewith to pay them. This King Chitarao has foot-soldiers paid by his nobles, and they are obliged to maintain six[1] *lakhs* of soldiers, that is six hundred thousand men, and twenty-four thousand horse, which the same nobles are obliged to have. These nobles are like renters who hold all the land from the King, and besides keeping all these people they have to pay their cost; they also pay to him every year sixty *lakhs* of rents as royal dues. The lands, they say, yield a hundred and twenty *lakhs* of which they must pay sixty to the King, and the rest they retain for the pay of the soldiers and the expenses of the elephants which they are obliged to maintain. For this reason the common people suffer much hardship, those who hold the lands being so tyrannical. Of these sixty *lakhs* that the king has of revenue every year he does not enjoy a

[1] *Seus leques* must be a misprint for *seis leques*.

larger sum than twenty-five *lakhs*, for the rest is spent on his horses, and elephants, and foot-soldiers, and cavalry, whose cost he defrays.

During his feasts and the almsgiving to his temples all these captains, who are thus like renters, must always attend the court, and of those whom this King always has about him and by whom he is accompanied in his court there are more than two hundred. These are obliged always to be present with the King, and must always maintain the full number of soldiers according to their obligations, for if he finds that they have a less number they are severely punished and their estates confiscated. These nobles are never suffered to settle themselves in cities or towns because they would there be beyond reach of his hand; they only go thither sometimes. But a concession is granted to the kings that are subject to him, namely they do not go to court unless they are summoned, and from their own cities they send to him their rents or tributes; yet the King of Bengapor is obliged to be always in camp, and he goes to court twice in the year.

The kings who are subject are these, besides this King of Bengapor, namely the King of Gasopa and the King of Bacanor and the King of Calecu and he of Batecala,[1] and these when they come to the Court of Bisnaga are not held in higher esteem than any other captains, either by the King or by the other nobles.

The captains and lords of this kingdom of Bisnaga, as well those who are at Court as those who are away from it, have each one his secretary who goes to the palace in order to write to him and let him know what the King is doing; and they manage so that nothing takes place of which they do not soon know, and day and night they are always in the palace. And the King also, when he leaves the palace, takes with him on his

[1] Above, pp. 121, 281, and notes.

own account secretaries, who write what the King says, and the favours he bestows, and with whom he spoke, and upon what subject, and what his determination was; and to these men is given a credit equal to that of the Evangelists, because they say that whenever the King speaks there must be something worthy to be recorded, and also that such a record is necessary for their remembrance. Thus no written orders are ever issued, nor any charters granted, for the favours he bestows or the commands he gives; but when he confers a favour on any one it remains written in the registers of these secretaries. The King however gives to the recipient of the favour a seal impressed in wax from one of his rings, which his minister keeps, and these seals serve for letters patent.

These Kings of Bisnaga eat all sorts of things, but not the flesh of oxen or cows, which they never kill in all the country of the heathen because they worship them. They eat mutton, pork, venison, partridges, hares, doves, quail, and all kinds of birds; even sparrows, and rats, and cats, and lizards, all of which are sold in the market of the city of Bisnaga.

Everything has to be sold alive so that each one may know what he buys—this[1] at least so far as concerns game—and there are fish from the rivers in large quantities. The markets are always overflowing with abundance of fruits, grapes, oranges, limes, pomegranates, jack-fruit, and mangoes, and all very cheap. It is said that in the markets they give twelve live sheep for a *pardao*, and in the hills they give fourteen or fifteen for a *pardao*. The King drinks water which they bring from a spring, which is kept enclosed under the hand of a man in whom the King has great confidence; and the vessels in which they draw the water come covered and sealed. Thus they deliver it to the women who wait on

[1] *E ysto he coanto a caça.* At the present day in Southern India game-birds are sold alive, generally with the eyes sewn up.

him, and they take it inside to the other women, the King's wives.

The greatest mark of honour that this King of Bisnaga confers on a noble consists of two fans ornamented with gold and precious stones, made of the white tails of certain cows;[1] he gives them bracelets also. Everything which the noble receives is placed on the ground. The King confers very high honour, too, if he permits a certain one to kiss his feet, for he never gives his hands to be kissed by any one. When he wishes to please his captains, or persons from whom he has received or wishes to receive good service, he gives them scarves of honour[2] for their personal use, which is a great honour; and this he does each year to the captains at the time that they pay him their land-rents. This takes place in the month of September[3] when for nine days they make great feasts. Some say that they do this in honour of the nine months during which Our Lady bore her Son in the womb; others say that it is only done because at this time the captains come to pay their rents to the King. Which feasts are conducted in the following manner.

The first day they put nine castles in a piece of ground which is in front of the palace, which castles are made by the nine principal captains in the kingdom. They are very lofty and are hung with rich cloths, and in them are many dancing-girls and also many kinds of contrivances. Besides these nine every captain is obliged to make each one his castle, and they come to show

[1] This evidently refers to the yak-tail whisks used in the service of idols in the temples and in the palaces of nobles. On occasions of ceremony at the present day any chief or noble who has a pretension to sovereignty, or who claims descent from a line of independent lords, proclaims his dignity by the use of certain insignia, and amongst these the yak-tail fan finds place. It is one of the most graceful of ornaments. The soft white hair is set in a metal handle of brass or silver and waved slowly by an attendant. Its material object was to keep away flies.

[2] *Pachari* for *pichhauri*.

[3] Above, p. 263.

these to the King. Each one has his separate device, and they all come like this during the nine days of the feast. The officers of the city are bound to come with their devices each day at night, just as in our festivals, and in these nine days they slaughter animals and make sacrifice. The first day they kill nine male buffaloes and nine sheep and nine goats, and thenceforward they kill each day more, always doubling the number; and when they have finished slaying these beasts, there come nine horses and nine elephants of the King, and these come before the king covered with flowers—roses—and with rich trappings. Before them goes the chief Master of the Horse with many attendants, and they make salaam to the King. And when these have finished making their salaam there come from within priests, and they bring rice and other cooked edibles, and water, and fire, and many kinds of scents, and they offer prayers and throw the water over the horses and elephants, just (as our priests do with) holy water; and they put chaplets of roses on them. This is done in the presence of the King, who remains seated on a throne of gold and precious stones; he never sits on this except only this once in the year. And this King that now reigns does not sit on it, for they say that whoever sits on it must be a very truthful man, one who speaks the whole truth, and this King never does so. Whilst this is going on there pass by the King fully a thousand women, dancing and posturing before him. After all the devices that have been prepared have been witnessed all the horses of the King pass by, covered with their silken trappings,[1] and with much adornment of gold and precious stones

[1] "Silken trappings." The original word is *patollas*. Later on (see p. 383), in describing the king's dress, Nuniz writes, "*os seus vestidos sao pachõiis*," &c. Both these words probably refer to the same Canarese word, *paṭṭuda*, "a silk cloth." Barbosa and Pinto use it in the form *patola*, Correa as *patolo*, and Peyton (in Purchas) as *patolla*. (Yule and Burnell's Glossary, *s.v. Patola*.) In Telugu, *pattu* = "silk."

on their heads, and then all the elephants and yokes of oxen[1] in the middle of the arena[2] in front of the palace. After these have been seen there come thirty-six of the most beautiful of the King's wives covered with gold and pearls, and much work of seed-pearls, and in the hands of each a vessel of gold with a lamp of oil burning in it; and with these women come all the female servants and the other wives of the King, with canes in their hands tipped with gold and with torches burning; and these then retire inside with the King. These women are so richly bedecked with gold and precious stones that they are hardly able to move.

In this way during these nine days they are compelled to search for all things which will give pleasure to the King.

The King has a thousand wrestlers for these feasts who wrestle before the King, but not in our manner, for they strike and wound each other with two circlets with points[3] which they carry in their hands to strike with, and the one most wounded goes and takes his reward in the shape of a silk cloth,[4] such as the King gives to these wrestlers. They have a captain over them, and they do not perform any other service in the kingdom.

And after these nine days are finished the Rao[5] rides out and goes to hold a review of the troops of his captains, and he goes a length of two leagues be-

[1] *Juntas.* The meaning is doubtful, but in all probability yokes of oxen are referred to. In the Canarese country these are often handsomely decorated and clothed when attached to travelling vehicles.

[2] *Terreiro.*

[3] *Rodas de bicos.* These may perhaps have been weapons such as in England were known as "knuckledusters."

[4] A free translation. The original runs, "*de maneira que o que fica de baixo d outro mais ferido vay, leva a fogaça, que he hũu pacharim,*" &c. It seems curious that the vanquished should be rewarded. *Leva a fogaça* is literally "takes the cake." For *pacharim* see above, p. 376, note 2.

[5] This is the only occasion on which the chronicler gives the king his hereditary title of *Râya,* usually spelt *Rao* by the Portuguese. *Râya* is the same as *Râja.*

tween the armed men. At the end he dismounts and takes a bow in his hand and shoots three arrows, namely one for the Ydallcão, and another for the King of Cotamuloco,[1] and yet another for the Portuguese; it was his custom to make war on the kingdom lying in the direction where the arrow reached furthest. After this is done the King returns home, and on that day he fasts and with him all the people of the land; and on the next day he goes to the river to bathe with all his people. Within these nine days the King is paid all the rents that he receives from his kingdom; for, as already said, all the land belongs to the King, and from his hand the captains hold it. They make it over to the husbandmen who pay nine-tenths to their lord; and they have no land of their own, for the kingdom belongs entirely to the King;[2] only the captains are put to charges on account of the troops for whom the King makes them responsible, and whom they are obliged to provide in the way of service. Every Saturday the dancing-girls are obliged to go to the palace to dance and posture before the King's idol, which is in the interior of his palace. The people of this country always fast on Saturdays and do not eat all day nor even at night, nor do they drink water, only they may chew a few cloves to sweeten the breath. The King always gives large sums in charity; in the palace there are always two or three thousand Brahmans who are his priests, and to whom the King commands to give alms. These Brahman priests are very despicable men; they always have much money, and are so insolent that even by

[1] The Qutb Shâh of Golkonda.

[2] Whether true or not, this statement, coming as it does from a totally external source, strongly supports the view often held that the ryots of South India were grievously oppressed by the nobles when subject to Hindu government. Other passages in both these chronicles, each of which was written quite independently of the other, confirm the assertion here made as to the mass of the people being ground down and living in the greatest poverty and distress.

using blows the guards of the door cannot hold them in check.

The captains and principal people use[1] at night torches of oil, from four to twelve torches (according to rank), those of highest rank having twelve at most. The King, however, must have a hundred or a hundred and fifty torches. There is much wax in the country, but they do not know how to work it. Every merchant who brings merchandise in horses and other things which he may have brought to sell to the King, if he desires an audience, has to offer him a present of a piece of goods or a horse of the best that he has brought, in order that he may obtain an audience and transact his business. And this not only to the King. You must perforce pay bribes to all the several officers with whom you have to deal. They will do nothing without some profit to themselves.

When any one suffers wrong and wishes to represent his case to the King he shows how great is his suffering by lying flat on his face on the ground till they ask him what it is he wants. If, perchance, he wishes to speak to the King while he is riding, he takes the shaft of a spear and ties a branch to it and thus goes along calling out. Then they make room for him, and he makes his complaint to the King; and it is there and then settled without more ado, and the King orders a captain, one of those who go with him, to do at once what the supplicant asks. If he complains that he was robbed in such and such a province and in such and such a road, the King sends immediately for the captain of that province, even though he be at court, and the captain may be seized and his property taken if he does not catch the thief. In the same way the chief bailiff[2] is obliged to give an account of the robberies in the

[1] When passing through the city, probably.
[2] *Meyrinho.*

capital, and in consequence very few thefts take place; and even if some are committed, you give some little present and a description of the man who stole from you, and they will soon know by the agency of the wizards whether the thief be in the city or not; for there are very powerful wizards in this country. Thus there are very few thieves in the land.

This King has continually fifty thousand paid soldiers, amongst whom are six thousand horsemen who belong to the palace guard, to which six thousand belong the two hundred who are obliged to ride with him. He has also twenty thousand spearmen and shield-bearers, and three thousand men to look after the elephants in the stables; he has sixteen hundred grooms[1] who attend to the horses, and has also three hundred horse trainers[2] and two thousand artificers, namely blacksmiths, masons, and carpenters, and washermen who wash clothes. These are the people he has and pays every day; he gives them their allowance at the gate of the palace. To the six thousand horsemen the King gives horses free and gives provision for them every month, and all these horses are marked with the King's mark; when they die they are obliged to take the piece of skin containing the mark to Madanarque, the chief master of the horse, so that he may give them another, and these horses which he gives are mostly country-breds which the King buys, twelve or fifteen for a thousand *pardaos*.[3] The King every year buys thirteen thousand horses of Ormuz, and country-breds, of which he chooses the best for his own stables, and he gives the rest to his captains, and gains much money by them; because after taking out the good Persian horses, he sells those which are country-bred, and gives five for a thousand *pardaos*, and they are obliged to pay him the money for them within

[1] *Farazes.*

[2] *Saneis que ensynão os cavallos.*

[3] Above, p. 361, and note.

the month of September; and with the money so obtained he pays for the Arabs that he buys of the Portuguese, in such a way that his captains pay the cost of the whole without anything going out of the Treasury.

This King has also within his gates more than four thousand women, all of whom live in the palace; some are dancing-girls, and others are bearers[1] who carry the King's wives on their shoulders, and the King also in the interior of the palace, for the king's houses are large and there are great intervals between one house and another. He has also women who wrestle, and others who are astrologers and soothsayers; and he has women who write all the accounts of expenses that are incurred inside the gates, and others whose duty it is to write all the affairs of the kingdom and compare their books with those of the writers outside; he has women also for music, who play instruments and sing. Even the wives of the King are well versed in music.

The King has other women besides. He has ten cooks for his personal service, and has others kept for times when he gives banquets; and these ten prepare the food for no one save for the King alone. He has a eunuch for guard at the gate of the kitchen, who never allows any one to enter for fear of poison. When the King wishes to eat, every person withdraws, and then come some of the women whose duty it is and they prepare the table for him; they place for him a three-footed stool, round, made of gold, and on it put the messes. These are brought in large vessels of gold, and the smaller messes in basins of gold, some of which are adorned with precious stones. There is no cloth on the table, but one is brought when the King has finished

[1] *Bois.* Hindu women of the Boyi caste. The Boyis are Telugus, and are employed as bearers of palanqueens and other domestic service in Southern India. Hence the Anglo-Indian term "Boy" for a servant.

eating, and he washes his hands and mouth. Women and eunuchs serve him at table. The wives of the King remain each in her own chamber and are waited on by maid-servants. It is said that he has judges, as well as bailiffs and watchmen who every night guard the palace, and all these are women.

The King never puts on any garment more than once, and when he takes it off he at once delivers it to certain officers who have charge of this duty, and they render an account; and these garments are never given to any one. This is considered to show great state. His clothes are silk cloths (*pachõiis*)[1] of very fine material and worked with gold, which are worth each one ten *pardaos;* and they wear at times *bajuris* of the same sort, which are like shirts with a skirt; and on the head they wear caps of brocade which they call *culaes*,[2] and one of these is worth some twenty cruzados. When he lifts it from his head he never again puts it on.

The punishments that they inflict in this kingdom are these: for a thief, whatever theft he commits, howsoever little it be, they forthwith cut off a foot and a hand, and if his theft be a great one he is hanged with a hook under his chin. If a man outrages a respectable woman or a virgin he has the same punishment, and if he does any other such violence his punishment is of a like kind. Nobles who become traitors are sent to be impaled alive on a wooden stake thrust through the belly, and people of the lower orders, for whatever crime they commit, he forthwith commands to cut off their heads in the market-place, and the same for a murder unless the death was the result of a duel. For great honour is done to those who fight in a duel, and they give the estate of the dead man to the survivor; but no one fights a duel without first asking leave of the minister,

[1] See above, note to p. 377.
[2] Telugu, *kuḷḷāyi*. See pp. 210, 252, 273.

who forthwith grants it. These are the common kinds of punishments, but they have others more fanciful; for when the King so desires, he commands a man to be thrown to the elephants, and they tear him in pieces. The people are so subject to him that if you told a man on the part of the King that he must stand still in a street holding a stone on his back all day till you released him, he would do it.

The officers of the King who go about the kingdom are these:—First the minister (*regedor*) of the kingdom, who is the second person in it, then the treasurer, with the scribes of the King's own lands,[1] the chief treasurer, and the commander of the palace guards (*o porteiro moor*), the treasurer of the jewels, the chief master of the horse. The King has no controller of the revenues nor other officers, nor officers of his house, but only the captains of his kingdom; of whom I will here mention some, and the revenues they hold, and of what territory they are lords,

Firstly Salvanayque, the present minister; he has a revenue of a million and a hundred thousand gold *pardaos*. He is lord of Charamãodel and of Nagapatão, and Tamgor, and Bomgarin, and Dapatao, and Truguel, and Caullim, and all these are cities; their territories are all very large, and they border on Ceylon.[2] Of this

[1] *De fazemda*. I think that the meaning is as given. It will be observed below that the kingdom was divided into provinces or estates, each one entrusted to a noble who farmed the revenue to his own advantage, paying a fixed sum every year to the king. In the case of Narvara, the treasurer of the jewels, his estate is described as "bordering on the country of Bisnaga," and as this expression cannot refer to the entire country ruled by the king, it must be taken in a limited sense as applying to the king's own personal lands—his home-farm, so to speak. The system is well known in India, where a prince holds what are called *Khâs* lands, *i.e.* lands held privately for his own personal use and benefit, as distinct from the lands held under him by others, the revenue of which last ought to go to the public purse.

[2] Note that Madura is not mentioned in these lists. And yet it would appear that a Nâyakka, or subordinate chief of Vijayanagar, had been

money he is obliged to give a third to the King, and two-thirds remain for him for the expenses of his *lascarîs* and horses, which he is obliged to maintain for the King, viz.: thirty thousand foot and three thousand horse and thirty elephants; so that he only gets the balance after deducting the expenses of this force. But in this way he acquires much wealth because he never maintains the whole force. And the King, whenever he wishes, takes away property of these nobles.

Another captain, Ajaparcatimapa,[1] who was minister of Crisnarao, has a revenue of eight hundred thousand *pardaos* of gold, and is lord of the city of Hudogary,[2] and of the city of Condovim,[3] and of the city of

ruling at that place since 1499. Mr. Nelson, in his work, "The Madura Country," gives the following list of Nayâkkas there :—

	A.D.
Narasa Nâyakka	1499–1500
Tenna Nâyakka	1500–1515
Narasa Pillai (a Tamulian)	1515–1519
Kuru Kuru Timmappa Nâyakka	1519–1524
Kattiyama Kâmayya Nâyakka	1524–1526
Chinnappa Nâyakka	1526–1530
Ayyakârai Veyyappa Nâyakka	1530–1535
Visvanâtha Nâyakka Ayyar	1535–1544

Four others are mentioned before we come to the great Visvanâtha Nâyakka, who founded an hereditary dynasty, though himself only a deputy of the crown. He ruled Madura from 1559 to 1563. Muttu Krishnappa (1602–1609) seems to have been the first to assume royal titles at Madura. His son, Muttu Vîrappa (1609–1623), is stated, in the narrative of the Portuguese writer Barradas (above, p. 230), to have paid a tribute in A.D. 1616 to the Vijayanagar king at Chandragiri of 600,000 pagodas; he had several vassal kings under him, and must have already obtained great power. It is possible that, in the time of Nuniz, Madura was not one of the greater provinces, but that it became so later.

The names Choromandel, Negapatam, and Tanjore are easy to distinguish in this list. "Bomgarin" I cannot identify, though the termination, *garim*, may represent *giri*, "mountain." "Dapatao" may be Devipatnam. "Truguel" seems to have some affinity with Tirukovil. It cannot be the "Truguel" mentioned by Barros and others as one of the fortresses given to Asada Khân by the king of Vijayanagar (above, p. 175), because those were close to Belgaum, while this "Truguel" was in the extreme south. "Caullim" may be Kayal.

[1] Above, p. 360, note 1. [2] Udayagiri. [3] Kondavîd.

Penagundim,[1] and of Codegaral[2] of Cidaota.[3] All these large cities border on the kingdom of Oria, and some of them with Cape Comorin (*cabo de Comarỹ*). These lands Crisnarao gave him when he made him minister and put out the eyes of Salvatinica, his minister, who was captain of them. He is obliged to serve with twenty-five thousand[4] foot, fifteen hundred horse, and forty elephants, and pays each year to the King three hundred thousand *pardaos*.

Another captain, who is called Gapanayque, is lord of these lands, namely of Rosyl,[5] and of Tipar, and of Ticalo, and of Bigolom.[6] These lands march with the territory of the Ydallcão, and in all these there is much wheat and grains and cattle and goats and gingely and cotton; and very fine cloth made of the last, for all the cloth that is manufactured is made of it. He has a revenue from these territories of six hundred thousand *pardaos*, and is obliged to furnish two thousand five hundred horse, and twenty thousand foot, and twenty elephants, and he pays every year to the King a hundred and fifty thousand *pardaos*.

Another captain called Lepapayque, who is lord of Vimgapor,[7] a land very rich in seed-plots and cattle-breeding farms, has a revenue of three hundred thousand *pardaos;* and is obliged to furnish twelve hundred horse and twenty thousand foot and twenty-eight elephants,

1 Pennakonda. 2 (?) Kanigiri, Nellore district.

3 Siddhout or Siddhavattam, Cuddapah district. Codegaral *may* represent Gandikota, the termination *giri*, "hill," being substituted for *kota*, "fort," *e.g. Gandigiri*.

4 The passage is incomplete, and I have rendered it as seems reasonable. It runs, "*vinte e cimco mill e quinhentos de cavallo e*," &c. Looking at the other lists of troops, it cannot be supposed that this chief had to provide 25,000 horse. It seems more probable that such a word as *piães* was accidentally omitted after *mill*, and that *mill* should have been repeated before *quinhentos*.

5 Perhaps Rachol, near Goa.

6 Bicholim (?).

7 "Bengapor" as elsewhere spelt, *i.e.* Bankâpur, south of Dhârwâr.

and he pays to the King every year eighty thousand *pardaos*.

The treasurer of the jewels, who is called Narvara, is captain of the new city which is called Ondegema,[1] and is lord of the city of Diguoty and of Darguem and of Entarem,[2] and of the other lands bordering on the lands of Bisnaga; they are all fields. They yield him every year four hundred thousand *pardaos*, of which he gives the King two hundred thousand, and the rest he spends on twelve thousand foot and six hundred horse and twenty elephants.

Another captain called Chinapanayque, the King's marshal, is lord of the land of Calalỹ[3] in the direction of Cochim in the interior, and of many other lands that yield him three hundred thousand *pardaos*; and he is obliged to pay the King every year one hundred thousand *pardaos*, and serves with eight hundred horse and ten thousand foot (*praços*).

Crisnapanayque is lord of Aõsel,[4] which is a large

[1] See the last sentence of the chronicle of Paes (above, p. 290), where a town "on the east" is called the new city which Krishna Deva built in honour of his favourite wife. The writer has evidently been confused in that statement, for it seems clear that the town so founded was Nâgalâpur, the old name for Hospett, with which it is distinctly identified in other places. This town "on the east" is said, in the sentence referred to, to bear the name "Ardegema," and the locality is hard to determine. "East" of what? If east of Nâgalâpur be meant, then Ardegema or Ondegema (*gema* probably represents *grâma*, "village") might have been a suburb of that town. If east of the capital be intended, I cannot identify the place. But these places evidently were close to the capital, bordering on the crown lands. This, I take it, is the meaning of "bordering on the lands (*terra*) of Bisnaga."

[2] These three places I cannot identify. "Diguoty" may perhaps be Duggavatti, in the Harpanhalli division of the Bellary district. "Darguem" suggests "Droog" or "Durgam." The word is applied to a hill-fort, of which there are many in the neighbourhood. One of the most important was Râyadrûg, south of Bellary. One of the ghât roads leading eastwards from Goa is called the "gate de Digui" in old maps.

[3] Possibly Kalale in Mysore, a place fifteen miles south of that capital. It is said to have been founded in 1504 by a noble who was connected with the Vijayanagar royal family (Rice's Gazetteer, ii. 255).

[4] Unidentified

city, and of other villages that I do not here mention as they have very difficult names. These lands yield him every year twenty thousand *pardaos* of gold, and he pays an annual revenue to the King of seven thousand *pardaos*, and serves with five hundred horse and seven hundred foot (*praços*).

Also Bajapanarque, who is captain of the country of Bodial,[1] which borders on Mamgalor[2] by the sea-coast. He is lord too of Guiana.[3] In this country there is much pepper and sugar-cane and cloth (of flax)[4] and much rice; but there is no wheat, nor other cloth, and it is a land of wax. It yields him three hundred thousand *pardaos* a year, and he serves with eight hundred horsemen and ten thousand foot and fifteen elephants. He pays the King ten thousand *pardaos*.

Mallpanarque, who was chief master of the horse to King Crisnarao, is lord of the country of Avaly,[5] which is in the interior of Calecu.[6] This land has much iron and much cotton, rice, goats, sheep, cows and buffaloes. He has a revenue of fifteen thousand *pardaos*, and is obliged to serve with four hundred horse and six thousand foot, and pays the King every year five thousand *pardaos*.

Another captain, called Adapanayque, who is the chief counsellor of the King, is lord of the country of Gate,[7] whence come the diamonds, and of many other

[1] Perhaps Budehâl in Mysore, which like Kalale was founded by a Vijayanagar officer, and contains several sixteenth-century inscriptions. It is in the Chittaldrûg division, forty miles south of that place.

[2] Mangalore.

[3] Unidentified.

[4] *Roupa*. Linen cloth. The word is not used of cotton, and the next sentence shows that cotton did not grow in that tract.

[5] I hazard the suggestion that this may be a mistake of the copyist for "Avâti." This place, now a village in the Kolar district of Mysore, was in the fifteenth century an important place, a ruling family having been founded here by the "Morasu Wokkalu" or "Seven Farmers" (Rice, "Mysore and Coorg," ii. 20). The description applies to it fairly well.

[6] Calicut.

[7] Either "the ghâts," or perhaps Gutti (Gooty). The rich Vajra Karûr diamond mines are about twenty miles south-west of Gooty, where are the remains of a very fine hill-fortress.

territories which yield him three hundred thousand gold *pardaos*, excluding the precious stones which form a revenue by themselves. He pays to the King every year forty thousand *pardaos*, with the condition that all diamonds which exceed twenty *mangelins*[1] in weight shall be given to the King for his Treasury. He serves with eight thousand foot and eight hundred horse and thirty elephants, and pays the King every year one hundred thousand *pardaos*.

Another Bajapanayque is captain of Mumdoguel,[2] which was a fortress of the Ydalcão, and was taken from him by Crisnarao when he took Rachol,[3] which was a boundary of it. This fortress of Mumdoguel with other territories yields him four hundred thousand *pardaos*, and he serves with a thousand cavalry and ten thousand foot and fifty elephants, and pays the King every year one hundred and fifty thousand *pardaos*.

In this way the kingdom of Bisnaga is divided between more than two hundred captains who are all heathen,[4] and according to the lands and revenues that they have so the King settles for them the forces that they are compelled to keep up, and how much revenue they have to pay him every month during the first nine days of the month of September. He never gives any receipts to them, only, if they do not pay they are well punished, and are ruined and their property taken away. All the captains of this kingdom make use of litters and palanqueens. These are like biers and men carry them on their shoulders, but people are not allowed to make use of litters unless they are cavaliers of the highest rank, and the captains and principal persons use palanqueens. There are always at the court where the King is twenty thousand litters and palanqueens.

[1] See note above, p. 368. [2] Mudkal. [3] Raichûr.
[4] *I.e.* of the Hindu religion, not Muhammadans.

These matters concerning (*i.e.* the power and greatness of) the kingdom of Bisnaga, though it may seem to you that I have exaggerated, yet the people of this country assert them to have been even more notable[1] in times past, and greater than they now are.

And in this kingdom of Bisnaga there is a class of men, natives of the country, namely Brahmans, who the most part of them never kill or eat any live thing, and these are the best that there are amongst them. They are honest men, given to merchandise, very acute and of much talent, very good at accounts, lean men and well-formed, but little fit for hard work. By these and by the duties they undertake the kingdom is carried on. They believe that there are Three Persons and only One God, and they call the Persons of the Most Holy Trinity "*Tricebemca.*" There is another class who are Canarese who have pagodas in which are (images of?) monkeys, and cows, and buffaloes, and devils, to whom they pay much honour, and these idols and monkeys which they adore they say that in former times this land belonged all to the monkeys, and that in those days they could speak. They have books full of fine stories of chivalry, and many foolish tales about their idols, such as it is out of reason for men to believe. But because of this, neither in the kingdom of Bisnaga nor in all the land of the heathen are any monkeys killed, and there are so many in this country that they cover the mountains. There is another class of men called Telumgalle;[2] when these die their wives are buried alive with them.

The King of Bisnaga is a Brahman;[3] every day he hears the preaching of a learned Brahman, who never married nor ever touched a woman. He urges in his preaching (obedience to) the commandments of God, that is to say, that one must not kill any living thing, nor take

[1] *Noveis* in the original, probably for *notaveis*.

[2] Telugus.

[3] This was certainly not the case.

anything belonging to another, and as with these so with the rest of the commandments. These people have such devotion to cows that they kiss them every day, some they say even on the rump—a thing I do not assert for their honour—and with the droppings of these cows they absolve themselves from their sins as if with holy water. They have for a commandment to confess their sins to the Brahman priests, but they do not do it, except only those who are very religious (*amiguos de Dios*). They give in excuse that they feel a shame to confess themselves to another man, and say that it is sufficient to confess themselves alone after approaching God, for he who does not do so does not acquire grace; thus they fulfil the command in one way or another. But they do it so seldom (in reality) that they (may be said to) neglect this command to confess.

This kingdom of Bisnaga is all heathen. The women have the custom of burning themselves when their husbands die, and hold it an honour to do so. When therefore their husbands die they mourn with their relations and those of their husbands, but they hold that the wife who weeps beyond measure has no desire to go in search of her husband; and the mourning finished their relations speak to them, advising them to burn themselves and not to dishonour their generation. After that, it is said, they place the dead man on a bed with a canopy of branches and covered with flowers, and they put the woman on the back of a worthless horse, and she goes after them with many jewels on her, and covered with roses; she carries a mirror in her hand and in the other a branch of flowers, and (she goes accompanied by) many kinds of music, and his relations (go with her) with much pleasure. A man goes also playing on a small drum, and he sings songs to her telling her that she is going to join her husband, and she answers also in singing that so she will do. As soon as she arrives at the place where they are always burned she waits with the musicians till her husband is burned, whose body they place in a very large pit that has been made ready for it, covered with much firewood. Before they light the fire his mother or his nearest relative takes a vessel of water on the head and a firebrand in the hand, and goes three times round the pit, and at each round makes a hole in the pot; and when these three rounds are done breaks the pot, which is small, and throws the torch into the pit. Then they apply the fire, and when the body is burned comes the wife with all the feasters and washes her feet, and then a Brahman performs over her certain ceremonies according to their law; and when he has finished doing this, she draws off with her own hand all the jewels that she wears, and divides them among her female relatives, and if she has sons she commends them to her most honoured relatives. When they have taken off all she has on, even her good clothes, they put on her some common yellow cloths, and her relatives take her hand and she takes a branch in the other, and goes singing and running to the pit where the fire is, and then mounts on some steps which are made high up by the pit. Before they do this they go three times round the fire, and then she mounts the steps and holds in front of her a mat that prevents her from seeing the fire. They throw into the fire a cloth containing rice, and another in which they carry betel leaves, and her comb and mirror with which she adorned herself, saying that all these are needed to adorn herself by her husband's side. Finally she takes leave of all, and puts a pot of oil on her head, and casts herself into the fire with such courage that it is a thing of wonder; and as soon as she throws herself in, the relatives are ready with firewood and quickly cover her with it, and after this is done they all raise loud lamentations. When a captain dies, however many wives he has thev all burn themselves, and when the King dies they do the same. This is the custom throughout all the country of the heathen, except with that caste of people called Telugas, amongst whom the wives are buried alive with their husbands when they die. These go with much pleasure to the pit, inside of which are made two seats of earth, one for him and one for her, and they place each one on his own seat and cover them in little by little till they are covered up; and so the wife dies with the husband.

CHAPTER XXIII

Of the ceremonies practised at the death of Brahmans.

WHEN a Brahman is sick, before he dies, they send to call the learned Brahmans who are his priests, so that they should come to pray, and console the sick man; and they talk to him of the affairs of his soul, and what he must do to save it, bidding him spend money in alms. After this ceremony is over they make the Brahman priests shave the sick man's head, and after the shaving they bid them wash it, and after the washing it is their custom to bring into their houses a cow with a calf,—there are very few Brahmans, however poor they be, who do not have one to live in their house,—which cow, when they have finished washing the man's head, they take a turban and tie it to its neck and put the end of the turban into the hand of the sick man, and he gives it and the calf in alms for his soul to those priests who perform these ceremonies. On that day he gives alms according to his position, and gives to eat to some Brahmans who are invited and who come there for the purpose. They believe that when these ceremonies are made for the sick man, if he is to live he is soon cured of his infirmity, and if not that he soon dies.

After the death of the sick man they have the ground washed upon which he lay, and after the washing they take cow-dung and spread it over the ground, and place the body on the top of this dung. They hold that a sick man who dies on a cot, or on anything soever except only on the ground, commits a mortal sin. As soon as the body is laid on the ground they make for it a bier covered with boughs of the fig-tree, and before they place the body on the bier they wash it well with pure water, and anoint it with sandal-wood (oil); and they place by the body branches of sweet basil and cover it with a new cloth, and so place it in the bier. Then one of his relatives takes the bier on one side, and they call three other Brahmans whosoever they may be to aid them to lift it; and so they carry it to the place where they are to burn it, accompanied by many Brahmans who go singing in front of the corpse. In front of all goes his son, if he has one, or next younger brother or nearest relative, with fire in the hand for the burning. As soon as they arrive at the place where they have to burn the body, they scatter money according to their ability, and then put the fire to it; and they wait there till the whole body is consumed, and then all go and wash their bodies in a tank and afterwards return each one to his house. The son or brother or relation who put the fire is obliged to sleep on the ground where the man died for nine nights, and after the lapse of nine days from the death come the priests and learned men and they command to shave the head of this man. During these nine days, they feed the poor and they give them the dead man's clothes, and they give the cot with its bed in alms to the priests, with some money in addition; if he is a rich man they give gardens and other things in alms to many Brahmans. When ten days are finished, and the son has been shaved, he goes to the place where they burned his father or his brother, and they perform many ceremonies over the ashes and bones that remain unburned; then they put them in a small vessel and make a pit in the ground and bury them in it, and keep them thus guarded and buried in order (afterwards) to send the bones to be thrown into a sacred river, which is distant from Goa over one thousand leagues.[1] There is a very large temple there, the object of many pilgrimages, and they hold that every pilgrim who dies there is saved, and goes to Paradise, and also every dead man whose bones are thrown into that river. In spite of this they in reality take very few people there. The heir or the father or son of the dead man is obliged,, from the day of the death, for eleven days to give food to twenty-seven Brahmans, and until twenty-one days to three others; until twelve days again he feeds seven Brahmans, and until twenty-seven days gives to eat to the three; on the last day of the month he gives food to three others, and thenceforward, until one year is finished, he gives meals once a month to three Brahmans. They do this in honour of the Trinity for the soul of the deceased. When this year is over he gives no more alms, except that each year, on the day on which the death happened, he feeds six Brahmans,—namely, three in honour of the Trinity, and three for the persons of his father, grandfather, and great-grandfather; who thus seemingly eat together. Thus he obtains favour with God, and for these expenses they beg alms of the Brahmans if they are poor. These give him all help for it. Before they dine they wash the feet of all six, and during the meal some ceremonies are performed by Brahman priests who come there for that purpose.

[1] The Ganges.

APPENDICES

APPENDIX A

DIAMONDS

HOWEVER much it may at first sight appear that our chroniclers have exaggerated in their description of the wealth of the Hindu sovereign and his nobles, and of the wonderful display of jewels made on days of high festival by the ladies of their households, an account of which is given us by Paes, I for one see little reason for doubt. Nuniz distinctly states (p. 389) that the diamond mines, in their day the richest in the world, were farmed out on condition that all stones above twenty mangellins in weight— about twenty-five carats—were sent to the Râya for his personal use, and there must have been many of these. Barradas (p. 226 above) states that, according to rumour, even after the downfall of the empire the king at Chandragiri in 1614 A.D. had no less than three large chests full of diamonds in his possession; and every traveller and chronicler has something to say on the subject.

The principal mines were on the north bank of the Krishnâ river, and in the Kurnool and Anantapur countries, notably at Vajra Karûr. Generically these are known as "the mines of Golkonda," and the phrase has passed into a proverb.

Linschoten (ii. 136) writes: "They (diamonds) grow in the countrie of Decam behinde Ballagate, by the towne of Bisnagar, wherein are two or three hilles, from whence they are digged, whereof the King of Bisnagar doth reape great profitte; for he causeth them to be straightly watched, and hath farmed them out with this condition, that all diamonds that are above twenty-five Mangellyns in waight are for the King himselfe (every Mangellyn is foure graines in waight).

"There is yet another hill in the Countrie of Decam, which is called Velha, that is the old Rocke, from whence come the best diamonds and are sold for the greatest price. . . . Sometimes they find Diamonds of one hundred and two hundred Mangelyns and more, but very few."

As regards the diamond "as large as a hen's egg," said to have been found at the sack of Vijayanagar and presented to the Âdil Shâh (above, p. 208), Couto (Decada VIII. c. xv.) says that it was a jewel which the Râya had affixed to the base of the plume on his horse's head-dress. Garcia da Orta, who was in India in 1534, says that at Vijayanagar a diamond had been seen as large as a small hen's egg, and he even declares the weights of three others to have been respectively 120, 148, and 250 *mangelis*, equivalent to 150, 175, and 312½ carats (Tavernier, V. Ball, ii. 433).

Dr. Ball has gone carefully into the question of the diamonds known as "Bâbar's," "the Mogul's," "Pitt's," "the *Koh-i-nûr*," and others, and to his Appendix I. I beg to refer those interested in the subject.

It is clear that this hen's egg diamond could not be the same as Sultan Bâbar's, because the former was taken at Vijayanagar in A.D. 1565, whereas Sultan Bâbar's was received by his son Humâyun at Agra in 1526, and could not have been, forty years later, in the possession of the Hindu king of the south.[1]

Dr. Ball has shown that probably the *Koh-i-nûr* is identical with the "Mogul's diamond." Was, then, this "hen's egg" diamond the same? Probably not. If we had been told that the "hen's egg," when found in the sack of Vijayanagar, had been cut, the proof *contra* would be conclusive, since the *Koh-i-nûr* was certainly uncut in A.D. 1656 or 1657. But there is no information available on this point.

The "hen's egg" was apparently taken by the Âdil Shâh to Bîjapûr in 1565, and it is not likely to have found its way, still in an uncut state, into the possession of Mîr Jumla in 1656.

The *Koh-i-nûr* was found at Kollûr on the river Krishnâ, probably in A.D. 1656. Mîr Jumla farmed the mines at that time, and presented it uncut to the emperor, Shâh Jahân. It is said to have weighed 756 English carats (Ball, ii. 444). It was entrusted to a Venetian named Hortensio Borgio, and was so damaged and wasted in his hands that, when seen by Tavernier in Aurangzîb's treasury in 1665, it weighed not more than 268½ English carats. In 1739 Nadir Shâh sacked Delhi and carried the stone away with him to Persia, conferring on it its present immortal name the "Mountain of Light." On his murder in 1747 it passed into the hands of his grandson, Shâh Rukh. Four years later Shâh Rukh gave it to Ahmad Shâh Durâni of Kâbul, and by him it

[1] Its history is known from A.D. 1304, when it was acquired by Alâ-ud-Dîn Khilji from the Rajah of Malwa.

was bequeathed to his son Taimûr. In 1793 it passed by descent to his son Shâh Zamân, who was blinded and deposed by his brother Muhammad; but he retained possession of the stone in his prison, and in 1795 it became the property of his brother Sultan Shuja. In 1809, after Shuja became king of Kabul, Elphinstone saw the diamond in his bracelet at Peshawur. In 1812, Shuja, being dethroned by Muhammad, fled to Lahore, where he was detained as a quasi-prisoner by Ranjît Singh, the ruler of the Panjâb. In 1813 an agreement was arrived at, and Shuja surrendered the diamond to Ranjît Singh. Ranjît often wore the stone, and it was constantly seen by European visitors to Lahore. Dying in 1839, the *Koh-i-nûr* was placed in the jewel-chamber till the infant Dhulîp Singh was acknowledged as Ranjît's successor. In 1849 it was handed over to Sir John Lawrence on the annexation of the Panjâb, and by him was sent to England to Her Majesty the Queen. In 1851 it was exhibited at the first great Exhibition, and in 1852 it was re-cut by an Amsterdam cutter, Voorsanger, in the employ of Messrs. Garrards. The weight is now $106\frac{1}{16}$ carats.

It would be interesting to trace the story of the "hen's egg" diamond after its acquisition by the Bîjapûr sultan, Ali Âdil.

H. de Montfart, who travelled in India in 1608, saw a very large diamond in the possession of the Mogul emperor Jahângîr at Delhi,[1] but this had been pierced. "I have seene one with the great *Mogor* as bigge as a Hen's egge, and of that very forme, which he caused expressly to bee pierced like a pearle to weare it on his arme. . . . It weighteth 198 Mangelins."

[1] De Montfart's "Survey of all the East Indies." Translation, edition of 1615, p. 34.

APPENDIX B

THE WEALTH OF THE DAKHAN IN THE FOURTEENTH CENTURY A.D.

WHEN Malik Kâfur, in the year 1310 A.D., during the reign of Alâ-ud-Dîn Khilji of Delhi, carried out his successful raids into the Dakhan and to the Malabar coast, sacking all the Hindu temples, ravaging the territory of Maisûr, and despoiling the country, he is said to have returned to Delhi with an amount of treasure that seems almost fabulous. Firishtah writes: "They found in the temples prodigious spoils, such as idols of gold adorned with precious stones, and other rich effects consecrated to Hindu worship;" and Malik presented his sovereign with "312 elephants, 20,000 horses, 96,000 *mâns* of gold, several boxes of jewels and pearls, and other precious effects."

When we come to estimate the amount of gold we are met with a difficulty, as there are many varieties of *mâns* in India, the variation being as much as from 19 lbs. in Travancore to 163¼ lbs. in Ahmadnagar. The Madras *mân* weighs 25 lbs., the Bombay *mân* 28 lbs. Hawkins, writing in 1610, gives 55 lbs. to the *mân*,[1] Middleton, in 1611, 33 lbs.[2] Now Firishtah had more to do with Ahmadnagar than any other part of India, and if his estimate was based on the *mân* of that tract, Malik Kâfur's 96,000 *mâns* of gold would have amounted to the enormous sum of 15,672,000 lbs. weight. It is hardly likely that Firishtah would have had in his mind the Travancore *mân*. Even if he was thinking of the Madras *mân*, which is not likely, his estimate of the weight of the gold carried off amounted to 2,400,000 lbs.

Whether we accept these amounts or not, there can be no manner of doubt that the richness of the temples was very great, and the reason is easy to see. The country had always been subject to Hindu kings, and treasures had year by year accumulated. The Brahmans exacted gifts and payments from the people

[1] Purchas, i. 218.

[2] See Yule and Burnell's Dictionary, *s.v.* "Maund."

on all occasions. Kings and chiefs, merchants and landowners, vied with one another in presenting rich offerings to their favourite places of worship; and when it is remembered that this practice had been going on from time immemorial, it need be no matter for wonder that the man who first violently despoiled the sacred buildings departed from the country laden with an almost incredible amount of booty. Colonel Dow, in his translation of the works of Firishtah (i. 307), computes the value of the gold carried off by Malik Kâfur at a hundred millions sterling of our money.

APPENDIX C

TABLES FOR REFERENCE

APPROXIMATE DATES OF REIGNS OF KINGS OF VIJAYANAGAR

The First Dynasty.

	A.D.
HARIHARA I.	1336 to 1343
BUKKA I.	1343 to 1379

(*Certain inscriptions imply that Kampa reigned from* 1343 *to* 1355, *and that his son Sangama was reigning in May* 1356.)

HARIHARA II.	1379 to end of 1399	
BUKKA II.	end of 1399 to Nov. 1406	
DEVA RÂYA I.	Nov. 1406 to 1412–13	
VÎRA VIJAYA	1412–13 to 1419	
DEVA RÂYA II.	1419 to 1444 (?)	
——— (?)	(?) 1444 to 1449	
MALLIKÂRJUNA	1452–53, 1464–65	*Confused period. The dates given are those of inscriptions.*
RÂJASÊKHARA	1468–69	
VIRÛPÂKSHA I.	1470–71	
(?) PRAUDHA DEVA RÂYA	1476–77 (?)	
RÂJASÊKHARA	1479–80	
VIRÛPÂKSHA II.	1483–84	
RÂJASÊKHARA	1486–87	

The Second Dynasty.

NARASIMHA	(?) 1490 to (?)
NARASA or VÎRA NARASIMHA	(?) to 1509
KRISHNA DEVA RÂYA	1509 to 1530
ACHYUTA	1530 to 1542
SADÂSIVA (*a prisoner all his life*)	1542 to 1567

The Third Dynasty.

RÂMA (*practically sovereign*)	1542 to 1565
TIRUMALA (*practically sovereign*)	1565 to 1567
„ (*actually king*)	1567 to 1575 (?)
RANGA II.	1575 to 1586
VENKATA I.	1586 to 1614

(*For the remainder see the text, pp.* 214, 216.)

GENEALOGY OF THE BAHMANÎ DYNASTY[1]

(According to the "Burhân-i Maâsir.")

- 1. ALÂ-UD-DÎN HASAN.
  - 2. MUHAMMAD I.
    - 3. MUJÂHID.
    - FATH KHÂN.
  - MAHMÛD KHÂN.
    - 4. DÂÛD.
    - 5. MUHAMMAD II.
      - 6. GHIYÂS-UD-DÎN.
      - 7. SHAMS-UD-DÎN.
  - AHMAD KHÂN.
    - 8. FÎRÛZ.
      - HASAN KHÂN.
      - MUBÂRAK KHÂN.
        - *Makhdûmah Jahân.*
    - 9. AHMAD.
      - 10. ALÂ-UD-DÎN II.
        - 11. HUMÂYÛN.
          - 12. NIZÂM.
          - 13. MUHAMMAD III.
            - 14. MAHMÛD.
            - *Fatimah.*
            - *A daughter.*
          - JAMSHÎD.
        - HASAN KHÂN.
        - YAHYÂ KHÂN.
      - MAHMÛD KHÂN.
      - MUHAMMAD KHÂN.

[1] This Table is taken from Major King's History (*Ind. Ant.*, xxviii. 121).

GENEALOGY OF THE BAHMANÎ DYNASTY[1]

(*According to Firishtah.*)

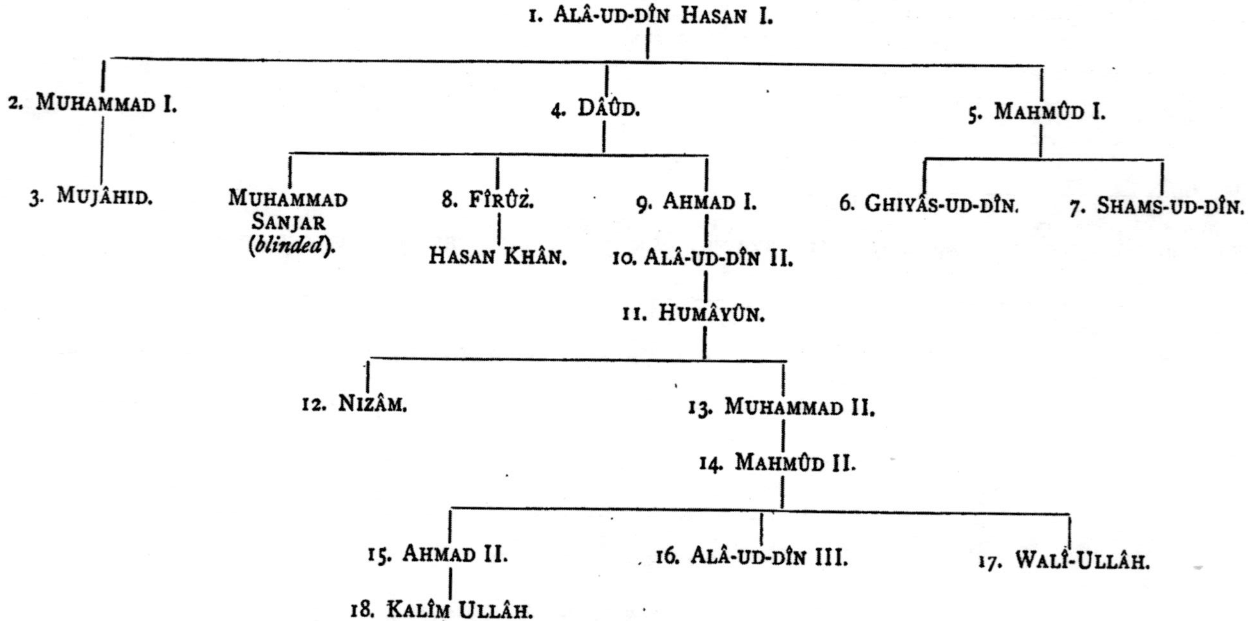

[1] This Table is taken from Major King's History (*Ind. Ant.*, xxviii. 121).

LIST OF THE BAHMANÎ SULTANS OF THE DAKHAN AT KULBARGA

(*According to Firishtah.*)

		A.D.	
1.	Alâ-ud-dîn Bahmanî I.	Aug. 3, 1347, to Feb. 2, 1358	
2.	Muhammad I.	Feb. 2, 1358, to April 21, 1375	
3.	Mujâhid	April 21, 1375, to April 16, 1378	
4.	Dâûd	April 16 to May 21, 1378	
5.	Mahmûd	May 21, 1378, to April 20, 1397	
6.	Ghiyâs-ud-dîn	April 20 to June 14, 1397	
7.	Shams-ud-dîn	June 14 to Nov. 15, 1397	
8.	Fîrûz	Nov. 15, 1397, to Sept. 24, 1422	
9.	Ahmad I.	Sept. 24, 1422, to Feb. 27, 1435	
10.	Alâ-ud-dîn II.	Feb. 27, 1435, to Feb. 13, 1458	
11.	Humâyûn	Feb. 13, 1458, to Sept. 5, 1461	
12.	Nizâm	Sept. 5, 1461, to July 30, 1463	
13.	Muhammad	July 30, 1463, to March 21, 1482	
14.	Mahmûd II.	March 21, 1482, to Dec. 18, 1517	
15.	Ahmad II.	Dec. 18, 1517, to (?) 1521 (?)	*Kings only in name.*
16.	Alâ-ud-dîn III.	1521 (?)	
17.	Walî-Ullâh	(?) 1521 to (?) 1523	
18.	Kalîm Ullâh	(?) 1523 to about 1528	

GENEALOGY OF THE ÂDIL SHÂHS OF BÎJAPÛR

- 1. ABÛ-L MUZAFFAR YUSUF ÂDIL.
  - 2. ISMÂÎL.
    - 3. MALÛ.
    - 4. IBRAHÎM.
      - 5. ALÎ.
      - TAHMASP.
        - 6. IBRAHÎM.
          - 7. MUHAMMAD.
            - 8. ALÎ.
              - 9. SIKANDAR.
        - ISMÂÎL.
    - *A daughter (m. Alâ-ud-dîn Imâd Shâh of Bîrâr).*
  - *A daughter (m. Ahmad Shâh Bâhmanî).*
  - *Maryam (m. Burhân Shâh of Ahmadnagar).*

	A.D.
1. YUSUF	1489 to 1510
2. ISMÂÎL	1510 to Aug. 27, 1534
3. MALÛ	Aug. 27, 1534, to Feb. 1535
4. IBRAHIM I.	Feb. 1535 to 1557
5. ALÎ I.	1557 to April 11, 1580
6. IBRAHÎM II.	April 11, 1580, to 1626
7. MUHAMMAD	1626 to 1656
8. ALÎ II.	1656 to 1659
9. SIKANDAR	1659 to 1686

GENEALOGY OF THE NIZÂM SHÂHS OF AHMADNAGAR

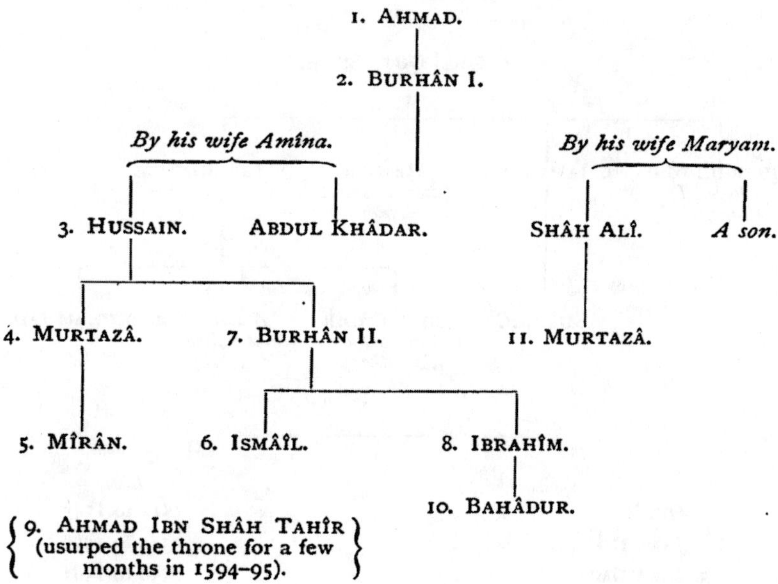

	A.D.
1. AHMAD	1490 to 1508
2. BURHÂN I.	1508 to 1553
3. HUSSAIN	1553 to 1565
4. MURTAZÂ	1565 to 1587
5. MÎRÂN	1587 to 1588
6. ISMÂÎL	1588 to 1590
7. BURHÂN II.	1590 to April 18, 1595
8. IBRAHÎM	April 18 to Aug. 6, 1595
9. AHMAD IBN SHÂH TAHÎR	Aug. 6, 1595, to 1596
10. BAHÂDUR	1596 to 1599

GENEALOGY OF THE QUTB SHÂHS OF GOLKONDA

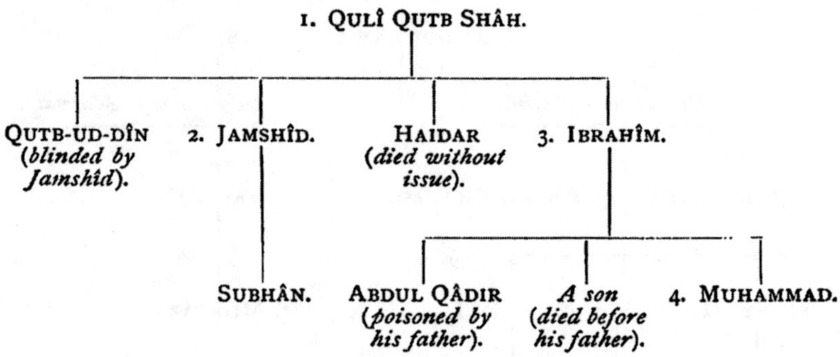

	A.D.
1. QULÎ	1512 to 1543
2. JAMSHÎD	1543 to 1550
3. IBRAHÎM	1550 to 1581
4. MUHAMMAD	1581 to 1611
5. ABDULLÂH	1611 to 1672
6. ABÛ HASAN	1672 to 1688

PORTUGUESE VICEROYS AND GOVERNORS OF GOA

(A.D. 1505 *to* 1568.)

	A.D.
DOM FRANCISCO DE ALMEIDA (*Viceroy*)	1505–1509
AFONSO DE ALBUQUERQUE (*Governor*)	1509–1515
LOPO SOARES DE ALBERGARIA (*Governor*)	1515–1518
DIOGO LOPES DE SEQUEIRA (*Governor*)	1518–1521
DOM DUARTE DE MENEZES (*Governor*)	1521–1524
DOM VASCO DA GAMA, CONDE DE VIDIGUERIA (*Viceroy*)	1524
DOM HENRIQUE DE MENEZES (*Governor*)	1525–1526
LOPO VAZ DE SAMPAIO (*Governor*)	1526–1529
NUNO DA CUNHA (*Governor*)	1529–1538
DOM GARCIA DE NORONHA (*Viceroy*)	1538–1540
DOM ESTEVÃO DA GAMA (*Governor*)	1540–1542
MARTIM AFFONSO DE SOUSA (*Governor*)	1542–1545
DOM JOÃO DE CASTRO (*Governor and Captain-in-Chief*)	1545–1547
" " (*Viceroy*)	1547–1548
GARCIA DE SÁ (*Governor*)	1548–1549
JORGE CABRAL (*Governor*)	1549–1550
DOM AFFONSO DE NORONHA (*Viceroy*)	1550–1554
DOM PEDRO MASCARENHAS (*Viceroy*)	1554–1555
FRANCISCO BARRETO (*Governor*)	1555–1558
DOM CONSTANTINO DE BRAGANZA (*Viceroy*)	1558–1561
DOM FRANCISCO COUTINHO, CONDE DE REDONDO (*Viceroy*)	1561–1564
JOÃO DE MEDONCA (*Governor*)	1564
DOM ANTONIO DE NORONHA (*Viceroy*)	1564–1568

[The above List is extracted from Mr. Danvers's work, "The Portuguese in India" (vol. ii. p. 487). The author continues the List to the present day.]

INDEX

THE END